HOW

WE GOT

HERE

BASIC
BOOKS

A MEMBER OF THE PERSEUS BOOKS GROUP

THE 70'S: THE DECADE

THAT BROUGHT YOU MODERN LIFE

(FOR BETTER OR WORSE)

Published by Basic Books,
A Member of the Perseus Books Group

A Cataloging-In-Publication record for this book
is available from the Library of Congress

ISBN-10: 0-465-04196-5   ISBN-13: 978-0-465-04196-1

TO MY WIFE, DANIELLE

ACKNOWLEDGMENTS

The idea for this book originated fifteen years ago in the Boston apartment of John Barnes, now an executive at Pfizer, and Dean Godson, now the chief leader-writer of the *Daily Telegraph.* John announced that a history of the 1970s desperately needed to be written. We all enthusiastically agreed, and here—belatedly—it is. I thank them for their inspiration and continuing friendship.

I owe more thanks than this page can hold to the Manhattan Institute and specifically to its president, Larry Mone, and its chairman, Roger Hertog. Without their generosity, this book could never have been finished. There were moments when my editor, John Donatich, probably darkly suspected that it never *would* be finished; among his many kindnesses were his stoic smiles through those moments.

Heartfelt thanks to the relatives and friends who read and commented on early drafts of the book: Linda Frum, Chris Gray, Nancy Lockhart, Jonathan Rauch, Florence Rosberg, Gerald Rosberg, and above all to my father, Murray, as trenchant but flattering a critic as any writer could hope for. My in-laws, Peter and Yvonne Worthington, hospitably permitted me to turn their barn into a paper-filled lair summer after summer, emerging only to eat and snarl. My happiest hours writing this book were spent in the garden laid out by my late mother, Barbara Frum, who glimmered glamorously through the 1970s in her Zandra Rhodes gowns. I dearly wish I could talk with her about those days again.

At various points along the way, I benefited from the assistance of some very able researchers: Aaron Solomon, Chris Stump, and Steve Taggart. I am grateful to them, as I am to Chris DeMuth of the American Enterprise Institute, John Dizard, Austen Furse, Mitzi Hamilton, Bill Kristol, Bob Newman, Doug Pepper, and Ken Whyte for their ideas and support.

My literary agent, Mildred Marmur, saved this book from capsizing as the storms of the New York publishing world heaved my publisher through three owners.

Finally and supremely, I thank my heroically patient wife and children. The enthusiasm of Miranda and Nathaniel for bellbottoms, Happy Faces, and the Temptations proves that life is a circle after all. My wife, Danielle, lovingly aided me the whole way, from the day the form of this book was conceived alongside the Central Park Carousel to the midnight hours when we together edited and re-edited the very last draft. The discussion of marriage appears in this book under the chapter title "Duty." It is due to her heavenly grace and nobility of spirit that ours has never been anything other than pure joy.

CONTENTS

LIST OF ILLUSTRATIONS

INTRODUCTION: Reading a computer print-out. © Archive Photos/Lambert.

PART I: A disgruntled message on a gas station sign during the U.S. gas crisis in the 1970s. © Ed Carlin/Archive Photos.

PART II: A dancer covered in metallic paint and wearing only a g-string raises his arms at the reopening of Studio 54, New York City, September 15, 1981. © Tom Gates/Archive Photos.

PART III: Actors John Belushi and Garrett Morris as Coneheads on the set of *Saturday Night Live*, 1975. © Joseph Sia/Archive Photos.

PART IV: A full-length portrait of two young women on a sidewalk, modeling metallic-colored leather hot shorts, tops and shoes, London, England, 1972. © Popperfoto/Archive Photos.

PART V: A full-length portrait of a young woman streaking past the Supreme Court on April Fool's Day, Washington, D.C., April 1, 1974. © Archive Photos.

PART VI: Tehran, Iran, November 19 (AP)—Burning an American flag in front of the American embassy. (APWirephoto) Sayad (333).

CONCLUSION: Astronaut James Irwin salutes in front of the landing module of Apollo 15 on the moon, August, 1971. © Archive Photos.

INTRODUCTION

"I PREFER THE DREAMS OF THE FUTURE TO THE HISTORY OF THE PAST." SO THOMAS Jefferson wrote to his friend John Adams in 1816. Could there be a more American sentence than that? The violence, poverty, and intolerance of the past was what Americans, in Jefferson's day and ours, had left their homelands to escape. The future was what they intended to build here. Americans often mock Europeans for refusing to accept reality—for dreaming of the days when the British Navy ruled the waves, when the Kingdom of Poland stretched from Berlin to Kiev, when Rome was the capital of the world. Yet Americans have lived in their dreams every bit as much as Europeans, maybe even more so. When Charles Dickens visited the United States in the 1840s, he mocked the locals' habit of pointing at a wooden schoolhouse in a clearing and describing the great university that would soon arise from it, or of calling the muddy lanes of New York and Washington "avenues" and "boulevards." But the locals were not lying. They were describing things not as they were, but as they must soon be. The magnificent future was not a speculation; it was, as one nineteenth-century newspaper editor said, a sure thing that simply "had not yet gone through the formality of taking place."[1]

That future has arrived. America at the beginning of the twenty-first century is rich beyond all reckoning. The Communist superpower with which it grappled for half a century lies shattered at America's feet, begging for American aid, technology, and investment. Past wrongs are being righted. The descendents of slaves sit on corporate boards and command fleets and armies; the grandchildren of coolies scoop up scholarships and prizes; women can go anywhere and do anything that men can. The United States leads the world in learning and the arts, in science and technology, in business and finance. Its shops are piled high with fresh plums in December and a hundred varieties of ice cream in August. At the flick of a switch, Americans can listen to the Brandenburg Concertos played more finely than they ever were for the Elector of Brandenburg himself; with a flash of plastic they can board a jet to Bali or Buenos Aires; with a tap of a key they can order any book in print delivered to their doorstep the next morning. Do they want to know what is happening in Sierra Leone? They can see it live on CNN. Are they worried about their daughter on her first day of university? They can call her pager from their car phone. Are they sick or in pain? The world's most fantastic medicine makes even more fantastic advances with every passing week. And unlike any previous great power—unlike Victorian Britain, unlike the caliphs of Baghdad, unlike imperial Rome—Americans can see nobody and nothing on the horizon who would dare to take, who could even imagine taking, all this away from them.

In every way that we can count, tally, or measure, these are America's best days, its high noon of empire. It's staggering to imagine what more Americans could wish for if they aren't satisfied with all that they have. And yet . . . and yet . . . they *aren't* satisfied. In fact, it seems that they feel less content, less secure, less proud of their country than they did forty years ago, when Jim Crow still ruled the South, Soviet bombers were aimed at Manhattan, a heart attack meant certain death, and $20,000 a year was a handsome wage. In those grimmer days, American publishing houses ground out books warning the country against (of all things!) complacency. Now, in an era when complacency seems like the most appropriate of all moods, the publishers are capitalizing on pessimism. On my bookshelf I see *The End of Affluence*, *Prozac Nation*, *The Time Bind*, *The War Against Parents*, *The Overworked American*, and *America: What Went Wrong?* The publishers know their market. In all but five of the thirty-five years since 1965, a majority—often an overwhelming majority—of the American public has told pollsters that the country is on the "wrong track." What matters, it turns out, are the things that cannot be tallied. Americans worry about deteriorating schools, about their inability to trust their neighbors, about the smut they see on television. They worry that the leaders ignore them and that the system is stacked against them. As then-Governor Bill Clinton said in his acceptance speech at the 1992 Democratic convention in New York, "[T]hose who play by the rules and keep the faith have gotten the shaft, and those who cut corners and cut deals have been rewarded. People are working harder than ever, spending less time with their children, working nights and weekends at their jobs instead of going to PTA and Little League or

Scouts." Americans feel that the country has lost its moral bearings. As Senator Bob Dole declared in *his* acceptance speech in San Diego in 1996, "To those who say . . . that America has not been better, I say, you're wrong, and I know, because I was there. I have seen it. I remember." The wistful strains of nostalgia waft through American culture, from the revival of cigars, ballroom dancing, and retro cars and home appliances to the proliferation of new housing developments that attempt to evoke front-porch, white-picket small towns.

Perhaps this yearning for old wisdom, old fashions, and old days is only to be expected in an aging country. In 1999, the median American was almost thirty-seven years old; he (or more precisely, she, since the average American is a woman) was twenty-eight in 1970. Since World War II, the mood of the country has reflected the moods of the colossal baby boom generation: rebellious when the boomers were teenagers, lustful when the boomers hit their twenties, covetous as they entered their thirties. Now, as they turn fifty, the mood of the country is shading into melancholy, tinged with the doubts and regrets of late middle age. Nevertheless, this yearning for the past springs from a deeper source than the aging of the baby boomers. Perhaps today's Americans, as they applaud the rhetoric of values, faith, and family, are disclosing something real and important about the present state of the American nation.

It is often said that we live in a time of unusually rapid change. If we are referring to economic and technological change, this isn't true. A Rip van Winkle who nodded off in 1930 and awoke in 1965 would have shut his eyes on a country where children were crippled by polio and adults died of strep throat; where workers walked or took the streetcar to their jobs in foundries and mines, on farms, or as domestic servants; where there were no federal old-age or disability pensions; where news was transmitted by paper and ink and goods were paid for in cash. He would have opened them on a world transformed by television and cars, subdivisions and shopping malls, antibiotics and the birth control pill, package tourism and universal high-school education, fast food and credit cards. A van Winkle who slept through the thirty-five years after 1965 would see hardly anything so dazzling compared to that.

But if we are talking about social and cultural change, the pace since 1965 has been positively bewildering. A 1965 van Winkle, familiar with long-distance telephones and DNA, would take the Internet and Dolly the Cloned Sheep in stride. But he would be left gasping by women bus drivers and the ubiquitous lottery ads, by the beggars on the sidewalks and the number of limousines on the streets, by the middle-aged men going to work in khaki pants and baseball caps and the young women sleeping in military barracks, by the homoeroticism of magazine advertising and the proscription of smoking, by the collapse of trade unions and the spread of mutual funds, by the millions of children in day care, the crumbling of the mainline Protestant churches, the automatic teller machines that offer service in both English and Spanish, and the replacement of beef by chicken as the staple of the American diet. In other words, the dizzying pace of change of the past thirty-five years has transformed not so much American tools as American habits, less America's material environment and more America's moral outlook, less the way Americans make things and more the way they feel things.

Have you ever seen a grown man cry? Before the 1970s, Americans agreed with Sir Walter Scott:

Woe awaits a country when
She sees the tears of bearded men.

Back then, Americans idolized the craggy, inexpressive man: the sort of man epitomized by Charles Lindbergh and Gary Cooper, Neil Armstrong and Sergeant York, John Wayne and Anthony McAuliffe (the general who replied "nuts" when the surrounding Germans called on him to surrender at the battle of Bastogne). But that man has been melted by a vast shift in the emotional climate, a kind of global moistening. The president wipes away tears when he tours hurricane disasters; coaches' voices catch at their teams' annual banquets; fathers snuffle at their daughters' weddings. In 1972, the front-runner for the Democratic nomination for president, Senator Edmund Muskie, destroyed his hopes by appearing to break down and weep during a reply to an editorial attack upon his wife by a New Hampshire newspaper. Today, those tears would float Senator Muskie into the White House.

Eaten any good meals recently? Not so long ago, American food was famously disgusting: "tasteless roasts, banal beefsteaks, cremated chops, fish drenched in unintelligible sauces, greasy potatoes, and a long repertoire of vegetables with no more taste than baled shavings." So complained H. L. Mencken in the 1920s, and the complaint still held true in the middle 1960s. Thirty years ago, the United States was a country of whisky drinkers and steak eaters. Today you can find a good risotto in Minneapolis and a tasty vindaloo in San Diego. The national tipple is no longer bourbon, but chardonnay.

When was the last time you heard a politician denounce Wall Street? On the campaign trail in 1948, Harry Truman accused the Republicans of wanting to fasten a "Wall Street economic dictatorship" on the country. People chuckled—that was the sort of thing that Democrats were expected to say. In those days only the rich owned stocks or bonds, and the chief of the AFL-CIO was one of the half-dozen most powerful men in the country. The thought that a day might come when shareholders would outnumber union members almost four-to-one—or that a Democratic candidate for president would cite a rising stock market as proof that his economic policies were working, as Bill Clinton repeatedly did in 1996—would have left old Harry gasping.

It meant something when the Romans stopped wearing togas. It meant something when French nobles stopped carrying swords. It meant something when Americans stopped spitting into cuspidors. Now it means something when you can buy a decaffeinated Sumatran coffee with steamed semi-skimmed milk and an almond *biscotti* on the ground floor of what used to be a discount woolens warehouse in the country that invented Nescafé. It means something that assistant professors specializing in Marxist analysis of the films of Buster Keaton own 401-K plans crammed full of General Electric stock. And it means something that Clint Eastwood felt obliged to weep on-screen in *In the Line of Fire*.

We live in a world made new, and made new not by new machines, but by new feelings, new thoughts, new manners, new ways. Yet, for all our world's newness, there is a distinctly autumnal snap in the air these days. As the largest generation in American history prepares to exit the stage, the country finds itself examining its character. A people once collectivist, censorious, calculating, conformist, taciturn, obedient, puritanical, and self-confident has mutated in the space of three and a half decades into a people that is individualist, permissive, emotional, enterprising, garrulous, rebellious, hedonistic, and guilt-ridden. Some of this change is for the better, some for the worse, but it is all puzzling and often uncomfortable.

During the making of the movie *Saving Private Ryan*, the studio publicity department released a photograph of the star, Tom Hanks, clad in GI battle dress, talking face to face with the director, Steven Spielberg, wearing his trademark T-shirt and baseball cap. It was a wonderful image, the Nineties meeting the Forties, and one found oneself glancing back and forth, from the man dressed as a warrior to the man dressed as a twelve-year-old, wondering—whither had the one man gone and whence had the other man come? When did this change happen? How? And why?

The usual answer is a phrase that is explanation and date all rolled into one: "The Sixties." Many of us carry in our heads what might be called the documentary-maker's version of that decade. As the Byrds sing "Turn, Turn, Turn," the camera cuts from images of Martin Luther King Jr. on the steps of the Lincoln Memorial, to dogs biting civil rights protesters in Birmingham, Alabama, thence to flower children in San Francisco, and then soldiers helicoptering down into a rice paddy, bombs dropping from the bay of a B-52, hippies smoking marijuana and flashing peace signs, Lyndon Johnson declaring he will not run again, tanks in the streets of Detroit, and finally Kent State. The events these images represent—the war, the protests, the assassinations—are usually thought to be the events that made the America we know.

The documentary-makers' history is not entirely wrong. But it is not enough. Imagine telling somebody in 1969 that within thirty years welfare would have been abolished! Imagine trying to explain that baby-boomer legislators would pass laws that permit the police to confiscate a car—on the spot and without trial—if they discover the fragments of a joint in the ash tray! Or that the first member of the Woodstock generation to become president would order more military interventions abroad than any president since FDR!

The exciting political events of the years from John F. Kennedy's inauguration to the withdrawal from Indochina formed our time, yes. But not in the way we usually choose to imagine. The documentaries would have us remember the 1960s as the era when the nation's young people took to the streets to protest the Vietnam War. But in fact "[a]lmost every public opinion poll taken during the war showed that youth, in the aggregate, disproportionately *supported* the war. (Surprisingly, the most 'dovish' age group turned out to be people over fifty-five.)"[2] The candidate who drew his support most disproportionately from young men was not Robert Kennedy or Eugene McCarthy, but George Wallace. The documentaries describe the 1960s as the decade in which the conscience of the nation was at last aroused against the evil of racial inequality. In fact, the crucial turn in public opinion occurred in the 1950s. Up until the mid-1960s, a plurality of white Americans believed that the country was moving "not fast enough" on civil rights. After the riots of 1965, pluralities consistently insisted that the country was moving "too fast."[3] And despite all that footage of stoned young people rolling in the Woodstock mud, the 1960s were not the era of sex, drugs, and rock 'n' roll. Only 5 percent of Americans had ever tried marijuana by as late as 1967. A majority of American brides still said they came to the altar as virgins in 1964. The number one song of 1969 was "Sugar, Sugar" by the Archies.

When you think of the 1960s, it's a great mistake to imagine them as represented by, say, Hillary Rodham Clinton. Two-thirds of the baby boomers never attended college. In 1966, almost all of the young men born in 1947—the year Hillary Clinton was born—were wearing their hair short, serving in the army or else taking jobs at the local plant, eating pork chops for dinner, and getting ready to marry the second girl they had ever slept with. The Berkeley Free Speech movement, the sit-ins at Columbia, the Harvard strike of 1969—for most American young people, the protests and love-ins of the 1960s were as remote and alien as the Newport regatta, the deb balls in the Plaza Hotel, or the rituals of Skull and Bones. For older Americans, they were a good deal more exotic than that. An influential book published in 1970, *The Real Majority* by Benjamin Wattenberg and Richard Scammen, observed that the typical American voter was neither young, nor poor, nor black. She was a 47-year-old machinist's wife living in Dayton, Ohio. And—as Wattenberg and Scammen did not quite say—as far as she was concerned, the 1960s were the 1940s, except that frozen vegetables had replaced canned. It was only in the next decade, the supposedly anticlimactic decade of the 1970s, that her world and that of people like her was turned upside down as Cambridge, Massachusetts, New Haven, Connecticut, Manhattan, and Northwest Washington were turned upside down by the 1960s. It was in the next decade that her husband dumped her, that she discovered cappucino, that her standard of living failed to rise for the first time in her adult life, and that she cast her first Republican ballot.

The Sixties, one-time Democratic activist Richard Goodwin later wrote, "contained a promise, an augury of possibilities, an eruption of confident energy."[4] They were a Promethean moment when everything seemed possible: the abolition of poverty, the overnight elimination of prejudice, unending economic expansion. But Goodwin is constrained to admit candidly that the 1960s were "a failure." The liberal dreams of social reform with which the decade began begat impossible hopes; the disappointment of those hopes spawned the radical movements of the decade's end; and the destructiveness and hatefulness of those radical movements in turn finished off liberalism's political prospects. "This country's going so far right you're not going to be able to recognize it," predicted Attorney General John Mitchell in 1970, and at least from an electoral point of view he was correct.

The vast size of the United States, the intense conservatism of a country where ordinary people have much to lose, the traditional preference of Americans for individual rather than collective self-improvement: These things make it difficult for reformers and dreamers to make much of a dent in the American consciousness. Even with television to spread the word, that would ordinarily have been true for the 1960s too. But the spark of rebellion lit in the 1960s did not sputter out, as previous sparks—the radical 1840s for example—had done. This time, it caught. A political upheaval was transformed into an upheaval in habits, beliefs, and morals, and not the habits, beliefs, and morals of an elite few, but of a quarter-billion souls spread across a vast continent. The origins of this upheaval can be traced far back in time: to the First World War, to the headturning new ideas of Darwin, Nietzsche, and Freud, and arguably even further still. But incendiary ideas only move from paper to life when they transform the behavior and beliefs of the mass of the people—when they cease to be known as the work of their author and are absorbed instead as the common property of humanity. In North America, it was in the supposedly quiescent 1970s that this absorption took place.

They were strange feverish years, the 1970s. They were a time of unease and despair, punctuated by disaster. The murder of athletes at the 1972 Olympic games. Desert emirates cutting off America's oil. Military humiliation in Indochina. Criminals taking control of America's streets. The dollar plunging in value. Marriages collapsing. Drugs for sale in every high school. A president toppled from office. The worst economic slump since the Great Depression, followed four years later by the second-worst economic slump since the Depression. The U.S. government baffled as its diplomats are taken hostage. And in the background loomed still wilder and stranger alarms and panics. The ice age was returning. Killer bees were swarming up across the Rio Grande. The world was running out of natural resources. Kahoutek's comet was hurtling toward the planet. Epidemic swine flu would carry off millions of elderly people. Karen Silkwood had been murdered for trying to warn us that nuclear reactors were poisoning the earth. General Motors was suppressing the patent on a hyper-efficient engine. Food shortages would soon force Americans to subsist on algae. There were, wrote a columnist for the *New York Times*, "fleeting moments when the public scene recalls the Weimar Republic of 1932–33."[5]

Disasters, though, can be liberating as well as destructive. In the 1970s the giant corporations that had dominated the American economy since the 1890s began to shrink, trade unions lost their power, the personal computer was invented, it became legal to ship a crate of lettuce across the country without asking the Interstate Commerce Commission for permission. In the 1970s the federal government lost its power to wiretap at will, conscription was suspended, price controls were discredited and repealed. Before 1970, America was a "love-it-or-leave-it" society. You didn't like Chevrolets? Tough. Your kid was home sick and wanted to watch a cartoon at ten on a weekday morning? Also tough. You wanted a checking account that paid interest? Again tough. You needed to pay less than $900 for an economy ticket to Paris? Tough once more. You'd like to own some gold coins? Fella, that's a very serious crime in these United States.

The gaudy characters of the 1960s are already seeping out of memory. In the gallery of forgotten celebrities, Abbie Hoffman is joining General Coxey, George Romney jostles against William McAdoo, Timothy Leary will soon vie for space with Madame Blatavsky. But the *social* transformation of the 1970s was real and was permanent. It left behind a country that was more dynamic, more competitive, more tolerant; less deferential, less self-confident, less united; more socially equal, less economically equal; more expressive, more risk-averse, more sexual; less literate, less polite, less reticent. But those are just words, aren't they? To really understand how the country has changed, we must study it minutely. This book is an attempt to do just that, to describe the most total social transformation that the United States has lived through since the coming of industrialism, a transformation (a revolution!) that has not ended yet. To describe—and to judge.

PART I

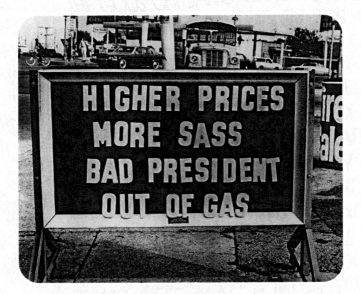

TRUST

FULL FAITH AND CREDIT

"Oil, steel, insurance, and the banks run this country. I'd go for public ownership of the oil companies if I didn't think the national politicians were a bunch of thieves."

—*Nixon supporter, Brooklyn 1974.[1]*

AT THE CLIMAX OF THE 1947 FILM CLASSIC, *MIRACLE ON 34TH STREET,* THE hero—a young lawyer determined to prove that a man who claims to be Santa Claus should not be institutionalized as a lunatic—opens the argument that will win his case by reading aloud a long description of the reliability of the U.S. Post Office. A weary district attorney urges him to get to the point: "The State of New York is second to none in its admiration for the Post Office Department." At which Santa's lawyer gives a signal, the doors to the courtroom are flung open, and postal workers march in with dozens of bags of mail addressed to "Santa Claus, North Pole" and deliver them to the man in the dock. Verdict for the accused. If the Post Office recognizes you as Santa, Santa you must be.

More than anything else in this ancient movie—more than the gloves on the women or the hats on the men—that scene opens a window onto a completely vanished America. Trust the post office? That's a lot crazier than believing yourself to be Santa.

Back then, however, it wasn't just the Post Office that Americans believed in. They believed in the Army and the Navy. They believed in the scientists who had built the atomic bomb and discovered antibiotics. They believed in their judges, their shop stewards, their ministers and priests. They believed in Social Security and also in the free-enterprise system that had fed and armed the American serviceman and all his allies, while simultaneously pumping unheard-of riches into the bank accounts of the folks at home. If the Americans of 1947 could see their country now, what would they think? What would they think of a former presidential adviser and U.S. senator accusing the U.S. government of having blown a domestic civilian airliner out of the sky with a ground-to-air missile, as Pierre Salinger has done? Or a football star being acquitted of murder because a jury chose to believe, against all the evidence, that he had been framed by the Los Angeles Police Department? Or the polls showing that ever-rising numbers of Americans feel certain that their tax money is wasted, their politicians are crooks, their democracy is manipulated by powerful interests? Americans lived through depression and war without succumbing to despair. How could a vastly richer and far more secure America have sunk so deeply into sourness and pessimism?

Americans have never been especially trusting people—they laugh at suckers as brutally as the French laugh at cuckolds and the British laugh at foreigners. But in the middle years of this century, they somehow reconciled their lack of confidence in their fellow man with a quite astonishing faith in their political and social institutions. The University of Michigan found in 1958 that 57 percent of Americans trusted the government in Washington to do the "right thing" most of the time; another 14 percent trusted it to do the "right thing" almost *all* of the time.[2] And the government in Washington was, even in those sunny days, one of America's *least* trusted institutions. Doctors and judges; generals and schoolteachers; clergymen and the presidents of corporations—in postwar America, all commanded a measure of trust from their fellow-citizens that today would strike most of us as downright gullible. Then, between 1967 and 1981, the United States sank into a miasma of self-doubt from which it has never fully emerged.

Some blame Watergate for this abrupt collapse of trust in institutions, but not very convincingly. For one thing, the decline in trust begins to appear in the polls as early as 1966, almost a decade before the Watergate was known as anything more than a big hole in the ground alongside the Potomac River. For another, the nation had managed unconcernedly to shrug off Watergate-style events before. Somebody bugged Barry Goldwater's apartment during the 1964 election without it triggering a national trauma. The Johnson administration tapped the phones of Nixon supporters in 1968, and again nothing happened. John F. Kennedy regaled reporters with intimate details from the tax returns of wealthy Republican donors, and none of the reporters saw anything amiss. FDR used the Federal Bureau of Investigation to spy on opponents of intervention into World War II—and his targets howled without result. If Watergate could so transform the nation's sense of itself, why did those previous abuses, which were equally well known to the press, not do so? Americans did not lose their faith in institutions because of the Watergate scandal; Watergate became a scandal *because Americans were losing faith in their institutions.*

The Vietnam war is a more plausible culprit for the loss of trust. The dates are right: 1965 to 1973. Certainly the war provoked in its critics a lacerating mood of fury against their government and their society. (In one of the great mad flights of oratory that characterized the antiwar movement, Norman Mailer charged: "It is self-evident that the *Reader's Digest* and Lawrence Welk and Hilton Hotels are organically connected with the Special Forces napalming villages."[3]) Since those critics numbered some of the most influential members of the society—its most prominent and admired professors, writers, clergymen—their fury could make itself heard. But Vietnam is ultimately an unsatisfying explanation. The twenty-eight years that elapsed between the withdrawal of the last U.S. troops from Indochina and the end of the century is a long time by Americans' forgetful standards: longer than from V-J Day to the 1972 election. Moreover, the social groups that supported the war have since 1973 seemed no less alienated than the war's critics. Finally, if Vietnam is responsible, why does a very similar loss of faith in institutions settle upon nearly every other advanced industrial economy at about the same time? The political scientist Ronald Inglehart compared surveys of confidence in the local police in nineteen different countries between 1981 and 1990. (He chose the police because it was the institution for which data were available in the largest number of countries.) In only four of the nineteen countries did the percentage expressing "great confidence" rise, and of those four, two were Argentina and South Africa, countries where a democratically elected government had replaced a less democratic one. In fifteen of the nineteen countries Inglehart surveyed, including Canada, Britain, Japan, and South Korea, the percentage of the population expressing "great confidence" in the police fell, often dramatically.[4]

Maybe the best way to explain the worldwide ebbing of trust in the 1970s is to re-examine the apogee of public confidence in the 1950s and early 1960s. Maybe what needs to be explained is not why latter-day Americans—and Canadians, Britons, and Japanese—trust so little, but why an earlier generation trusted so much.

Think for a moment of how the world looked in 1900. For most people, life was almost unimaginably hard, but more frightening than the hardship of life was its chanciness. In the happy United States, some people born poor could—with effort and luck—rise to great wealth. Others, no less hardworking, ended their lives as maimed beggars because a bolt had sheared or a sprocket slipped. A tornado could wipe out ten years of work on the farm, a strike could bankrupt the merchants who supplied the workers' wives. We can look back on that world and see order, progress, and rising standards of living. Those in the middle of it certainly noticed the progress, but they saw no order. And order is something human beings crave.

One could tell the entire political, social, and cultural history of the United States and Western Europe from 1900 to 1960 as the story of an ever-more successful attempt to impose order on a recalcitrant world. That's what Britain's New Liberals tried to do after 1906 with their pioneering National Insurance programs; that's what Democrats and Republicans in the U.S. Congress were seeking when they created the Federal Reserve in 1913. Orderliness was the underlying theme of the New Deal and of the similar attempts to guide and regulate the market that were tried in fascist and democratic Europe before and after World War II.

For a reasonable span of time, this enforced order held. A West German who saw a gleaming industrial democracy arising out of the rubble of

Hamburg, a Briton who could for the first time visit the doctor without worrying about the bill, an American veteran who returned from war not to the slums of Brooklyn but to a neat house in Levittown, a car, and a refrigerator—these people had every reason to think that their societies were functioning brilliantly. *Things worked.* And when things work, it's natural to try more of the same. Have Keynesian economic policies driven the unemployment rate down to 4 percent? Then double-Keynesian policies should drive it down to 2 percent. Have frugal welfare payments mitigated the misery of the poor? Then generous welfare payments should abolish that misery altogether. Has a slight relaxation of discipline made schools more humane without diminishing standards? Then even laxer discipline should yield even better results. Unfortunately, every human idea, even the very best, is true only up to a point. Equally unfortunately, we usually only ascertain where that point is by bumping into it—hard. In the 1970s Americans did not merely bump into the limits of the ideas that had governed the midcentury world, they crashed. The distrust and despair that seized them were the wounds from that collision.

The 1950s are often described as conservative. In political terms, that is not quite right. The Fifties were the highwater mark of the New Deal coalition in the United States and social democracy in Western Europe. As conservative a politician as Senator Robert Taft sponsored bills calling for huge public-housing construction programs. Free-market economists like Britain's Lionel Robbins forcefully advocated massive government support for the universities and the arts. But if we use the word conservative to mean "cautious, averse to change, incremental," then the 1950s were a very conservative decade indeed. A war-battered world hungered for tranquility, stability, and the appearance of continuity. So, while public opinion in those years favored leftish policies, voters in the democratic countries consistently selected old men with right-of-center backgrounds to carry those policies out. Dwight Eisenhower—who at sixty-two was the oldest man to be elected president since James Buchanan in 1856—was actually the baby of the bunch. Alcide de Gasperi was sixty-four when he became the leader of post-Fascist Italy. Louis St. Laurent, the elegant corporate lawyer who governed Canada for most of the 1950s, was sixty-six when he ascended to the prime ministership in 1948. Shigeru Yoshida formed the first postwar Japanese government at age sixty-eight and stayed in office until age seventy-six. Charles de Gaulle was sixty-eight when he resumed power in France; he hung on past his seventy-ninth birthday. Konrad Adenauer was first elected chancellor of West Germany in 1949 at seventy-three, and won his last election at eighty-one. Winston Churchill returned to the British prime ministership in 1951 aged seventy-six and refused to quit until 1955.

The reality of change, the appearance of continuity—it was a formula that satisfied the peoples of the Western world for a decade and a half after the war. Not even the harsh recession of 1958–60 (the first severe downturn since the war) depressed public confidence. But no democracy remains grateful forever. As standards of living rose, as pensions and unemployment programs grew ever more plentiful, as the danger of renewed depression and a third world war seemed to abate, the self-confidence and ambition of the democracies surged and their patience with their own faults thinned. In 1957, Adenauer won his last election as West German chancellor on the slogan, "No Experiments." Five years later, at a convention in Port Huron, Michigan, the founders of the Students for a Democratic Society issued their famous statement denouncing this elderly caution. The United States, the Port Huron Statement complained, was pervaded by a "feeling that there simply are no alternatives, that our times have witnessed the exhaustion not only of Utopias, but of any new departures as well." "For most Americans," the statement continued, "all crusades are suspect, threatening." It was time, they argued, for that hesitation to be cast aside.

"His was a generation of winners," Richard Goodwin would later write of his boss and hero, John F. Kennedy. The old men who led the world in the 1950s had seen and suffered too much cruelty and stupidity to believe in Utopia. But to the rising men of the 1960s—the sergeants and lieutenants who had come of age during World War II and in the breathless years of reconstruction immediately afterward—the accomplishments of

the 1950s seemed almost offensively paltry. The world leaders elected between 1960 and 1968 with rare exceptions shared two traits: They were relatively young and they believed in the limitless potential of their societies,
their governments, and themselves. Kennedy was forty-three in November
1960, the youngest man ever to be elected president.[5] Harold Wilson was
forty-eight when he was elected prime minister of Great Britain in 1964, in
a campaign in which his labor party promised to melt the British class system under the "white heat" of technology. Pierre Trudeau was an almost
preternaturally youthful forty-nine when he assumed the prime ministership of Canada in 1968; Willy Brandt, a vigorous fifty-six when he became
West Germany's first Social Democratic chancellor in 1966. Aldo Moro and
Kakuei Tanaka were both striplings of forty-seven when they seized control of the dominant political parties in Italy and Japan, control they retained until their deaths no matter who sat in their countries' revolving
prime ministerial chairs.

These young leaders would no longer abide the restraints that had
bound the sad-eyed old men who had preceded them. No experiments?
Without experimentation, how would social justice ever be attained? Nobody was quite sure how to define a just society, but however defined, the
societies of the Western world, and especially of the United States, were
generally agreed to have fallen well short. It was likewise generally agreed
that the situation had to be rectified immediately. No less a moral authority than Martin Luther King Jr. explained in 1964 "Why We Can't Wait." And
why should we wait? Money was piling up in government treasuries. The
universities were crowded with self-confident experts offering solutions to
the problems of poverty, urban overcrowding, racial animosity, air pollution, juvenile delinquency, anomie and alienation, and all the other social
evils that had previously seemed inescapable elements of the human condition. Publishers poured forth books on pollution, on poverty, on racial
prejudice, breaking their readers' hearts with the horror of the situation,
pleading the urgency of immediate action. Everyone remembered the
mighty battles triumphantly waged by the mass mobilization of the 1940s.
If such victories could be won in time of war, why could not equal victo-

ries be won in time of peace? We had conquered Nazism. Why not poverty? The Marshall Plan for Europe had been a success. Why not a Marshall Plan for the cities? During his campaign for the 1968 Democratic nomination, Robert Kennedy liked to quote (without credit) George Bernard Shaw, "Some see things as they are and say 'why?' I dream things that never were and say, 'why not?'" All the faith and trust heaped up in the years when everything went right were wagered in the 1960s on the gamble that a Great Society—a Just Society—a Caring Society could be built now, in our time. The mood was Promethean: "[T]he Great Society," declared Lyndon Johnson in the speech that introduced the term, "is not a safe harbor, a resting place, a final objective, a finished work. It is a challenge constantly renewed, beckoning us toward a destiny where the meaning of our lives matches the marvelous products of our labor."[6]

In a story as old as the Greeks, overweening pride brought condign disaster. Daniel Patrick Moynihan, who had served all three of the decade's presidents, offered this piercing explanation of why the grand ambitions of those years so often left behind only regret and bitterness. "Wishing so many things so, we all too readily come to think them not only possible, which likely they are, but also near at hand, which is seldom the case. We constantly underestimate difficulties, overpromise results, and avoid any evidence of incompatibility and conflict, thus repeatedly creating the conditions of failure out of a desperate desire for success. . . . I believe that this danger has been compounded by the increasing introduction into politics and government of ideas originating in the social sciences which promise to bring about social change through the manipulation of what might be termed the hidden processes of society."[7]

The great gamble of the Sixties was lost—lost not only in the jungles of Vietnam and the serpentine schemes of the Nixon White House, but in the inflation, demoralization, and failure of the Great Society and its analogues throughout the developed world. Moynihan's point about the social sciences is a very profound one. Just as the authority of the traditional élites of Europe collapsed after they led Europe into the catastrophe of the First World War, so the prestige of the new élites that had emerged in the twentieth-century United States was indelibly tarnished by the disappointments of the soaring hopes of the 1960s. In 1918 the kings and bishops, squires and headmasters who sent the young to the trenches lost the confidence of their people. That same fate now befell the corporate managers and federal bureaucrats, the progressive clergymen and self-confident professors who had presided over the disappointments and defeats of the promises of the Sixties. The story was the same in almost every advanced Western democracy: The old men of the 1950s earned trust; the young men of the sixties squandered it. Britain, Canada, West Germany, France, all went through experiences very like America's. America's only distinction is to have gone through it all first and to have been marked by it most profoundly.

THE LAW IS CRAZY

IN THE 1971 TOUGH-COP CLASSIC, *DIRTY HARRY,* CLINT EASTWOOD IS GIVEN THE news that the deranged serial killer he has captured will be released back onto the streets of San Francisco, because he violated the killer's rights. "It's the law, Harry," the exasperated district attorney tells him. "Then the law is crazy!" Eastwood fires back.

People expect their government to protect them from attack and assault, and before 1965, American governments had by and large succeeded. Pre–1973 crime statistics are not very reliable, but without stretching them farther than they ought to go, we can say that between 1915 and 1965 the United States became steadily safer and more peaceful. Saloon brawls, range wars, lynchings, slum murders, anarchist violence, the feuds of the Hatfields and McCoys—these lingered on in the folk memory. But on the whole, prosperity, temperance, and education had done their mollifying work. The crime rate dropped, feuds vanished, the police grew more courteous and professional, and men whose great-grandfathers had carried Bowie knives and Colt revolvers accoutered themselves with slide rules and attaché cases. It was unusual, even in New York City, for an apartment door to have a chain lock: An ordinary bolt sufficed to discourage vacuum-cleaner salesmen, peeping toms, and the other nuisances of urban life. Burglar alarms were gewgaws for the ultra-rich. Heiresses and mobsters might be followed around by bodyguards, but ordinary citizens trusted the cops to come when needed, and come fast.

In the early 1960s—slowly at first, then with accelerating speed—the safety and civility of mid-century America crumbled. One's chance of being robbed, raped, assaulted, or murdered nearly tripled between 1960 and 1980, with the biggest single jump in crime occurring in 1974. Crime was raging so desperately out of control that an entirely new system of counting it had to be invented. Since the 1920s, the FBI had calculated the crime rate by toting up reports to local police departments. Although academic criminologists might grumble about sloppy police record-keeping, the FBI's method made good-enough sense. When crime is generally low, confidence in the police will be relatively high and most crimes, at least most serious crimes, will be reported. But as the crime wave of the 1960s and 1970s tore up American cities, citizens simply ceased bothering with the useless trip to the police station to report that their purses had been snatched, that they had been stabbed, that they had been raped. The police came under intensifying pressure from local political figures to protect their city's or town's image by shaving their reports. Future U.S. Attorney General Edward Levi estimated in 1973 that more than one-third of all crimes were going unreported. That same year the Justice Department introduced a more scientific technique for measuring crime, the victimization survey. Pollsters interviewed statistical samples of the population, and asked them whether they had suffered a crime in the past year. The first of the new reports arrived in the summer of 1975, and its results were horrifying. It found that 37 million Americans—meaning one household out of every four—had suffered a rape, robbery, assault, burglary, larceny, or auto theft in 1973. In cities of more than 100,000 population, the victimization rate was one household out of every three.

A feeling of constant and imminent menace pervaded the country, and especially its big cities. The 1974 movie, *Death Wish*, captures the mood of dread. Charles Bronson plays a New York architect, a self-described "bleeding-heart liberal," whose wife is murdered and whose daughter is raped by three thugs who force their way into the family's apartment. The police do not catch the killers. They do not much try. They fill out forms, make some routine inquiries—and then forget about it. As a precinct captain explains, the city is suffering thirty murders a week. How could anyone investigate them all? A friend gives Bronson a gun, and he begins to prowl the streets and subways at night. Never has Manhattan looked more terrifying. The wind is chill; the streets are empty; the few law-abiding pedestrians pull their collars up around their ears, and hear and see nothing. At first by accident, then deliberately, Bronson tempts muggers to attack him. It seldom takes him long. The criminals are lurking everywhere. They approach their victims in total arrogance, without even a glance over their shoulder for the police. *They* know the police aren't coming. And in fact, the only police action we see in the movie is a furious manhunt to capture Bronson, the vigilante killer.

The corruption, indifference, or malevolence of the police is taken for granted in the decade's movies, and in particular its two most colossal commercial successes, *The Godfather* and *The Godfather Part II*. In the first *Godfather*, a Sicilian man comes to Don Corleone because a bribed police officer has dropped the charges against his daughter's rapist. The don reproachfully asks the man why he went to the law instead of to his friends. The makers of *The Godfather* were of course attempting to score an ironic mid–1970s point: The police and the courts are just as crooked as the gangsters. But the audiences that thronged the theaters were cheering Don Corleone without irony. Here at last was a leader who maintained order and dispensed justice, who upheld clear and certain rules and punished those who violated them, who heeded the moral sense of his community rather than championing those who defied its norms.

A 1979 survey by the National Education Association discovered that 110,000 teachers, one out of every twenty members of the union, had been the victim of a physical attack by a student in the 1978–79 academic year. A Gallup survey taken in July 1975—in the middle of the worst economic downturn since 1937 and the steepest rise in the cost of living since the collapse of the Confederate dollar—asked city-dwellers to name their worst problem. Five percent cited inflation. Eleven percent identified unemployment. *Twenty-one percent* named crime. A majority of adults, and more than three-quarters of women, living in large cities told pollsters that they were afraid to walk in their own neighborhoods at night. The sociologist Jonathan Rieder lived for a year in the early 1970s in the Jewish and Italian New York neighborhood of Canarsie, near Kennedy airport. He described a meeting in a synagogue basement after a rash of muggings and beatings near the local subway station. An old man with a thick Yiddish accent demanded to know why the neighborhood could not get more police: "So broken ribs and shoulders are not enough? We need a murder too?" A somber elderly woman said, "I am locked up like in the ghettoes of Europe." "I am afraid of people knocking down my door. I still am not free."[8]

Franklin D. Roosevelt, the president who was a hero to everyone in that basement, had declared "freedom from fear" one of the four freedoms for which World War II was being fought. Only a decade before, New Yorkers had enjoyed that freedom. In November 1965, New York and the entire Northeast were plunged into darkness by a power failure, but the dimming of the lights did not unravel the fabric of civilization. "Although many merchants feared looting and violence, the police reported little such trouble. Many New Yorkers even seemed merry. There was the same air of revelry that often accompanies a heavy snowstorm," reported the *New York Times* the following morning. Only five people were arrested for looting.

A dozen years later, on July 13, 1977, New York's power went out again. This time New York exploded into horrifying urban mayhem. "The marauders had moved almost as though on signal at the start of the power blackout, and continued brazenly through daylight hours even though city police were on a full mobilization," the *Daily News* reported "Youths in the Bronx could be seen trucking off supermarket goods in shopping carts. . . . The looters had no pattern: hit-and-run break-ins struck parts of Manhattan and Queens and whole streets of stores were ripped off in Brooklyn and the Bronx. In the Bronx, thieves used the cover of darkness to steal 50 new Pontiacs from Ace Pontiac, 1921 Jerome Ave. at 177th Street. When the cars were recovered later in parts of the city, they were found stripped clean of parts. . . . In Yonkers, a Molotov cocktail and eggs were thrown at passing patrol cars. Twenty persons were arrested for looting in Getty Square, near City Hall. In the Sunset Park section of Brooklyn, youths were seen driving their car up on the sidewalk to a targeted store. Ropes or chains were tied between the protective grating of the store and the car's back bumper. The car then pulled away, the grating tumbled off, and the looters swept into the store." More than 550 policemen were injured; 4,500 looters were arrested.

Arrested—but almost certainly not punished. American society had made a quiet, collective decision in the 1950s and early 1960s to view crime more indulgently. This disinclination to arrest and punish was inspired by two powerful emotions, pride and guilt.

Pride: Mid–century Americans felt much more certain than we do now that they had unlocked the secrets of human behavior. In the era of B. F. Skinner, explaining human conduct in moralistic terms exposed one as sadly out of date. Just as "madness" had been transmuted into "mental illness" and "idleness" into "unemployment," so "crime" was reinterpreted as "delinquency," an unfortunate inability to bring one's conduct into line with the expectations of society. And as it was cruel and futile to jail the mentally ill and the unemployed, it was very nearly as foolish to jail the delinquent. The intelligent thing to do, from everybody's point of view, was to rehabilitate the delinquent or—even better—prevent delinquency from arising in the first place by rooting out the causes of crime. True, there was the awkward difficulty that nobody could agree on what those all-important causes might be. Was crime a psychological problem? Or was it sociological? But whatever caused crime, thoughtful Americans refused to accept punishment as anything but a last desperate resort, and they judged the need for punishment a failure as much of society as of the delinquent himself.

Guilt: In the 1960s, punishing crime stringently inevitably meant punishing blacks disproportionately. Before World War II, crime and race were two quite distinct subjects in the northern and western states. Of the 2,100 felons sentenced to New York state penitentiaries in the year ending in June 1941, some 1,600 were white.[9] The stereotypical criminal in the cities of the North was the Irish tough in his knit sweater and derby hat, the Sicilian hoodlum with his greased hair and knife, or the Jewish bootlegger and pimp (of the 2,100 convicts sentenced in 1941, 145 had been raised in what the state called the "Hebrew" faith).[10] Between 1940 and 1960, however, some two million blacks migrated northward in search of better opportunities. As the sons and grandsons of the migrants came of age, the face of crime in the north and west darkened. In the 1960s, blacks, 12 percent of the population, committed more than half of the nation's serious crimes. Embarrassed judges and juries refrained from convicting and jailing criminals. Parole boards set prisoners free earlier and with fewer questions asked. Reported crime rates more than doubled between 1960 and 1970, but the total number of criminals in prison actually *fell*, from 212,953 federal and state inmates in 1960 to 196,429 in 1970.[11]

Policing lapsed. The population of the city of Los Angeles, for example, grew by 30 percent between 1950 and 1966. Over those same sixteen years, the Los Angeles Police Department added 698 officers to its 1950 roster of 4,442, an increase of only 15 percent. The death penalty was quietly abandoned. Although the number of murders in the United States jumped from nine thousand in 1960 to fifteen thousand in 1970 and more than twenty thousand in 1975, only three men suffered the maximum punishment for first-degree murder in the whole United States in the fourteen years between 1965 and 1979—despite a Supreme Court decision in 1976 reaffirming capital punishment's constitutionality.

Ex-convicts could no longer be denied the right to vote, the California Supreme Court held in a seven-zero decision in March 1973. In February 1975, Vaughan Booker of Pennsylvania, who was serving a life sentence for killing his wife, was made a deacon of the chapel of Graterford State Prison, the first convicted murderer ordained by the Episcopal Church. It neatly symbolized the new tenderness toward criminality when the *New York Times* in 1977 purged from its stylebook the rule that convicted felons were to be referred to only by their last names. Henceforward they were to be "Mr.," "Mrs.," or "Miss," just like everyone else.

Since the causes of crime were increasingly attributed to society, rather than the criminal, the federal government and the states very logically hurled themselves with enthusiasm into the task of social reform: building public housing, funding summer jobs for youth, boosting welfare payments, squeezing the unemployment rate toward 3 percent, outlawing discrimination in hiring, housing, and public accommodation, appropriating billions of dollars of federal aid for early childhood education, and on and on in fulfillment of all the most precious hopes of every criminologist ever to bring home a degree from the fabled University of Chicago sociology department. No gardener ever attacked root causes more vigorously. Alas, the more tenderly society tried to salvage its delinquents, the more crime it got. We're still arguing over precisely what went wrong. Was it that welfare weakened family structures and multiplied the number of fatherless young men seeking to prove their manhood? Did criminals rationally assess the risks of getting caught and decide that crime paid better than it used to? Did the relatively declining pay for unskilled work after 1973 lure uneducated young men into criminal careers? Did a century of black rage and resentment finally explode into an undeclared guerila war? Or was it perhaps a little of each and every one of these explanations, and a dozen others beside, that caused the post–1960 crime surge? For our story what matters is not the origins of the crime wave, but its result. In the span of a very few years, the explosion of criminality utterly discredited the liberal ideas that had governed American public life since the war. It was already true in 1965 that a majority of Americans felt that the courts treated crime too leniently, but this sort of law-and-order conservatism remained a redneck view. In 1965, the majority of *college-educated* Americans still believed that the courts either were getting crime right or should become more lenient still.

When the question about the leniency of the courts was repeated in 1974, the college graduates were nearly as furious at the courts as their less-credentialed neighbors. A crushing 85 percent majority damned the courts as too soft, and this time there was no difference between the replies of men and women or between high-school dropouts and holders of postgraduate degrees.[12] Between 1949 and 1973, the proportion of Americans expressing "great confidence" in the Supreme Court plunged from 83.4 percent to 32.6 percent in the University of Michigan's poll, and to 28 percent in the Lou Harris poll—the steepest drop for any branch of government.

Crime was to the liberalism of the 1960s, Moynihan observed, what communism was to the liberalism of the 1940s: the issue that "forced the left-liberal intellectuals of the country to see that the masses really were not with them on issues of fundamental importance."[13] Americans had trusted their political leaders, their university professors of criminology, their liberal newspaper columnists, their judges and district attorneys— and in return their daughters had been raped, their mothers robbed on the way home from church, their cars stolen, their houses burgled. Understandably, they boiled with rage. In the three years 1965–68, the proportion of Americans who said they believed in the death penalty jumped to 48 percent from 38 percent. Over the next eight years, the proportion jumped again, to 67 percent. (By 1997, 75 percent of Americans expressed support for the death penalty.)[14] It was crime that convinced Americans that George Wallace was right: Those pointy-headed know-it-alls in the black robes and at the college lecturer's rostrum really could not "park a bicycle straight."

After 1969, Richard Nixon's Supreme Court chipped away at the more extreme pro-defendant precedents of the Warren Court. Prison sentences extended longer, more cops were hired, new prisons built. Alas, it was like chasing a diesel train on a unicycle. By the late 1970s, some 40 million serious crimes were being committed in the United States a year. Only about 142,000 criminals per year were being sent to jail.[15] Americans drew a stern conclusion from that grim arithmetic: If the authorities cannot and will not protect my family, I must do the job myself. Between 1959 and 1973, the percentage of Americans who owned a handgun jumped from 32 percent to 42 percent.[16] Membership in the National Rifle Association tripled over the fifteen years after the Watts riot from 600,000 in 1964 to 1.9 million in 1981.[17]

Above all, Americans responded to crime the way they always have responded to bad situations: by hitching up their wagons. America was still to a very surprising degree a pre-suburban country in 1965. Camden, New Jersey; Oakland, California; Bridgeport, Connecticut; Gary, Indiana, and other smaller centers of heavy industry might have lost some of their railroad-age gleam, but Detroit, Chicago, Queens, Cleveland, and Los Angeles still throbbed with blue-collar life. If the great cities of America could not guarantee them the life they wanted, however, the urban working class was ready to move on, farther and farther out from the crime and welfare of the decaying cities. And these refugees from the ravaged cities of industrial America did not much appreciate it when the leaders whose policies they blamed for wrecking their old neighborhoods then told them that they were bigots for seeking homes where their kids could play on the streets without fear of having their bikes stolen.

ON THE LINE

EARLY IN 1970, A REPORTER FOR *FORTUNE* MAGAZINE TOURED THE AUTO-mobile plants of Michigan. On the streets below his New York office, long-haired protesters were fighting with hard-hatted construction workers. In the Midwest, the protesters *were* the workers. "The visual evidence of a new youthful individuality is abundant in the assembly plants," the reporter wrote. "Along the main production lines and in the subassembly areas there are beards, and shades, long hair here, a peace medallion there, occasionally some beads—above all, young faces, curious eyes. Those eyes have watched carefully as dissent has spread in the nation. These men are well aware that bishops, soldiers, diplomats, even Cabinet officers, question orders these days and dispute commands. They have observed that demonstrations and dissent have usually been rewarded. They do not look afraid, and they don't look as if they would take much guff. They are creatures of their times."[18]

It was not the war in Vietnam that was sparking dissent in these young men, but their work on the line. A twenty-two-year-old assembly worker at the Ford plant in Dearborn told *Fortune* that his job was "boring, monotonous." He felt himself to be "just a number." A thirty-two-year-old worker at Cadillac complained that his job stunted his mind. "They tell you to do the job the way it's wrote, even if you find a better way." A thirty-one-year-old union committeeman complained: "You're like in a jail cell—except they have more time off in prison. You can't do personal things, get a haircut, get your license plates, make a phone call." Line workers even had to request permission to visit the bathroom. Older workers tolerated this petty authoritarianism. They had seen worse in the army, and they had mortgages to pay. But at the beginning of 1970, one-third of the line-workers at the Big Three automakers were younger than thirty.

If these young workers were chafing against low pay or meager benefits, their unions would have been glad to champion them. But the disaffected workers' grievances were not economic. They were rebelling against the conditions of their work, not the remuneration for it—against bossiness, not the boss. On that issue, their unions were wary. When United Autoworkers President Doug Fraser observed that "the young workers won't accept the same old kinds of discipline their fathers had," he appeared to understand that the discipline he imposed was scarcely more welcome than that imposed by Henry Ford II.

The discontent on the line expressed itself not in protest but in spontaneous acts of sabotage. One-quarter of Ford's assembly-line workers quit in 1970. Unexcused absences from work doubled at Ford and General Motors between 1961 and 1970, spiking upward most sharply in 1969–70. In the spring of 1970, 5 percent of General Motors' workers were missing without excuse on any given day. On Fridays and Mondays, up to 10 percent of the workforce failed to show up. At GM's most troubled plant, a Chevrolet factory in Baltimore, absenteeism shot up from 3 percent on a typical day in 1966 to 7.5 percent in 1970. Disgruntled workers took to vandalizing cars, especially the expensive models. *Fortune* reported that "screws have been left in brake drums, tool handles welded into fender compartments (to cause mysterious, unfindable and eternal rattles), paint scratched, and upholstery cut."[19]

Rebellion flared hottest at the auto plants, but the surly mood observed by *Fortune*'s reporter in Detroit was echoed across the nation in the 1970s. In a poll that asked whether "hourly paid workers in your company are more conscientious about their work than a generation ago, or less," only 2 percent of managers deemed the workers of 1970 more conscientious than the workers of 1950; 63 percent condemned them as less conscientious.[20] The workers did not like their managers any better than their managers liked them: A 1977 survey of 159 firms found more job dissatisfaction than at any time since the survey was first taken in 1952.[21]

This mutual hostility took aback a country that had come to expect peace and quiet on the job. In 1960, the bloody labor unrest of the late nineteenth and early twentieth centuries had receded into the half-forgotten past. The Taft-Hartley Act of 1947 and the booming prosperity of the postwar years calmed the labor violence of 1877 to 1937 with a new deal: Management won the right to run its factories in what it regarded as the most efficient way; and in return unionized American blue-collar workers earned the highest wages in the world, wages that exceeded those of the lower echelons of the white-collar workforce. But that new deal was rooted in a world that had not long left to live, not, at any rate, on American soil—a world in which wealth was earned with brawn and sweat.

"We Americans love big things!" Theodore Roosevelt had proudly boasted, and as if to vindicate him, mid–century America had built big dams, big towers, and big bridges. Every one of the seven tallest buildings now standing in the United States was built before 1974,[22] as were eight of the ten tallest dams,[23] and all twenty of the longest-spanned bridges.[24] Huge automobile plants and steel mills hulked over the mid–century landscape. Twelve thousand men worked at U.S. Steel's great Duquesne Works in the Monangahela Valley; 18,000 men labored at its South Works, Chicago's single largest employer in 1945. Big firms loomed large not just physically, but also economically. The twenty-five biggest American corporations of 1969 employed almost 7 percent of the U.S. labor force; the twenty-five biggest of 1998 employed only 4.5 percent. Big corporations predominated emotionally as well. The glamour companies of late twentieth-century America were relatively small. Microsoft, for instance, employed only 30,000 people in 1998. The exciting companies of 1969 were behemoths like General Motors, ITT, and Union Carbide.

Supervising and controlling so many hundreds of thousands of workers might seem an impossible task. Modern companies despair of it, and re-engineer themselves as federations of virtually independent units. The managers of the 1960s were, however, undaunted. Working in a world of giant units came naturally to them. The chief executive officer set broad strategic goals. His staff conveyed those goals to the division managers. The division managers issued orders to *their* subordinates. At long last, via an immense chain of command of steadily diminishing power and importance, the directives from HQ reached the unit leader, the foreman, the sergeant of the American industrial army. He in turn barked them out to the men on the line, insisting that they be executed to the letter.

Charlie Chaplin satirized the dehumanizing quality of this system in the 1930s, but one can see why mid–century managers gravitated to it. The men on the American factory line in the early days of this century were the rawest of industrial recruits: peasants newly arrived from the miserable villages of Russia or Italy, Okies fleeing the dust bowl of the Southwest, displaced black sharecroppers only a generation or two removed from slavery. Working by the clock rather than by the hours of the sun and the seasons of the year, working in noise and soot rather than in the open air, working surrounded by machines that could kill a man in an instant: These were alien experiences for them. They did not always speak English and they could less often read it. Setting them at a simple, repetitive task under the watchful eye of a foreman ensured that they did their unfamiliar work steadily, without undue risk to machines or men. In a world in which distance was large and communication less than instantaneous, a *millefeuille* of supervisory management also seemed to serve a genuine function: Headquarters needed to be in New York, where the money was borrowed and the dividends paid, while the factories needed to be in the Midwest, where the coal and iron came from, and only the post office and a costly long-distance telephone connected them.

But institutions are conservative things, which do not easily recognize when a once-functional behavior has become dysfunctional. "I think we've just gone through a decade of rather surprisingly bad decisions by businessmen worldwide. Some of them so bad that nobody could have guessed it," complained the president of truck-engine maker Cummings Motor in 1976.[25] "Your people aren't lazy and incompetent! They just look that way," cheerfully proclaimed the business best-seller of 1970, *Up the Organization* by former Avis president Robert Townsend. "They're beaten by all the overlapping and interlocking policies, rules and systems encrusting your company."[26]

The young workers of the postwar economy chafed against the restrictions and controls that their parents had accepted. With Patrick McGoohan in the cult television series *The Prisoner*, they shouted, "I am not a number! I am a free man!"—only to hear back the sinister off-camera reply, "You are number six." These disaffected baby boomers became increasingly willing to accept a new accusation against American business. Not only did it grind the face of its workers and undercut and destroy its virtuous small competitors, as the muckrakers of 1900 charged, but it cheated and bored its customers. At first, this discontent expressed itself in the complaint that the products of American industry were excessively luxurious. "The disparity between what modern man needs and what the modern corporation produces appears to be widening," argued two critics of American capitalism in the 1974 radical classic *Global Reach*,[27] and as proof they cited the wood-veneered American color television set, with its chunky dial that was always breaking off in your hand and that cost the average worker more than a week's pay. A simple one-channel black-and-white television set could be manufactured for only $9, the authors asserted, and wasn't that really good enough? Americans, though, have seldom been an ascetic people. The baby boomers might buy books praising a Soviet one-channel television or a Volkswagen Beetle, but what they yearned for—without yet knowing it—was a sleek black 49-inch full-color digital monster, with 500-channel cable reception, a built-in DVD player, and a remote control that could double as NORAD's nuclear-missile console. They wanted a Lincoln Navigator with a walnut dashboard, satellite geopositioning locator, and six-zone air conditioning. What irked the new generation of consumers about the goods manufactured by American industry was not that they were too costly, but that they were too crummy.

Mass production is a radically egalitarian institution. In the early 1960s, the doctor and his plumber used exactly the same telephone, sat on very similar chairs, drove virtually the same car (the doctor's was called a Cadillac and was upholstered more luxuriously, but was otherwise indistinguishable from the plumber's Chevrolet), and unless they lived in a very big city, shopped in the same department store. It would be wrong to exaggerate the homogeneity of mid-century America—there were plenty of Southern sharecroppers and destitute widows without the means to buy much of anything at all—but it would be fair to say that the gap between the goods available to the middle- and the upper-middle classes was much smaller thirty-five years ago than it is today. As American incomes became more unequal after 1973, however, American industry's virtuosity at delivering adequate goods at low prices stopped impressing its customers. The doctor who had once contentedly snapped pictures with a Kodak Instamatic now wanted a Nikon. Instead of a Philco radio, he headed to the stereo shop for a brushed-steel Yamaha amplifier and pre-amp. He put aside Johnny Walker as he discovered single malts, and traded in his Caddy for a Mercedes or Jaguar. His wife stopped shopping on the top floor of Sears, and headed out to the Saks Fifth Avenue that had opened at the new mall.

The 1970s were the decade when imported manufactured goods began to arrive on American shores in appreciable numbers. In only four years, 1975 through 1978, the U.S. trade deficit with Japan multiplied by ten, from $1.7 billion to $11.6 billion.[28] By 1979, one-quarter of all the manufactured goods sold in the United States were made abroad, up from near-zero in the early 1960s.[29] Toyota, Honda, Nissan nameplates crowded the parking lots. In 1981, the Reagan administration struck a deal with Japan to cap car sales in the United States at 1.67 million a year, or one new car of every four then sold.

American business pitifully tried to keep up by decking out its mass-produced goods with ever-more absurd veneers of pseudo-luxury: the "*Coreentheean* leather" of the Chrysler Cordoba touted by actor Ricardo Montalban in a commercial that every junior high school boy learned to mimic. The results, alas, were goods that were simultaneously costly *and* crummy. A vast tsunami of shlock roared through American homes in those years. The remains of the great wave still litter basements and garages across the land: boxes of unspooled eight-track cassettes, discarded pieces of orange modular chesterfields; spongy nylon Pierre Cardin track suits; clock radios that snapped after the third use. People may have bought the stuff, but they were not long fooled by it. In 1966, when asked by the Lou Harris poll to rate the job business was doing bringing them goods of high quality, 75 percent of Americans offered a grade of "good" or "excellent." When the question was repeated in 1971, only 47 percent of Americans said that business was doing a good or excellent job. A 1977 survey by the University of Michigan's National Opinion Research Center found that 27 percent of American workers felt so ashamed of the quality of the products they were making that they would not want to buy them for themselves.

"I AM NOT A CROOK"

"I AM NOT A CROOK." WHEN PRESIDENT NIXON PRONOUNCED THAT SENTENCE before an audience of newspaper executives in November 1973, he pointed the gun at his own temple and pulled the trigger. It might have been wiser, in fact, for him to go on television and proclaim—yes, I *am* a crook. With Americans as cynical as they then were, they might well have refused to believe him.

An ABC News poll conducted within days of the "I am not a crook" comment found that 59 percent of Americans did not believe "much of what the president says these days." Still the damning details tumbled out. The famous eighteen-minute gap—a series of almost certainly deliberate erasures in a potentially damning tape—was revealed by Special Prosecutor Leon Jaworski later that same month. Eight weeks later, on January 25, 1974, a California state official reported that the deed donating Nixon's vice presidential papers to the National Archives had been backdated by more than a year to qualify for a half-million dollar tax deduction. In March, Nixon confessed that his earlier denials of knowledge about the payment of hush money to the Watergate burglars had been false. He had indeed known all along. In July the Supreme Court ruled that Nixon must surrender all his White House tapes to Jaworski. The "smoking gun" tape that proved Nixon was aware of the Watergate cover-up from its inception was promptly discovered, and on August 8, 1974, the president announced his resignation. Vice president Spiro Agnew had resigned ten months before, on October 10, 1973, and pled "no contest" to charges of corruption during his tenure as governor of Maryland.

American politics have seldom been pure. But in the past, Americans were able to absorb the news of the Tweed Ring or Teapot Dome or the influence-peddling of the Truman years without losing faith in the ultimate goodness of their political system. The system worked despite the inevitable human weaknesses of the men who led it. Educated Americans had long understood that the story of George Washington and the cherry

tree was a myth. It was understood and accepted that presidents sometimes had to lie about military and intelligence matters. President Dwight
Eisenhower lied in 1960 when he denied that the United States was spying
from the air on the Soviet Union; Franklin Roosevelt lied about his prepa-
rations for war. But with the semi-exception of Warren Harding, the dozen
presidents to occupy the White House between 1884 and 1960 were all
men of unquestioned *personal* integrity. There were scandals of course.
But the scandals never touched the man at the top. Even Harding was
never proven guilty of anything worse than negligence and credulity.
("Harding wasn't a bad man," Alice Roosevelt Longworth cruelly quipped.
"He was just a slob.")

Watergate, however, uncorked a flood of disturbing revelations about
the institution of the presidency. One abusive president the country could
perhaps shrug off. Between 1960 and 1974, the country was governed by
three in a row. Nixon's financial maneuvers were shabby, but they
amounted to a nickel on the dollar compared to the depredations of Lyndon Johnson, who used his power in the Senate and the White House
grossly to enrich himself. Johnson extracted licenses from the Federal
Communications Commission for Texas television stations—he took the
precaution of applying in his wife's name—and he leaned on industry for
gifts and favors. Testifying before the House of Representatives in November 1973 about illegal contributions to the Nixon campaign, the head of the
country's largest milk producers' cooperative revealed that he had also
struck a deal with then-President Lyndon Johnson to lease Johnson's
personal plane from a Johnson family holding company at a price the
milk producers regarded as "plush." After Johnson left office, the milk producers tried to renegotiate the onerous contract. Johnson refused. Their
president realized that they had better just knuckle under. "It became
plain to me," he testified, that he was "in no position to charge the
immediate past president of the United States with being party to a fraudulent transaction." Luis Salas, a Texas judge, confessed in July 1977 that he
personally certified 202 ballots that he knew to be fraudulent in order to
win Lyndon Johnson's first Senate election for him. Johnson's margin

of victory in the August 1948 Democratic primary was only eighty-seven votes. "Johnson did not win the election," Salas said. "It was stolen for him."[30]

As the son of one of the country's richest men, John F. Kennedy had no need to scrounge for dollars. He had, however, other vices, and the country now learned of them. In December 1975, William Safire—a former Nixon speechwriter who became a columnist for the *New York Times*—broke the story that Kennedy had had a sexual affair with Judith Exner, née Judith Campbell, at the same time that she was sexually involved with gangster Sam Giancana, who also happened to be Kennedy's co-conspirator in anti-Castro plots. Exner published her autobiography in 1977,[31] triggering an avalanche of JFK sexual revelations: his wartime romance with a Danish woman believed by the FBI to be a German spy, his smuggling of prostitutes into the White House swimming pool, even his liaison with Marilyn Monroe. (A relationship between Robert Kennedy and Monroe had been rumored since 1964, when a California investigator, Frank Cappell, published a pamphlet titled "The Strange Death of Marilyn Monroe," but the much briefer JFK-Monroe connection was hushed up). Because Lyndon Johnson preyed on stenographers rather than starlets and Mafia molls, his sexual adventuring remained secret until his bloodhound biographer Robert Caro sleuthed it out in the 1980s.

Maybe the country could have shaken off even all this. But there was *still* more. Watergate inspired a national revulsion against petty political corruption—and emboldened U.S. attorneys all over the country to believe that it was their job to root it out. Indictments of office-holders by federal grand juries climbed from sixty-three in 1970 to 337 in 1976. Two-thirds of these indictments ended in convictions. The prosecutors thought they were cleaning up the system. Possibly they even succeeded. But the more zealously Washington tried to perfect the country, the more defective the country looked. April 1973, for instance, was one of the most sensational months in the Watergate investigation. John Dean testified before the Senate Watergate committee, and Nixon's chief of staff, H. R. Haldeman, and his chief domestic adviser, John Ehrlichman, both resigned. And here's what a conscientious citizen who opened his newspaper to the inside pages would have read over those same few weeks:

On March 28, two Chicago alderman were indicted for accepting bribes for their role in a rezoning scandal. On April 3, a Democratic state legislator in Maryland was indicted for distributing forty pounds of heroin. On April 6, the mayor of Miami and two Dade County judges were indicted for taking bribes to reduce the sentences of convicted felons. On April 10, a Maryland state senator was indicted for tax evasion. On April 12, the district attorney for Queens, New York, was indicted for blocking prosecution of a fraud in which some of his aides had been involved. On April 19, former Illinois Governor Otto Kerner—the chairman of the famed Kerner Commission convened by President Johnson to investigate urban riots—was sentenced to three years in prison and fined $50,000 on conspiracy, perjury, fraud, bribery, and income-tax charges. The former revenue director for the state received an equal sentence the same day.

Over the course of the remaining sixteen months of the Watergate scandal, more than a dozen senior administration officials were forced to resign. Two attorneys general were indicted—one, John Mitchell, went to jail. So did both Haldeman and Ehrlichman. Over those same sixteen months, a former Republican congressman from Pennsylvania was convicted of criminal mail fraud, the president of the Newark city council pled guilty to income tax fraud, a sitting Democratic congressman from New York was indicted for helping a Mafia figure obtain government contracts, one Republican member of the Senate Watergate committee gave up reelection to fight an indictment for bribery, the mayor of Camden, New Jersey was indicted for corruption and perjury, the lieutenant governor of California was indicted for perjury, the former chief judge of the U.S. Customs Court was indicted for perjury in a corruption case, and the chairman of the Securities and Exchange Commission resigned after confessing to repeated perjuries in connection with the Watergate investigation. In March 1975, Otto Kerner's misery got company when a former governor of Oklahoma, David Hall, was convicted of bribery and extortion. The next month, George Hansen of Idaho became the first sitting congressman since 1956 to be sent to jail. Hansen's distinction did not last long. In March 1977, two other members of Congress were indicted for taking bribes from a South Korean businessman. In 1979, seven members of Congress, one of them a U.S. senator, were indicted after they took money from FBI agents posing as rich Arabs seeking help with an immigration petition. (All of the seven were ultimately convicted.)

The corruption leaked down the chain of command from local politicians to local cops. In 1973, the United States was rocked by three sensational exposes of police misconduct: one in Indianapolis, another in Philadelphia, a third in New York City. A six-month series of articles in the *Indianapolis Star* charged that "a multimillion dollar narcotics business in Indianapolis, fed by hundreds of burglaries and robberies, flourishes because of collusion among some policemen, the county judicial system, and narcotics peddlers." The *Star* accused the chief of police and his deputy of accepting bribes to protect prostitution, narcotics, bootlegging, and gambling rackets. Both men were fired. In March 1973, a fourteen hundred-page report by the Pennsylvania Crime Commission was made public. It concluded that corruption was "on going, widespread, systematic, and occurring at all levels of the police department" of the city of Philadelphia, and estimated that four hundred officers were receiving payoffs from racketeers and prostitutes. Corruption on the New York force inspired the 1973 best-seller and hit movie, *Serpico.*

The corruption extended from the politicians to the businessmen who paid their bills. Nixon's fund-raisers had squeezed corporate America to fund his extravagant re-election campaign. Executive pay was a lot lower in the 1970s than it is today, and the amounts extracted often exceeded the donors' ability to pay. The president of American Airlines, for instance, was asked for a gift equivalent to one-quarter of his salary. With airlines then tightly regulated by the president's appointees on the Civil Aeronautics Board, he felt in no position to refuse. Businessmen like him often succumbed to the temptation to find a way to pay for the donation out of the company treasury, either by reimbursing themselves for their campaign donations or by creating a slush fund that could give cash gifts undetected.

This was illegal. Corporate gifts to political campaigns had been outlawed in 1907, and the managers of a company that violated the ban could face criminal charges. But since Nixon, not corporate America, was their target, the Watergate prosecutors offered illegal donors what the 1970s called "an offer they couldn't refuse": lenient treatment to any corporation that voluntarily confessed its infractions of the campaign finance laws. The prosecutors were nearly trampled by the ensuing stampede of sinners to the penitents' bench. What the corporations had to confess was more than just an occasional lapse of judgment. In 1974–75, Americans learned that their great corporations had for decades been ignoring the laws meant to protect their democracy from the plutocrats—and that the two great political parties had connived to help them.

Some companies would build up reserves in secret bank accounts overseas and then smuggle the money into the country—literally, in briefcases filled with twenties and hundreds. At Braniff Airlines, for example, the company would end each year with a small surplus of unaccounted-for cash taken in by gate agents who failed to record ticket sales properly, which often happened in those days when airline tickets were still written out by hand and often paid for in cash. Braniff used that money to build a campaign slush fund; $40,000 from the fund went to Nixon. Companies with overseas operations were in a position to give even more. Officers of 3M smuggled more than $630,000 in cash into the United States in the 1960s and 1970s to give to political campaigns. Northrop, a major defense contractor, gave $476,000 to the Nixon campaign; $50,000 of that money was used to buy the (short-lived) silence of the Watergate burglars. By early 1976 the Watergate special prosecutors office had successfully prosecuted eighteen American corporations for illegal donations to the Nixon campaign.

Campaign law-breaking seemed so prevalent that the Securities and Exchange Commission, still reeling from the forced resignation of its chairman, decided in 1975 to audit *all* the political activities of publicly traded companies. It quickly discovered that the gifts U.S. companies made at home were dwarfed by the vast scale of their political influence-buying abroad. Northrop was revealed to have spent $30 million to grease its arms sales overseas. Exxon had contributed $44 million, most of it illegally, to Italian political parties, including the Italian Communist Party, and had then falsified its records to hide its actions. Gulf Oil had made payoffs in Bolivia and given a helicopter to the country's president. Gulf had also secretly contributed millions to the South Korean ruling party. The oil company's chairman and two senior officers resigned in disgrace. Lockheed had bribed the prime minister of Japan. RJ Reynolds admitted to millions of dollars of illegal campaign contributions at home and abroad. Alcoa and its subsidiaries confessed to paying bribes to secure their bauxite mines in Jamaica. United Brands, the successor to United Fruit, dispensed more than $1 million to senior officials in Honduras in 1974 to ward off confiscation of its plantations in that country. Altogether, thirty major companies were investigated, sued, or ordered to change their ways of doing business.

One might well wonder who the villains really were in these bribery cases. Did these companies bribe politicians or were they succumbing to threats? But Americans were in no mood for philosophical musings. Of the three presidents after 1960, the first stood exposed as a womanizing rogue who abused the FBI and IRS, who was implicated in assassinations and attempted assassinations, and who wiretapped Martin Luther King, Jr. The second owed his political career to stuffed ballot boxes, had corruptly enriched himself, had lied the country into Vietnam, and had also wiretapped King. The third had orchestrated a campaign of lies to cover up multiple crimes, had chiseled on his income tax, had chosen a corrupt governor as his vice president, and had bankrolled his campaigns with illegal corporate gifts. "I am not a crook"? It was looking like a good working assumption that everybody was a crook.

To weed the crookedness out, Americans hastily erected a vast internal system of snooping and checking, culminating in the independent counsel law of 1978. This law transferred responsibility for enforcing honesty in the executive branch from the attorney general to an outside official appointed by a three-judge panel. But these endless investigations—there would be seventeen between 1978 and 1999, most lasting for years and costing millions or tens of millions of dollars—only stoked suspicions. If government were honest, the investigations would scarcely be needed in the first place, would they?

The events of the 1970s have now slipped into the past. The young voters who cast their first ballot in the 2000 presidential election were born on the tenth anniversary of the Watergate burglary. Watergate is to them a story as creaky as the struggle over the New Deal was to those adults born in the first year of the baby boom. Yet the New Deal is not remote—its crown jewel, Social Security, costs you 12.6 percent of every paycheck—and neither is the explosion of scandalous revelations we sum up as Watergate. Echoes of that explosion can be heard to this day in the awkward silence that fills the room every time a national leader appeals to the American people for their trust.

WILD AND CRAZY GUYS

ON SUNDAY, JUNE 26, 1977, THE *CHARLOTTE OBSERVER* PUBLISHED A STINGING front-page inquiry into the finances of Charlotte's most famous resident, the evangelist Billy Graham. The newspaper's story charged that the Graham ministry had amassed a mysterious trove of $22 million in land, stocks, bonds, and cash, and went on to insinuate that Graham was connected to organized crime. Land owned by his ministry, the paper said, was "secretly bought" from a company whose president "was reputed to have been in the business of helping mobsters disguise money they acquired illegally." The *New York Times* and the Associated Press picked up the story the next day. Soon newspapers across the country were referring as a matter of course to "Graham's secret fund." Five books purporting to expose Graham were published over the next year and a half. In one book, he was accused of enriching himself personally and of offering a famous (Jewish) gangster $10,000 to come to Christ at a rally in Madison Square Gardens. Another book, a novel, featured graphic sex scenes involving an evangelist whose life was based upon Graham's.

It would take months for the unexciting truth to emerge. The *Observer*'s story was groundless. Graham's personal finances were austere. He took only a modest salary from the ministry, had turned down many lucrative proposals from television and the movies, and owed his own personal wealth to the good luck that had placed his parents' farm directly in the path of Charlotte's growth. The very large royalties from his 1977 bestseller, *Angels: God's Secret Agents*, were donated to his alma mater, Wheaton College. The $22 million "secret fund" had been amassed entirely unsecretively to build a bible college in Asheville, North Carolina. The land had been bought in an equally above-board way for the college's construction. All of these facts had been readily available to the editors of the *Observer*. It made no difference. Billy Graham was the biggest icon in the town of Charlotte, and so it was under his nose that the local newspaper felt compelled to draw a mustache.

Media organizations are susceptible to fashion, to put it mildly, and the fashion of the 1970s was "investigative journalism." No longer would reporters brainlessly transcribe the events of the day. Instead, like Woodward and Bernstein, they would go hunting for big game. They would track down wrongdoers, bag them, collect Pulitzers, and get rich. And if a few innocent reputations were besmirched along the way—well, that's what the correction columns were for.

It even made a kind of business sense. Newspapers were a troubled industry in the 1970s. New York began the decade with four dailies and ended with three, Chicago started with three and finished with two, Los Angeles sank from two to one. Even the nation's capital would have been reduced to a monopoly town had Sun Myung Moon not been able to afford to lose tens of millions of dollars a year subsidizing the *Washington Times* after the 1981 demise of the *Washington Star*. If newspapers were to survive in the television era, they needed a distinctive niche, and investigation promised to be it—or so the papers' editors said when their publishers ventured onto the news floor to complain after enduring a particularly withering evening at the country club.

Investigative journalism was not, however, fated to remain a newspaper exclusive. As television cameras shrank in size and weight, television news became more mobile and adventuresome. Television went to war in Vietnam, broadcast police dogs and truncheons from Birmingham, showed the world the murder of Robert Kennedy, and flew to the moon with Neil Armstrong. In the mid-1960s, television for the first time outdistanced newspapers as the most trusted source of news. By 1975, more than one-third of all Americans said they relied *exclusively* on television for their news.[32]

Curiously, politicians were among the last Americans to understand the new medium's significance. In 1964, Democrats and Republicans actually fought out their internal political battles on the floor of their respective party conventions in foolish disregard of the whirring cameras. George McGovern delivered his address accepting the 1972 Democratic presidential nomination from a stage crammed with defeated rivals and party panjandrums, just like Harry Truman in 1948, on the apparent theory that it was more important to keep the president of the pipefitters' union happy than to look good on television. Four years later, the Democrats had cleared the thick-necked union bosses and the glum losers off the stage, but they had not yet learned to check their camera angles. The shot from the camera on the left of the rostrum reached up and above the speaker's head to take in a bored conventioneer reading a paper throughout Jimmy Carter's acceptance speech.

However little the politicians understood it, television was remaking their world. Television was in fact the *only* American institution to show a rise in public confidence in the 1960s and '70s. This may not be as much of a paradox as it seems, because—as one shrewd observer of the medium has observed—television wins credibility for itself by attacking the credit-worthiness of everyone else. Television journalists "help define public affairs as suspect; in effect, they direct suspicion away from themselves to other persons and institutions. They have assisted the audience to project their mistrust and to select targets for their mistrust . . . " Hence the slogan of a local television station in my town and a good many others: "Channel Seven—we're on *your* side."

Nothing on television worked harder to spread mistrust than the revolutionary public-affairs show *60 Minutes*, which first aired in the fall of 1968. Seven years later, it was the most-watched show on television, the first and only public affairs show to win the fantastically lucrative number-one slot. *60 Minutes* pioneered almost every one of the techniques of television investigative journalism: the carefully re-edited interview, the surprise "gotcha" visit to a malefactor's home or office, the hidden camera, the rejection of any pretense of objectivity. Week after week, it treated America to the crimes and misdeeds of its two favorite targets: the Pentagon and big business. Land fraud in Arizona, the evils of nuclear power, game-show cheating, Tupperware's manipulative selling techniques, the abusiveness of credit checks, phosphate mining, unsanitary conditions in slaughterhouses, carcinogens in hair dye—on and on the roster of villainy went. By the late 1970s, the other networks were all desperately producing their own imitations of *60 Minutes*, and local television was replicating its techniques. Australian television created a *60 Minutes* of its own, mimicking the original's methods, anti-corporate outlook, and even its name, and similar knock-offs, with similar points of view, could be seen on the British and Canadian Broadcasting Corporations.

Possibly, though, it was less the content of the television of the 1970s that fanned public distrust than it was the style; possibly Mike Wallace mattered less than comedian Steve Martin. Martin was a deceptively ordinary-looking man—conservatively dressed, his prematurely white hair cut short—who wore silly hats, told almost painfully unfunny jokes, and yo-deled at his audience in an unspecifically foreign accent, "I am a wild and crazy guy!" The point to Martin's act was that his material was excruciatingly unfunny—and that he knew it and expected the audience to know it too. Television critics liked to say that Johnny Carson was "better than his material," but Carson at least *had* material. Martin invited his audience to laugh at the old-fashioned vaudeville corniness of the assumption that any modern American might conceivably be amused by "material." Elevated to stardom by frequent guest appearances on *Saturday Night Live*, the hippest program on the air in the mid-1970s, Martin taught a whole generation of young people the distant, cool, ironic sensibility summed up by the gesture he popularized—the four-fingered drawing of double-quote marks in the air.

In the 1960s, chat shows aimed at big audiences invited onto their chairs and sofas show–business figures, of course, but also novelists, adventurers and explorers, politicians, even academics. And when these figures from the land of real life ventured onto the television stage, something remarkable—by our lights—happened: They were treated with something very like dignity. They were expected to be amusing, of course, but they were not regarded by host and audience alike as intrinsically ridiculous figures who could command the camera's affection only if, like Bob Dole on the Letterman show after his 1996 election defeat, they consented to act the buffoon. The television of the 1970s taught its audience that nobody was entitled to that sort of respect, least of all the ludicrous bigshots who once imagined they could take it for granted.

THE PARANOID MOMENT

THE HEROES OF MANY OF THE MOST POPULAR BOOKS AND MOVIES OF THE 1970s share a common problem: Their government is trying to kill them. Robert Redford is hunted down by America's intelligence services in 1975's *Three Days of the Condor* because he has learned too much about their murderous inner workings. Jack Lemmon discovers that the U.S. embassy in Chile is complicit in the kidnapping of his daughter in the 1982 movie, *Missing.* Warren Beatty's 1974 *Parallax View* portrays the U.S. government recruiting social misfits to assassinate dissenters. The middle-aged businessman hero of Robert Ludlum's 1972 thriller, *The Osterman Weekend*, is told by the CIA that one of his best friends is a Soviet agent, only to discover that it is his supposed CIA protector who is really out to get him.

Not so long before, America's spies had been seen as vigilant defenders of democracy. The liberalism in vogue in the 1950s was a self-consciously tough-minded liberalism: cool, worldly, knowing. Arthur Schlesinger Jr. evangelized for this liberalism in the deft character sketches in his monumental, if not always reliable, three-volume history of the New Deal. Bad liberalism was sentimental about the poor, like Frances Perkins. Good liberalism was caring but unillusioned, like Harry Hopkins. Bad liberalism was self-righteous, like Harold Ickes. Good liberalism accepted human frailty, like Tommy Corcoran. Bad liberalism was pacifist, like Henry Wallace. Good liberalism met force with force, like Dean Acheson. Bad liberalism was naïve about power, like poor failed Woodrow Wilson. Good liberalism knew how to use power, like the glorious FDR—or like the ruthless but principled James Bond. Joseph Conrad had envisaged the secret agent as the paradigmatic modern man in a 1907 novel, but it was Ian Fleming's spy who captured the imagination of postwar America. Bond is simultaneously an organization man and an individualist. He has access to the truth in a world of deception. Above all, he can do wrong for a greater good without losing his moral bearings.

Modern writers with a polemical quarrel with the 1950s like to represent those years as a time of moral näivete, the era of Ozzie and Harriet. In fact, Americans of the 1950s made something of a fetish of moral complexity. They perceived their country to be locked in a shadowy war against a totalitarian enemy. The enemy used dark methods—blackmail, propaganda, manipulation, counterfeiting, murder—and could only be defeated by an adversary willing to use those same methods. Democracies forbid themselves to do such things. But if democracy did not do them, it would lose the shadowy war. The way out of the dilemma was to recruit a small band of men willing to lose their souls for the sake of heaven—who would commit the unspeakable acts necessary for the defense of democracy and then protect democracy a second time by keeping those acts a deadly secret. The idea that America's most heroic defenders must of necessity go unacknowledged and unrewarded appealed to the pop existentialism of the 1950s. Years later, William F. Buckley recalled the mood of the time in a series of spy novels set in the tensest moments of the cold war. In the second of the novels, *Stained Glass*, the young CIA man Blackford Oakes is assigned to assassinate a charismatic young German political leader. Axel Wintergrin is brave, decent, admirable in every way—but his determination to reunify his country threatens to trigger a general war between the United States and the Soviet Union. Oakes befriends Wintergrin, warns him, attempts to avoid responsibility for his death, but ultimately cannot escape. Years later, Oakes meets Allen Dulles, the CIA head who ordered the ficticious murder. Oakes tells Dulles that the United States did the wrong thing. Dulles replies, "'I believe you are right. I believe Wintergrin was right. The Russians—I believe—would in fact not have moved. But do you want to know something I *don't* believe, Oakes?' his voice was strained. Blackford was silent. 'I *don't* believe the lesson to draw is that we *must not* act because, in acting, we may *prove* to be wrong. And *I* know'—his eyes turned to meet Blackford's—'*that you know that Axel Wintergrin thought so too.*'" "Both men," Buckley sadly notes of Oakes and Wintergrin, "had read Camus."[33] It was not credulity but a self-conscious sophistication that led a man like Senator Leverett Saltonstall, a liberal Republican from Massachusetts, to offer in 1966 this explanation for Congress's ignorance of the activities of the Central Intelligence Agency: "It is not a question of reluctance on the part of CIA officials to speak to us. Instead, it is a question of our reluctance, if you will, to seek information and knowledge on subjects which I personally, as a member of Congress and as a citizen, would rather not have."

The United States managed to get surprisingly far into the century of total war without much in the way of an intelligence service. After 1940, however, the country more than made up for lost time, and an alphabet soup of spy services was entrusted with the emergency powers of wartime. From a legal point of view, World Wars I and II did not end until 1976, when Congress finally declared a formal end to the national emergency proclaimed in April 1917. Not until 1976 would there exist a congressional committee specifically charged with oversight of the intelligence agencies. Given the breadth of the powers Congress had entrusted to the president, the real shocker was that the abuses were not even more numerous and more flagrant.

The shattering of half a century of government secrecy began in March 1971, when thieves broke into the FBI office in the aptly named town of Media, Pennsylvania, and stole a thousand files. In dribs and drabs over the next few weeks, the Media burglars released items from those files to a large number of newspapers, giving every one of them—even the *Harvard Crimson*—its own little exclusive. The files offered a glimpse into the FBI's domestic intelligence operations and showed that the agency was keeping eyes on a troublingly wide range of people: local antidraft activists, a black student group at Pennsylvania Military College, and the radical daughter of a liberal congressman, Henry S. Reuss of Wisconsin. The Media revelations jolted the country. House Majority Leader Hale Boggs of Louisiana denounced the "secret police prying and spying" of the FBI, and charged that his home phone had been tapped, as had been the phones of three antiwar senators: Democrats Birch Bayh of Indiana and Wayne Morse of Oregon, and Republican Charles Percy of Illinois. Senator Harold Hughes, a Democrat from Iowa, bitterly accused President Nixon of fostering a "trend toward repression" via "the relentlessly increasing emphasis on wiretapping, bugging, no-knock entry, subpoenaing of private notebooks and tapes from news reporters, increased surveillance by the government of dissident political groups and the attempts by the government to intimidate the communications media." Senator Sam Ervin of North Carolina, who had opened hearings into the Nixon administration's surveillance program the previous month, declaimed in his opening statement, "When people . . . grow afraid to speak their minds freely to their government or anyone else, . . . then we shall cease to be a free society."

To the Nixon administration, these accusations were shockingly, monstrously unfair. What had Nixon done that Presidents Johnson and Kennedy had not done? As attorney general, Robert Kennedy had ordered the wiretapping of Martin Luther King Jr.—a story broken by Drew Pearson in 1968, evaded by Kennedy until his death, and confirmed in 1975. The King tap was only one of untold hundreds ordered by the Kennedy administration, an administration that Lyndon Johnson implicitly chided in a January 1967 State of the Union address that condemned the "bugging" and "snooping" of the recent past. Not that Johnson was any more averse to bugging and snooping than the Kennedys: His Justice Department renewed the order to eavesdrop on King.[34]

Indeed, it was one of the conceits of the early Nixon days that Republicans respected civil liberties better than Democrats. Warren Harding calmed the spy scare of 1919–20 and released Socialist Party leader Eugene Victor Debs from the prison to which the Wilson administration had sent him for opposing the draft. Woodrow Wilson segregated the federal civil service and the District of Columbia's streetcars; Franklin Delano Roosevelt pioneered the political use of the IRS (among his victims: Joseph P. Kennedy); Harry Truman threatened to draft the miners to end a peacetime coal strike; and John F. Kennedy used the FBI to frighten the steel companies into rolling back a price increase. President Kennedy was implicated in three murder plots against heads of state: Ngo Dinh Diem of South Vietnam, Rafael Trujillo of the Dominican Republic (cut down by CIA-provided weapons), and Fidel Castro of Cuba. "We were running a god-damned Murder, Inc., down there in the Caribbean!" Lyndon Johnson is said to have burst out when he was briefed on his predecessor's secrets.

But the precedents of the past were going to be harder for the Nixon administration to escape than its more high-minded members hoped. For one thing, there was the character of their boss—a man who was determined to prove himself every bit as tough as his longtime opponents and who had succumbed to the fatal delusion that the limits of the permissible were defined not by the law, but by what his opponents had managed to get away with.

Nixon was motivated by more than his personality flaws, however. He and his national security adviser Henry Kissinger were attempting to extricate the United States from Vietnam with a particularly complex three-way diplomatic carom shot. They would seek a rapprochement with China in order to push the Soviet Union into a détente with the United States, and they wanted détente with the Soviet Union so that they could squeeze North Vietnam harder without fear of international repercussions. Each step of this intricate minuet required the strictest secrecy—and when secrets leaked, as they did almost from the moment the administration began, Nixon and Kissinger were prepared to use fair means or foul to identify the culprits and fire them. The Nixon administration's first national-security wiretaps were installed in the spring of 1969 on the phones of four journalists and a dozen national-security aides after the leak of confidential information on the administration's arms-control negotiating strategy.

No leak inflicted consequences as lasting and fateful as that of the Pentagon Papers by a former Department of Defense consultant named Daniel Ellsberg in the spring of 1971. The Pentagon Papers were forty-seven volumes of documents on the origin and conduct of the Vietnam War assembled on orders of Secretary of Defense Robert McNamara. McNamara was a character who would have fascinated Euripides: a man of palpitating moral doubts entirely lacking in moral courage. He had concluded by mid–1966 that the Vietnam War was futile and unwinnable. Yet he continued to preside over it, knowingly wasting thousands of lives and tens of billions of dollars. His motive, as best as anybody can tell, was nothing so vulgar as careerism (indeed, by quitting in 1966 McNamara would have made himself a hero to the Harvard-Georgetown-Hyannisport world, the only world whose good opinion he ever cared for), but rather an inability to look his president in the face and honestly deliver bad news. Unable to do the job himself, McNamara decided to assemble the most damning possible antiwar dossier, set it before the president, and let the documents do the talking. The idea was idiotic. Lyndon Johnson was not the sort of man to be talked out of a policy by anything so feeble as a pile of dusty old papers. *He* was in Vietnam for a cluster of psychic, political, and ideological reasons far beyond the ken of a Gradgrind like McNamara. Johnson believed that the American electorate tilted rightward, not leftward, and that if a civil-rights-and-welfare-spending Democratic president abandoned Vietnam to communism after 25,000 Americans had lost their lives battling it, the United States would plunge into a right-wing reaction that would make McCarthyism look like the harmless Toryism of Sir Walter Scott. Maybe Johnson was wrong about that, but that's what he thought, and the papers were not going to change his mind. McNamara eventually figured that out and permitted Johnson to shunt him to a do-gooder job at the World Bank even before the papers were completed. Ellsberg, one of the redactors of the Papers figured it out too, but he was not prepared to go so quietly.

The Pentagon Papers demonstrated how eagerly the Kennedy administration had embraced war in Vietnam. They showed President Kennedy pressuring South Vietnam's Diem to accept American ground troops as early as 1961, and they implicated Kennedy in the 1963 coup that ousted and murdered Diem. The Papers discredited the official version of the August 1964 attack by North Vietnamese gunboats on the destroyer *Maddox* that had provided President Johnson with his legal authority for war. U.S. naval forces in the Tonkin Gulf had been raiding North Vietnamese territory for six months *before* the attack on the *Maddox*; the North Vietnamese had every justification for firing on the ship. The Papers also revealed that the text of the Tonkin Gulf resolution had been drafted long before the attack on the *Maddox*, as had the plans for the bombing of North Vietnam. They also unveiled some potentially awkward information about friendly governments, notably the information that the supposedly neutral Swedes had provided considerable diplomatic assistance to the United States in the middle years of the war.

The Nixon administration fought and lost a legal battle to enjoin publication of the Papers. The first installment appeared in the *New York Times* on June 13, 1971. Even before the Supreme Court handed down its six-to-three decision in favor of the *Times,* Ellsberg had made the lawsuit moot by providing selections from the Papers to the *Washington Post* and other newspapers. The Supreme Court judgment in the Pentagon Papers case is usually described as a grand victory for press freedom, but it might be more accurate to call it a grand defeat for the ideal of national security. For half a century, courts had generally held that national security must prevail over freedom of the press. It is too often forgotten that the 1919 Oliver Wendell Holmes opinion in *Schenck* v. *United States* that resoundingly argued that freedom of speech can be curbed only to prevent a "clear and present danger" *upheld* the government's power to lock up protesters for distributing anti-draft pamphlets. Another much-quoted Holmes opinion, *Abrams* v. *United States,* this time favored pamphleteers. But *Abrams* was a *dissent*—the majority of the Court affirmed the government's power to suppress subversive speech.

True, through the 1940s and 1950s the Supreme Court took a progressively broader view of free speech. Those were the romantic days of the First Ammendment, when Justice Hugo Black was always pulling his little paperbound copy of the Constitution from his breast pocket, intoning "no law abridging the freedom of the press means *no law,*" and smiting the Philistines who wanted to ban *Ulysses* or *Lady Chatterley's Lover.* In those days, the defense of free speech was a defense of High Culture. Who would ever have believed that the day would come when the First Amendment would demand of its avatars that they speak up for Ice-T's "Cop Killer" or Nazis who wanted to march in front of Jewish old folks' homes or child pornographers on the Internet? And in those romantic days, the small-town dogmatism and Puritanism of state officials sent the court a gratifying sequence of easy cases. The Court held in 1942 that soapbox orators must be allowed to speak their mind unless their words were reasonably likely to spark a riot.[35] It held in 1943—with the country at war!—that public school students could not be made to salute the flag.[36] In

1957 it overturned the obscenity laws of all forty-eight states when it held that a sexually explicit book or film fell afoul of the law only if it possessed "no redeeming social importance."[37]

Deep into the 1960s, the Supreme Court almost invariably deferred to the federal government's understanding of national security. As late as 1968, in an opinion written by the liberal Chief Justice Earl Warren, the Court rejected a claim that the burning of a draft card was a form of political speech protected by the First Amendment.[38] With the Pentagon Papers case, that long tradition of patriotic self-restraint came to an end. Before the federal government could suppress the publication of leaked national security information, Justice Potter Stewart held, it must prove that the leak would do "irreparable" harm to the national interest, an almost insuperable legal barrier. On remand, the trial courts rejected the government's contention that the papers disclosed intelligence-gathering methods and other important national secrets. The "real tragedy" of the *Times*'s decision to publish the papers, Hubert Humphrey said, was that it corroded faith in government. The Pentagon Papers documented how deceitfully the Vietnam War had begun, and they suggested too how readily the U.S. government would exploit claims of national security to spare itself political embarrassment.

The courts never again fully trusted invocations of national security. In 1972, in the first major national security case after the Pentagon Papers case, the Supreme Court drastically reduced the attorney general's thirty-year-old power to wiretap alleged subversives. Unless there was a substantial connection between the alleged subversive and a foreign power, the Court held, the government must go to a judge, show cause, and obtain a warrant before placing the tap. Perhaps the definitive word was delivered by Judge Gerhard Gessell in the midst of the trial of the White House operatives who organized a burglary of the Beverly Hills offices of Daniel Ellsberg's psychiatrist. The defendants, Gessell ruled in May 1974, could not invoke "national security" as a justification for their crime. He did not believe, he wrote, that the president had any power to order warrantless searches. But even if the president possessed such power, the court "rejects the contention that the president could delegate his alleged power to suspend constitutional rights to non-law enforcement officers in the vague, informal, inexact terms noted above. . . . Whatever accommodation is required between the guarantees of the Fourth Amendment and the conduct of foreign affairs, it cannot justify a casual, ill-defined assignment to White House aides and part-time employees granting them an uncontrolled discretion to select, enter, and search the homes and offices of innocent American citizens without a warrant."

Fatefully, however, the person whose faith in government was most utterly corroded by the leak of the Pentagon Papers was Richard Nixon. Nixon had at first been inclined to shrug off Ellsberg's leak. After all, the Papers followed the story only up to the spring of 1968: They made Kennedy and Johnson look bad, not him. Henry Kissinger changed Nixon's mind. The defense of government secrets, Kissinger argued, must not be influenced by partisan feeling, with Republicans acquiescing in leaks embarrassing to Democrats and Democrats doing the same to Republicans. Nixon had been elected custodian of all the nation's secrets. If the Papers contained information damaging to relations with allies or that tended to undercut support for a war that must be ended with honor, however recklessly begun, Nixon was responsible for keeping them sealed. The courts' acquiescence in the Ellsberg leak convinced Nixon that the regular mechanisms of government could not be trusted. Ellsberg was, after all, one of the authors of the nation's nuclear warfighting plans, and the perceived urgent need for information about him—what else he might divulge, what influence could be brought to bear on him—led to the creation of the White House Special Investigations Unit, the Plumbers. No Papers, no Plumbers. No Plumbers, no Watergate.

The 1972 McGovern campaign was one of the more hysterical in recent American politics. Harry Truman had let loose some savage remarks in 1948, but even he compared his Republican opponent to Hitler only once. George McGovern did it habitually. The Watergate break-in, he repeatedly declared, was "the kind of thing you expect under a person like Hitler."

Nor did McGovern relent after his defeat in November. At Oxford University in January 1973, he warned that the United States had moved "closer to one-man rule than at any time in our history." Perhaps McGovern was an extremist, but more level-headed Democrats echoed his harsh accusations. Delivering the Democratic reply to the 1973 State of the Union message—which Nixon chose to present in writing rather than in person—Senator Edmund Muskie intoned on national television that, "We in Congress fear, as all Americans fear, the threat of one-man rule." After the firing of Special Prosecutor Archibald Cox in October 1973, anticorporate activist Ralph Nader lost his composure altogether: "Every citizen in this land must strive to reclaim the rule of law which this tyrant has been destroying month by month, strand by strand."

The struggle between Nixon and his critics was like one of those movie saloon fights that smashes up not only the combatants, but the piano, the mirrors, and the bar. Nixon's adversaries denounced him as a rogue president, a lawless monster entirely unlike his sainted predecessors (including General Eisenhower, who was retrospectively rehabilitated by Democratic partisans for the occasion). Nixon replied by letting slip a few truths about what those sainted predecessors had really been up to. It was Nixon who divulged the information that Presidents Kennedy and Johnson had surreptitiously taped conversations in their offices ("an outrageous smear" sputtered Joseph Califano, a former Johnson aide, but it was true). It was Nixon who contended, at an August 1973 news conference, that Kennedy and Johnson had burglarized "on a very wide scale." When the story broke in the spring of 1973 that Nixon had proposed using the Internal Revenue Service against 575 big Democratic contributors—a proposal immediately vetoed by Treasury Secretary George Shultz—somebody leaked to *Time* magazine evidence that the Kennedy and Johnson administrations had *actually* done what the Nixon administration had in the end decided *not* to do. President Kennedy had ordered the IRS to audit eighteen right-wing groups and the Fair Play for Cuba committee, and then later to audit nineteen left-wing groups. There was no George Shultz in the Kennedy administration, and the orders were carried out. The Kennedy IRS had then quite illegally released to law-enforcement agencies the tax returns of groups it deemed subversive. During the Johnson administration, the IRS had set up its own security program, which maintained files on almost nine thousand persons and nearly three thousand organizations. And although nobody ever proved any political connection, it is an odd coincidence that private citizen Richard Nixon was audited three times between 1961 and 1968.

This tit-for-tatting had its effect on the public. Even as Nixon's poll numbers plunged, a large and consistent majority continued to agree that Nixon's actions were no different from those of past presidents. The tit-for-tatting may have had its effect within government too. It set in motion the prolonged tragedy of the House of Atreus that has gripped Washington since 1973, with Republicans and Democrats investigating and prosecuting each other to enforce the ever-stricter standards of probity demanded by the accumulating mountain of post-Watergate ethics laws. Many Nixon loyalists believe to this day that "Deep Throat"—Woodward and Bernstein's Watergate source—was someone very close to the top of the CIA who wanted Nixon hustled out of town before he revealed any more Kennedy-vintage shenanigans. That's the thesis, for example, of John Ehrlichman's 1976 novel, *The Company*. But if knifing Nixon to save itself was the CIA's plan, it failed as miserably as did its Kennedy-era schemes to topple Fidel Castro by passing him drugs that would cause his beard hair to fall out. E. Howard Hunt told the Watergate grand jury in May 1973 that the CIA had provided his team with false identification, tape recorders, and cameras for the burglary of Ellsberg's psychiatrist. Grand jury secrecy being rather less than it is cracked up to be, then as later, the story appeared almost immediately in the *New York Times*. That whiff of CIA-Nixon collaboration set into motion the *Times*'s top investigative reporter, Seymour Hersh.

In the fall and winter of 1974, Seymour Hersh detailed in the *New York Times* the CIA's involvement in the 1973 Chilean coup and in domestic illegalities, triggering a scandal in many ways more shocking than Watergate. The CIA's charter forbade it to operate on U.S. soil. Catching agents and traitors who spied upon the United States was the job of the FBI, a law-enforcement agency obliged, in theory anyway, to comply with the Fourth, Fifth, and Sixth Amendments. Early on, though, the CIA had chosen to disregard its charter. From the early 1950s until 1973, the CIA had reviewed every letter addressed to or from the Soviet Union: 28 million pieces in all, of which 215,000 had been opened and read without any legal authority. In 1967, acting on the belief that there were foreign intelligence connections to the American New Left, the CIA and the FBI jointly created a domestic espionage program known as Operation Chaos, just like the bad guys in the old "Get Smart" series. Chaos opened files on some thirteen thousand people, of whom seven thousand were American citizens.

Senator Frank Church of Idaho hastily put himself in charge of a Senate committee to investigate CIA wrongdoing. His fellow Democrat, Representative Otis Pike of New York, assumed a similar role in the House. Large portions of the Pike committee's scathing and supposedly secret report were leaked to a radical New York newspaper, *The Village Voice*. The Ford administration tried to head off the congressional committees by appointing a commission chaired by Vice President Nelson Rockefeller, but instead of protecting secrets, the existence of the Rockefeller commission probably encouraged the spilling of more. Church—a grandstander looking for an issue to ride into the 1976 Democratic presidential nomination—was forced to go even farther to control the headlines. What ensued was in some ways a ludicrous spectacle—Republicans and Democrats vying to outdo each other's protestations of horror and surprise at information that for three decades they had worked overtime to avoid.

Since 1947, the CIA had been responsible for thousands of covert operations. It had overthrown or tried to overthrow governments in Guatemala, Indonesia, Laos, Ecuador, and Iran. It had sponsored guerilla attacks upon the seacoasts of China and North Vietnam. It had recruited a 35,000-man secret army in Laos during the Vietnam War, not informing Congress until years later. The agency had overseen a secret assassination program in Vietnam that killed some 20,000 Viet Cong cadres. It had been deeply involved in Chilean politics since at least 1964 and was implicated in the coup that overthrew Chile's elected Marxist president, Salvador Allende, in September 1973. In pursuit of truth serums and brainwashing drugs, it had experimentally dosed American citizens with LSD and other psychotropic drugs without their knowledge or consent. In 1953, one of those human guinea pigs, an army scientist named Frank Olson, had killed himself while under the influence of the drug by jumping out the window of the New York Statler Hotel. (The CIA had company. In September 1975, the Army confessed to thousands of abusive drug experiments between 1953 and 1969.) The agency had cooperated with the Mafia in a series of attempts upon the life of Fidel Castro. When those failed, the CIA infected Cuba's pigs with swine disease, killing half a million of them.

It was like peeling wallpaper. Tear away one strip, and a bit of the next panel comes off with it until finally the whole wall is bare. The CIA revelations led directly to the exposure of the secrets of the FBI, especially its spying upon the civil rights movement. It was only in 1972 that Americans had learned of the Tuskegee syphilis experiments begun in the 1930s—experiments that had left black victims of venereal disease untreated even after a cure had been found. Now they learned that the FBI had regarded Martin Luther King Jr., and his associates as subversives, and had conducted a surveillance program on King second only to that ordered by Bobby Kennedy against Teamsters' boss Jimmy Hoffa. Nor was it only blacks who were spied upon. The FBI had opened files on more than one million Americans, opened more than ten thousand letters a year without warrants, and committed at least 239 illegal burglaries since 1960. Its agents apparently provoked some of the crimes the bureau was supposed to be preventing, including five Molotov bombings in 1973 and 1974 intended to make it seem that one far-left faction was warring upon another.

It seemed that the country was ruled by mysterious agencies that answered to no one. At a press conference in July 1975, President Ford felt obliged to insist that "there are no people presently employed in the White House who have a relationship with the CIA of which I am personally unaware." Suddenly the CIA, and the intelligence services generally, found themselves despised and mistrusted. Congress, the press, the universities looked on them as the henchmen of Third World dictators, fomenters of secret wars, and (after the beard story!) irresponsible nutcases. President Carter signed an executive order forbidding assassinations and directed his CIA director, Stansfield Turner, to purge the agency of its old covert operators.

The we're-all-on-the-same-side spirit that had once rendered treason odious and cooperation with the national security forces a patriotic duty evaporated. In the early 1970s, a former CIA agent, Philip Agee, founded a newsletter that began publishing the names and addresses of CIA agents in foreign countries. One of the men Agee identified, Robert Welch, the Athens station chief, was murdered in December 1975. Welch's killers were never apprehended. After that, the public identification of CIA agents became something of a sport for the left-wing press worldwide. The Paris radical newspaper *Liberation* published the names of forty-four alleged CIA spies in France in January 1976. It said that it "did not wish the death of anyone," but commented that retaliation was a risk that agents of the CIA ran. *Liberation* added twelve more names to its list the next day. The London weekly *Time Out* published the names of sixty alleged agents in England, Italy's *La Republica* published the names of eight in that country, and a left-wing Dutch weekly named seven who allegedly operated in the Netherlands. The American media never went so far as that, but they went far enough. The journalism magazine *MORE* asked twenty American editors and publishers what they would have done in a situation like Welch's. The replies were printed in January 1976. Only six of the twenty—Walter Cronkite, William Shawn of the *New Yorker*, William Rusher of *National Review*, Norman Podhoretz of *Commentary*, William Thomas, editor-in-chief of the *Los Angeles Times*, and the syndicated columnist Jack Anderson—replied with an unequivocal no. The editor-in- chief of UPI said he would publish. So would the executive editor of the *Miami Herald*. "Of course I would publish his name," said David Sanford, editor of the *New Republic*. "The threat of death is an occupational hazard suffered by persons who would be covert agents of the CIA abroad." The editor of *News-*

day would have published—but would first have generously given the CIA time to get its man out of the country.

Under this mood of suspicion, the government had greater and greater difficulty winning convictions in national-security cases, even when the accused were clearly guilty. In August 1973, it took a federal jury in Gainesville, Florida, only eight hours to acquit seven members of Vietnam Veterans Against the War and one associate of conspiring to disrupt the 1972 Republican convention. Seventeen radicals who raided a draft office in Camden, New Jersey, in 1971 were acquitted by a jury in May 1973, apparently because one of those involved in planning the raid had been an FBI informant. Charges against another eleven Camden defendants were dropped the following month, after the trial judge told jury members they could acquit if they found the government's police methods "fundamentally unfair." The Berrigan brothers—two Catholic priests accused of an immense list of illegal acts—were freed after their jury deadlocked in April 1972. The riot convictions of five of the Chicago Seven—who had provoked violence at the 1968 Democratic convention in Chicago—were overturned on appeal in November 1972. And in October 1973, the government was constrained to drop its case against Weatherman, members of a radical group responsible for a campaign of bombings, when the judge ordered the prosecution to tell him about the "espionage techniques" it had used to acquire its evidence.

Through the 1960s, wild-eyed radicals had flung one seemingly paranoid accusation after another at the FBI, the CIA, and the Pentagon. In the 1970s, so many of these allegations turned out to be true that many Americans had trouble accepting that there could be any accusations that were *not* true. Louder and louder doubts were heard about the official verdicts on the assassinations of John F. Kennedy, Martin Luther King Jr., and Robert Kennedy—so much so that in 1978, the House of Representatives gave the go-ahead to a select committee that opened the halls of Congress to every conspiracy theorist who had once skulked on the margins of American life. The committee's final report, released in July 1979, endorsed two conspiracy theories out of three. President Kennedy, it said, had likely been the victim of the Mafia, King of a conspiracy of right-wing

St. Louis businessmen, and Robert Kennedy of the Palestinian terrorist Sirhan Sirhan acting alone. More important than the report's findings was its very existence, which lent the authority of Congress to the charge that the investigations of these killings had been negligent at best and deceitful at worst. To believe a report issued by the chief justice of the United States, drawing on the resources of the entire federal law enforcement apparatus—that marked one as a chump. The outstanding conspiracy theory of the 1970s—the bookend to the 1960s attacks on the work of the Warren Commission—was the conviction that American prisoners of war had been left behind in Vietnam. This belief inspired the first "Rambo" movie, *First Blood*, by far the most commercially successful Vietnam film. What motive the government in Washington would have for forsaking POWs was never very clear. But then, the motive did not have to be clear. As John Travolta, playing an eyewitness to what appeared to be the accidental death of a local politician, frets to another character in the 1981 Brian De Palma movie *Blow Out*: "If they can get away with killing him, they can get away with anything." The script did not explain who "they" might be. It didn't have to. Everybody could be counted on to supply his own sinister antecedent to the pronoun. You can begin to see what Henry Kissinger was thinking of at his famously gloomy January 28, 1975, press conference when he pronounced that there was "a crisis of authority" crippling the Western world.

PART II

DUTY

THE GREAT REBELLION

"Honor Thy Self."

—*Magazine ad for Johnnie Walker Black whisky, c. 1972.*

IT'S 1912. OFF THE BOAT FROM PALERMO, ONTO THE DOCKS OF THE LOWER EAST Side of New York, step a young bricklayer and his wife, shuffling nervously down the gangway toward a life of hardship. The young Sicilians will never feel at home in their new country. They will never speak the language properly, never adjust to the climate or the strange sounds and smells of city life, never trust the police, never emerge from the slums of Mulberry Street. They will endure these sacrifices, and countless more, all for the sake of their children. But things do not get much easier in the next generation. The bricklayer's son will come to manhood in the midst of the Great Depression, and then be drafted, sent to boot camp, and shipped out to combat—quite possibly to land at Anzio and point a gun at his first cousin. If he survives, he'll return home, get a job, marry, father four children, and encumber himself with a mortgage on a house in Bensonhurst or Canarsie, all before the age of thirty-two. He lives this way, shouldering his obligations in war and peace, because it's never occurred to him that there is any other way to live.

Stories like that were *the* American story of the first sixty-five years of this century. Instead of a boat from Europe, it might have started on a farm in Nebraska, or a coal town in Kentucky, or a sharecropper's shack in the Mississippi Delta. But each of these family sagas shared the same somber themes: hardship and sacrifice, duty and obligation. Life was labor and toil, and its rewards were never to be reaped by oneself, always by one's children. Then something astonishing happened. Sometime after 1969, millions of ordinary Americans decided that they would no longer live this way.

An early 1970s advertisement for hair dye featured a lovely blonde simpering, "This I do for me." The ad would have spoken more directly to the times had it only added: "and this, and this, and this." One could fairly call it the greatest rebellion in American history. It may have lacked the blood and gunpowder of the political rebellions of the past. There was no Boston Tea Party, no firing upon Fort Sumter. But it was more earthshaking than any of the violent uprisings of the past. In hundreds of thousands of kitchens, offices, and classrooms across the continent, Americans in their multitudes shucked the duties and broke the rules that their parents and grandparents had held sacred. From now on, Americans would live *for themselves*. If anyone or anything else got in the way—well, so much the worse for them. "Clear your mind then," advised one of the many bluntly titled best-sellers of the 1970s, *Looking Out for Number One*. "Forget foundationless traditions, forget the 'moral' standards others may have tried to cram down your throat, forget the beliefs people may have tried to intimidate you into accepting as 'right.'"[1] Another best-seller urged, "When you say 'I should do this,' or 'I shouldn't do that,' you are also in many cases allowing yourself to be trapped by the past, following rules set down by parents, teachers or other mentors that may no longer have real meaning for you in our crisis culture."[2]

These were not, of course, new ideas. "I shun father and mother and wife and brother when my genius calls me," wrote Ralph Waldo Emerson before the Civil War. Nietzsche made a career out of the same thought in the 1880s; Ayn Rand made a fortune out of it in the 1950s. But in years past, few Americans could muster the nerve to live up to this bracing credo. You don't find many self-sufficient individualists in small towns (as Sinclair Lewis complained in *Main Street*), and you find fewer still in immigrant tenements. For all Emerson's popularity, in his day and for a century afterward an American would have been ill-advised to execute the great man's advice. Country clubs blackballed men who left their wives. Even as rich and powerful a figure as Nelson Rockefeller suffered for defying society's conventions. In 1961, the 53-year-old Rockefeller, then governor of New York, divorced his first wife. Two years later he married 36-year-old Margaretta "Happy" Murphy, who had the previous month divorced *her* husband and surrendered to him custody of their four children. Rockefeller had been the overwhelming favorite for the 1964 Republican presidential nomination. The remarriage knocked twenty percentage points off his popularity among Republican voters almost overnight. "Rockefeller's problem," reported pollster Lou Harris, "is his divorce and remarriage. . . . Make no mistake about it, it is a crippling element particularly among women, and has just about destroyed his chances." This was true even in permissive states like California, one of the few states in which Rockefeller still held his lead among Republicans into the summer of 1964. Unfortunately for him, the new Mrs. Rockefeller bore a son three days before the June California primary. This reminder of the scandal wiped out Rockefeller's lead in the state, delivering the primary—and the nomination—to Barry Goldwater.[3]

Americans today may look back on these events as proof that their elders were absurdly easy to shock. It would be more accurate to say that those elders were shocked by different things. Had Rockefeller been in the habit of making unsuccessful passes at his female employees, his behavior would have seemed ludicrous rather than scandalous in 1964. Had he been photographed on a yacht trip in the company of a pretty woman, no broadsheet newspaper in America would have deemed the story fit to print. But abandoning his wife of more than twenty years for a younger woman— that was an offense that outraged the country. "Have we come to the point in our life as a nation," thundered Connecticut Senator Prescott Bush, father of the future president, "where the governor of a great state—one who perhaps aspires to the nomination for president of the United States—can desert a good wife, mother of his grown children, divorce her, then persuade a young mother of four youngsters to abandon her husband and their four children and marry the governor?"

In 1964, the answer was no. Two decades later, the question would be almost incomprehensible. Rockefeller and Murphy were consenting adults. They had fallen in love. Why shouldn't they be together? What right had their former spouses to trap them in a loveless marriage? And why would the former spouses want to? To travel the mental distance between our time and the time immediately before ours, we need to understand the outlook that would have found the behavior of a Bob Packwood or a Gary Hart unpleasant or comic, but that of a Nelson Rockefeller wholly unacceptable.

Contemporary Americans value sincerity above almost everything else. Mid–century Americans cared less about sincerity and more about responsibility. Their classic movie, *Casablanca*, celebrates two men and a woman who stifle their true feelings of love and jealousy in order to do their respective duties. It was not that the moral standards of mid–century were so impossibly high. Americans then were actually rather less inclined than we are to demand perfect sexual fidelity.[4] But what they did demand was that adults live up to the obligations they had shouldered. They would not have blamed Nelson Rockefeller for ceasing to love his wife. They would not have expected to hear about it if he had discreetly sought other companionship. But when he discarded the wife to whom he was bound, and then lured another woman away from the responsibilities to which she was bound, they turned their backs on him as a moral outlaw.

It was this ethic of responsibility that the young couple from Palermo carried in their shabby luggage and that the Americans of the 1970s overthrew and replaced. Fittingly, in the middle year of that decade, 1975, Nelson Rockefeller was sworn in as Gerald Ford's vice president. By then, the Happy Murphy brouhaha looked as quaint as some sepia-tinted photograph of Lily Langtry. Why shouldn't a rich and powerful man take a younger and prettier wife? Why should he be expected to live up to the oppressive expectations of others? What mattered—as the people of the 1970s assured each other as they talked about their marriages and relationships over endless glasses of suddenly chic California white wine—was "doing what was right for *you*."

BY ANY MEANS NECESSARY

IN APRIL 1976, WEST POINT INSTRUCTORS NOTICED DISTURBING SIMILARITIES IN the 823 exams they were grading for a third-year electrical engineering course. The exam had been a take-home paper—meaning that students worked on it in their own rooms, using their texts and notes—and that created abundant opportunities to cheat. But who could imagine that the gray-clad cadets summoned to serve "Duty, Honor, Country" would ever exploit those opportunities? The West Point honor code proclaimed that a cadet neither cheated nor tolerated cheating in others, but after a month of investigation, it became clear that the school had been senescently living in the past. By August, the school had convicted ninety-four cadets of cheating, and another forty-four had quietly resigned. Nasty rumors of an even larger scandal could not be hushed. In April, the *Washington Post* quoted unnamed cadets complaining that the cheating scandal was much bigger than the school was willing to admit. In June, a cadet named Timothy Ringgold publicly charged that half the test-takers, more than four hundred students, had been involved in the cheating ring. Ringgold did not substantiate his charge, but three months later, in a gesture that suggested that West Point felt remorse for singling out some students for punishment while others escaped, the secretary of the army announced that the expelled and dishonored cadets of the class of '77 would be permitted to apply for admission to the class of '79.

Students have always cheated, even at West Point, but sometime after 1970 they seem to have begun cheating with a new brazenness. In a survey of high school students, the proportion admitting that they had cheated at least once on a test jumped from 34 percent in 1969 to 60 percent in 1979.[5] That same survey found a rapid increase in the number of students who had stolen high-school property as well. In October 1973, the Educational Testing Service required the fingerprinting of all LSAT exam-takers after some law-school applicants were caught hiring others to write the test for them. A Carnegie Foundation report issued in April 1979 lamented a "general decline in integrity on campus": Mutilation and theft of library materials were reported at 80 percent of institutions. Nearly half the students surveyed by Carnegie, 47 percent, said that they believed they must "beat the system" in order to succeed; nearly one in ten undergraduates condoned cheating. In August 1973 the All-American Soapbox Derby stripped that year's prize-winner of his title and $7500 scholarship prize when it discovered that he had used an illegal electromagnet to get a head start over the other cars.

When the kids weren't cheating, they were stealing. "Lately," *New York* magazine reported in 1970, "the situation has become so bad on Lexington [Avenue] in the fifties that groups of stores hired an armed guard, and farther up Lexington, in private-school land, boutique owners call each other daily to pass along warnings and tales." Girls, perhaps emboldened by the new feminist movement, were becoming particularly light-fingered. "One of the startling youth shoplifting statistics," *New York* observed, "is the ratio of girls to boys: 20 to 1. 'Many of the teenyboppers have a mean streak,' [one owner] insists. 'They'll take half a pair of shoes for the simple joy of screwing the establishment and then take it home and put in on the mantle or drop it in a sewer.'"[6] It's not as if the adult world were setting teenagers much of an example. The Internal Revenue Service estimated that revenue lost because of income-tax chiseling rose from 17 percent of the tax due in 1973 to 21.8 percent in 1978.[7] Over those same five years, the FBI reported that criminal frauds by men jumped by 13.2 percent while frauds by women—who were for the first time arriving in large numbers in jobs that gave opportunities to embezzle—rocketed up 49.2 percent.

For more than a century, individualists, bohemians, and dissidents had dreamed of a world in which human beings could make their own moral choices, unpressured by the conventions of society. "In this age," John Stuart Mill wrote in 1859, "the mere example of nonconformity, the mere refusal to bend the knee to custom, is itself a service."[8] The nonconformists now got their wish. "It has occurred to me," wrote a former *Time* editor in a 1972 memoir, "that I've lived all my life for other people, not for their sake, like a saint, but on their say-so. Be nice to your mother. Don't slap your wife. Responsible fatherhood. Succeed at the job. Pick up your socks. Don't offend anyone. Don't make waves. Conform. What do they expect? Do it. What is one's social role? Play it. I'm tired of all that."[9] So tired, in fact, that he quit his job, left New York, and moved to Pago Pago.

In one best-seller of 1973, *How I Turned Ordinary Complaints Into Thousands of Dollars*, a New York lawyer name Ralph Charrel divulged his secrets for getting satisfaction for his grievances. Unhappy about an inept washing machine repair, he telephoned the manufacturer's vice president of customer relations, conned him into thinking Charrel was a friend of the company's CEO, and extracted a new machine. He flew to California and discovered that his rental car was not ready—so he lied to the woman at the counter, told her he was a movie producer in a desperate hurry, and got a fancier car immediately. His phone company failed to correct an erroneous bill; he filed challenges to its pricing policies at the state regulatory body. When Charrel's landlord wanted to demolish his apartment building, he took advantage of New York City's rent-control laws to extract a larger apartment in another building at the same price, plus payment of his moving and hotel expenses, plus $25,000 cash. He endlessly threatened anyone who offended him with a lawsuit. (Which, believe it or not, the canon of professional ethics forbids lawyers to do.) Litigious pests like Charrel have been around as long as there have been law courts. What was unusual about Charrel was the self-justification he offered. His book contended that middle-class Americans should feel *entitled* to lie and cheat. "More and more often, we are forced to deal with unaccountable employees of large conglomerates, or faceless bureaucrats whose telephones are busy, out of order, or worse, left unattended while they filch an extra coffee break or otherwise extend their on-the-job semiretirement. Shoddy, overpriced goods and poor services are a commonplace." Lies and threats are, under the circumstances, excusable forms of retaliation.

One has to wonder if something like this line of thought was at work in the minds of the exam cheaters, shoplifters, tax evaders, and embezzlers who proliferated in the 1970s. Politicians lie. The sons of the rich avoid the draft, but the sons of the poor ship out to Vietnam. The daughters of the rich attend private school, while the daughters of the poor are bused across town. Inflation enriches owners of real estate and other hard assets, even as it reduces the standard of living of wage-earners. *The system is crooked. They're robbing me. They owe me.* In 1964, according to the University of Michigan's annual poll, fewer than one-third of Americans endorsed the complaint that "the government is pretty much run by a few big interests looking out for themselves"; 64 percent took the sunny view that government is run "for the benefit of all." Fourteen years later, the proportions were almost exactly reversed. Sixty-seven percent glumly espoused the "few big interests" answer; only 27 percent endorsed the "for the benefit of all" alternative.

Sourness and cynicism pervaded the America of the 1970s, and the sourness and cynicism have never quite lifted. It was to this cynicism that the great movies of the early 1970s spoke, and in turn the movies, books, and television of the 1970s inculcated a deeper cynicism still. In 1969, Francis Ford Coppola and George Lucas co-founded the first domestic independent production company to have much commercial success, American Zoetrope. Their venture opened the way for a burst of cinematic creativity in the United States during the early 1970s—arguably the finest period of American movie-making. It was in the early 1970s that the gangster movie displaced the Western. Criminal enterprise, not the opening of the continent, suddenly seemed the defining American metaphor. In *Chinatown*, which competes with *The Godfather* as the movie of the period most admired by cinephiles, Jack Nicholson plays a private detective who discovers that Los Angeles is built on theft and murder: the theft of water rights from neighboring towns and the murder of anyone who knows the truth. *Chinatown* won an Oscar in April 1975 not for Jack Nicholson's magnificent acting—he lost to Art Carney in the long forgotten *Harry and Tonto*—but for its paranoid classic screenplay. Cynicism about law seeped so deeply into American culture that a Watergate conspirator could, not altogether disingenuously, invoke it as an excuse for his misdeeds. In May 1973, Jeb Stuart Magruder, the deputy director of the 1972 Nixon re-election campaign, attempted to extenuate his actions in testimony to the Senate Watergate Committee by noting that he had seen "people I was very close to breaking the law [in antiwar protests] without any regard for any other person's pattern of behavior or belief. So consequently when these subjects [Gordon Liddy's plans to spy on and disrupt the Democratic campaign] came up, although I was aware they were illegal, we had become somewhat inured to using some activities that would help us in accomplishing what we thought was a cause, a legitimate cause . . . "

"You say a good cause hallows even war?" said Friedrich Nietzsche's prophet Zarathrustra. "I say unto you, a good war halloweth any cause." Much the same might be said of a good antiwar. The Vietnam War hallowed lawbreaking and elevated it to the status of an eloquent form of social protest. That raised the question of why other people, with grievances just as fierce, were not entitled to do the same. Why shouldn't the overburdened taxpayer protest the rapacity of the IRS by undercounting his income? Why shouldn't the anxious college student protest the harsh competitiveness of academia by cheating on exams? Why shouldn't the hard-pressed housewife protest inflation by slipping a package of steak under her coat? The power of the old answers to these questions was fading in the 1970s, and it has never really recovered.

THE NEW WORK ETHIC

DURING THE 1973–74 FOOTBALL SEASON, THE NEW YORK LIFE INSURANCE Company broadcast a television ad in which a bespectacled man in white shirt and tie finds himself on a football field surrounded by uniformed hulking giants. Without warning, the ball is thrown into his hands. He starts to run. The camera cuts to the stands. There is his wife, cheering, "Come on, Hubby, make it for the mortgage!" There is his daughter, shouting, "Come on, Daddy, make it for my college education!" Somehow he manages to trip his way past the astonished players and cross the goal line. Wife, daughter, and dog charge joyously onto the field. A voiceover announces that New York Life can help you carry your ball too. It was an advertisement that summed up exactly what increasing numbers of American men thought was wrong with their lives. One writer commented sourly that the poor schnook with the football "thinks he is being supported by the cheers of his family from the stands." In fact, "Every cheer is a pressure."[10] It may be degrading to women to be regarded as sex objects; it was every bit as bad for men to be regarded as success objects.

When the first baby boomers graduated from college, it was often predicted that they would turn their backs on the competitive, materialistic ways of their parents. That was the thesis of, among others, Yale Law Professor Charles Reich in his 1970 book *The Greening of America*. The United States and the world were, Reich claimed, trembling on the cusp of a new consciousness (he called it "Consciousness III") that would scorn life-wasting work and give itself up instead to ecstasy and play. Even at the time, Reich's breathless generalizations made sensible people wince. Nobody winced, though, at Alvin Toffler's eminently serious *Future Shock*, which extrapolated from the rapidly rising productivity statistics of the 1950s and 1960s to conclude that Americans would soon have more leisure on their hands than they would know what to do with.

Nowadays, Toffler's prophecies sound like a bad joke. As Mom furiously negotiates with clients on her cellphone while racing to pick up Meredith or Emma from ballet class and Dad slaves into the late hours of Saturday night to ready himself for a Monday morning deposition in London, the world of Reich and Toffler seems impossibly remote. But is it really? We all think we know that Americans are working longer and harder than ever. On the other hand, federal statistics show no very impressive increase in the length of the average working day over the past quarter century, and Americans have sufficient free time to have increased their television-watching by hundreds of hours per year since 1970.[11] Can it truthfully be claimed that Americans in general work harder than they did in the day of the plow and the laundry tub, the blast furnace, and the wood stove? The frantic pace of life is very much a middle-class and professional-class phenomenon, the product of two inter-related events: the rush of educated women into the work force and changing ideas about the meaning of work.

Toffler and Reich correctly perceived that the old hard-grinding work ethic was fading as society's need for it diminished. Where they erred was in supposing that a leisure ethic would take its place. Instead, the old work ethic was replaced by a new work ethic, in which one worked to fulfill oneself rather than to support others. The new ethic demanded no less than the old: Seventy percent of the college-educated young people of the early 1970s said they would *not* welcome "less emphasis on work" by society. But the purpose and motive for work—that they did want changed, with less emphasis on competition and money, and more on self-fulfillment and self-expression.[12]

The GI generation, its children came to believe, had been made miserable by "the obsession with achieving and the compulsion to accumulate status and prestige at the expense of one's personality and life."[13] In July 1974, *The New England Journal of Medicine* reported on the results of a now-famous Boston University medical experiment. The researchers had divided a sample of 2,750 men into two groups, based on their psychological profile. One group, "Type A," was perfectionist, tense, active, energetic, and reluctant to relax. The other, "Type B," was placid and accepting. Men with Type A behavior were twice as likely to suffer heart attacks as men with Type B. Within months, the phrases "Type A" and "Type B" had embedded themselves into American English and their implications had soaked into American culture. Over the half-decade from 1968 to Watergate, the pollster Daniel Yankelovich conducted a series of surveys and interviews of the attitudes toward work of new college graduates. Fully two-thirds of the new graduates of 1973, were "career-minded."[14] But what it meant to *be* career-minded had changed dramatically since the 1950s. The Depression-seared GIs had cared most about a job's money, prestige, security—security above all. They were all too ready to believe, as critics of the Organization Man lamented, that "to make a living these days you must do as someone else wants you to do."[15]

After a brief moment of anti-materialistic giddiness in the late 1960s, the college-educated baby boomers decided they agreed with their parents about the importance of money. They differed from them, however, on the importance of prestige. Only 28 percent of the college students of the early 1970s considered "prestige" an important consideration in choosing a job. More than 60 percent considered "the ability to express oneself" important. Nor was that just empty anti-elitist talk. Over the next twenty years formerly prestigious but underpaid professions—schoolteaching, the foreign service, the clergy—conspicuously failed to attract talent, while occupations that were once regarded as humiliatingly servile but now seemed "creative"—hairdresser, chef, dressmaker—would boom.

There was much mockery in the 1980s of the title inflation at the top of the corporate organizational chart. (*New York Times* columnist Maureen Dowd once imagined what would happen to the U.S. government if super-agent Mike Ovitz took charge of it: "Secretary of the Treasury? Secretary of Defense? Nobody's a secretary any more—make them all vice presidents!") But nobody laughed in the 1970s when illustrators became "graphic artists," beauticians became "makeup artists," and dressmakers became "fashion artists." In the austere 1950s, people engaged in the fine arts sneered at and kept their distance from commercial art. But that boundary blurred and then vanished altogether in the 1970s. The hot art form of the 1970s was photography, and its most acclaimed practitioner, Richard Avedon, happily snapped pictures of models in dresses for commercial fees. It was in the 1970s that movie actresses like Jane Fonda and Meryl Streep began referring to themselves as "artists," a self-description that would have seemed as odd in the 1950s as it would now to hear Naomi Campbell or Laetitia Casta claim the title. The zeal for art reached down into the high school curriculum, promoting English into "language arts" and drama into "theater arts." In 1970, an aspiring American artist boarded the bus to New York City. By 1980, quite moderate-sized towns—Minneapolis, Austin, and Winnipeg—had a black-garbed "art scene," even if most of its members earned their living as bartenders.

This trend toward expressive work was accelerated by the rush of women into the workforce. Before 1970 it was uncommon for a married woman to work outside the home, and even more uncommon for a mother of young children to do so. By 1980, half of married mothers of children under six worked for wages. Second thoughts have now developed about this trend, and it's common to hear it attributed to economic necessity—to the productivity and earnings slowdown that occurred in the 1970s. There's some truth to that explanation, but only some.[16] After all, if wives were being driven to work by economic necessity, we would expect the poorest women to be affected most. In fact, it's the wives of husbands who are in the middle of the income curve who are the likeliest to work. Wives whose husbands' wages rank in the top 10 percent are actually more likely to work for pay than women whose husbands' wages rank in the poorest 10 percent.[17] The entry of women into the workforce was caused at least as much by new ideas about the meaning of work as by the need for more family income. "I must find something interesting to do for myself in the world," the mother in the 1978 tearjerker *Kramer vs. Kramer* writes to her son, explaining why she has left home and him. "Everybody has to, and so do I. Being a mommy is one thing, but there are other things too." The Ms. Foundation's widely distributed children's recording "Free to Be: You and Me" drilled the same thought into hundreds of thousands of tiny ears:

> *The Sun is filled with shining light*
> *It blazes far and wide*
> *The Moon reflects the sunlight back*
> *But has no light inside.*
> *I think I'd rather be the Sun*
> *That shines so bold and bright*
> *Than be the Moon, that only glows*
> *With someone else's light*

In the late 1970s, 72 percent of Americans professed to spend a "great deal" of time thinking about their inner lives.[18] An older work ethic would have condemned that self-absorption as a distraction from the proper subject of one's thoughts—the external world and one's tasks in it. The older ethic saw work as an end in itself, and praised or condemned behavior according to whether it helped or hindered one's work. The work done in farmer's fields and mine shafts, on the girders of skyscrapers or the assembly line, behind the counter or the adding machine, was dirty, exhausting, arduous, boring, dangerous. Interesting work was a privilege reserved for a lucky few. "Sure it was a rotten job," was one World War II veteran's appraisal of his career. "But what the hell. I made a good living, I took care of my wife and kids. What more do you expect?"[19] Those were hardscrabble values, formed in hardscrabble times. As America grew richer, it automated or exported to poorer lands its nastiest, loneliest, and most arduous jobs. It required fewer longshoremen to break their backs moving crates onto piers, fewer meat handlers to hold frigid carcasses inches away from whirring blades, fewer tannery workers stinking of acid, fewer merchant sailors thousands of miles from home, fewer cottonpickers spending half their lives bent in two. The American workplace became safer and more pleasant;[20] it required less manual labor and more thinking and imagination.

No company better symbolized this new imaginative economy than Apple Computer. It was founded in 1976 by a fruitarian (like a vegetarian, only minus the vegetables) druggie dropout from Reed College named Steve Jobs and a former long-distance telephone service thief named Steve Wozniak, and incorporated the following year. Apple created the first home computer in 1977. In 1979 it unveiled a word-processing program created by Paul Lutus, a one-time hippie panhandler. At the beginning of 1977, the company was valued at $5,309. At year end 1980, publicly traded Apple was valued by the market at $1.8 billion, more than the Ford Motor Company or the Chase Manhattan Bank.[21] Nothing could have been less hardscrabble than Apple. The company's only assets were the inventions of its employees, who had to be pampered and kept interested or they would walk out the door. So they were permitted to arrive when they pleased and to leave when they pleased, helping themselves to juice from the company refrigerator, taking their compensation in stock as well as cash, deciding for themselves what they would work on and how. Apple was an extreme case. But it bred imitators, first up and down the highways of Silicon Valley, and then throughout America. Apple was for the mass-production American economy of the late 1970s what the Pennsylvania

Railroad was for the agricultural and natural-resource economy of the 1870s: the harbinger of things to come. There the parallel stopped, for the high-tech workplace of the 1970s promised to undo the rigid order and strict time-tabling of the post-Civil War industrial workplace and to usher in a world in which millions of workers, not just a lucky few, would taste the satisfactions of creation.

The changing nature of work changed the meaning of work. Because one was working for identity and personhood, rather than for duty, one's attachment to work was both stronger and yet at the same time more conditional than it had been. The job could demand eleven-hour days; it could not tell workers when those days were to begin or end. (Texas Instruments abolished time clocks for workers paid by the hour.) It could require overalls emblazoned with the company logo, but not a white shirt or short hair. (IBM, possibly the starchiest company in America, junked its notorious white-shirt rule.) It could demand the full attention of mothers of infants; it could not demand that one call the boss "Mister." (The Walt Disney Corporation introduced a new policy requiring everyone from the president of the company on down to wear tags marked with their first name only.) Executive dining rooms and reserved parking spots began vanishing from company headquarters. Robert Townsend of Avis quipped, "If you're so bloody important, you better be the first one in the office."[22] Townsend made himself the first CEO to advocate the contemporary "Are we having fun yet?" style of management. You can see Townsend's influence on a walk through the bookkeeping and data processing floors of an up-to-date company. Look in the cubicles: The staff have festooned their walls and cluttered their desks with satirical cartoons, kitten calendars, mugs with jocular messages, party balloons, Dracula hand puppets, dried flowers, Magritte reproductions, and Xeroxed copies of last night's Letterman Top Ten. In the boss's office are a basketball hoop and a Snerf gun.

The new work ethic was conditional in another way too. If work failed to provide fulfillment and meaning, there was no discredit in quitting it. Between 1970 and 1980, the proportion of married middle-aged men (that is, men between forty-five and sixty-four) who were neither at work nor looking for work nearly *doubled*, from 8.8 percent to 15.7 percent.[23] What were these forty- and fifty-year-old men doing with their time? Many of them were being seduced away from the world of work by more lucrative government benefits. Fewer than one and a half million Americans drew a federal disability pension in 1970; nearly three million drew one by 1980. For those men who could not produce an injury, juicier Social Security benefits made early retirement a far more beguiling prospect. One could quit work at sixty-two in 1980 by accepting a pension somewhat smaller than that offered to those who worked until sixty-five, but still much more generous than the pension that had been available even to a sixty-five-year-old as recently as 1969. Americans had once believed that man must work, at whatever work he could get. Anything was better than taking handouts. "Dependence begets subservience and venality," Thomas Jefferson wrote in *Notes on the State of Virginia*, "suffocates the germ of virtue, and prepares fit tools for the designs of ambition." But if work was valuable only to the extent that it was interesting, dependency might be an acceptable choice if the only work available to that person was uninteresting—or, in the phrase of the time, "dead end."

In the early 1960s, welfare had taken the form of a small weekly cash payment. It could stave off destitution, but was in no sense a substitute for a paycheck. In the late 1960s, welfare payments were raised. More importantly, they were supplemented by a battery of other benefits: Medicaid health coverage, food stamps, special aid to pregnant women and mothers of young children, federal and state housing assistance. For the first time in American history, a poor person who was neither elderly nor crippled could eke out a livelihood from the state. In 1968, only 4.1 percent of American families were headed by women on welfare; by 1980, 10 percent of families were.[24]

If idleness attained a new respectability, so too did wealth won by chance. American state governments had long sternly proscribed gambling. No state except Nevada permitted casino gambling in 1970, and only three had a state lottery: New York, because it needed the cash, New Jersey, because it was unwilling to see its commuters' loose change end up in the New York treasury, and New Hampshire, which saw the lottery as an alternative to taxes.[25] The legislatures that maintained these bans were motivated by the paternalistic impulse to protect poor people from wagering away the rent money. But there was something else at work too: the vestiges of the Puritanical condemnation of windfall wealth, money won by tempting fate. In the 1970s, those vestiges vanished. New York legalized off-track betting in 1971. In 1972 those former bastions of Puritan probity, Massachusetts and Connecticut, instituted state lotteries, as did Michigan and Pennsylvania. By decade's end, fourteen of the fifty states, including seven of the ten biggest, had adopted some form of legal lottery, and New Jersey had thrown Atlantic City open to casinos.[26] On the side of every bus, overhead at every cigarette stand, interrupting the local newscasts were the inescapable ads for lotteries, teaching in thirty-second bursts a whole new attitude toward wealth. Instead of patient accumulation throughout a lifetime of work and saving, there was a new and better way—guess the lucky numbers, pick the lucky cards, and—"Hey, you never know!"

THE COURAGE TO DIVORCE

A SOCIETY IN WHICH PEOPLE ARE ENCOURAGED TO PUT THEMSELVES FIRST IS not likely to be a society in which many people celebrate their golden wedding anniversaries. "[I]f it comes down to your marriage or your identity, we think your identity is more important," advised the authors of 1972's *Open Marriage*,[27] and their opinion was representative. During the first sixty-five years of the twentieth century, about one American marriage in twenty ended in divorce. Since 1980, more than two marriages out of every five—nearly half—have ended in divorce.

The United States had never seen anything like it. No society had ever seen anything like it. The divorce rate had briefly spurted after World War II, as returning soldiers and their wives figured out that the marriages hastily contracted during the excitement of war were not always suited to the quiet of peacetime. Those divorces, however, predominantly involved newly married people who were quickly correcting a youthful mistake. The divorces of the 1970s, by contrast, shattered the marriages of the middle-aged. In 1972, an overwhelming 84 percent of Americans in their forties were married. Ten years later, only 67 percent of forty-something Americans were. "Do you think most Americans getting married today expect to remain together for the rest of their lives?" the pollster of the Associated Press and NBC asked in 1978. Sixty percent responded "no." George Segal and Natalie Wood co-starred in 1980 in a comedy titled, *The Last Married Couple in America.*

Americans had once admired husbands and wives who sustained marriages under difficult circumstances and put their obligations to others ahead of their own personal happiness. In the 1970s the real heroes were those who chucked their marriages. "Joanna is a very unhappy woman," says the warring couple's best friend in *Kramer vs. Kramer.* "You may not want to hear this, but it took a lot of courage for her to walk out of here." Indeed, remaining in a marriage was often proof of one's *lack* of courage, according to a book recommended by that paragon of American normality, Ann Landers. "It is clear that all-too-many married couples live together while having emotionally divorced each other long ago. These are cowards."[28]

What was truly admirable was fearlessly to put one's own needs first. *New York* magazine in 1972 printed the story of a 31-year-old mother of four from the Baltimore suburbs. After a decade of marriage, she was bored and restless. She closed the door on her house behind her, moved to New York, took a job, divorced her husband. "Was I spoiled because I was taking so many other people—like my husband and children, just to pick some at random—over the hill with me in my decisions? Or was I moral in the deepest sense because I would no longer in the name of sacrifice to others—like my husband and children, just to pick some at random—let slip away the one life I was given as wholly mine to do something with?"[29]

Divorce was not only moral, it was healthy. "It has been our experience with patients and friends," trilled the psychologist authors of one of the first popular "how-to" divorce guides, "that both spouses, after an initial period of confusion or depression, almost without exception look and feel better than ever before. They act warmer and more related to others emotionally, tap sources of strength they never knew they had, enjoy their careers and their children more, and begin to explore new vocations and hobbies."[30] Divorce was emancipating even when it came unwillingly. In the 1978 movie, *An Unmarried Woman*, director Paul Mazursky cast Jill Clayburgh as a New York wife whose husband abandons her for a woman he met while buying shirts at Bloomingdale's. After a spasm of humiliation and anger, Clayburgh flourishes. She takes an exciting new job managing an art gallery and rediscovers her sexuality with an artist who is both better-looking and wittier than her husband. Along the way she learns to preserve her independence at all costs. When the artist invites her to come to the Hamptons with him for the summer, she refuses in order to remain alone in the hot, sticky city. For an upper-class New Yorker, there could be no greater sacrifice.

It's one of the favorite clichés of journalism to refer to the mid–century years as "a more innocent time." In many ways, however, they seem to have been a time of fewer illusions than our own. The radios of the 1940s swung to jazzy, arch tunes about love—"This can't be love because I feel so well"; ours ululate with gushy odes to undying passion—"Oh, aye-uh-aye will ul-weeeez love yoo-ooo-ooo-ooo." Earlier generations expected less and were disappointed less. "Don't complain about the things they're not," sang the chorus of sailors in *South Pacific*'s "There Is Nothing Like a Dame," "be grateful for the things they've got." The chorus of women in *Showboat* replied, "Tell me he's lazy, tell me he's slow, tell me I'm crazy, maybe I know." Marriage was tough, marriage was burdensome, but if you made the best of it, didn't grumble, and whistled while you worked you might find at the end that it wasn't so bad after all. But the tongue-biting, looking-the-other-way, shoulder-shrugging and yes-dearing that preserved the marriages of mid–century from altar to grave looked about as appealing to the Americans of 1970 as a dinner of Spam and canned wax beans. The self-sacrifice required to save a faltering marriage, even the lesser dose necessary to preserve a moderately happy marriage, was regarded by those who had grown up in a less arduous era as a betrayal of one's sacred obligation to oneself. "Of course I don't want to lose my husband," wrote a professedly moderate feminist in 1973. "But if our relationship depends on my constantly striving to fit a particular image so I won't lose my man, it isn't worth it."[31] A male New York publishing executive with a Yale degree who'd fled to a new life in Santa Fe, New Mexico, in the early 1970s complained, "[My] marriage represents a side of me, the socially acceptable part. And I live in conflict between that side, the face that pleases other people, and what I am learning is another part of me, a part I like better."[32]

If male executives had wearied of the expectation that they should live for others, their wives were positively seething against it. The trend-sensitive editors of *New York* magazine observed that women's liberation had progressed from being a joke in the spring of 1969, to ubiquity by the fall, to absolute and complete hegemony by early 1970. The rebellion commenced on the island of Manhattan, but by the end of 1970, Gloria Steinem was jetting off to address Women's Republican clubs from Schenectady to Pasadena with stops at Scranton, Columbus, Jefferson City, Colorado Springs, and Boise in-between. "James Kunen, resident radical writer at Columbia and author of *The Strawberry Statement*, thought he was safe until the night the Minute Rice commercial came over the tube. Laura Jacknik, his fiancée, was scraping plates. Preconnubial bliss on Second Avenue. Suddenly the voice-over announces, "Yesterday it was dolls. Today it's Daddy's supper." On the screen is a little girl, maybe 9 or 10, happily whisking up rice on the kitchen stove. Transition shot to father gobbling up rice at the dinner table. Mother announces that his little daughter made it. Close-up of little daughter. Head dipped, biting her lip, proud but demure. Jim was just sitting back, thinking, *Now there's a beautiful thing. I'd be damn proud to have a daughter like that . . .*'There it is. Look! *Typical!*' Laura wound up and let go her first plate against the wall. Unscraped. Every time the commercial comes on now she throws something. Newspapers, ashtrays. She has run out of plates. . . . Don't laugh! Humor is irrelevant. Men of the women's liberation movement have learned not to laugh."[33]

Centuries of women before Laura Jacknik had circumscribed their lives for the sake of husband and family. But nobody was circumscribing life for anything in 1969. The boys were refusing to march off to war. Why must the girls march off to the kitchen? Men were refusing to submit to authority. Why must women submit to men? The divorce epidemic charged that question with special bitterness. After all, *The Feminine Mystique* had been published in 1963. Although it is now remembered as the match that ignited an insurrection, for six years after its publication, not much happened. The spark that sputtered in 1963 blazed in 1969–71. Why?

One reason surely must be the peculiar situation of the baby-boom generation. Before World War II, higher education for women had been extraordinarily rare. Those women whose families could send them to college to earn a B.A. generally came from privileged backgrounds and typically married affluent men, and, the first thing that privilege and affluence in those days purchased was domestic help. A woman with a college degree seldom scraped her own plates. After World War II, democratization of education—the vast increase in the number of B.A.-holders—and the equalization of incomes repealed the exemption of educated women from domestic drudgery. "Today," the witty historian Frederick Lewis Allen observed in 1952, "the daughter of comfortably situated parents had better know how to cook well."[34] As the numbers of these educated drudges grew, so did the revolutionary potential of their underemployment. Aprons bearing the motto "For This I Went to College?" suddenly began appearing upon American housewives in the early 1970s—and then vanished, as the aprons came off.

Another spark-enhancing puff came from the macho style of the antiwar movement. The young men who defied the Vietnam draft very naturally wanted to scotch any imputation that their unwillingness to fight might be motivated by cowardice, that they lacked—that favorite Sixties word—"balls." Hence the famous belligerence of the New Left. Nobody would call a young man who occupied the dean's office and faced down the guns and tear gas of the campus police a coward, right? Hence too the left's brutal attitude toward women, summed up most notoriously by

Stokely Carmichael's quip that the position of women in The Movement was "prone." The women of The Movement had obligingly served the coffee while their men bravely confronted Lyndon Johnson's police state. But as the war wound down, it began to occur to some of these women that they had been played for saps.

No situation comedy of the 1970s was complete without a scene in which a long-suffering woman denounces her chauvinistic husband or boyfriend and walks out the door. In real life, it happened at least as often the other way round: *first* the breakup, *then* the outburst of rage. Much ink has been spilled on the question of whether it was men or women who rebelled first against the strictures of marriage.[35] What one can say for certain is that the demographics of sex in the 1970s favored men more starkly than at any other time in the century. Men typically marry women a few years younger than themselves; women typically choose men a few years older. No news there. But against the background of the baby boom, that tendency had huge consequences. A forty-five-year-old man divorcing his forty-year-old wife in 1977 would be able to choose his second mate from the enormous generation born after 1946. His ex-wife would have to look for a husband among the comparatively tiny numbers of men born between 1927 and 1937. This was not a theoretical problem: The proportion of women aged twenty-five to thirty-four who had been divorced and had not subsequently remarried nearly tripled between 1950 and 1975.[36]

The sudden determination to rewrite family law in sex-neutral ways bolstered the male demographic advantage. Before 1970, most states drew a distinction between uncontested divorces, which could proceed relatively quickly, and contested divorces, which could drag on for years. This imposed a powerful incentive on the more-eager party, usually the husband, to come to terms with the less-eager, typically the wife. In 1969 California rewrote its divorce laws to eliminate the distinction between contested and uncontested divorce, and over the next eight years all but three of the fifty states followed. The usual new rule was that an unhappy spouse need only remove himself from the house and wait a few months. After six months' or a year's separation, a divorce would be granted at the request of either party. The wife's leverage was gone.[37] Nor did the law's tilt against the unwilling spouse halt there. The 1969 California divorce reform put an end to the old bias in favor of maternal custody: Either parent could apply to have the children live with him or her. The California lawmakers and their imitators in the rest of the country were moved by the ideal of sexual equality, but the new unisex custody rules put a powerful new weapon in the hands of husbands, who, by threatening to apply for custody, could bring pressure on their wives to scale down their financial demands. Feminist writers, like Susan Faludi in *Backlash*, express great puzzlement at the plunging size of divorce settlements in the 1970s. But it should be no mystery. Enhance the bargaining power of husbands, weaken the bargaining power of wives, and smaller settlements are exactly what you can expect. "They're all pigs underneath, you know," says one of Erica Jong's bitter characters in her 1977 novel about her divorce. "Even my illustrious Alan—with his cute vasectomy scar and his men's c.r. [consciousness-raising] group. You can take it as a rule of thumb. Pigs is pigs."[38]

With extremely rare exceptions, feminist writers chirruped unconcernedly through this vast collective trauma. (One of those exceptions published a surprisingly successful 1979 book titled, directly enough, *Women Who Kill*: "Women who kill find extreme solutions to problems that thousands of women cope with in more peaceable ways from day to day."[39]) In her 1976 pop-psychological megahit *Passages*, Gail Sheehy assembles testimonial after testimonial to the transformative power of divorce—so much so, she said, that "I began to wonder if divorce is a *rite de passage*. Is this ritual necessary before anyone, above all herself, will take a woman's need for expansion seriously?"[40] To many of the new feminists, in fact, the abandoned middle-aged woman fully deserved her fate, condign punishment for having once accepted dependence on a man. "I cannot get excited about women who are threatened by the thought of being responsible for their self-support *without* alimony," sniffed one female proponent of easier divorce. "Perhaps thirty or fifty years ago economic conditions totally excluded women. Currently, opportunities are available to both men and women. . . . Women can no longer live off the complaint that they had no awareness of their alternatives as teens, as wives and mothers, or as career women. The past is past. And what women are accountable for is what they choose and do now."[41] The revocation of the old promise that marriage meant "assured support as long as they live may be one of the best things that could happen to women," wrote feminist sociologist Jessie Bernard in her influential 1972 textbook, *The Future of Marriage*. "It would demand that even in their early years they think in terms of lifelong work histories; it would demand the achievement of autonomy. They would have to learn that marriage was not the be-all and end-all of their existence. It would not free them from the necessity of knowing how to take care of themselves. It would save them from the pitfalls of too much security. All this would actually be a blessing in a not very impenetrable disguise, for if it is good for men to be saved from normlessness by hemming them in, it is good for women to be forced out of their security. It costs too much."[42] Other feminists might protest against the sexual objectification of women. Bernard understood, to the contrary, that liberation would force women to think ever more obsessively about their beauty. "If commitments are to be limited, women will have to learn to remain attractive. Indeed, they can do so, well on into their fifties and even, folk clichés to the contrary notwithstanding, beyond."[43] And after that—if they make it so far? "Living with oneself can be an exciting odyssey."[44]

It was an odyssey that more and more women began embarking upon. There were only 480,000 divorces in the entire United States in 1965. In 1969 there were 640,000, in 1971 773,000, and in 1975 more than 1 million. By then, divorce was so pervasive that even the religious denominations most hostile to it—high-church Protestants and Roman Catholics—had to make their peace. In October 1973, the general convention of the Episcopal Church voted to recognize the validity of civil divorce, ending the long delays for remarriage within the church that Episcopalians had once faced. The Catholic Church relented too. Between 1968 and 1981, the number of annulments granted jumped seventy-sevenfold.[45]

One million American children lost their families to divorce in each year of the 1970s,[46] but the experts counseled parents not to worry. "We see no reason for parents to apologize to their children for deciding not to be married anymore. *Children would not feel so 'wronged' if their parents did not feel so sorry."* If parents put a positive spin on their separation, the children would not embarrass them by crying and carrying on. One wise mother is supposed to have phrased her announcement thus: "Children, I have good news for all of us. There is going to be more happiness in this house from now on. Daddy and I have decided not to live together anymore, and we will all be happier because of this." "Whew!" the woman's nine-year-old daughter replied, "I thought you were going to tell us that we had to get rid of the kitty!"[47] Only now, as those children reach maturity and tell their stories, are we beginning to hear the children's own version of events. How many scenes were there like this one, from a novel by the daughter of a famous journalist? "'Let's write him letters,' Mom said. 'If we tell him how much we miss him, he'll come back.' Mom's eyes were puffy and red, but she smiled a wide, hopeful smile. 'I love my little girls,' she said. 'He loves his little girls.' My heart started to race. I thought maybe Dad didn't know how much we missed him. So we wrote, furiously, on pads of white paper. . . . I wrote 'I love you,' just 'I love you,' at least one hundred times all over my blank white page."[48]

I AIN'T A-MARCHIN' ANY MORE

ON APRIL 16, 1862, AN EMBATTLED CONFEDERACY ADOPTED THE FIRST CON-scription law in the history of the English-speaking world. Until then, although individual Englishmen might sometimes be sentenced or impressed into involuntary service on land or sea, or required to perform militia exercises on the village green, the assertion by a government of the power to commandeer every able-bodied young man and send him away to fight and die far from home had seemed the very essence of French, German, or Russian despotism. But the century of total war would demand total mobilization.

No country, not even the Soviet Union or China, would put more men and women into uniform during World War II than the United States: 12

million by V-E Day. When the war ended, so did the draft. But peace had not truly returned, and two years later, at the same time as he appealed to Congress for military aid for Greece and Turkey, President Truman reinstated the draft. For the first time in its history, the United States would field a large, standing conscript army. (Britain too: The draft ordered in that country in 1939 would not be lifted until 1962.)

Midcentury America thus became a country of soldier-citizens and citizen-soldiers. Almost every able-bodied male served, even Elvis. The military shaped fashion: the unpleated khaki cotton pants that every man wore on the weekends, the aviator sunglasses, the buzz cuts. Military experience weighed upon the schools: What were the gym classes of the 1950s but basic training without guns? And upon the ballot box: None of the eighteen men nominated by either major party for the presidency between 1912 and 1944 was a veteran; in the eleven elections between 1948 and 1988, the winning candidate invariably was. The service obtruded anytime two American men met in a foreign place. "Where'd you serve?" was as all-purpose a conversation-starter in 1959 as "What do you do?" is now. Then came Vietnam.

The legitimacy of the draft in the United States fluctuates according to its equity. The Confederate draft allowed plantation owners to exempt one white for every twenty blacks they owned, and resentment of this privilege badly damaged support for the Richmond government among non-slaveowners. The horrific New York draft riots of 1863 were provoked in part by the provision that permitted rich men like Grover Cleveland and Theodore Roosevelt Sr. to buy their way out the Union Army. The universal drafts of World War I, World War II, and the 1950s, by contrast, were accepted without dissent.

No draft in American history, however, fell as unequally upon the different classes of society as did the Vietnam draft. High school dropouts were four times as likely as college graduates to be drafted and twice as likely to see combat. This fact was not lost on the lower-class Americans, white and black, who did the fighting and dying. During the war, some upper-class antiwar protesters would profess incomprehension of how the draftees could dislike them. By demanding an end to the war were they not the draftees' best allies? The population on whom the draft fell did not see it that way, and the smoldering of their resentment would heat American politics for the next three decades, periodically combusting into open flame—flame that never burned hotter than during the trial of William Calley, commander of the troops who perpetrated the My Lai massacre. On March 16, 1968, Lieutenant Calley had led a platoon of soldiers of the Americal Division into the steamy hamlet of My Lai, one hundred miles south of the city of Hue. Calley's platoon had been unsuccessfully chasing guerillas for weeks in a counterattack following the Tet Offensive, losing dead and wounded to invisible mines and snipers. Calley had been told that the concentration of huts known as My Lai was a Viet Cong base. He was ordered to burn the hamlet to the ground.

When the Americans entered My Lai there were, as usual, no guerillas in sight. There were no men of fighting age at all, only about two hundred old men, women, and children. Confrontation with these helpless people uncorked some horrible reservoir of savagery in the Americans. They turned their guns on them, killing every one, stopping their ears to their desperate begging and their dying shrieks. The women were raped before being killed. At least one was gang-raped. It was the worst American atrocity of the war.

Word of the massacre at My Lai quickly reached the Americal's commanding officers. They chose to do what American officers in Vietnam too often did when faced with bad news: Hush it up. But the horrible story could not be hushed. It seeped through the army in Vietnam. An officer in another division heard of it and reported the crime to the Department of Defense. Early the following year, Seymour Hersh broke news of it in the U.S. press. A Pentagon investigation culminated in the court-martial of Lieutenant Calley; Calley's immediate superior, Captain Ernest Medina; and three other men. On March 29, 1971, Calley was convicted by a military court at Fort Benning, Georgia, of the premeditated murder of twenty-two Vietnamese civilians. Two days later, he was sentenced to life imprisonment. Medina and the other officers were either acquitted or had the charges against them dropped for lack of evidence. None of the enlisted men at My Lai was ever tried.

My Lai is remembered as a turning point in the war, and indeed it was, but not in the way people usually think. In the twenty-four hours after the military court declared Calley's guilt, the White House received more than five thousand telegrams and fifteen hundred phone calls. The messages ran one hundred to one in Calley's favor. Congressional liberals like Senator Abraham Ribicoff of Connecticut joined with conservatives like Georgia's Herman Talmadge to condemn the verdict. Representative Don Fuqua, a Democrat from Calley's home state of Florida, proposed inviting Calley to address a joint session. "We are his accusers. Let us invite this American serviceman here to tell his story."

The governor of Indiana ordered all state flags to be flown at half staff for Calley. The governor of Utah criticized the verdict as "inappropriate" and the sentence as "excessive." Governor Jimmy Carter of Georgia proclaimed "American Fighting Man's Day," and urged Georgia motorists to drive all week with headlights on. The Arkansas legislature approved a resolution asking for clemency. The lower house of the Kansas legislature demanded Calley's release from prison. So did the Texas Senate and the state legislatures of New Jersey and South Carolina. The draft board in Quitman, Georgia, wired the White House that so long as the Calley verdict stood, it would not induct any more young men. Members of draft boards in Athens and Blairsville, Georgia, and in Elizabethtown, Tennessee, resigned. A Poughkeepsie, New York, radio station invited listeners to call in their opinions. It received more than two thousand calls in just one hour. Only thirty-six defended the verdict.

Alabama Governor George Wallace visited Calley in the Fort Benning stockade and called on President Nixon to pardon him. Wallace then spoke at a rally in Calley's defense at Columbus, Georgia, alongside Governor John Bell Williams of Mississippi. The Columbus rally was just one of a series of demonstrations across the nation; Jacksonville, Florida, Los Angeles, Kansas City, and Dallas quickly followed. By the end of the first week after Calley's conviction and sentencing, 79 percent of Americans polled expressed disapproval of the verdict. Within the month, a Tennessee recording company announced that it had sold more than 200,000 copies of a song titled "The Battle Hymn of William Calley."

On this one issue, populist hawks and campus doves could agree. Calley was—in words attributed to an anonymous soldier that were widely repeated in articles of the time—"just another victim of a war nobody wanted to fight." An antiwar activist said, "The attempt, I suppose, is basically . . . to take the monkey off the individual's back, take it off Calley's back, and put it a step higher—let the generals do what they will with the monkey once it's on their back."[49] Populist hawks similarly saw Calley as an ordinary American boy thrust into a dangerous situation in a war the elites started, bungled, and then wanted to bug out of—and they were instantly ready to believe that when the military condemned Calley, it was attempting to appease the *New York Times* and the president of Harvard and the Episcopal bishop of New York by sacrificing an unlucky grunt.

It was the baby boom that made the inequity of the Vietnam draft possible. In 1964, the boys born in 1946 turned eighteen—and for the first time since 1940, the U.S. military had more manpower available than it needed. Twelve months later, the number of able-bodied eighteen-year-old males jumped by another 35 percent. Altogether, some 27 million men passed through their draft-eligible years between 1965 and 1973. Only 11 million of them ever served in the military and only 1.6 million—6 percent of the total—served in Vietnam. An eighteen-year-old was more likely to be drafted in the peacetime year 1959 than in 1968, the most violent year of the Vietnam War. But if the chances of serving in Vietnam were low, the possibility could never be dismissed from one's mind. Until the Nixon administration instituted the lottery system in November 1969, which let young men know at once whether they were likely to be called or not, the draft-eligible could not be certain until they turned twenty-six whether they would be summoned by the army. "For every man taken, two or three others were dodging from deferment to deferment like children playing hide and seek. All the while they concentrated on the draft, they were delaying decisions about marriage and family and career and were becoming increasingly angry."[50] *Fortune* conducted a poll of elite college students in the spring of 1970 and found that fully half of them damned the United States as a "sick" society. One of the most promising of those students, a young Rhodes Scholar named Bill Clinton, observed in a 1969 letter to the commander of his local ROTC that the best members of his generation felt themselves "loving their country but loathing the military."

The military knew itself to be loathed. "You are facing a world," Vice President Spiro Agnew told the 1971 graduates of the Air Force Academy, "where your efforts, your patriotism, your sacrifice will probably be denigrated." The percentage of Americans expressing "great confidence" in the military dropped from 61 percent in 1966 to 27 percent in 1971—a figure that would not significantly rebound until the Gulf War. A March 1971 Gallup poll found that half of all Americans thought the nation's military budget "excessive." (In 1960, when the military consumed almost twice as much of the nation's total income as it did in 1971, only 18 percent of those polled regarded the defense budget as "excessive.") One telling indicator of how low the military had sunk came in 1974, when General William Westmoreland ran for governor of South Carolina. In one of the most conservative states of the union, the former commander of the Vietnam army was crushed in the *Republican primary* by a former dentist, State Senator James B. Edwards.[51]

The army that splashed ashore at Danang in 1965 may have been as magnificent a force as the United States ever fielded, superbly trained, keen to fight, resolute under fire. But it never threatened Ho Chi Minh with the one thing he feared, the loss of his hold on power. That would have required an invasion of North Vietnam, which President Johnson ruled out at the very beginning of the war. Instead, the United States commenced a war of mass slaughter, on the theory that if only it could kill enough Vietnamese Communists, Ho would knuckle under. This deluded strategy did worse than lose the United States its war: It corrupted the U.S. army. At the same time as Westmoreland was failing, his civilian superiors in Washington were demanding day-by-day statistical measures of success. The disparity between the truth and the news that President Johnson wanted put intense pressure on every officer through the ranks to lie—to report progress where there was none, to count dead civilians as dead guerillas, to assert that an artillery barrage must have killed some of the enemy even when no bodies could be found. Sustained lying corrupts any organization, and perhaps an army most of all.

This army was in trouble already. Unlike the armies of earlier wars, in which men served with their units for the duration, the Vietnam army rotated enlisted men in for twelve-month tours of duty and officers for six month tours. This clockpunching war encouraged a man to hunker down and wait his war out. With every airplaneload of reinforcements, a little more of the turbulence of Sixties America was imported into the army, and with every returning soldier some of the army's demoralization was released back home. In June 1971, the Nixon administration estimated that as many as 39,000 soldiers had become addicted to heroin in Vietnam. Ten percent of the men still remaining in Vietnam were estimated to be heroin users, half of them regular users. Two months later, Flora Lewis reported in the *New York Times* that five men who handled nuclear weapons had been caught under the influence of marijuana, hashish, or, in one instance, LSD. Newspaper accounts described marijuana being smoked openly at the bases in Germany and South Korea, with harder drugs readily available to anyone who wanted them. (In 1979, the year the army launched a harsh crackdown on drug use, almost 9,000 men would be disciplined for drug offenses in West Germany alone.) The Pentagon reported that incidents of "fragging"—attacks by enlisted men on officers—doubled between 1969 and '70, from ninety-six to 209. Thirty-nine of the fragged officers of 1970 were killed.

Racial tension crackled through the armed forces, erupting frequently into deadly riots. On May 22, 1971, a fight between black and white airmen erupted at Travis Air Force Base near Marysville, California. Three blacks but no whites were detained by military police. Two days later, two hundred black airmen marched on the stockade to protest the one-sided arrests. They were repulsed by police. They returned to barracks in an ugly mood, and a comment by a white airman in the hearing of the marchers triggered a four-hour riot in which ten airmen were injured and ninety-seven arrested. A fireman died of a heart attack while fighting a blaze set by black airmen at the base's officers' quarters.

The retiring commander of the Atlantic Fleet, Charles Duncan, admitted that the navy had suffered "dozens" of hushed-up incidents of racially motivated sabotage, culminating in a multimillion dollar fire aboard the carrier *Forrestal*. Shortly after Duncan's moment of candor, racial violence erupted on two other aircraft carriers, the *Constellation* and the *Kitty Hawk*. The seemingly unprovoked *Kitty Hawk* incident was particularly vicious. According to the Senate subcommittee that looked into the matter, black sailors "armed with chains, wrenches, bars, broomsticks and perhaps other weapons, went marauding through sections of the ship, seeking out white personnel for senseless beatings . . ." Three white men were very seriously injured. Many others, both white and black, were hurt less gravely.

This was the sinister background to the Nixon administration's decision to transform the draftee army of the postwar era into an all-volunteer force in 1973. But the same antimilitary sentiment that forced an end to the draft also threatened to stunt the new volunteer force. In each of the first seven months of recruiting for the volunteer force, the army fell short of its enlistment quota. The services were forced to lower their standards and then—as Congress failed to raise military pay and benefits in pace with inflation—to lower them again. Only 3 percent of enlistees in the first six months of the volunteer army had even a partial college education; back in 1961, fully 18 percent of the enlisted men had some college.[52]

The unloved new volunteer army failed dismally in its first fight. In May 1975, Cambodian armed forces seized an American trawler that had strayed within their waters, the *Mayaguez*, and took the fifty-man crew hostage. President Ford ordered an 1,100-man Marine force to free the ship. Early reports announced a stunning success: The *Mayaguez* had been liberated, the crew saved, and all with the loss of only one marine. A sadder truth dribbled out over the next few days. The Cambodians had downed three helicopters before the action commenced, and twenty-three servicemen had been killed in a helicopter crash in Thailand while preparing for the mission to start. Count those dead, and total American casualties in the rescue amounted to thirty-eight marines dead and more than fifty wounded. If the U.S. military could suffer such losses in an attack on *Cambodians*, it made you wonder how the country would fare in a fight with the Russians. And if it had not learned from Vietnam the imperative of confessing to bad news, when would it learn?

This was still not rock bottom. President Carter's new secretary of the Air Force, John Stetson, acknowledged in February 1977 that pilots were quitting at a rate 50 percent higher than before 1973. There were some 130,000 cases of unauthorized absence or desertion in 1977—a record worse than in any year of the Vietnam War. That same year, the military discharged 40 percent of all recruits prematurely for causes such as "apathy" and "bad attitude."[53] Marijuana use continued to rise. In October 1979, the Department of Defense revealed that for the first time since the inception of the all-volunteer force, *none* of the services—not even the normally over-subscribed air force—had met its recruiting quotas for the year. The men the services were able to attract were worryingly often of very low quality. The armed forces require applicants to take an IQ test. Aspiring soldiers with IQ scores that would rank them among the brightest 10 percent in the general population are Category I, and so on all the way down to Category V. People in Category V are not permitted to serve, and the services hope to minimize the number of men from Category IV. Even during World War II, when the army was pressing rifles into the hands of almost every able-bodied man, only 21 percent of America's servicemen were rated as having Category IV IQ scores. In 1979, a dismaying 46 percent of new Army recruits were drawn from Category IV. Recruitment difficulties tempted sergeants to fiddle the numbers: 479 sergeants were fired in November 1979 in the worst of the decade's recurring recruiting scandals. In despair, the joint chiefs recommended the reinstatement of draft registration in November 1978.

During the Reagan defense build-back of the 1980s, military pay recovered and so did the caliber of the young people attracted to the service. But the steady improvement of military competence and esprit since 1981 was not purchased with money alone. It was obtained in very great part by isolating the American military from American society and cultivating in it ideals and codes of conduct that were becoming more exotic in civilian life. In a civilian world that values innovation, ingenuity, and risk-taking, the military offers a home to those who crave tradition, stability, and security. Against a civilian world that seems dedicated to ever-greater personal autonomy, the military stands for ever-more alien order and discipline.

A gulf has opened between these two worlds wider than at any previous point in modern American history. Even in the pacifist 1930s, 4.7 million Americans under age forty had worn the uniform.[54] In 1998, by contrast, the youngest man for whom military service was a normal part of life was fifty-three years old. Soldiers and civilians are increasingly strangers. What little they know of each other, they do not like. Soldiers are more religious and more politically conservative than their civilian peers, and their officers are even more so. In 1996, 67 percent of officers identified themselves Republicans. Only 7 percent called themselves Democrats.[55]

Through the 1980s and 1990s, civilian society has repeatedly attempted to remake the military in its own more easy-going image: repealing the ban on uncloseted homosexuals in uniform, sex-integrating the barracks, relaxing penalties for breaches of discipline. But where the public sees modernization, the military sees degeneration. Since the 1970s, the defended and the defenders have come to resemble two mutually uncomprehending societies, which honor warring ideals and uphold incompatible values.

WON'T YOU BE MY POSSLQ?

"PERHAPS I IMAGINE IT," A NEW YORK JOURNALIST OBSERVED IN 1973, "BUT IT seems to me that fewer and fewer of the songs young people listen to now contain lyrics such as 'You belong to me forever,' 'If you leave me, I'll die,' 'Now that you're mine, I'll never let you go' and the like—the kind of lyrics I grew up with and that always brings to mind images of chains and fetters . . . "[56] Her ears were not deceiving her. As they watched their parents' marriages dissolve, the middle-class young people of the 1970s decided that they wanted to stay a healthy distance from this terrifying institution. "It isn't pathetic any more to be single. As a friend of mine had the wit to reply when someone asked if she were married, 'Good God, no, are *you*?' As much as anything, an unmarried person nowadays is the object of envy."[57] By 1980, almost a quarter of American households contained only one person.

Middle-aged Americans allowed their imaginations to run wild when they thought of the fun these swinging singles must be having. *Newsweek*'s July 1973 cover story on single life was illustrated with a photograph of a slim, sexy blonde in a bikini. If only! The young (and especially young women) stayed single not out of desire, but out of fear. "Romantic love," wrote a feminist named Caroline Bird in 1970, is "a put–up job utilized to trap women into giving up their identities."[58] It's telling that movies that wanted to represent single life as carefree tended to be set in the past, like George Lucas's *American Graffiti*. Movies set in the present-day depicted single life as depressing and dangerous, like 1977's *Looking for Mr. Goodbar*, the story of a young teacher compulsively drawn to singles bars who is murdered by one of her pickups, or *Saturday Night Fever*, a dark picture of sexual exploitation in Italian Brooklyn. That cinematic darkness corresponded to something very real in American life. Between 1973 and 1980, the proportion of Americans who described themselves as feeling a "hungering for community" rose sharply, from one in three to one in two.[59] Americans who turned eighteen between 1971 and 1975 were three times as likely to kill themselves as those who turned eighteen between 1962 and 1966.[60] "I think I'm typical of my generation," sighed a prematurely experienced young woman in a mid–1970s interview. "To live a life of continuous affairs is a big blank. You get nothing from it. But what's the alternative?"[61]

One alternative was quasi-marriage, or what used to be called shacking up, but now carried the wonderfully bureaucratic Census Bureau designation, Persons of Opposite Sex Sharing Living Quarters. (This mouthful prompted *New York Times* columnist Russell Baker to rewrite Christopher Marlowe's line, "Come live with me and be my love," as "Won't you be my POSSLQ?") By 1979, more than one million U.S. households were made up of an unmarried man and woman. This arrangement, once shocking, had lost almost all of its illicit glamour. Instead, it seemed to offer a hopeful Third Way—a relationship more lasting than an affair, minus the unrealistic expectations "that it will last forever," "that it means total commitment," that one person "can fulfill all your needs, economic, physical, sexual, intellectual, and emotional."[62] Best of all, cohabitation based the future of the couple not on some external authority, but on their own desires. "I really don't feel I have to go to somebody and hear them say, now, you're really married," a seventeen-year-old girl confided in a survey of adolescent sexuality conducted by the Episcopal Church. "I feel that I'm living with somebody and I love him very much and I feel that, you know, like if I tell the person I'm living with that I'm married to you—like spiritually—and he tells me the same thing, then we're automatically married as far as I'm concerned. Not because we go to a priest and he tells us we're married and he gives us a piece of paper. We married because we want to. And I think that's more lasting than a piece of paper."[63] Alas for her, cohabitation proved even less lasting than the piece of paper. And when it failed, it left behind feelings of disappointment and betrayal every bit as acute as those inflicted by divorce.

Until the mid-nineteenth century, courts throughout the English-speaking world reasoned much as that seventeen-year-old girl did, and treated a couple who publicly stated their intention to live together as man and wife. This common-law marriage (as it was called) offended the Victorians' preference for legal clarity—what exactly counted as a statement of intention?—and in 1843 the British House of Lords ruled that a marriage was invalid unless officiated by a clergyman or some other person with legal authority. Most of the rest of the English-speaking world conformed to the Lords' decision, although the laggard state of California waited until 1895. That's how the law stood when the newly divorced actor Lee Marvin invited a singer named Michelle Triola to set up housekeeping with him in December 1964. The relationship lasted almost six years. After it ended in the summer of 1970, Marvin sent Triola support payments for a few months, but he remarried in 1971 and the payments ceased. Furious, Triola legally changed her name to Michelle Triola Marvin and sued Marvin for half the $3.6 million she said he had earned over the years they lived together. The newspapers humorously dubbed her demand "palimony."

The lower California courts bluntly rejected Triola Marvin's claim. Even if Lee Marvin had promised to support her in exchange for her companionship, they ruled, enforcing that promise would be tantamount to enforcing a contract for prostitution. In 1976, however, the California Supreme Court reversed the courts below. Censorious attitudes to cohabitation had fallen behind the times. "The mores of society have indeed changed so radically in regard to cohabitation that we cannot impose a standard based on alleged moral considerations that have apparently been so widely abandoned by so many." The court's assessment of public opinion was accurate. By decade's end, more than half of all Americans held that it was morally acceptable for a man and woman to live together outside of marriage.[64] On remand in the spring of 1979, Lee Marvin was ordered to pay Michelle Marvin $104,000.

Federal and state authorities quickly moved to punish businesses and individuals who saw cohabitation as an immoral act or proof of bad character. In 1974, a Trenton, New Jersey, woman filed suit against the State Farm insurance company for denying her automobile insurance because she was living unmarried with a man. The suit evolved into a huge class-action that ended in the abject surrender of the insurers. Soon after, President Ford signed legislation written by Republican Senator William Brock forbidding discrimination in consumer credit on grounds of marital status. Banks could no longer refuse a mortgage to a couple who wanted to buy a house together on the grounds that they were not married. New Jersey forbade landlords to refuse apartments to unmarried couples in 1970; most of the other states soon followed. The handful of holdouts were brought to heel by a federal statute in 1988.

As roundly as marriage had been denounced for its injustice to women, the new cohabitation regime soon showed itself even worse. A woman and man would move in together in the first flush of romance. Years would pass. (Five years typically: The Marvins were spot-on average). The woman would gradually come to depend on the man economically, usually just as the man was losing interest in her sexually. Suddenly the woman would find herself on her own, without any claim on the earnings and assets accumulated by the man during the course of the relationship. Confronted with these genuine injustices, courts haphazardly had to work out new rules. The effect of these new rules was to blur the once-sharp boundary between marriage and non-marriage.

Griswold v. *Connecticut*, the 1965 case that created a constitutional right to buy contraceptives, conferred that right only on *married* couples. The new sexual regime could not, however, halt there. In March 1972, the Supreme Court handed down its decision in *Eisenstadt* v. *Baird*, extending a constitutional right to purchase contraceptives to unmarried and married couples equally. Unlike *Griswold*, which was written by Justice William O. Douglas with characteristic boldness and disregard for precedent, *Eisenstadt* speaks in the quiet, careful tones of Justice William Brennan. *Eisenstadt* is usually treated as nothing more than an afterthought to *Griswold*, but it is in fact the most radical and portentous case of the sexual revolution. In *Eisenstadt*, a six-to-one majority of the nation's supreme tribunal declared it unconstitutional for a state to differentiate between sexual relations within marriage and sexual relations outside marriage: "It is true that in *Griswold* the right of privacy in question inhered in the marital relationship," Brennan reasoned. "Yet the marital couple is not an independent entity with a mind and heart of its own, but an association of two individuals each with a separate intellectual and emotional makeup. If the right of privacy means anything, it is the right of the individual, married or single, to be free from unwarranted governmental intrusion into matters so fundamentally affecting a person as the decision whether to bear or beget a child."[65] *Griswold* was a case about *marriage*. The intimate lives of married couples, Justice Douglas said, must be exempted from the police power of the state because of the unique importance and sacredness of the marital relationship. *Eisenstadt* was a case about *sex*. The intimate lives of individuals, Justice Brennan held, must also be exempted from scrutiny—not out of deference to marriage, but out of deference to the importance and sacredness of sexuality. An institution had been replaced by a network of millions of individual sexual relationships.

Every era tacitly places one liberty ahead of all others; one that must always prevail when values conflict. For late 18th-century Americans, that liberty was freedom of religion. For late 19th-century Americans, it was the right to own and dispose of property. For late-20th-century Americans, it was sexual freedom. So completely were the principles of *Eisenstadt* taken to heart that in 1974 a federal judge declared unconstitutional a New York State law banning the sale of contraceptives to unmarried *minors*. Even the language of marriage began to shift. Forward-looking people stopped referring to "husbands and wives" and took up first the gender-neutral term "spouses," and then later, in deference to cohabiting non-married couples, "spouse" gave way to the vaguer "partner."

If living together out of wedlock was now a protected right, having children out of wedlock must logically also be protected. The Supreme Court struck down a series laws that distinguished between the offspring of wed and unwed unions, explicitly repudiating in 1977 an argument that states had any legitimate interest in buttressing "legitimate family relationships." 1977 was also the year that a major survey by the Centers for Disease Control found that children born out of wedlock were 250 percent more likely to be abused than children born to married parents. As far as the Court was concerned, however, illegitimacy was not a vast social crisis in the making. It was just another lifestyle choice.

"I don't care if I'm an unwed mother. I mean, so what? I mean if people don't like it, screw them." So declares an unmarried pregnant college student in a popular 1974 novel.[66] She was blustering, and went on to admit that she did worry what her mother might say. But her need to worry was coming to a rapid end. By 1979, three-quarters of all Americans thought it was "morally acceptable" to be single and have children. A respectable minority of Americans even argued that illegitimacy was actually to be *preferred* to the husband-wife family. "The mother-child relationship is the essential human relationship," wrote the poet Adrienne Rich in her 1976 book, *Of Woman Born*. "In the creation of the patriarchal family, violence is done to this fundamental human unit."[67]

Even in the 1970s, most people did eventually succumb to marriage—if rather later than their parents and grandparents. Over the first sixty years of the twentieth century, as the country flourished and wages rose, the average age of men at first marriage fell: from nearly twenty-six in 1900 to a low of twenty-two and a half in 1959. There was a gradual rise in the age of men at first marriage through the 1960s—and then a sudden and unprecedented rise between 1971 and 1980, from twenty-three to nearly twenty-five. Women's age at first marriage also rose at a fast clip by historic standards, from under twenty-one in 1971 to twenty-two in 1980. The marriages to which the baby boomers succumbed were, however, very different from the marriages of the past. The proportion of Americans who agreed that men and women had equal responsibility to care for young children doubled, from 33 percent in 1970 to 60 percent in 1980.[68] A much-cited series of studies of public opinion in the typical American city of "Middletown"—which was in fact Muncie, Indiana—were conducted in the 1920s, the 1950s, and then the 1970s. In the 1920s, 52 percent of the teenage girls in Muncie agreed that "being a good cook and housekeeper" was the most desirable quality in a mother. By the mid–1970s, 76 percent *disagreed.* And while women were refusing to run the house, men were mutinying against their ancient obligation to pay the bills. By 1973, barely half of college-educated youth regarded being a "good provider" as a very important quality in a man.[69]

The new marriage gave rise to new kinds of weddings. As Americans chafed against the old rules and obligations of marriage, a vogue for untraditional—indeed, defiantly anti-traditional—weddings spread from the self-consciously rebellious to respectable society. Those were the days of blue-jeans weddings on the shores of the ocean, of weddings solemnized by captains of ferries and tugboats, of pregnant brides attended by pregnant bridesmaids, of . . . well, read the *New York Times* society pages of 1971 yourself. "WESTPORT, CONN., July 11—Miss Wendy Gailmour and David Newton were married here today in the woods outside the rough sawn cedar house the bridegroom designed and built and in which they will live. The bride, whose feet were bare, wore a Mexican wedding dress and carried tiger lilies she had picked up at the side of the road." The

Times did not describe the groom's costume, but a journalist who interviewed the couple later reported that he wore an old shirt, khaki pants, and sandals. As the Westport address suggests, the couple were not hippies. He was a prosperous middle-aged businessman, and she was a teacher. "We decided to have a wedding that would mean something to us," they explained.

In *The Future of Marriage*, Jessie Bernard offered an example of the sort of ceremony she thought should replace the old religious wedding service: a ceremony with no role for the church and precious little for the state, one that forthrightly accepts the likelihood of impermanence, and incidentally one that lets the woman do most of the talking.

THE BRIDE: This ceremony marks the beginning of a time in which we will try to create as best we can a true and honest marriage. We might fail. We hope not. We feel that certain things in the world as it is will impede our efforts. We first reject the legal vestiges of the definition of marriage that treats two people as one, and that one being the husband, such as laws that require a woman to maintain her legal residence at the place of her husband's. We also reject the traditional definition of marriage that divides human activity into two parts—one for men and one for women. Work done by men at the expense of their identity as part of a home and as a parent diminishes their humanity. Homemaking and child raising done by women at the expense of their need to establish their self-sufficiency cannot but injure, restrict, and confine not only women but also their husbands and the children in their care.

We would like to share with you a few decisions that we have made regarding our marriage. I will keep my maiden name.

GROOM: I will keep my name. Neither of us will, in the event of separation or divorce, ask for or accept alimony, but we both recognize our responsibility for child support.

THE BRIDE: We recognize that neither of us to the exclusion of the other is solely responsible for the support of the other or of any children.

GROOM: I don't think men should view the liberation of women as a threat. Too often the man is trapped in the role of the breadwinner, in effect, the hero; and the consequences, if related only in terms of ulcers, are not always pleasant.[70]

Alas, these vows did little good for the marriage at which they were actually used, the 1971 wedding of Derek Shearer, the future Clinton foreign policy adviser and U.S. ambassador to Finland. The marriage quickly disintegrated, and Shearer remarried in 1976.

Fashions come and fashions go. Nineties brides did not wear peasant dresses. They sold a chunk of their stock-market portfolios to pay for the tulle and organza extravanganzas their mothers had scorned. There seemed to be a smallish reversal of the vogue for retaining one's maiden name. But if the clothes and customs of the 1970s went out of style, the habits of mind Jesse Bernard celebrated became more deeply entrenched than ever. Fathers no longer gave away their daughters; the girl clomped up the aisle herself. It caused a sensation in 1981 when Diana Spencer omitted the line of the wedding service in which she promised to "obey" Prince Charles. It caused an equal sensation in 1999 when, at her wedding to Prince Edward, Sophia Rhys-Jones vowed she would obey. But even royalty cannot turn back the clock. What made the traditional vows traditional was that they were *the same for everyone*—each couple made its own individual marriage within the context of overarching norms. Those norms have been bulldozed and dynamited. A bride may recite the beautiful old words of Archbishop Cranmer, but she cannot restore their social meaning. She is having the same do-it-yourself wedding as her friend who plights herself before a yellow-robed monk on the top of a hill; she has merely decided that hers will have a traditional rather than a Tibetan theme.

At the threshold of the twenty-first century, the new egalitarian marriage that prevails in the United States is ricketier than the old traditional marriage ever was. A child born in the year 2000 has less than a one in two chance of reaching his eighteenth birthday with both his father and mother continuously present in his home. In 1995, barely half of American women over the age of eighteen were married and unseparated. Optimists profess to see all sorts of harbingers of greater marital stability, but the truth is that American society is steadily leaving marriage behind. In 1997, half of all American households earned more than $37,000 a year and half earned less. Among those earning less—that is across the whole vast lower half of society—an absolute majority of children were born outside of wedlock. A once-universal institution was dwindling into an upper-middle-class idiosyncrasy, like bottled water or cotton shirts.

LET'S TALK ABOUT ME!

BELIEVE IT OR NOT, THERE WAS A TIME WHEN AMERICANS THOUGHT OF THEM-selves—and were thought of by others—as a taciturn people. The Puritan heritage and the rigors of frontier life had instilled in Americans a mistrust of garrulity, of the blatherskate, of the flibbertigibbet. "Speak not but what may benefit yourself or others; avoid trifling conversation," urged Benjamin Franklin in his autobiography, and even into the mid-twentieth century, Americans wanted to think of their heroes as men of few words, like Gary Cooper or John Wayne. But the public display of one's suffering, one's wrongs, one's pitiableness, one's misfortunes, which would have seemed shameful, ignoble, even disgusting before World War II, became in the 1970s the distinctive American national style. Don't bottle it up; you have a right to tell others how you feel. It was, said the author Tom Wolfe, the undeclared motto of the 1970s: "Let's talk about *me!*"

On April 10, 1975, Betty Ford, the first lady of the United States, entered Long Beach Naval hospital. The first lady's spokesman confessed that Mrs. Ford was to be treated for drug addiction. Two weeks later, Mrs. Ford volunteered that she was an alcoholic as well. These were personal and private secrets of a sort that Americans had once desperately concealed and publicly acknowledging them took considerable courage. Betty Ford may have suspected she had no choice—her secrets were in danger of being spilled by a newly uninhibited press. But she also seems to have believed she was rendering a public service, by rescuing addiction from the dark obscurity to which it had been superstitiously consigned, as cancer and mental illness had been rescued before it. The first lady's frankness taught millions of people that addiction can be successfully treated—but that success requires the addict and family to abandon their face-saving lies and confront the truth.

This was a lesson that Americans badly needed to learn in the coke-snorting 1970s. Unfortunately, they learned it only too well. A dozen years before, Jacqueline Kennedy had dazzled the Washington press with the discretion and delicacy with which she coped with her husband's womanizing. Twenty years before that, Eleanor Roosevelt had bitterly closed her well-bred mouth on the news that her old rival Lucy Mercer had been visiting with President Roosevelt on the day of his death. But Mrs. Ford apparently believed that there was no disclosure too embarrassing to lay before the American public—and the public agreed. She became the most popular first lady since Mrs. Kennedy, hailed and applauded for her courage and honesty.

It's true that the old wall of discretion had begun to crumble well before the 1970s, thanks, in very large part, to the profession of psychiatry. Freudian psychoanalysis had arrived in the United States before World War I, and the exodus of German and Austrian Jews in the 1930s landed on these shores representatives of every psychiatric clique, sect, and heresy. Freudianism reached its apogee of prestige in this country in the 1950s, when a psychiatrist played by Ingrid Bergman could—without anybody laughing or coughing—solve a crime in Alfred Hitchcock's 1946 *Spellbound* by interpreting dreams, and when clinical psychological terms and the new coinages of Freudianism ("paranoia," "repression," "transference") flooded middle-class speech. Still, the cost, lengthiness, and verbalism of the Freudian system guaranteed that psychoanalysis would remain very much a minority practice. In the 1970s psychotherapy was at last democratized. New and cheaper methods of treatment were developed; Blue

Cross, employer health plans, and Medicaid were enlarged to include mental health coverage; and a tsunami of psychological books, articles, lectures, and television appearances broke upon the nation. The Westside Los Angeles telephone book for February 1970 discloses 135 psychologists' offices. By February 1980, there were 233. A psychologist became the lead character of a situation comedy, *The Bob Newhart Show*. With this professional help, Americans in the 1970s began talking their heads off. "Let it all hang out" had in the 1960s been a slogan of the self-consciously countercultural. Half a decade later, every Buick owner in the country understood how very dangerous it was to keep his feelings bottled up.

Classic Freudianism, for all its hostility to religion and traditional ideas of morality, nevertheless remained very much a doctrine of the respectable *Mitteleuropäische* bourgeoisie. Freud suspected that some nasty impulses lurked in the unconscious mind, and he believed that the ultimate goal of therapy was to subdue these impulses and reassert the supremacy of reason and self-control in the individual's life. Freudianism originated in the lands of Kafka and Wagner, of the Brothers Grimm and the Thirty Years' War. Whatever their other failings, strict Freudians were in no danger of being conned into an excessively optimistic view of human nature. But as psychotherapy was Americanized—and even more, Californianized—all those dark Central European anxieties were dismissed as outdated gloom. The mind did not resemble Dracula's castle, with horrors unimaginable chained in its dungeons; it was like a Santa Monica sea house whose windows had become a little grimy. Polish them up, let the outside in and the inside out, and the owners will once again enjoy the sunlight, the ocean zephyrs, and the aroma of orange blossoms.

What these popular psychologists taught—and what the American reading public snapped up by the millions in paperbook editions—was a heady creed. They unabashedly asserted the absolute priority of oneself and one's desires. "If we can learn to love and nurture ourselves," opined the authors of *How to Be Your Own Best Friend* (350,000 copies in print by early 1974), "we will find ourselves richer than we ever imagined." The amazingly astute title of that book was taken from what one of the authors regarded as a great moment in his career of psychotherapy. Counseling a grieving man, the psychologist said, "'You look as if you've lost your best friend.' He said, 'Well, I have.' And I said, 'Don't you know who your best friend is?' He thought for a moment, and tears came into his eyes. Then he said, 'I guess it's true—you are your own best friend.'"[71] One of the decade's most successful self-help books, *Your Erroneous Zones*, sold four million copies between its publication in 1976 and the end of the decade. The author, Wayne Dyer, furiously attacked even the most minimal obligations of ordinary courtesy, which he termed "musterbation," the "shoulds" that crimp the free spirit. Contemporary America was oppressed, Dyer wrote, by the rule that "You must go to a wedding or send a gift, even if you don't like them. You just don't ignore invitations even when you want to. You may feel resentful about buying the gift, but go through the motions anyhow because that's the way things are supposed to be done. Conversely, attending funerals that you'd rather not go to, because you're supposed to. You must attend such formal functions to show that you grieve or respect or have the appropriate emotions."[72] (Dyer, as this quotation suggests, rejected conventional grammar as thoroughly as he repudiated conventional etiquette.)

Only *you* can decide what's right for *you*. In February 1980, when the Marine Corps discharged a woman sergeant for posing nude in *Playboy*, the magazine issued a statement saying, "We are stunned by the military's response. . . . All the women who took part in the pictorial made it clear they were proud of their military service." *They* were proud of their service; what business had the stuffy old Marines to object? Sergeant Bambi Linn Finney was, after all, only taking to heart the advice in *Effectiveness Training for Women*, a handbook published in 1979 to accompany a popular series of courses, that "one of the basic ways to meet personal needs, and bring about changes, is through self-disclosure . . ." A psychologist named Penelope Russianoff barged her way to fame as the country's leading teacher of assertiveness to women. For $150, she led her students through ten weeks of drills and workshops that helped them put their needs first. A graduate of the course, a painter, described what it did for her. "[O]ne occasion stands out; it sounds silly, but it was important. I moved my studio from a small room (the dining room) to the biggest room in the house. I took over the center of the entire place. I have to see my paintings from everywhere, from every viewpoint; they have to be the focal point so I can judge them and experience them. Before I was married, my work space was at the center of my living quarters. But when I got married, the main room became the living room. It seemed the acceptable thing. But I gradually knew I needed to take over the living room. I agonized silently for months about it before making the switch. Then suddenly one day I did it. I got a friend to help me. I had to move all the furniture, even a piano. When my children and my husband came home, it was all done. They had to accept it. There were some hard moments, but I knew I needed it. It was my life and my work at stake."[73] True, the marriage ended in divorce, but no technique can solve *all* one's problems.

PBS persuaded a California family, wonderfully named Loud, to permit the network to install a camera in their home and film everything that happened there. The highlights were edited into a twelve-part series called *An American Family*, and broadcast in the fall of 1973. In 1978, William Morrow issued *Mommie Dearest*, in which the adopted daughter of the movie star Joan Crawford exposed every one of her mother's cruelties and vices to public view. More elegantly, the son of Harold Nicolson and Vita Sackville-West published his *Portrait of a Marriage* in 1973, baring the homosexuality and mutual adultery of a couple who had once been best known for their literary accomplishments, their beautiful garden, and their diplomatic service to England. Not so long ago, it was considered highly improper for former cabinet members to publish memoirs about their time in office. Dean Acheson waited for almost twenty years before publishing *Present at the Creation*, and even then made a point of never quoting President Truman directly. Of the twenty-three men and women to serve in President Eisenhower's cabinets, only one, Agriculture Secretary Ezra Taft Benson, published a memoir, and it was discreet to the point of tedium. Of the thirty men and women to serve in President Reagan's cabinet, a dozen published, as did his chief speechwriter, his first economic policy adviser, and two of his budget directors—and it was only a handful of these writers who didn't have some cruel or hurtful story to tell about the president they had served.

It was a new American style. Phil Donahue's Dayton, Ohio, talk show migrated to Chicago in 1969 and entered national syndication in 1970. It introduced a whole new genre of programming to tens of millions of viewers. Day after day, ordinary Americans caught in problems both ordinary and not-so-ordinary confessed the most minute and humiliating details of their lives to Phil and his studio audience: drunkenness and wife beating, transvestism and credit-card debt, incest and obesity. Before *Donahue*, the entertainer who offered the public a prurient spectacle had felt compelled to adopt a stance of outraged morality. The direct ancestor of the Donahue show had been the breach-of-promise trials of the nineteenth century. In front of an enthralled town, a weeping pregnant girl accused a young man of having lied to her about marriage; the young man would defend himself by arguing that the girl was no unblemished virgin. The Walter Winchells of the radio age continued that tradition. They were angered, appalled, shocked by the juicy story they were about to unveil. Phil Donahue's innovation was to dispense with the old humbug and substitute a new humbug of his own: the non-judgmental hearing, with the studio audience as a combination of jury and dispenser of absolution. Donahue taught all his audiences, in the studio and at home, to react to the squalid, the disgraceful, the immoral exactly the way he did—with an attentive ear and a sympathetic nod of the head. Along the way, he taught his audiences to talk the way his guests did—without any tincture of hesitation, reserve, or modesty.

By 1979, 39 percent of all Americans—and close to 60 percent of educated young Americans—agreed that "people should be free to look, dress, and live the way they want, whether others like it or not."[74] J. Edgar Hoover, a notorious judger of values, had famously fired an FBI agent he spotted with a copy of *Playboy* under his arm. In July 1979, FBI director William Webster formally terminated virtually all supervision of the private lives of his agents. "We are trying to say out of people's private lives unless their conduct—and the emphasis is always on conduct, not personal beliefs—impacts upon the effectiveness of that individual and the bureau." If even the FBI felt it could no longer draw draw value judgments, the non-judgmental millennium had truly arrived.

Among the harbingers of that millennium were Vince Mathews of New York City and Wayne Collett of Santa Monica, California, the gold and silver medalists in the 400-meter run at the 1972 Olympic games. On the winners' platform, the two men slouched and chatted throughout "The Star-Spangled Banner." As Mathews stepped down, he twirled his medal around his finger.[75] Four years before, in Mexico City, the U.S. team's black sprinters had bowed their heads and struck the clenched-fist salute during the medal ceremony. Upsetting as it was to many at home during that season of riots and assassinations, the 1968 incident made a serious point in a dignified way. But Mathews and Collett had nothing to say. They were rebels not only without causes, but without content.

The endless self-expression of the 1970s was uttered in a strangely in-expressive new idiom: a halting language of semi-digested bits of psycho-logical theory ("relationships," "centering," "neurosis") and salvaged fragments of drug-user slang, all uttered in the stammering inarticulation affected by the student radicals of the 1960s. One wonders whether a large part of the appeal of the "you knows" and "kind ofs" and "I'm likes . . ." that settled on American speech like a blanket of dust clogging the gears of a once-clean machine was that Americans retained some residual aware-ness of the shamefulness of the thoughts they were expressing. To come right out and say that one is leaving one's wife because she is no longer as pretty as she was requires a more candid hard-heartedness than most men can summon up. Better, much better, to scuttle backward, covering one's retreat with meaningless broken shards of jargon, separated by grunts, ums, and ah-ah-ahs.

SATAN'S SPAWN

THINK OF ALL THOSE OLD MOVIES IN WHICH A BEAUTIFUL YOUNG WIFE LOOKS UP at her husband with dewy eyes and says, "Darling, I have some wonderful news." In the movies of the 1970s, pregnancy is not so happy. Actress after actress discovers that the child she is carrying is quite literally Satanic. In *Rosemary's Baby*, a pregnant Mia Farrow learns that the baby she's carrying is the Antichrist. In *The Omen*, Gregory Peck and Lee Remick make the same dreadful discovery about their child. Monster-babies drive the plot of the 1970s cult classic, *It's Alive!* And of course a demonic child was the star of one of the decade's most hugely successful movies, *The Exorcist*.

It's hard to remember an era when American popular culture was as nervous of children as in the 1970s. The protagonists of all the most successful situation comedies of the 1970s—*The Mary Tyler Moore Show, The Bob Newhart Show, Rhoda, The Jeffersons, Three's Company*—were cast as childless. (The exceptions prove the rule: *All in the Family's* Gloria announced her pregnancy in the show's 110th episode, in an attempt to perk up ratings. Bea Arthur's Maude had a grownup daughter, but as if to make up for it, Maude herself had an abortion.) With tens of millions of baby-boomer women entering their peak fertility years, statisticians expected a follow-on boomlet beginning in the middle 1970s. Instead, the number of twenty-something women rose and rose while the number of births dropped and dropped. Fewer babies were born in 1971 than in 1970, fewer in 1972 than in 1971, fewer in 1973 than in 1972. The number of births hit bottom in 1974, when just 3.1 million babies were born, down from 4.3 million in 1957. Eighteen New York City hospitals closed their maternity wards in the early 1970s.[76] The total U.S. birth rate plunged to the lowest level seen since the 1930s, to *half* the level that prevailed in the 1950s.

People bear fewer children in economically troubled times. But the Americans of the 1970s did not merely postpone children, as the Americans of the 1930s did. They actually changed their minds about wanting them. In 1945, half of all adult Americans thought the ideal family contained four or more children. As late as 1967, 40 percent of Americans— and 45 percent of American women—thought that four or more was the ideal family. Six years later, in 1973, only 20 percent of American adults— and only 12 percent of college-educated women—thought that four or more children was the ideal. A majority of Americans thought two children ideal in 1980; back in 1936, only 29 percent would have been content with two.[77] The Americans most immune to the economic woes of the 1970s actually turned against childbearing most strongly. In 1971, upper-crust Bryn Mawr conducted a survey of the college's five most recent graduating classes (1966, '67, '68, '69, and '70). About three-quarters of the alumnae participated. They reported giving birth to more than seventy babies. In 1975, the college repeated the survey of recent graduates (1971, '72, '73, '74, '75). Again, three-quarters of the alumnae responded. This time, they reported a grand total of *three* babies.

Abortion and birth control are obviously part of the explanation of the baby bust, but only a part. New York State liberalized its abortion law in 1970, and other states soon followed. The U.S. Supreme Court handed down *Roe* v. *Wade* in January 1973, which recognized abortion as a federal constitutional right. Abortion, once a crime so dreadful as to verge on the unmentionable, edged toward the center of sexual life. In 1975, federal statisticians counted 272 abortions for every one thousand live births; in 1976, they counted 312. New York City recorded 676 abortions for every one thousand births in 1976; in Washington, D.C., the number of abortions actually *equaled* the number of live births. From the late 1970s until the mid–1990s, the number of abortions in the United States seldom dipped below the 1.5 million mark.

Nevertheless, it would be a big mistake to seek a technological explanation for the crash in the birth rate. The women of the 1950s and early 1960s had big families not because they lacked the means to control their fertility—in that case, they would have borne nine or fourteen children apiece rather than three or four—but because they wanted big families. Married women had ready access to diaphragms, and even unmarried women could get them with only a little trouble: The 1879 Connecticut statute overturned by *Griswold* had not been enforced in decades. The birth-control pill appeared on the market in 1961, a decade before the birth rate plunged.

It was women's preferences, not contraceptive techniques, that changed in the 1970s. The women of the 1970s wanted small families—often, they wanted no family at all. Only 50 percent of non-college young women and only 35 percent of college-educated young women regarded having children as "very important" in 1973.[78] These women were unenthusiastic about children because they believed, perfectly correctly, that children would inhibit their freedom and compromise their individuality. "Motherhood: Who Needs It?" demanded Betty Rollins in a famous 1970 article in *Look*. "Even the most adorable children make for additional demands, complications, and hardships in the lives of even the most loving parents."[79] Theologian Rosemary Radford Ruether, argued in her 1975 book *New Woman, New Earth*, "Each generation of women has been sacrificed to its own children. History has been the holocaust of women."[80] It was past time, she and others felt, for the holocaust to end. The adults of the 1970s were adamant: Their needs came first. The truest single detail in a film packed with reminiscences of 1970s daily life, *The Ice Storm*, was the middle-class dinner party at which the children carried and cleared the plates for their parents' friends. In 1973, it would have seemed excruciatingly pretentious to hire a tuxedoed waiter to serve dinner in a private home and shockingly retrograde for the woman of the house to do it. The solution (almost unthinkable in the child-obsessive 1990s) was to assign the task to the kids.

"If a mother has a life of her own, the daughter will love her more, will want to be around her more," promised Nancy Friday in her 1977 bestseller, *My Mother/My Self*. "She must not define herself as 'a mother,' she's got to see herself as a person, a person with work to do, a sexual person, a woman. It isn't necessary to have a profession. She doesn't have to have a high IQ or be president of the PTA to have this added life. So long as she isn't just sitting home, chauffeuring the kids and baking cookies, giving her children and herself the feeling that their life is hers."[81] Wayne Dyer advised, "[I]f you make your children more important than yourself, you are not helping them, you are merely teaching them to put others ahead of themselves, and to take a back seat while remaining unfulfilled. . . . Only by treating yourself as the most important person and not always sacrificing yourself for your children will you teach them to have their own self-confidence and belief in themselves."[82] This teaching found its audience. By the late 1970s, 66 percent of American adults surveyed agreed with the statement "parents should be free to live their own lives even if it means spending less time with their children."[83]

Leaving the care of one's children to others became a test of one's commitment to female independence and equality. "Easing the burdens of motherhood and supporting abortion reform are essential tasks, yet they both imply a continuation of a powerless female responsibility for children and for birth control," complained the feminist writer Phyllis Chesler.[84] The National Opinion Research Center found in 1977 that 55 percent of women agreed that "a working mother can establish just as secure and warm a relationship with her child as a mother who does not work." By 1985, 67 percent of women agreed.

In the past, working women had endeavored to place their children in the care of a relative, typically their own mothers. That sense that children whose mothers worked ought at least to be cared for in the family was fading. In 1977, only 13 percent of the children of working mothers attended day-care centers; by 1985 centers took care of 23 percent of the children of a much larger cohort of working mothers. President Nixon vetoed a comprehensive national day-care plan in 1971, but his view that child care was a family responsibility was already obsolete.

It was every bit as important to put oneself first in one's intimate life as in one's worklife. "No marriage should be sustained for the sake of the children," urged a popular divorce book.[85] Once the divorce had occurred, there was no reason to be bashful about one's sexuality. "In my clinical practice, I've found that those single parents who feel good about themselves and have a healthy respect for their own needs are best equipped to be good parents," cooed Mary Mattis, a psychologist who had spent the 1970s counseling divorced women.[86] Parents must encourage their children, she continued, to "understand a parent's needs." She offered a helpful example of how best to do that. A twelve-year-old boy barged into his mother's bedroom in mid-afternoon to tell her about his big score in a Little League game. (This propensity of children to pop up when they're least wanted inspired one of the most characteristic inventions of the 1970s, the adults-only condominium complex.) He interrupted the mother grappling with her new boyfriend. The son ran out, furious; the mother dressed and caught up with him to impart the decade's new wisdom. Just as she respected his closed door when she suspected he was masturbating, she said, she expected him to respect her closed door. This—the psychologist claimed—calmed the boy. He asked, "'Are you going to have sex again now?' 'Probably not . . . . You know how it is. You can't always get back into masturbating if I've just left the room, can you? We'll probably want to be alone together after bedtime. What are you planning to do now?' . . . . 'I was going to ask if I could go and play with Roger. His mom said I could stay for supper if I liked hamburgers.'" And the boy walked happily off to his friend's house, proving that *Hamlet* might have had a happier ending if only Gertrude had mastered modern communication techniques.[87]

In the past, experts had worried about divorce because it undermined the authority of parents. This was just what the new advocates of divorce liked about it. "The multimarriage family can be seen," *The Courage to Divorce* argued, "as an extended kinship system that provides relief from the suffocating relationships children often encounter and endure in the intact nuclear system."[88] After all, the children had to learn to live for themselves too. The divorced single mother was no longer the stern guardian of Puritan morality who so haunted the collective memory of the 1970s. ("Who first takes our hand away from our genitals, who implants pleasure or inhibitions about our bodies, who lays down The Rules and with her own life, gives us an indelible model?" Nancy Friday demanded.[89]) She was now a friend to her children, almost a sister—just as she was in the 1977–78 television comedy *One Day at a Time*, the first regularly scheduled show to feature a divorced family.

Divorced or married, the parents of the 1970s found it uncomfortable and awkward to exert authority over their children. The boomers who had been raised on the not exactly stern Dr. Spock turned when their own children arrived to Penelope Leach, an English baby guru whose first book appeared in the United States in 1978. Leach popularized the new child psychology of the era, which held that the word "no" crushes children's fragile self-esteem. It might seem paradoxical that the same era could at once so indulge and so neglect its children. But is it? Indulgence follows neglect as surely as hangovers follow booze. The parents of the 1970s may have been more obsessive about their children than the parents of earlier times, more determined to buy the right educational toys, more frantic about placing them in the right school. But this sort of obsessiveness flows much more from the parent's own ego than from the needs of the child. There was much talk in the 1970s of how male sexual hunger transforms women into objects. Parental obsessiveness can do the same to children. Objects? Some were prepared to venture further still, and treat children as commodities. One of the brightest legal minds of the 1970s, Richard Posner of the University of Chicago, a future Reagan appointee to the Seventh Circuit Court of Appeal, proposed that the chaotic system of adoption be replaced by the straightforward sale and purchase of children.[90] He was only slightly ahead of his time. Twenty years later, the sale and purchase of offspring would become a familiar feature of American life, as sperm banks, egg donors, surrogate mothers, and international adoption enabled those with cash to acquire their dream baby. The fateful step toward this baby market of the future was taken on July 25, 1978, when a healthy six-pound girl was born in Lancashire, England: the first human being to have been conceived in a petri dish.

PART III

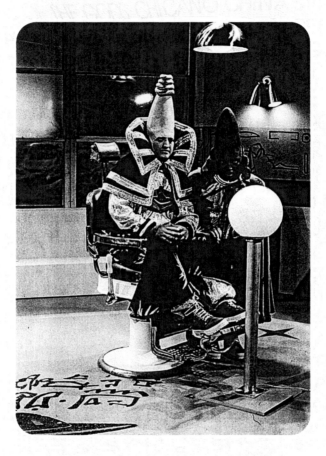

REASON

BEYOND REASON

"Sometimes when we touch,
The honesty's too much,
And I have to close my eyes
And cry."

—*Dan Hill, "Sometimes When We Touch."*

ONE AFTERNOON IN THE SPRING OF 1977, PROVOKED BY ONE CONDESCEND-ing comment too many, the wife of the prime minister of Canada raced up the stairs of the official residence in Ottawa, and tore to bits with her bare hands a tapestry hanging above the landing. She was offended not by the tapestry's earth tones or big nubby knots, but by the words embroidered into it: "*la raison avant la passion*"—reason before passion—the favorite motto of her cold, cerebral husband, Pierre Elliott Trudeau. Margaret Trudeau would commit much worse excesses before the marriage was finally dissolved: smuggling drugs in the prime ministerial luggage, engaging in liaisons with rock stars and playboys, allowing herself to be photographed squatting on a step at Studio 54 visibly without underwear. The tapestry attack may not actually qualify as one of those excesses. It could be thought of as just an especially exuberant way of expressing the mood of the time.

It was a mood that celebrated the emotive and intuitive and denigrated the rational and the intellectual. "Trust your feelings, Luke," was the advice that the spirit of wise old Obi-Wan Kenobi whispered in the climactic moments of 1977's *Star Wars*, and young Skywalker obediently shut his eyes and put his faith in the Force—and not his on-board computer—to aim the shot that would destroy the evil Death Star. It was in their feelings that the Americans of the 1970s put their trust. They drank white wine and luxuriated in the caressing music of Jackson Browne and James Taylor and Joan Armatrading. (*Show Some Emotion* was the title of Armatrading's 1977 hit album.) In the early 1970s, it was estimated that there were some 5,000 "encounter" groups in New York City. The leader of one of them expressed the spirit of the age in a magazine interview: "We're all so locked up in ourselves, we've got so many defenses going that we've forgotten how to feel. We're physically tight and so emotionally tight that we don't dare let go for fear of finding out what we really feel. The point is to get rid of those blocks, both emotional and physical, so we can start growing as human beings again."[1]

What an amazing turn of events. Only a generation before, the United States had been the homeland of efficiency and practicality, a country so uncongenial to dreamers, artists, and poets that they fled for Europe as soon as they could scrape together the boat-fare. And yet, if we cast our mind back only a little further, the turn of events might not seem so amazing after all. The "Oprah-ization" of public life is usually talked of as it were a brand-new thing. It is in reality the return of something antique. A hundred years ago, middle-class life in Britain and America was bathed in the gush of emotions. Reread the poetry of Swinburne or the orations of Daniel Webster, glance at the paintings of Frederick Leighton or old photographs of the obsequies of General Grant if you doubt it. The wry, laconic anti-emotionalism of a Jimmy Stewart or a Prince Philip is a last relic of the early-twentieth-century reaction against the overwrought romanticism of the Victorians. Bob Dole brought to his political speeches the same sensibility that Ernest Hemingway brought to his novels. Hemingway's generation had learned in the fire and slaughter of the First World War to mistrust the man who put his hand on his heart while wiping a tear from his eye. Frederick Lewis Allen recalled the terse manners of his contemporaries: "During the whole three years and eight months that the United States fought [the Second World War], there was no antiwar faction, no organized pacifist element, no objection to huge appropriations, no noticeable opposition to the draft. Yet there was also a minimum of crusading spirit. . . . They"—the men and women of the 1940s—"didn't want to be victims of 'hysteria.' They felt uncomfortable about flag-waving. They preferred to be matter-of-fact about the job ahead. . . . These people were unstintedly loyal, and went to battle—or saw their brothers and sons go— without reservation; yet they remained emotionally on guard. . . . disillusioned and deadpan. . . . "[2]

We think now of the dislike of emotional fuss and show as generically old-fashioned. It is probably truer to say that the laconic style we associate with the GI generation came into fashion in the 1920s and went out in the 1970s, to be replaced by a style reminiscent of the moist, voluptuous sentimentality of a hundred years ago, with the teary television interview replacing black crepe. This was the style of the two party conventions in 1996. It is the style of the most-talked-about mass movement of the 1990s, the evangelical Promise Keepers, who brought stadiums full of middle-aged husbands and fathers together to weep and hug. It is the style of contemporary American evangelicalism. And it is the style of the most successful politicians of the age—the Bill Clintons and the Tony Blairs—as they explain how this or that policy will "save the life of a child." The gurus of the 1970s taught, and we today still seem to believe, that to delve honestly into one's feelings requires one to shut down the analytical lobes of the mind. "People often talk about wanting to be spontaneous, to live out of their feelings," reported the authors of *How to Be Your Own Best Friend.* "They have locked themselves into intellectual boxes, where they hardly know what they feel any more. They become desperate to experience plain, simple emotion. They think if they could throw away their minds, they would be free."[3]

This jargon of the 1970s had a surprisingly respectable history. In the aftermath of World War II, the Army sought techniques to improve the efficiency of small fighting units: the crew of a tank, an infantry squad. It commissioned studies on collective problem-solving, and one set of those studies, conducted in 1946 at New Britain Teacher's College by an MIT professor named Kurt Lewin, found something interesting. As a group of five to seven people worked on a problem, tempers sometimes flared: "Bob, why must you always jeer at everything I say!" "Because, Fred, everything you say is stupid, that's why!" And soon the group was so angry that all work stopped. Underlying the anger, however, was truth. Bob really was jeering; Fred really did talk before thinking. If certain rules were set for the discussion—no criticism of personalities, only of ideas; accept all statements about feelings as true, and then try to understand where those feelings come from, and so on—Bob's and Fred's failings could be addressed without poisoning relations between them. Thus was born Transactional Analysis, so called because it studied specific interactions between particular people over a short period of time.

Transactional Analysis quickly migrated from the military to the business world and thence into the general arsenal of psychotherapy. Along the way it got a new name—group therapy—and a new mission. If an individual could be shown how he mishandled six randomly chosen strangers, he would learn from that experience how to better handle all the other people in his life. But something else happened along the way. The Transactional Analysis *technique* (avoid judging the whole person; stick to the problem before us here and now) was transmuted into a philosophy of life, in which "frankness substitutes for tact, self-expression for manners, non-verbal techniques for language, and immediacy for responsibility."[4] This philosophy condemned abstract reasoning and celebrated nonjudgmental acceptance. Suddenly, the airwaves and newspapers were crammed full of psychological experts blaming rational thought for the ailments of American society. "Armed with their theory," *Psychology Today* charged in 1972, "thinking types go out to do battle with the world. . . . [T]hey can easily become rigid, narrow-minded, and dogmatic. Such pejorative terms as 'martinet,' 'opinionated,' 'difficult,' and 'arrogant' frequently are employed to describe these individuals."[5] Spread-collared business consultants echoed the psychologists. "The majority of businessmen are incapable of original thought because they are unable to escape from the tyranny of reason"— those words of the legendary ad man David Ogilvy are approvingly quoted in the 1984 publishing phenomenon, *In Search of Excellence.*[6]

The condemnation of rationalism was seized upon by the burgeoning environmental movement. It was out-of-control rationality that was fouling the air, ensnaring workers in bureaucracy, estranging mankind from the earth. "There is just no escape from it," moaned the 1974 best-seller, *Zen and the Art of Motorcycle Maintenance*. From what? "The whole thing . . . the whole organized bit . . . the system." Sensing that this wasn't a very helpful definition, the narrator continued: "The 'it' is a kind of force that gives rise to technology, something undefined, but inhuman, mechanical, lifeless, a blind monster, a death force. Something hideous they are running from but know they can never escape."[7] An editorial in *New West* magazine, the California counterpart to Clay Felker's influential *New York*, complained: "Increasingly, we have handed over our destinies, our bodies, our lives to specialized experts. The short-term effects have been dazzling in some cases. Over the longer range, however, our dependence on expertise is creating a paralyzing sense of individual helplessness. And the experts have often been wrong. They showed us how to defeat the Vietcong with technology. They concocted deadly pesticides to increase food production. They devised indestructible plastic substances to take the place of metal and wood. But somehow, in their feverish specialization, they missed the larger picture . . . "[8]

The man in the white coat had been the hero of the hour in the 1940s and 1950s. His radar saved Britain in 1940, his atomic bombs compelled Japan's surrender, and his hydrogen bombs deterred Joe Stalin from invading Western Europe. Twenty-five years later, that same scientist stood arraigned for defoliating and napalming Vietnam, and one best showed one's opposition to that war by turning one's back on modern science and its works.

In retrospect, there is something sweetly comic about the back-to-the-land trend of the 1970s. Who but Americans would display their rejection of materialism and industrialism by buying ten-speed bicycles crafted from materials developed for the space project? Yet for all the folly and self-indulgence of the anti-rationalists, they were onto something real.

For half a century, America's leaders had worked to gather their society under greater control, to make it less volatile, more predictable, more legible. Their economic techniques had smoothed out the violent business cycles of the nineteenth century. Their schools taught similar curricula in similar ways from one ocean to another. Regional accents were smoothed away by television. Local products disappeared as supermarkets replaced corner stores. Zoning ordinances ensured that similar people lived in similar houses within similar neighborhoods. Psychologists kept an eye peeled so that the odd and the eccentric could be speedily treated. The welfare state's taxes and benefits tried to ensure that nobody rose too high or sank too low. In the blue-and-white cards of the Social Security system America acquired its first national identity card; in the Scholastic Aptitude Test, its first national exam; in the Selective Service system, its first peacetime conscription.

Most of these innovations had been initially welcome. Americans who had endured the terrible uncertainty and risk of a wide-open society—Americans who had lived through the Depression, who had kept house in the old tenements, who knew the dread of the summer polio season—were cheerfully willing to exchange the dangers and terrors of the old world for the carefully managed security promised them by the experts. But almost as soon as the bargain was ratified, a new generation of Americans began to question it. They demanded to know: What had they given up? And to whom?

West of the U.S. Capitol and south of the Mall, squeezed into a few blocks alongside the Potomac River, lies the tiny Southwest quadrant of Washington, D.C., the hottest, swampiest district in a hot and swampy town. In the early 1950s, Southwest D.C. was a slum. It contained some of the oldest private homes in the district, brick rowhouses built in the days of Benjamin Harrison and wooden frame structures that dated back to the Civil War. Southwest was home to fish markets and barbershops and clapboard churches and cheap brothels and venerable trees, not to mention some 45,000 people, most of them black and poor.[9] Between 1954 and 1958, in the grandest urban renewal project of the Eisenhower years, the federal government razed almost 90 percent of those buildings, cut down all the trees, expropriated all the shops, and displaced more than half the population. In place of the grime and noise and neighborliness of the old city streets—in place of the horse-drawn watermelon carts and the old women who knew your mother—sprang up a clean, concrete, Corbusian landscape amidst the on and off ramps of interstate highways.

To forward-looking architects and planners, urban renewal made self-evident sense. Jumble would give way to order, decaying houses and ram-shackle shops to hygienic high-rises, chaos to rationality, an all-black neighborhood to a deliberately integrated one. "The universal demand for 'conscious' control or direction of social processes is one of the most characteristic features of our generation," the great free-market economist, Friedrich Hayek wrote in an essay published in 1959. "That anything is not consciously directed as a whole is regarded as itself a blemish, a proof of its irrationality and of the need to completely replace it by a deliberately designed mechanism."[10]

It was against the background of the previous generation's faith in central planning and control that the 1970s' rebellion against rationality has to be understood. Consciously created order looked beautiful in the plans and blueprints; in life it was brutal, alienating, and inhuman. The anti-rationalists saw Southwest Washingtons everywhere: in psychiatry, in nuclear power plants, in table manners. They wanted to do to every one of those Southwest Washingtons exactly what was done in August 1973 to another huge urban renewal project—the thirty-three high-rise towers of St. Louis' Pruitt-Igoe project: Blow 'em up. The 1970s were the decade in which Americans turned against Modernist architecture. Young architects bewildered their Bauhaus elders by delighting in Robert Venturi's *Learning From Las Vegas*, which praised the gaudy horrors of the seedy old Las Vegas strip. That supremely sensitive cultural weathervane, the architect Philip Johnson, scandalized his old colleagues by sticking a Chippendale broken pediment atop his 1984 Madison Avenue AT&T Tower (now the Sony building), and—maybe even worse!—facing the building in stone. Victorian art and architecture returned to fashion. In the 1960s, a careful young man could collect Tissot drawings on a foreign service salary.[11] After 1975, it was a taste only an Andrew Lloyd Webber could afford to indulge. *Old House Journal*, the bible of historic home restoration, began publishing in 1973.

Americans turned against overweening architects at exactly the same moment as they were rejecting cocksure schemes of economic control, overbearing doctors, austere apostles of High Culture, strict enforcers of good order and good deportment of every kind. It was a revolution not so much against institutions, as against the cool, methodical habits of mind underlying those institutions. "[T]o tear down a factory or to revolt against a government or to avoid repair of a motorcycle because it is a system is to attack effects rather than causes," *Zen and the Art of Motorcycle Maintenance* proclaimed, "and as long as the attack is upon effects only, no change is possible. The true system, the real system, is our present construction of systematic thought itself, and if a factory is torn down but the rationality which produced it is left standing, then that rationality will simply produce another factory. If a revolution destroys a systematic government, but the systematic patterns of thought that produced that government are left intact, then those patterns will repeat themselves in the succeeding government."[12] Alas, like all revolutions, this one attacked what was good in the old regime of rational thought just as fiercely as it attacked the bad: ideals of serious scholarship just as much as the excesses of Bauhaus architecture; orthodox religious faith as much the planned economy; modern physics as much as Freudian psychiatry. All too many Americans had felt like cogs in the wheel. Resentment against the crimping and cramping of the individual personality inspired not only the New Left, not only the Berkeley Free Speech Movement and the Students for a Democratic Society, but also the 1964 Barry Goldwater campaign: "[E]ach member of the species is a unique creature. . . . The conscience of the Conservative is pricked by *anyone* who would debase the dignity of the individual human being. . . . dictators who rule by terror equally with those gentler collectivists who ask our permission to play God with the human race."[13]

Those were days in which Americans still carried draft cards, still were expected to show up at the Department of Motor Vehicles once a year and line up all afternoon to exchange old license plates for new. Queues and licenses: That was just the way things worked. But a challenge had been hurled. Why must things work that way? Why must I accept them? The intense questioning of those days has lost its focus and intensity. But it has not ceased to prick. Like a drop of ink in a bucket of water, the questions have blurred, lost their shape, become indistinct, and finally vanished— but in vanishing, they have tinctured the whole bucket.

CRUNCHY GRANOLA

WHEN I WAS SEVENTEEN I KNEW (AS DID EVERY OTHER YOUNG MALE IN MY home town of Toronto) that the place to take a date one hoped to impress was Mr. Greenjeans, an old warehouse hung with plants that served what everyone said was the best spinach salad in the city. (Take a huge mass of uncooked spinach leaves, add chopped-up hardboiled eggs and bacon, and douse in sunflower seed oil and raspberry vinegar.) The owners of Mr. Greenjeans had put into effect one of the iron laws of 1970s-era marketing: If you want people to eat in your joint, festoon it with vegetable matter. F. Scott Fitzgerald called the 1890s the cut-glass decade, because every home that aspired to gentility plopped a cut-glass bowl on its sideboard. In the same way, the 1970s might be called the spider-plant decade. What made a house a home were plants suspended from every wall and over every window. The plants had to be supported by macramé nets. With them you needed hand-made plates and blemished glassware from the Yucatan or Portugal in which you served granola and grainy muffins (if breakfast), salad (for lunch), and paella or fettuccine (at dinner). Furniture was upholstered in earth tones—browns, oranges—and piled high with nubby pillows. Plaster was stripped off the walls to expose the underlying brick, and the broadloom lifted up to reveal the maple flooring. The family wore skirts and shirts made from coarse Peruvian cloth or colorful batiks from Indonesia. Everything was rough, unfinished, crude. In the center of it all stood the only aesthetically tolerable machinery: a $3,000 assemblage of gleaming brushed-steel stereo components—

woofers, subwoofers, monster cables, a turntable precise to the ten-thousandth of a second, amplifiers that could boost the final twitterings of a dying bird louder than the roar of a Super Bowl crowd. A Santa Fe couple who lived this way told an interviewer about a visit from city friends and their ten-year-old daughter. The little girl had refused to sit down on the knocked-together straw-seated chair offered to her. "[T]he child," the hosts realized, "had mistaken the rough-hewn, textured quality of the chair for dirt. Can you imagine a life with no textures? Kids are growing up in a smooth world, where everything is made out of plastic Formica."[14]

Formica was the miracle stuff of the 1950s—smooth, futuristic, artificial, easy-to-clean, cheap. It symbolized the Space Age, the triumph of American industry. Twenty-five years later, that was precisely what was wrong with it. "In general," the environmentalist Barry Commoner wrote in his 1971 book, *The Closing Circle*, "the growth of the U.S. economy since 1940 has had a surprisingly small effect" on the fulfillment of basic human needs. "That statistical fiction, the 'average American' now consumes each year, about as many calories, proteins, and other foods (although somewhat less of vitamins); uses about the same amount of clothes and cleaners; occupies about the same amount of newly constructed housing; requires about as much freight; and about the same amount of beer (twenty-six gallons per capita!) as he did in 1946. However, his food is now grown on less land with much more fertilizer and pesticides than before; his clothes are more likely to be made of synthetic fibers than of cotton or wool; he launders with synthetic detergents rather than with soap; he lives and works in buildings that depend more heavily on aluminum, concrete, and plastic than on steel and lumber; the goods he uses are increasingly shipped by truck rather than rail; he drinks beer out of nonreturnable bottles or cans rather than out of returnable bottles or at the tavern bar. He is more likely to live and work in air-conditioned surroundings than before. He also drives about twice as far as he did in 1946, in a heavier car, on synthetic rather than natural rubber tires, using more gasoline per mile, containing more tetraethyl lead, fed into an engine of increased horsepower and compression ratio." Commoner's dismissiveness about the achievements of the American economy since 1946 makes the eyes goggle. Between 1940 and 1970, the number of Americans living in poverty plunged from about one in three to about one in seven. The advancing economy delivered, among other benefits, near-universal indoor plumbing, the polio vaccine, vacations and old-age pensions, tumbling long-distance telephone prices, refrigerators, and television sets. But to those fortunate people who had already enjoyed most of those good things in 1946, Commoner's haughty judgment sounded more than plausible.

The 1970s were the time when the word "Wonder" in "Wonder Bread" acquired its present ironic connotations. Norman Mailer let loose an amazing attack on the stuff. He denounced an America that "took the taste and crust out of bread and wrapped the remains in waxed paper and was, at the far extension of the same process, the same mentality which was out in Asia escalating, defoliating. . . . "[15] But back when the new bread was introduced, it was indeed a wonder. Before World War II, bread would begin to spoil within hours of purchase, even in the tightest breadbox. Alas, the preservatives that triumphed over mold and other contaminants had their dangers too—and because these dangers issued from the hand of man, they carried a sharp sting of betrayal. The first modern food panic struck in 1959, when Health, Education, and Welfare Secretary Arthur Fleming recommended two weeks before Thanksgiving that shoppers avoid buying cranberries, because some berries from the west were feared to have been contaminated by a weedkiller associated with cancer of the thyroid. State and city authorities across the country banned cranberry sales, and supermarkets yanked cranberries and cranberry sauce off their shelves. In the end, the scare fizzled out, and most canners were able to slap reassuring labels on their products in time for the holiday. At a campaign stop in Wisconsin, a big cranberry state, Senator John F. Kennedy pointedly drank two glasses of cranberry juice. Still, the scare prodded Congress into passing the law that made possible the innumerable scares yet to come: the Delaney amendment to the Food and Drug Act, which forbade the Food and Drug Administration to consider any food safe if it contained even the smallest amount of an additive that produced cancer in lab animals. When Congress said small, it meant small. To get cancer from the tainted cranberries of 1959, a human being would have had to eat 15,000 pounds of them each day, and keep it up for years. Unfortunately for the country's eleven-year-olds, the Delaney amendment only applies to artificial ingredients. Otherwise it would have banned turnips, which contain one hundred times as much antithyroid potency as the weedkiller that sparked the 1959 panic. In fact, most fruits and vegetables are veritable germ-warfare factories of natural toxins, which have evolved to deter bugs and other hungry pests.

The Delaney amendment represented a remarkable reversal in American thinking. When Congress passed the first pure food law, in 1906, it was nature—dirt and germs—that was perceived as dangerous and science— boiling, scrubbing, and disinfecting—that offered safety. From the Delancy amendment, a public that had once been told to trust what came out of cans and bottles received its first instruction in a new wisdom: Safety lay in returning to nature, in preferring sugar to sweeteners, brown sugar to white sugar, honey to brown sugar.

Hitherto, the menace of food additives had been an obsession associated with the far-right wing. In the 1964 movie *Dr. Strangelove*, it is a mad ultrapatriotic general who worries that his precious bodily fluids are being polluted. The political left, by contrast, championed industrial progress, scientific research, and greater human control over the environment. In the 1960s and 1970s, the two ideological poles suddenly shifted—or converged. Suddenly it was progressive to dislike progress. The American Council on Education surveyed college freshmen in the fall of 1972, and was astonished by the hostility it discovered to science and technology. In findings published the following spring, it reported that only 6.9 percent of students wanted careers in engineering, down from 9.8 percent in 1966. Only 1.9 percent were interested in careers in science, down from 3.3 percent six years before. (The promoters of the products created by science and technology were regarded with even greater disdain. "[A]dvertising is regarded as almost the *last* vocational choice by the top 20 percent of campus talent," a vice president of the glamorous 1960s firm Doyle, Dane, and Bernbach lamented to *Advertising Age* in December 1970.) Again and again students insisted that they wanted "people-oriented" work. Who could blame them? Scarcely a year would pass between 1969 and 1982 without a major food and drug scare: cyclamates in 1969, hormones in beef in 1972, nitrites the same year, red dye number two in 1976, hair dyes and saccharin in 1977, coffee in 1981.

Not even American medicine escaped the surge of anti-technological feeling. Americans had good reason to venerate their doctors. Americans who fell sick in 1930 enjoyed only a marginally better chance of recovering than the Americans of 1730. That's not hyperbole. In the summer of 1924, sixteen-year-old Calvin Coolidge Jr. walked out of the White House and onto the tennis court to hit a few balls. He had neglected to wear socks with his tennis shoes, and he developed a blister on his foot. The blister welled up, burst, and became infected. Days later, the president's son was dead.

Much that we now find incomprehensible about the medicine of mid-century—the doctors' priestly garbs of white, their omnipresent gloves and masks, their fanatical insistence on removing husbands and relatives from delivery rooms, their preference for formula from sterilized bottles over breast milk as food for babies—was a holdover from the early years of this century, when doctors knew *why* people got sick, and had a fair idea of how to *prevent* them from getting sick, but were absolutely helpless to *cure* them if they did get sick. Doctors had learned then to put their faith in hygiene. After the discovery of antibiotics in 1942, the old germicidal struggle no longer had to be waged so desperately. But it is hard for a profession to change its ways, and doctors, as they basked in their fantastic postwar prestige, were not inclined to listen to anyone who suggested that they should. If anything, their new triumphs reinforced their worst habits. As doctors got better at curing, they put less effort into consoling; as the machinery in the hospitals improved, they became more resistant to visiting the sick at home; as their power to help grew, so did their insistence on controlling the way that the help was delivered. Patient resentment was inevitable, and it was aggravated by the bitter sexual politics of the 1970s. The medical profession was then overwhelmingly male, and doctors' manner toward women was often condescending. Grievances against gynecologists and psychiatrists fueled many of the first consciousness-raising sessions. Feminists quickly decided that they had more strenuous objections to medicine than the insensitivity of some doctors. They were in rebellion against the most fundamental axioms of medical science.

One million copies of the women's health manual *Our Bodies, Ourselves* had been sold by 1976, instilling in its readers such wisdom as this: "I see an aggressive, masculine system in which diseases (and even normal states like pregnancy) are considered enemies to be conquered through drugs and surgery. I think healing needs to be feminized to include the gentler conceptions of sects like homeopathy. Homeopathy concentrates on the whole patient—body, mind, and spirit—rather than on the disease or on one isolated organ of the body. It strives to build up the person's strength so he or she can resist illness." High-technology childbirth was especially galling. "The woman who is about to give birth is removed from her loved ones, taken to a cold and sterile delivery room, strapped to a table, her legs spread apart and elevated, her knees in stirrups, her arm attached to an intravenous bottle, her belly to an oscilloscope. She looks up into a spotlight. Gleaming instruments and masked strangers surround her. No longer is the American mother an active childbearer, nor has she been since the days of the midwives. Now, strapped down and drugged, she is the object on which the doctor works and her unborn baby is 'the intrauterine patient.' The physician, who regulates women's access to abortions and sterilizations, also controls childbirth and he has transformed it from a natural event into a physician-centered operation. In the late 19th and early 20th centuries, doctors did develop aseptic techniques, x-ray technology, anesthesia, and blood transfusion—advances which reduced deaths in the small number of seriously abnormal deliveries. But even though more than 90 percent of births are normal, doctors use scientific advances not just for difficult deliveries but for routine cases as well and in doing so, turn nativities into technological nightmares."[16]

When invented, that technology had seemed miraculous, not nightmarish. In 1940, 376 out of every 100,000 mothers died while giving birth; by 1975 maternal mortality had plunged to 12.8 out of every 100,000. But as memories of dangerous deliveries faded, "natural," "tribal," "non-western," and "herbal" displaced "scientific" and "modern" as the highest accolades of medical praise. Women's health clinics—which brought babies into the world without the aid of anesthetic or antibiotics—popped up across the land like toadstools after a hard rain, thirty-nine of them by 1976, and in such unlikely venues as Tallahassee, Florida, and San Diego.

The revulsion against technology ran strong enough to sustain the decade's largest mass protest movement, the campaign against nuclear power. Alexis de Tocqueville observed during the French revolution of 1848 how slavishly the men of the Second Republic mimicked the rhetoric, gestures, and even the costumes of the men of the First. Likewise, the antinuclear movement of the 1970s self-consciously modeled itself on the protests of the 1960s. Nuclear power, Ralph Nader insistently repeated, was "our country's technological Vietnam," and it was to be opposed in exactly the same way—not with the technical arguments, expert testimony, facts, and statistics that one might have expected in what was, allegedly, a scientific controversy, but with slogans, songs, sit-ins, passionate speeches, and dark accusations. As with Vietnam, the protesters possessed a certain nugget of truth. The nuclear generation of electricity was a technological marvel that flunked basic economic tests. But the antinuclear movement did not stop there, any more than the anti-Vietnam protesters stopped at pointing out that the Indochina commitment exceeded America's real security needs. It was not nuclear power's economic doubtfulness that had protesters staging rallies under the shadow of the hourglass-shaped cooling tower of the local reactor; it was the protesters' fear and hatred of a technology created for war and now used by gigantic corporations to sustain America's consumerist way of life. The protesters damned nuclear power not merely as wasteful, but as murderous—and they had a martyr to prove it. Karen Silkwood had died in a car crash on her way to present evidence of unsafe practices at the Kerr-McGee power company's Oklahoma plants to a newspaper reporter. An autopsy showed Silkwood's bloodstream dangerously high in tranquilizers, but the antinuclear activists unshakably believed that Kerr-McGee's goons had forced her off the road, a version of events cautiously endorsed by Meryl Streep's filmed biography of Silkwood.

Protesters had convinced four states (California, Iowa, Maine, and Wisconsin) to impose a moratorium on nuclear construction within their borders even before the Three Mile Island reactor near Harrisburg, Pennsylvania, accidentally released radioactive coolant into the atmosphere in March 1979. Three Mile Island would have caused a panic at any time, but by one of those flukes that makes a Hollywood producer's fortune, the accident occurred in the same week that the scaremongering antinuclear movie *The China Syndrome* was released. Pennsylvanians threw their belongings on top of their cars and drove furiously away from Harrisburg. Hundreds of people were arrested attempting to disrupt reactor sites in Arkansas, California, Colorado, Indiana, New York, South Carolina, and Vermont. Some 65,000 people marched on Washington in May to demand the immediate shutdown of all nuclear power plants. President Carter, who had bragged during the 1976 election campaign of having been a Navy nuclear engineer, invited seven of the organizers to meet with him in the White House. The federal Nuclear Regulatory Commission imposed a three-month moratorium on the issuing of construction and operating licenses for new plants. In August 1979, New York State forbade the construction of any more new nuclear plants. When Massachusetts Senator Edward Kennedy challenged President Carter for the Democratic nomination in 1980, he adopted opposition to nuclear power as one of his issues. By then, the Seabrook plant in New Hampshire (the epicenter of the protests because of its proximity to the universities of New England) was under almost permanent siege. A march on the Pentagon over the April 26, 1980, weekend led to more than 300 arrests for trespassing and defacing government property, the biggest mass arrest since the anti-Vietnam May Day rally of 1971. (The Pentagon of course has nothing to do with civilian nuclear power, but old habits die hard.)

By then, the fight was over. Utilities and government agencies had filed forty-two requests for licenses for new nuclear plants with the Nuclear Regulatory Commission in 1973. Two were filed in 1978, and they were the last two of the twentieth century.

So the antinuclear power movement prevailed. Or had it? In 1979, some 13 percent of America's electricity was generated by nuclear power; by

1998 the figure was approximately 20 percent, where it is projected to stay until the end of the first decade of the new century. The Barry Commoners and Ralph Naders who once equated nuclear power to slavery managed to get through the 1980s in cheerful indifference to its rising importance. At the very moment that the reactors commissioned in the early 1970s were coming on-line, the antinuclear movement subsided, its activists' zeal absorbed by protests against the defense and foreign policies of President Reagan. And even though nuclear power is expected to dwindle in importance after 2010, it has been driven from the marketplace not by picketers, but by the competition of cheaper gas-turbine generators.

Yet the antinuclear movement did not truly lose. Every time the country is convulsed by some new mass panic—brain tumors inflicted by cell phones, cancer from transmission wires, immune-system disorders from breast implants—the vanished spirit of the antinuclear movement comes to life again. The conviction that nature is benign and science is dangerous and the mistrust of claims of scientific expertise are now permanent features of the American scene.

THE GOLDEN AGE OF CRANKS

"IN FIVE YEARS, FROM 1971 TO 1975, I DIRECTLY EXPERIENCED EST, GESTALT THERapy, bioenergetics, rolfing, massage, jogging, health foods, tai chi, Esalen, hypnotism, modern dance, meditation, Silva Mind Control, Arica, acupuncture, sex therapy, Reichian therapy, and More House. . . . "[17] So wrote Jerry Rubin in 1976, in as perfect an evocation of the spirit of the time as anybody has put to paper. America has always been the promised land of confidence men and hucksters, the happy hunting ground of P.T. Barnum and Charles Ponzi. But seldom did hucksters hunt with greater success than in the 1970s.

In 1972, a twenty-four-year-old Israeli named Uri Geller appeared in the United States claiming the ability to perform amazing feats. He could bend keys made of solid metal, twist forks at a distance of fifty feet, restart stopped watches. These stunts are, of course, the stock-in-trade of every dinner-theater magician, and other professional magicians rapidly saw through them. How could Geller bend seemingly unbendable keys? asked the stage magician James "the Amazing" Randi. "He didn't. They were bent already; he just reveals the bend by sleight-of-hand movements that make you think it's bending." When Johnny Carson (a one-time stage magician himself) invited Geller onto the *Tonight Show* in August 1973, Carson asked Randi to safeguard the props—with the result that every one of Geller's tricks failed. What made Geller something more than just another lounge act was his skillful reading of the temperature of his times. Stage magicians normally eschew mumbo-jumbo. Following the great Harry Houdini, who made a vocation out of exposing the table-rapping frauds of spiritualists, they cheerfully confess that they achieve their effects by sleight of hand. Geller, by contrast, claimed that his tricks were achieved by mysterious psychic powers, powers conferred on him, he later said, by extraterrestrials.

What Geller had glommed onto was the rising respectability of curiosity about the paranormal. It is unlikely that many more Americans believed in ghosts in 1975 than in, say, 1935. What changed over those forty years was the composition of the audience for the eerie. In Richard Condon's 1960 novel, *The Manchurian Candidate*, one character tells a newspaper reporter, "Always ask for their astrology sign because people love to read about astrology if they don't have to ask for it directly"—the implication being that asking for it directly was somehow embarrassing. Faith in horoscopes, or in any other uncanny phenomena, contravened the tenets both of orthodox Christianity and of modern science, the two dominant faiths of mid-century America. Had you peered into the future in 1960, you would have guessed that the star of astrology was fated to sink even lower, as the spread of higher education led more Americans out of superstition into enlightenment. Only one in ten of those Americans born in 1905 had any post-high school education, after all, while one in three of those born in 1955 did.[18]

Instead, tales of spirits and prophecy from the stars moved from the cabins of the Ozarks and the palm-readers' booths at county fairs into college dormitory rooms and suburban kitchens. The University of Rhode Island instituted an "occult studies" program. The CIA quietly funneled money to researchers in psychokinetics and telepathy. The retired chairman of Stanford University's material sciences department set himself up as a psychic healer. Time-Life Books instituted a new series on the occult. Stephen King published his first novel, *Carrie*, in 1974. Spooky movies— *Close Encounters of the Third Kind, The Exorcist*—topped the box-office charts: The actress Jane Seymour made her film debut in the 1973 James Bond movie *Live and Let Die* as a tarot-reading fortune-teller. In the spring of 1978, four of the five *New York Times* fiction best-sellers took the eerie and bizarre as their topics: J. R. R. Tolkien's posthumous *The Silmarillion*; *The Amityville Horror*; Carlos Castaneda's *Second Ring of Power*; and *Gnomes*, by the Dutch writer Wil Huygen and the illustrator Rein Poortvliet. Between 1976 and 1982, the number of working astrologers in San Francisco jumped from twenty-three to thirty-three. In 1976 the city had to make do with only five occult-supply shops. By 1982 it boasted ten. In the thirty-three years before 1968, eleven books were published about the Bermuda Triangle; in the seven years between 1968 and 1975, publishers cranked out twenty-seven.[19] Newly tenured professors of women's studies at Smith College and the University of California at Santa Cruz gathered in fields at midnight to celebrate reconstructed pastiches of the witches' sabbaths of baroque Europe. Gallup reported that 32 million Americans admitted to a belief in astrology in 1976, and Simon & Schuster published books by astrologers warning that their charts predicted climactic disaster.[20] The Internal Revenue Service recognized acupuncture as a deductible medical expense in January 1973. Ida Rolf taught the affluent of Manhattan and California that their neuroses originated in their vertebrae, Arthur Janov promised them that they could relieve depression and anxiety by lying on the floor and screaming, and L. Ron Hubbard charged them thousands of dollars to speak into tin cans and release the 65-million-year-old Thetan spirits lurking within their bodies. It was not the poor or the ignorant who learned from Peter Tompkins's *The Secret Life of Plants* to coo to their hibiscus bushes, or who paid to have their biorhythms charted, or who employed personal psychics.

One person who profited spectacularly from the recrudescence of magical thinking was a Swiss hotelier named Erich von Daniken. Von Daniken believed or at any rate wrote that the earth had been visited by extra-terrestrials before the dawn of history. These spacemen had, he theorized, brought the first civilization to ancient earth. The record of their visit was preserved in the scriptures of the world's religions, and artifacts inspired by these spacemen could still be found. The story of Eve, he said, was an account of a cloning; the myth of the golem preserved memories of the astronauts' robots; and the Bhagavad-Gita preserved the memory of ancient atomic wars. Von Daniken published his first book, *Chariots of the Gods*, in Switzerland in 1968 and in the United States in 1970; its sequel, *Gods From Outer Space*, was published in the United States in 1971. Paperback editions of the two books sold more than 6.5 million copies in the United States by 1974, and many more in Britain and Europe. A profitable movie was made as well. Von Daniken's methodology was not exactly scrupulous. Von Daniken claimed that the great trident carved by pre-Columbian Indians in Pisco Bay, Peru, cannot be seen from the sea when in fact it can; that it pointed toward the Nazca lines of the Bolivian highlands when in fact it does not; that it was carved into solid rock that Indian tools could not have cut when in fact it was carved into layered salt that those tools could cut. Yet, for all their glaring inaccuracy, von Daniken's science-fiction fantasies satisfied the needs of an age that hungered for mysteries. In its content, the God-Is-a-Spaceman theory may have been scientistic flim-flam; for its adherents, it came to be a substitute faith.

Both science and religion rest in the end upon things external to oneself: the physical universe, in the case of science; the commands of God, in the case of religion. Magic looks inward. If you can only learn the right jumble of phrases, sky charts, or spells then *you* will be the master. In a society that was rapidly losing confidence in institutions, magic was appealing because it assured individuals that they could control their destiny unaided. As one of the basic psychic-healing texts put it: "Ultimately, you get exactly what you want. . . . If you or a friend of yours have some illness, one of the things you're going to want to do in the course of your psychic healing is to find out what it is the person is getting out of that condition. Another thing you're going to want to know is whether he is willing to 'let go' of the illness."[21]

This is an individualism run amok, an individualism that not only refuses to be bound by the laws of society, but even by the laws of nature. No crank of the 1970s expressed a more extreme version of that individualism than Werner Erhard, creator of what may be the paradigmatic self-improvement movement of the decade, *est*, or Erhard Seminar Training. Erhard, who began his career as Jack Rosenberg, a used-car salesman from Philadelphia, ditched his wife and three children in 1960 and ran off to California. After dabbling in various human potential movements, he unveiled his own in 1971. Training would take place over two consecutive weekends; trainees would be locked in a room for up to fifteen hours a day, forbidden to use the washroom, and then yelled at by trainers. Erhard contended that individuals could control absolutely every aspect of their existence. He would shout at trainees, "You are an asshole!"—by which he meant someone who denied that he controlled his own life—and then when they agreed to "take responsibility" for whatever ill had prompted them to seek out *est*, he would announce, "You are omnipotent." "You are god in your universe," he would say. "You caused it. You pretended not to cause it so that you could play in it, and you can remember you caused it any time you want to." *New York* magazine reported in 1978 the case of a man who had stopped wearing eyeglasses because he had decided to "take responsibility" for his bad eyesight. Less comically, *The American Journal of Psychiatry* reported in March 1977 a series of psychotic episodes suffered by people who had attended *est* seminars, including that of a man who became convinced that he could survive without air and immersed himself in his swimming pool to demonstrate it. Three quarters of a million people enrolled in one Erhard program or another between 1971 and 1988, including Hollywood figures Valerie Harper, Cher, John Denver, Cloris Leachman, Raul Julia, and Peter Guber. At their peak, Erhard's enterprises were grossing as much as $30 million a year. Then Erhard was hit by accusations of sexual molestation from one of his daughters, a colossal IRS tax lien, and a tough story by *60 Minutes*. He fled the country in 1991. The tax case was eventually settled, but Erhard's empire never recovered.

And yet, our language shows the lingering impact of *est*. Every time someone says "I take responsibility for that," or when we assure a friend who has got into trouble that we "support" him, or ask to be left alone by saying that we "need our space"—we are chatting away in *est*-speak. The essence of *est*-speak is its clever packaging of moral evasion as moral responsibility. What, after all, does it mean to "take responsibility"—as Attorney General Janet Reno ostensibly did after the conflagration of the Branch Davidian compound in Waco, Texas, that left eighty-six people dead? She was not defending her action as right or proper under the circumstances, but neither was she apologizing or expressing remorse. Certainly she was not resigning. What she was saying, evidently, was that the action she took was taken by her. Beyond that, she had nothing to add. In a similar vein, we might wonder what it means when we tell an errant friend that we "support" him? That we condone what he has done? Probably not. That we will forgive him if he makes amends? Then we should emphasize not our support, but our expectations. That we will remain his friend no matter what he has done and whether he apologizes or not? But that's a contemptible thing to say, isn't it?

DUMBING DOWN

THE CATALOGUE OF THE UNIVERSITY OF TEXAS AT ARLINGTON TOUTED AN EXCITing new offering for the fall semester of 1973: a credit course in belly-dancing. It cannot be said with absolute certainty that this was the first college credit course in belly-dancing. The United States is a big country, and perhaps somebody beat UT to it. But the University of Texas was certainly leading the plunge toward a new definition of university-level work.

The two decades after the end of the war were a time of rising standards in American education. Average scores on the Scholastic Aptitude Test hit their all-time high in the spring of 1963. Virtually all American teenagers attended high school. The once-tiny universities expanded at an even more blinding clip. We may snicker now at the era's often awkward pretension to culture—quiz shows, the Boston Pops, *Time* magazine cover stories about Arnold Toynbee, the oh-so-serious painters in turtlenecks smoking and arguing in the Red Lion bar. But risible as the pretensions of the 1950s could be, they reflected a genuine and admirable aspiration to democratize high culture without debasing it. Mid–century America was materially egalitarian but intellectually hierarchical, an outlook precisely the opposite of our own. Modern America is prepared to tolerate vast inequalities of wealth. What it will not tolerate is any claim of intellectual or cultural inequality. The 1950s were offended by John D. Rockefeller's pious self-justification, "the good Lord gave me my money." Modern Americans are offended by Saul Bellow's mocking query, "Where is the Tolstoy of the Zulus?"

As the Bellow example suggests, our impatience with claims of cultural excellence is very closely linked to racial politics. After three hundred and fifty years of slavery and segregation, it was hardly surprising that standardized tests should find a big gap between the skills of black and white Americans. Only 15 percent of black IQ test-takers score as well as the median white test-taker. A 1977 study by the Educational Testing Service found that 75 percent of the blacks admitted to law school over the previous few years would have been turned down had their applications been weighed on the academic merits alone. One response to these dismal facts might have been patience. Desegregation was barely a decade old in the mid–1970s. Black educational attainments had been rising handsomely for half a century (the average black IQ score in the 1980s was higher than the average white score in the 1920s).[22] In time the gap was bound to close. Patience, however, had fallen out of style. Black Americans had waited patiently since 1863, more than long enough. So the institutions that had once counted on standardized tests to pick candidates objectively for civil service jobs, university admission, and professional school now began to cast about for subterfuges to evade those tests. In 1976, Jane Mercer, the chairman of the department of sociology at the University of California in Riverside, devised "race-norming," a technique that graded test-takers according to their performance relative only to test-takers of the same race. If the fifth-best white test-taker received a score of 95 for answering 95 out of 100 questions correctly, then the fifth-best black test-taker would also receive a 95, even if she answered only 80 out of 100 questions correctly. Race-norming found its widest use in civil service examinations; universities and law schools preferred to use the less scientific method of the quota and the straightforward double standard. The technique could be used to even things up between the sexes too. In April 1979, the Army announced that while male recruits would be expected to score 50 out of 100 on its selection test, women would be required to score only 31.

It can be humiliating to be on the receiving end of a double standard, and no matter how often those enforcing the double standard assure you that it is perfectly fair, in the end a handout will sting. "Those of us who have graduated professional school over the past fifteen to twenty years, and are not white," writes Yale law professor Stephen Carter, "travel career paths that are frequently bumpy with suspicions that we did not earn the right to be where we are. We bristle when others raise what might be called the qualification question—'Did you get into school or get hired because of a special program?'—and that prickly sensitivity is the best evidence, if any is needed, of the principal costs of racial preferences."[23] Some called on educators to soothe that prickly sensitivity by abolishing the standards that had made the double standards necessary in the first place. At a July 1971 meeting of the largest black legal organization, the National Bar Association, the group's president, Edward Bell, a Detroit attorney, demanded the abolition of bar examinations. In 1976, John Ryor, president of the country's largest teachers' union, the National Education Association, called for radical reform of the Scholastic Aptitude Test to ensure equality of black and white scores. A federal judge ruled in 1979 that the state of Florida had violated the U.S. Constitution when it required high-school graduates to pass a literacy test before receiving their diplomas. One could pile on a hundred more examples. Bar exams, the SAT, and literacy tests all survived this ordeal of criticism, but they did not survive unscathed. The idea that seemingly objective academic and intellectual standards were somehow arbitrary, unjust, even racist, had been injected into the American bloodstream, and there it lingers to our day.

The critique of objective academic standards was especially welcome in the 1970s, because the attainments of *all* American students, white and black, had begun to slip. In the spring of 1963, the average score on the verbal portion of the SAT was 478 out of 800; the average score on the math portion was 502. Over the next decade, the verbal score declined by about 7 percent and the math score by about 4 percent. American educators explained away the decline by pointing to the big increase in the number of students taking the SAT between 1963 and 1970 and to the changing demographics of those students: more minorities, more students from low-income backgrounds, and so on. But after 1970, the demographics of the test-takers stabilized, and the decline continued regardless. Verbal scores declined by almost another 10 percent between 1970 and 1980, and math scores by a further 6 percent. Scores dropped noticeably on College Achievement Tests and the Test of Standard English as well. If test scores were in reality as arbitrary and unimportant as educators liked to say, this long, unchecked slide ought to have been a matter of supreme unconcern. But few people believed in their heart of hearts that the slide did not matter. The College Board commissioned an inquiry by former Labor Secretary Willard Wirtz. Wirtz reported back in 1977, blaming excessive television viewing, easier textbooks, and "a decade of distraction" as the main villains. Most educators, however, preferred to accept the etiology offered by the federal Office of Education. The Education Office administered the National Assessment of Educational Progress test, arguably the broadest test in the country: 71,000 randomly chosen students aged nine, thirteen and seventeen, took it. Results had fallen precipitously between 1973 and 1977. The culprit? With considerable chutzpah, the Education office put the blame on the school districts that still retained traditional curriculums. They were, the office charged, narrowing students' minds and hampering their learning.

So, in the face of the havoc wrought by the educational innovations of the 1960s, still more progressive teaching methods were introduced. New math gave way to newer math. Phonics was replaced by "whole word" reading. The tough old biddies who once taught school were replaced by eager young people charged with safeguarding the pupils' self-esteem. Test scores dwindled regardless.

No surprise, really. In a close study of the origins of the decline of SAT scores between 1970 and 1980, Charles Murray points out that the average score slipped not because the average student got worse, but because the scores of the very best students were declining.[24] Murray provocatively argued that schools had faced a harsh dilemma: A demanding curriculum frustrated the least capable students and sent dropout rates upward; an easy curriculum stunted the most capable students and depressed test scores. Post-Sputnik, most districts had opted for the first of these twin evils. Then alarm at the high dropout rate caused them to reverse course and opt for the second.

The dumbing down of the curriculum was encouraged by changes within the teaching profession. The 1970s were the decade in which teaching was transformed from a low-paying, relatively prestigious profession to a relatively well-paid, unprestigious occupation. Despite the higher pay, however, the intellectual attainments of the people attracted to teaching tumbled even faster than the national average. The September 1979 issue of the magazine of Phi Delta Kappa, the education school honor society, reported that the average verbal SAT score for college seniors who said they intended to teach had plunged by twenty-six points between 1973 and 1979, from 418 to 392. The drop for college-bound high school seniors as a whole was only eighteen points. The math scores of would-be teachers plunged by twenty-nine points against fourteen points for all college-bound seniors. The key to the seeming mystery is unionization. In March 1971, the National Education Association affiliated itself with the American Federation of State, County, and Municipal Employees. Five months later, at a bitter three-week convention in Fort Collins, Colorado, the NEA voted to exclude school administrators from membership. As the NEA reinvented itself, it became ever more effective at squeezing pay raises for its members out of local governments. At the same time, it transformed the nature of the teaching profession. The inept and lazy gained a huge new increment of job security. Assignments would be distributed by seniority rather than skill. Teaching rosters once filled with the enthusiastic young en route to marriage and by the experienced elderly—retired military officers, housewives whose children had grown up—came to be dominated by lifers in their forties and fifties who stuck to their jobs for the pay and the pension. And as the American government unleashed a money inflation to mask the country's fiscal troubles, so American educators tried to hide the failings of the schools by inflating grades. In 1969, only 18 percent of college undergraduates reported a cumulative average of B+ or higher; in 1975, 36 percent reported a B+ or better average, according to a 1977 study by Berkeley Professor Martin Trow. Some professors may have been preserving their students' draft deferments, but the trend continued after the draft stopped. The students, and parents, of the 1970s had learned to expect more praise for less achievement.

How could their teachers deny them? The young people of the 1970s had been plopped in front of a television set at an early age (*Sesame Street* first aired in 1969, assuaging the consciences of parents about letting their three-year-olds watch television). They had grown up "a generation characterized by poor verbal skills, inability to concentrate, and a reluctance to read. Even the boom generation's language tics—usages such as 'like' and 'y'know' and 'sort of'—bespoke its lack of precision."[25] We are accustomed to thinking of the *Howdy Doody* audience as television's first victims, and so it was, but compared to what was to come later, the youth of the 1950s seem positively bookish. A Cleveland State University study conducted in the mid–1970s found that the number of hours devoted to television, records, and movies by eighteen to twenty-four year olds shot up from 13.9 per week in 1965 to 18.5 per week in 1976.[26] Between 1977 and 1988, the proportion of high school seniors who reported reading a book, magazine, or newspaper "almost every day" diminished from 62 percent to 46 percent.[27] A 1979 Gallup survey found that one-quarter of American young people had never read the Bible. By 1982, the National Opinion Research Center reported, only 42 percent of Americans in their late twenties read a newspaper every day, and only about one-quarter of those in their early twenties.

The 1970s saw the emergence of a whole new literary genre, the "novelization"—that is, the putting into book form of plots and characters already familiar from the movies or television. (The *Star Trek* series was among the most successful.) A publisher who produced novelizations suggested to one reporter "that many people who buy novelizations of movies would find it hard to read a book if they hadn't already seen the film which did the work of visualizing characters and settings for them."[28] William Paley, chairman of CBS, worriedly observed, "There is a desire on the part of young people for messy shows. They don't want a good beginning, middle, and an end. They want the damn thing to sort of float around, and they either read something into it that the older generation can't, or they feel comfortable in not having things too carefully spelled out. The spirit of it is more important than the story part."[29]

Even the very best educated young people, the bright young men and women of Harvard and Vassar, now struggled with the written word. Pollsters had been asking Americans since the 1950s where they got most of their news. Among the population as a whole, television overtook newspapers in the early 1960s; among the college-educated, the fateful moment was 1972. The early 1970s were also the moment at which artistic young people with something to say decided that they wanted to make a "film"— as a movie now came to be called—rather than write a novel. "[A]ny critic of talent who devoted himself in the fifties to writing about ambitious current novels could expect to be read with far more attention and discussed with far more intensity than he would ten years later," Norman Podhoretz observed in 1967.[30] Novels kept being written, to be sure, but they had moved from the center of cultural life to the periphery. Robert Gottlieb, the chief editor at the storied publishing house of Alfred A. Knopf, told *Publishers Weekly* in 1972, "My impression is that many fewer young men and women coming out of college are desperate to get into publishing now than fifteen years ago. . . . [M]ost of those hundreds of young people who used to come into publishing, or try to come into publishing, because they 'loved to read' . . . most of them were really coming because it was, at that time, 1955 or 1960, a great glamour industry. Those same young men and young women now all want to be in movies or in who knows what else—the record business."

Even those young people who did still love to read were influenced in odd ways by the strange new theories swirling about university literature departments, theories that rejected the austere New Criticism of the 1950s, with its emphasis on pure aesthetics ("a poem doesn't *mean*; a poem *is*"). In 1964, students aspiring to a B.A. in English at the University of Chicago were required to take nine courses in English literature plus a year of English history. By 1989, Chicago had cut its requirements in half; the survey of English history had been dropped and even Shakespeare was no longer compulsory.[31] An ever more radical rejection of artistic and intellectual standards steamrollered through the academic world. Undistinguished writers of the right race, sex, or nationality—like Alice Walker or the soon-to-be notorious Rigoberto Menchu—displaced Milton and Dryden. The great hope of the 1950s that a democratic polity could sustain a high culture had been defeated. The very idea of "high culture" was discredited and discarded. In his introduction to the massive catalog of the Orsay collection, the lavish new museum that opened in Paris' grand old Gare d'Orsay in 1978, the influential art critic Robert Rosenblum boasted, "The Musée d'Orsay is now the grandest international statement of what might be called a Postmodernist view of nineteenth-century art. In this view, the Modernist belief in a century aesthetically polarized into the blacks and whites of left wing/right wing, hero/villain, genius/daub has dissolved into infinite shades of gray. Instead of a battlefield, we have a huge family of artists whose connections with one another are far more subtle and binding, for they shared the experience of living together through some or all of the same decades in Western history."[32] Upholding standards, according to Columbia professor Edward Said's *Orientalism*, the academic book that ranks almost certainly as the most influential and most frequently cited of the 1970s, is never a disinterested act of judgment. Instead, Said contended, the act of judging is always and necessarily an assertion of power, grounded in ideology and self-interest. "[T]he general liberal consensus that 'true' knowledge is fundamentally nonpolitical (and conversely, that overtly political knowledge is not 'true' knowledge) obscures the highly if obscurely organized political circumstances obtaining when knowledge is produced."[33] There is no truth; there is only political muscle.

GOD MOVES TO DALLAS

"THE THIRD GREAT AWAKENING"—THAT'S WHAT TOM WOLFE CALLED IT IN 1972, A whoosh of rushing religious enthusiasm to match the great revivals of the 1740s and the 1840s. Wolfe had his eye primarily on the bulging ranks of the exotic new religious cults. In a speech to the Catholic Press Association in April 1977, George Gallup claimed that some six million Americans had tried transcendental meditation, five million had tried yoga, and two million had tried one variant or another of Oriental religions, from the comparative respectability of orthodox Buddhism to the cults of Hare Krishna and the Bhagwan guru. By one estimate, some three hundred new religious movements appeared in the San Francisco Bay area between 1964 and 1973.[34]

Strange sects have always flourished on the margins of American life, but the cults of the 1970s popped up at its very center. Their glassy-eyed converts loitered in the country's airports, selling carnations and distributing weird religious literature. The new cults proselytized not among hard-pressed farmers or the ignorant poor of the inner city, but among the lost children of the vast new American middle class. A 1971 study of thirty-one Hare Krishna devotees found that the average income of the families in which they had been raised exceeded $20,000, a solidly middle-class income at the time. A sociologist interested in the cult interviewed fourteen

Bay Area proselytes. All were white, seven had been raised in prosperous California suburbs, all had begun college, but only two had finished.[35] These young people, raised by indulgent parents, semi-educated by sloppy schools, their appetites prematurely jaded, had been granted radical personal freedom without ever having absorbed the self-discipline needed to make that freedom a blessing rather than a curse. They were searching for meaning in their aimless lives and they had money in their pockets—the eternal conditions for suckerhood.

Krishna Consciousness had been founded in New York City in 1965 by A. C. Bhaktivedanta, a seventy-year-old immigrant from India. A successful businessman back home, he spotted more profitable opportunities in America. He opened his first temple in the East Village and attracted a motley crew of followers, including the poet Allen Ginsberg. He relocated his movement to a former coin laundry near San Francisco's Haight-Ashbury in early 1967. From as few as 150 converts in 1968, he had acquired some four thousand more by the summer of 1974, as well as a chauffeur driven Mercedes. Fifty-four Krishna temples, usually located near a college or university, preyed on psychologically troubled students, especially those with a history of drug use. "Stay high all the time, discover eternal bliss," read the sign outside one temple. That promise, plus the offer of a free meal, lured students inside. There, "the incense, paintings of ancient scenes, and pictures of the swami seemed calculated to convey a distinctly alien impression to the visitor. The strange musical instruments, the cherished ritual embellishments (such as a pillow that holds the Gita), and the prayers in Sanskrit (a language understood by none of the devotees) fortified the exotic symbolism."[36] Hare Krishna was cobbled together out of a pastiche of Indian folkways, Hindu beliefs, and Age of Aquarius millennarianism. It taught that human history moved in cycles and that we had come to the end of the materialistic age of Kali-Yuga. A new age of peace, love, and unity lay just around the corner—if only people would accept it. In practice, Hare Krishna amounted to an exercise in mass self-hypnosis: rhythmic chanting and clapping culminating in surges of ecstasy, all the more exquisite because of the sexual denial imposed on Krishna followers.

The price of this ecstasy was the surrender of one's critical faculties. "Why should I go back to college when I have already learned everything there is to know through Krishna?" asked one devotee, a twenty-year-old woman, who had previously studied at San Francisco City College. A temple leader interviewed after one chanting session rejected even an interest in study of the Hindu scriptures. "Vedic knowledge is transcendental and cannot be understood by educational procedures. It is something that one can study, but simply studying it will only take you so far. In order to understand it, one must practice it." What Krishna and the other cults offered—and what a remarkable number of young Americans found attractive and comforting—was absolute submission to the will of another. "Someday," one devotee predicted, "there will be only one political party. People will not vote, they will chant."[37]

Bhaktivedanta had his competitors. In September 1974, a roly-poly South Korean named Sun Myung Moon began his mission to America. Moon's followers believed him to be the incarnation of God, sent to earth to preside over the amalgamation of all races and the unification of all faiths. Hence the name of his church, the Unification Church, and hence too his church's most conspicuous rituals, its mass, interracial weddings in football stadiums. Moon was a skillful businessman, if not always a law-abiding one: He was sentenced to federal prison for tax fraud in 1982. He showed too a keen eye for political advantage. He granted the daily newspaper he founded, *The Washington Times*, editorial independence, and its elegant design and trenchant editorials—not to mention President Reagan's habit of reading it first every morning—soon won it real influence in the capital. Despite his political acumen, however, Moon probably had no more than ten thousand adherents in the United States by the end of the 1970s. Much more immediately successful was the eight-year-old guru Maharaj Ji and his "Divine Light" mission. His handlers proclaimed the boy the "perfect master," the reincarnation of Christ, Buddha, and so on. The boy himself showed much more interest in his collection of stereos, rock-band equipment, and cars than in the Hindu mish-mash taught by his mission. But he found U.S. disciples all the same, including one of the Chicago Seven defendants, Rennie Davis. In 1972, Ji's American followers chartered six Boeing 747s to transport themselves to India for a Divine Light jamboree.

The truly big news in American religion in the 1970s was not the rise of outlandish new religions but the shifting balance of power among the old, spectacularly symbolized by the election of Jimmy Carter in 1976. Baptists had been the most numerous southern denomination since the early nineteenth century, but they had only once before elected one of their own, Harry Truman, to the White House. Of the twelve pre-Carter southern presidents other than Truman, seven—Washington, Jefferson, Madison, Monroe, Harrison, Tyler and Taylor—were Episcopalians, and four—Jackson, Polk, Andrew Johnson and Wilson—were Presbyterians, conforming to the old tradition that ranked the old national churches of England and Scotland as the most prestigious in the United States. (The twelfth, Lyndon Johnson, was raised a Disciple of Christ, but as president worshipped most often in Episcopal churches.) An old joke brutally summed up the hierarchy of American Protestantism: "An Episcopalian is a Presbyterian with a trust fund, a Presbyterian is a Methodist with a college education, and a Methodist is a Baptist with shoes." That would change. Of the four presidents since 1976, both of the southerners, Clinton and Carter, were Baptists, and one of the northerners, Reagan, had been raised in a tiny evangelical sect.

The 1950s had been the Indian summer of elite Protestantism, the last days when the chaplain of Harvard College still counted for something in the world of American religion. Between 1955 and 1965, membership of the Episcopal Church grew by more than 22 percent, and the best-known Protestant clergyman in America was the rector of Fifth Avenue's Marble Presbyterian Church, the Rev. Dr. Norman Vincent Peale. For Catholics, the 1950s were a Golden Age. The parochial schools bulged with the fourth, fifth, and sixth children of women who forswore birth control. The edicts of the conservative archbishop of New York, Francis Cardinal Spellman, were approvingly communicated to his flock by the nation's biggest newspaper, *The Daily News*. The full Americanization of the church was ratified by the election of the first Roman Catholic president in 1960. As for Jews, while there remained too many clubs they could not join and corporations at which they were unwelcome, they had obtained a place in society that would have seemed secure beyond imagining even twenty years before.

In fact, the 1950s were happy days for all American denominations. The membership of almost every one jumped between 1955 and 1965. New churches and synagogues popped up on what had once been farmer's fields, orange groves, scrubland, or desert. In 1958, 49 percent of Americans told George Gallup that they had attended church the previous Sunday, a peak never equaled before or since. Congress amended the phrase "one nation indivisible" in the Pledge of Allegiance to "one nation *under God* indivisible," and voted to inscribe "in God we trust" on the coinage. Still, some people questioned the reality of the return to religion. Critics sniffed something duty-bound and unlively in the ostentatious religiosity of the period. They wondered whether the decade's enthusiasm for interfaith dialogue and alliances was less a sign of tolerance for others' beliefs than of flickering confidence in one's own. On the visit to California that resulted in *The Loved One*, the militantly Catholic Evelyn Waugh was introduced to a "non-denominational" minister. Ever after, Waugh rumbled in his letters, "What on earth does it mean to be non-denominational?" He would likely have been equally stumped by President Eisenhower's deservedly famous statement, "A system of government like ours makes no sense unless founded on a firm faith in religion—and I don't care which it is." The 1950s surely did not *look* like a renewed Age of Faith. There was something terribly faith*less* about the shabby, budget-conscious churches of the raw suburbs, built by architects who seemed to be thinking more about weddings and coffee klatches than worship and contemplation. The 1950s were a reverent rather than a fervent age. People came to church because they thought they ought. When "doing as you ought" suddenly ceased to wake Americans on Sunday mornings, the jerry-built chapels of the suburbs and the crumbling old churches downtown emptied out as rapidly as they had filled up.

Between 1965 and 1975, most big denominations surrendered all the gains they had made between 1955 and 1965, and then some. Northern Lutheran membership dropped by 5 percent, United Methodist membership by 10 percent, southern and northern Presbyterian membership by 7 percent and 12 percent respectively, and membership in the United Church of Christ, the merger of the various New England Congregationalist churches, by more than 12 percent. Hardest hit among the Protestant denominations were the once-mighty Episcopalians, who lost a startling 16.7 percent of their lofty adherents.

The blows to the Roman Catholic Church were, if possible, more punishing. Seventy-five percent of American Catholics claimed to have attended mass in the past week in 1957; by 1975, weekly mass-going had dropped to 54 percent. (Both these percentages are almost certainly inflated but there's no reason to think that the 1957 number was more inflated than the 1975 number.) The proportion of Catholics who said they attended church "practically never" or "not at all" doubled between 1966 and 1975. More ominous still was the crumbling of the zeal and self-confidence of the Catholic clergy. A 1971 survey of five thousand priests, about 10 percent of the nation's total, and 250 bishops by the renegade Catholic priest Andrew Greeley spotted serious breaches in support for Rome's teaching on divorce, birth control, and the all-male priesthood.[38]

Among all Americans, both Catholics and Protestants, the percentage who expressed a "great deal" of confidence in organized religion plunged from 40 percent in 1967, the first year the question was asked, to 20 percent in 1979, about where it has remained ever since. Americans voted with their checkbooks too. Discreet signals of financial distress began to be emitted by the Episcopalian, Presbyterian, and Lutheran church organizations.

So long as the Vietnam War lasted, the decline in the wealth and influence of the mainline churches was partially offset by a remarkable surge in the media-worthiness of their leading clergymen. Their pews might be empty, but William Sloane Coffin of Yale and Bishop Paul Moore of New York could still make news by denouncing the bombing of Hanoi. From the perspective of the press, it was the ultimate "man bites dog" story: The spiritual advisers to the establishment joining the cause of the shaggy and radical. But the thing about man-biting-dog stories is that they depend on a degree of manly self-restraint. When the in baskets of the news organizations begin to overflow with press releases from men announcing their intention to chew on the haunch of a St. Bernard next Tuesday, man-biting-dog stories become as tedious as dog-biting-man. That's what happened to Coffin and Moore. After Vietnam came welfare rights, ecology, migrant farmworkers, Nestlé's baby formula, South African apartheid, nuclear disarmament, and on and on. Perhaps these causes were individually worthy—most journalists were predisposed to think that they were—but the information that William Sloane Coffin and Paul Moore had taken them up ceased sometime after 1971 to qualify as anything remotely resembling news.

Alexis de Tocqueville suggested in the 1830s that one reason the American clergy possessed much more spiritual influence than the clergy of Europe was the former's willingness to eschew the political power that the clerics of Europe hungered for. In the 1960s, a great many liberal clerics disregarded that advice, with results that Tocqueville foresaw. By virtue of the time he spends with the sick and the sad, even a very worldly minister acquires insight into the human soul unavailable to the comfortable and secure in his congregation. But it was an exceeding rare liberal Protestant or progressive Catholic minister who had anything to say about welfare or grapes or South Africa or nuclear weapons that his congregants had not already read in the *New York Times*. Why should they waste a Sunday morning listening to the same editorial twice?

Unfortunately for them, the leaders of the big northern Protestant denominations and the American Roman Catholic church explained their predicament in terms exactly the opposite of Tocqueville's. They convinced themselves that they were losing adherents because their religion was too authoritarian, its doctrines too demanding, its moral edicts too strict, its ritual too formal, its ministers too aloof. They responded with the remodeled churches we know today, with priests called "Father Bob," and by jettisoning fusty old hymns and replacing them with songs that sound as if they were written by Joan Baez. Ministers hung hand-knotted tapestries in the apse of the church and delivered breezy short sermons in conversational language. The Episcopalians had successfully updated Book of Common Prayer in 1927, retaining the familiar beauty of Cranmer's language but clarifying some of his Elizabethan linguistic obscurities. In 1974 they revised the 1927 version. This time, rather than clear the dust gently away with an archaeologist's brush, the church applied a massive sandblaster. One of the world's most beautiful liturgies collapsed into one of the world's silliest. Not content with the renovation of their rituals and liturgy, the mainline denominations also upended their teachings on faith and morals. In particular, they gutted the traditional strictures against nonmarital sex, extending their blessing to everyone in a "loving, committed relationship."

Most contentiously of all, the churches rethought the place of women. The evangelical churches had long hearkened to women preachers—the most famous was Aimée Semple McPherson in the 1920s—and the Quakers and Unitarians allowed women an extensive role. But the more ritualistic denominations barred women from holy orders. They believed that the officiant of communion stood in the place of Christ, and that since Christ had come to earth as a man, the figure who represented him must likewise be a man. To ordain women would, they feared, cast away the most visible symbol of the old doctrine that Christ was both divine *and* human, a doctrine ratified more than fifteen hundred years ago in the Nicene creed and held to this day by almost every Christian sect and faction. On the other hand, to refuse to ordain women would constitute a rejection of the new doctrine of the absolute equality of the sexes. Hmmm. The Nicene creed, the equality of the sexes; the equality of the sexes, the Nicene creed. . . .

It was an easy enough call. The Episcopalians voted to approve women deacons in 1970. At a ceremony in North Philadelphia in July 1974, four Episcopal bishops joined to defy church rules and ordain eleven women deacons as priests. Two weeks later, the Episcopal House of Bishops hurriedly gathered to deny the validity of the ordinations. This was a last-gasp protest. Within two years, the Episcopal Church and the Canadian Anglican Church had formally approved women priests, as did the Church of England. The Presbyterians and Lutherans moved rapidly to catch up with the Episcopalians, and the American Catholic church inched closer and closer to women priests with every passing year. The first woman rabbi was ordained in 1972 by the Reform seminary in Cincinnati. Other denominations took even bolder steps. The northern California conference of the United Church of Christ voted on April 30, 1972, to approve the ordination of America's first openly homosexual minister.

To the manifest bafflement of the mainline Protestants, the bold reforms failed to halt the decline in membership. Women bishops followed women priests; acoustic guitars were replaced by electric guitars; ministers ascended to ever loftier peaks of grooviness; racism replaced pride as sin number one; and still the pews emptied, gifts dried up, and vocations diminished. By some counts, the number of Muslims in the United States exceeded the number of practicing Episcopalians by the mid–1990s.

Politics cut a peculiarly ugly swath through the Catholic church. The American Catholic bishops tried futilely to weave a "seamless garment" out of the pet causes of left and right: opposition to abortion *and* to the death penalty, support for a generous welfare state *and* for anticommunism, equal condemnation of homosexuality *and* of homophobia. A 12,000-word papal letter released on May 14, 1971, made bows to all the causes of the Sixties: the disparity between rich and poor nations, the liberation of women, youth protests, urban problems, the alienation of a consumer society. It praised socialist movements for aspiring toward a more just society, while reaffirming the church's rejection of Marxism. Alas, the seams in the "seamless garment" were impossible to ignore. After the 1978 election of Karol Wojtyla as Pope John Paul II, the Vatican moved toward a more robust anticommunism even as the American Catholic church flirted with the Soviet-funded nuclear freeze movement and the communists of Central America. Individual Catholics faced an awkward choice. On the one hand, the leftward migration of many local parishes offended and alienated parishioners; on the other hand, the principal check on the excesses of local parishes—the authority of the Vatican—was equally offensive and alienating. American Catholics did not like it when their priest told them to support the Sandinistas and they equally did not like it when the Pope told their priest to cut it out. Parishioners were simply no longer willing to be told what to do. While fewer than one-third of married white Catholic women used a forbidden means of birth control in 1955, two-thirds were violating church rules by 1970, the journal *Science* reported in January 1973.

Sociologists had predicted for a century that advancing modernization would sooner or later corrode religion, and the prolonged resistance of the United States to this trend had seemed to many intellectuals both odd and faintly disturbing. It was much more in a mood of relief than dismay that *Time* magazine titled a 1966 cover story on religion, "Is God Dead?" To the surprise (and horror) of the editors of *Time* and of the academic sociologists they quoted, the reply to that query turned out to be a sharp "no." Episcopalianism and Presbyterianism might be ailing, but God was doing fine. He had simply relocated to Dallas.

The years in which mainline Protestantism collapsed were the very years in which evangelical Protestantism boomed. An exhaustive *Los Angeles Times* report in February 1980 estimated that there were some fourteen hundred radio stations, thirty-six television stations, and sixty-six cable systems devoted in whole or principal part to religious broadcasting. Some $600 million was spent that year to purchase air time for televised evangelism; each week a total of 129 million people tuned in. In 1980, the big eight televangelists—Oral Roberts, Pat Robertson, Jim Bakker's PTL Club, Jerry Falwell, Billy Graham, Rex Humbard, Jimmy Swaggart, and Robert Schuller—grossed an estimated $310 million. Commentators on religion worried that televangelism might displace brick-and-mortar churches and destroy spiritual community. But the opposite seems to have been true. The evangelical and pentecostal Christians to whom the television evangelists preached were joining churches with new-found enthusiasm. Between 1965 and 1975, as the Lutherans, Presbyterians, Congregationalists, and Episcopalians were withering, the ranks of the Church of the Nazarene grew by 8 percent, those of the Southern Baptists by 18 percent, those of the Seventh-Day Adventists by 36 percent and of the pentecostal Assemblies of God by 37 percent. And the growing denominations built bible colleges, schools, and publishing houses as well as churches.

Four things seem to have made the difference between thriving and shriveling churches. First, the thriving churches were evangelical—that is, they elevated the preaching of the Gospel over the sacrament of communion. The cool, wary GI generation had been embarrassed by the overt emotionalism of full-throated evangelicalism. But the churches that continued to grow after 1965 were precisely those that eschewed ritual and instead embraced the emotional, even the ecstatic. They treated the congregation as an audience to a performance rather than as witnesses to an event. The starkest physical difference between the grand new evangelical palladiums and the old-fashioned churches of the mainline denominations is the substitution of padded movie-theater seats for unupholstered wooden pews. The successful churches demanded less from worshippers (including less in the way of dressing up—the 1970s were the decade in which middle-class white Americans stopped wearing suits and ties to church) and offered more: a more intense and fulfilling emotional experience at a minimum, and in many cases miraculous healings and solutions to personal problems.

Second, the thriving churches emphasized forgiveness over rectitude. Not that the new churches condoned immorality. But while the American church of mid–century, whether it was St. Xavier's or the Second Wesleyan, urged its adherents to avoid sin, the burgeoning evangelical churches promised that even the worst sinners could be "born again." Donna Summer, the chanteuse who had belted out some of the raunchiest disco hits of the 1970s, announced in January 1980 that she had become a born-again Christian. Nobody saw anything odd about that. Who could imagine her announcing that she had become a Presbyterian? Mid–century churches taught an ethic of conduct. At the time, this often seemed prune-faced: An entire generation of comedians would joke about their terrifying "Catholic school flashbacks." But prim as the mid–century churches may have been, they were also optimistic. They assumed that a functioning majority of society could be expected to lead reasonably moral lives—enough of a functioning majority that the moral could effectively disapprove of the immoral. The message of the evangelical churches may at first have seemed more saccharin—one evangelical church distributed to its members tiny sparkling stickers bearing the message "You are loved"—but underneath was a much more pessimistic assessment of humanity. They assumed that very large numbers of their congregants would fail to live up to the moral standards taken for granted at mid–century, and promised to love them anyway.

This shift from an ethic of rectitude to an ethic of forgiveness might be seen as a resurgence of the deep Christian belief that we are all wrongdoers. Or it might be that in 1975, there was more to forgive than there was in 1955. Whatever the cause of the shift, it certainly seems to have worked. Not only did evangelical churches add members faster through the 1970s than non-evangelical, a trend that continued to the end of the century, but the more evangelical the church, the more likely its members were to attend services. Through the 1970s, the Baptists consistently showed the highest turnout of any Protestant denomination; Episcopalians the lowest. On the other hand, a church that embraces every sinner the instant he announces his intention to turn over a new life is creating what might politely be called perverse incentives. That all-too-recurrent late twentieth-century moment in which a disgraced public figure tearfully informs us that God has forgiven him occurred far less often in the more bracing moral clime of half a century ago.

Third, the thriving churches are eschatological rather than theological. One of the striking things about the big new evangelical American churches is how far behind they have left the old doctrinal quarrels that used to divide Protestants. Many of the biggest evangelical churches have no denominational affiliation at all. They are simply "Christian." Others have affiliations that reflect only the happenstance of their pastor's background. Robert Schuller, for example, was raised in the Dutch Reform tradition and so his famed "crystal cathedral" in Orange County is titularly Reform as well. In practice, that identity means little. American evangelical Christianity is not much interested in the unresolvable metaphysical disputes that have embittered Christian sects against one another for centuries. What does exercise evangelicals is Prophecy—by which they mean working out from the tangled hints dropped by the Christian Bible a coherent account of the End of the World.

The account goes more or less as follows. The world is entering into the Last Days, as proved by, for example, the return of the Jews to the Holy

Land. As the Last Days begin, sincere Christians will suddenly be bodily snatched up to heaven, in what is called "the Rapture." During the ensuing chaos, a demonic ruler, Antichrist, will try to conquer the world. War will erupt. Millions will perish. And then Christ will return to earth, accompanied by the enraptured Christians, to inaugurate a thousand years of earthly government before the Final Judgment. This story is broadly familiar to anyone who pays attention to religion, or, for that matter, watches late-night television. But as recently as three decades ago, it was not familiar at all. True, the promise of a Millennial Christly Kingdom has appealed to dissenting Christian sects since the Middle Ages, and the version of Millennarianism expounded on American television sets was worked out more than a century and a half ago by the Englishman John Darby, founder of the Plymouth Brethren sect. True, too, Lyman and Milton Stewart, the Los Angeles businessmen who published *The Fundamentals*, the series of pre-World War I tracts that gave the name to the movement we call Fundamentalism, inscribed the Millennium story alongside the inerrancy of the Bible as an essential component of Protestant faith. For all that, a Christian who in 1955 applied an "In Case of Rapture This Car Will Be Unoccupied" bumper sticker to his car would attract puzzled looks from his neighbors. The Millennium story did not command the attention forty years ago that it does now, in part because the GI and cold-war generation took ill to prophecies of war. They were frightened enough already; they did not pay the pastor to frighten them still more. More important still, the big church-going public of the 1950s was a practical population, interested in practical solutions to practical problems, not spooky speculations. The most-read religious book of the 1950s was Norman Vincent Peale's *The Power of Positive Thinking*, a guide to the perplexities of everyday life.

By contrast, the most-read religious book of the 1970s, *The Late Great Planet Earth* (ten million copies sold between 1970 and 1977), was a blood-curdlingly vivid description of the End Time. The sequel to *The Late Great Planet Earth, Satan Is Alive and Well and Living on Earth*, sold three million copies in the five years after it was published in 1972, and a novel premised upon the Antichrist story, *The Omen,* sold more than six million copies. It was made into an immensely successful movie as well. Hal Lindsey, the author of *The Late Great Planet Earth* and *Satan Is Alive and Well,* fully understood that his brand of prognostication was a product of its time. He told *Publishers Weekly,* "If I had been writing 15 years earlier, I wouldn't have had an audience. But a tremendous number of people were beginning to worry about the future, and they were looking everywhere for answers. The turn to the occult, astrology, Eastern religion, and other movements reflected the fear of what was going to happen in the future. And I'm just part of that phenomenon."[39]

The final difference between the thriving and decaying churches is that the thriving churches were politically conservative, while the declining churches tilted to the left. Almost all the branches of American Christianity, the theologically traditional as well as the more liberal, have been drawn to social reform. One can match the abolitionism of the New England Congregationalists against the temperance crusades of the Baptists and the decency campaigns of the Roman Catholics. What divides left-wing social activism from traditionalist is the locus of the sin to be stamped out. The left has usually been drawn to collective problems (segregation, poverty, sexism, the war in Vietnam); the traditionalists, to individual vices and weakness (drunkenness, drug addiction, abortion). The glory days of liberal Protestantism happened to be those in which Americans believed in the efficacy of collective action to remedy collective problems. As that faith waned after 1965, those Protestant churches that had committed themselves to it when it seemed progressive suddenly found themselves looking hopelessly out of date. The politically left-tilting Protestant churches faced a second, and even graver, problem. Perhaps not fully consciously, the mainline churches were gambling in the 1960s that if they tilted to the left politically, they could hold onto the young and disaffected without alienating their more conservative adherents. The gamble went spectacularly wrong. The young and disaffected gave up on church anyway, while the tradition-minded quit the First Methodist in disgust and reaffiliated with the People's Christian Church out on Route 272.

And when, in the fullness of time, those disaffected young people ceased to be quite so young, they did not return to the faith of their youth. They took up instead a vague, post-biblical spirituality—a spirituality that the dying mainline churches began to digest in one last pathetic attempt at accommodation. By the 1990s, the old tripartite scheme of Catholic-Protestant-Jew was retreating before new trichomoty: the secular, the spiritual, and the traditional. The secular did not go to church at all; the spiritual cobbled together a lukewarm syncretic faith out of bits and pieces of Buddhism, mysticism, and paganism; and the traditional made new homes for themselves in the evangelical churches, the more conservative Catholic dioceses, and Orthodox Judaism.

The United States in 1980 was, as it had been in 1960, the most religious industrial country on earth. But the form of its religiosity had been dramatically altered. The post–1980 American faith was more emotional, more forgiving, more individualistic, more variegated, and often more bizarre. It was less obedient, less ritualistic, less intellectual. It concerned itself more with self-fulfillment and less with social reform. Americans yearned as fervently as ever for a direct encounter with the transcendental, but they chafed against the authority that had once guided them toward that encounter. They hungered for religion's sweets, but rejected religion's discipline; wanted its help in trouble, but not the strictures that might have kept them out of trouble; expected its ecstasy, but rejected its ethics; demanded salvation, but rejected the harsh, antique dichotomy of right and wrong.

APOCALYPSE NOW

THE ICE AGE WAS RETURNING! THE SKYSCRAPERS OF NEW YORK WOULD VANISH under a mile-high ice sheet, pitiful Canadian refugees would stream southward toward Panama, and millions would starve as the world's crops failed in the new cold weather. And all of this was going to happen within a very few more years, the newspapers warned.

As the Dead Sea Scrolls remind us, the impulse to declare that the End Is Nigh has been driving men to grow beards and retreat into the deserts for millennia. One of the strange tendencies of modern life, however, has been the institutionalization of scaremongering, the willingness of the mass media and government to lend plausibility to wild surmises about the future. The crucial decade for this odd development was the 1970s.

One of the most terrifying of those scares was instigated by a professor named Paul Ehrlich in a 1968 book, *The Population Bomb*. "The battle to feed all of humanity is over. In the 1970s the world will undergo famine—hundreds of millions of people are going to starve to death in spite of any crash programs embarked upon now."[40] In a style exactly like that of the Rand Corporation and the United Nations, Ehrlich produced a range of scenarios, from best-case to worst-case. The worst case led to the total extinction of mankind in a nuclear holocaust. Here's the best case: "In 1974 the United States government finally realizes that the food-production balance in most of Asia, Africa, and South America is such that most areas cannot attain self-sufficiency. American expeditionary forces are withdrawn from Vietnam and Thailand, and the United States announces it will no longer send food to India, Egypt, and some other countries which it considers beyond hope. A moderate food rationing program is instituted in the United States." The pope, yielding to pressure from enlightened Catholics, then endorses birth control and abortion, and urges reduction of birth rate. Alas, even in the best case, "Famine and food riots sweep Asia. In China, India and other areas of Asia, central governments weaken and then disappear." Russia falters. "Famine and plague sweep the Arab world." "Most of the countries of Africa and South America slide backward into famine and local warfare." There is what Ehrlich calls a "major die-back." Afterward, the rich countries impose central economic planning and forced population-control program upon the poor. Ehrlich came to the reluctant conclusion that this optimistic scenario was unrealistic because it presupposed "a maturity of outlook and behavior in the United States that seems unlikely to develop in the near future."[41]

The media displayed a limitless appetite for this malarkey. Ehrlich was invited onto *The Tonight Show* with Johnny Carson some twenty-five times in the 1970s. Ehrlich's fabulous success inspired imitators. Through the 1970s, grim-faced pundits stepped forward to urge Americans to accept in the name of realism and ecology the imminent deaths of tens of millions of Third Worlders. In a 1974 article, the environmentalist Garrett Hardin coined the phrase "lifeboat ethics" to describe the policies he recommended. If you're in a lifeboat after a shipwreck, it's tempting to save everyone bobbing in the water around you. But take aboard too many, and the boat is swamped and everyone drowns. For this reason, Hardin opposed any emergency food aid to the starving. Aid, he warned, only encouraged breeding. Also popular was the idea of triage, a phrase borrowed from military medicine. After a battle, doctors divide the wounded into three categories: the least wounded, who will recover without help; the badly wounded, who will probably die even with help; and the moderately wounded, who will survive only if they get treatment. Then they concentrate their efforts on the last group. In just such a way, argued the 1967 book *Famine 1975!*, the United States ought to rationalize its food aid. Libya might be able to survive without aid—it falls into category one. Overpopulated India is doomed no matter what—if falls into category two. But Pakistan shows potential for self-sufficiency and should therefore be assisted.[42] It must be stressed that despite the sensational title, the proponents of triage were highly regarded scholars, and their contentions were repeated in magazines like the *Atlantic Monthly.* The overpopulation fright found a popular audience too, with movies like *Soylent Green* (a 1973 film set in 2022, when 40 million people live in New York City and only the very rich can afford fruit or meat) and *Logan's Run* (a 1976 movie about a future society that kills its members at age thirty) depicting a world so short of food that only planned murder and high-tech cannibalism sustain civilization.

If anything, serious thinkers were even more alarmed than Hollywood. Almost immediately upon taking office in 1977, President Carter appointed a commission of doomsayers, led by Gerald O. Barney of the Rockefeller

Brothers Foundation, to analyze environmental trends and offer recommendations. The commission's report, dubbed *Global 2000*, was delivered immediately before the 1980 election.[43] It predicted continuing high population growth, stagnating food production, a rapid decline in oil production after the mid-1990s, skyrocketing mineral and commodity prices, and severe water shortages in the Third World. These bad tidings seemed to have heavily influenced President Carter's thinking. They undergirded his energy plans, and may have accounted for the despair and pessimism that he radiated through the 1980 campaign and that did so much to cost him the election.

Carter's pessimism flew in the face of the available facts. Julian Simon, an economist who made a career out of debunking scare stories, noted that between 1948 and 1979 world food production per person rose by about 37 percent. The rise would have been more impressive still but for the collapse of agriculture in Mao's China.[44] It was true that Africa immediately south of the Sahara had suffered a terrible famine in 1974–75. But as with most famines, people starved because of malign politics, rather than an absolute shortage of food. In the west of Africa, the government of Mali refused to distribute emergency food supplies in the countryside in hope of crushing rebellion among the Tuareg nomads. In the east, the new revolutionary government of Ethiopia was using a Stalin-style famine to force through a Stalin-style collectivization of agriculture and bolster its power. There was no necessity for triage. More than sufficient stocks of food existed to save all the victims of crop failure if, and this was the crucial if, the governments of the starving did not impede the delivery of the food for reasons of their own.

If fears of disaster were so unconvincing, why did they find such a large audience? "The unconscious mind wants to be taken seriously, and not to be laughed at," the historian Edward Shorter has observed. People therefore express their anxieties in terms compatible with the spirit of the age. They reported visits from demons in the 1690s; their descendents reported visits from extra-terrestrials in the 1990s. Someone whose ancestor believed her skin tingled because she had been cursed now believes her skin tingles because of multiple chemical sensitivity. And when a modern society feels troubled, as it did in the 1970s, it looks for scientific-sounding grounds for its premonitions of doom.

"The world is unhappy. It is unhappy because it does not know where it is going and because it senses that if it knew, it would discover that it was heading for disaster." So French President Valery Giscard d'Estaing observed in 1974, and with apparent reason. The Arab oil boycott had turned the lights off all over Europe, a global inflation was squeezing living standards, the long postwar boom seemed to have ended. Further in the background, there lurked deeper anxieties. Some feared that the relative position in the world of Europe and America was declining relative to Africa and Asia: Between 1900 and 1975, Europe's share of world population dropped from 24 percent to 16 percent; that of the United States, barely held steady at 5 percent.[45] Others suffered anxiety because the great meaning-providing intellectual systems of the past—Marxism, Freudianism, and so on—were collapsing under the weight of contradictory evidence. What more satisfying revenge could there be on the Arabs and Africans who had turned off the oil spigot than to imagine them dying for lack of American grain? And for intellectuals who yearned for a substitute for their ebbing socialist faith, ecology seemed to offer an exciting new justification for an authoritarian elite of central planners. After all, food *was* more expensive in 1974 than it had been in 1967. Was it not logical to infer that it would be more expensive still in 1981?

Apocalyptic fantasies were stoked above all by the discomfort with children that suffused the new self-oriented culture of middle-class Americans and Europeans. Listen again to Ehrlich as he offers suggestions on what steps should be taken to save the planet. First he recommends killing all pets—the world could not afford useless mouths. Then on to human babies: "Many of my colleagues feel that some sort of compulsory birth regulation would be necessary . . ." Ehrlich himself was not quite ready to go so far as that; instead he would raise income taxes steeply on families with children. Further, "luxury taxes should be placed on layettes, cribs, diapers, diaper services, expensive toys," and "a governmental 'first marriage grant' could be awarded each couple in which the age of both partners was twenty-five or more." There could be state prizes for each period of five years in which a couple delayed childbirth and bonus grants for vasectomies. Abortion must be legalized, and sex education in the schools geared to de-emphasizing the reproductive purposes of sex. Poor countries must accept compulsory sterilization of their people. "A cancer is an uncontrolled multiplication of cells; the population explosion is an uncontrolled multiplication of people. . . . We must shift our efforts from treatment of the symptoms to the cutting out of the cancer. The operation will demand many apparently brutal and heartless decisions. The pain may be intense. But the disease is so far advanced that only with radical surgery does the patient have a chance of survival."[46] Ehrlich urged his readers to join his mission to eradicate the disease of humanity, by, for instance, commending friends who had no children or at most one and waggling their eyebrows at those who created three or more. (Despite the complete discrediting of all the rest of Ehrlich's scheme, the anti-child evangelism he favors continues. Ask any mother of three about the casually insulting comments she receives from total strangers. One of America's richest men, David Packard, left his fortune to a foundation dedicated to population restriction; another, Warren Buffett, has pledged to do the same.)

Credit Ehrlich at least with recognizing that the creed he was expounding was religion, not science. He understood that the severing of the connection between sex and reproduction and the deliberate withholding of life-saving assistance from famine-wracked countries was incompatible with Christianity, or indeed any known monotheistic religion. He therefore recommended that the ancient faiths of mankind be jettisoned and replaced with a "new pantheism" and a new ethics that attached less value to human life. His followers would, however, borrow arresting images from the old religions: Noah's Ark, for instance. Like Noah, the United States could save anyone only by first recognizing that it could not save everyone. There was more than a hint that just like the vicious generations in Genesis whose sins provoked God to drown them, the Third World millions must go under for their sin of uncontrolled reproduction. Indeed, it could be argued that a softened version of Ehrlich's creed has already become the faith of hundreds of thousands of college-educated, professional people. In 1937, Walt Disney had his Snow White pray to an unmistakably Christian God. The religion in *Pocahontas* and *The Lion King* is, however, strictly pagan.

The dietary and clothing restrictions that environmentalists impose on themselves; the secular mass performed every day over the recycling bins with cans, bottles, newsprint, and compost each carefully placed within its own holy container and left by the curb to await resurrection—what else is this but religion?

Since the 1970s, hundreds of prophets have competed to win souls for their distinctive version of the new faith. Some prophets warned that climate change, not overpopulation, would usher in the apocalypse. A report written for the Central Intelligence Agency in 1974 by Reid Bryson of the University of Wisconsin warned that the benign interglacial period under which human civilization had blossomed over the past ten thousand years was coming to an end. Now the world hovered on the brink of upheaval almost beyond comprehension—a frigid period that would dramatically shrink crop production and trigger global famines lasting for at least forty years, and maybe for centuries.

It was Professor Bryson's good luck that the CIA decided to declassify his study in the spring of 1976, after an especially nasty winter. The story was splashed onto page one of the *New York Times*. Later that year, Stephen Schneider, a scientist with the National Center for Atmospheric Research in Boulder, Colorado, put Bryson's warnings of global cooling into a talked-about book, *The Genesis Strategy*. The world, said Schneider, owed the prosperity of the 1950s and 1960s to a favorable climate. Alas, "since 1940, and particularly during the 1960s, there has been a sharp reversal of this warming trend in the Northern Hemisphere. . . . In fact, average temperatures in the Northern Hemisphere have recently appeared to be moving toward lower levels reminiscent of times immediately prior to the twentieth century." Schneider favorably quoted a 1974 warning from the International Federation of Institutes of Advanced Study that "the direction of the climactic change indicates major crop failures almost certainly within the end of the decade. This, coinciding with a period of almost non-existent grain reserves, can be ignored only at the risk of great suffering and mass starvation."[47]

Schneider's book excited a frenzy of glacier hysteria. Television reports, magazine features, the front pages of local newspapers all explained how the glaciers came and went in cycles and that a renewed glaciation was due at any moment. "We feel," said Walter Orr Roberts, a former observatory director at the National Atmospheric Research Center, in a 1976 colloquy with reporters at the Aspen Institute, "that the downturn of temperatures since 1950—and rapidly in the '60s—probably represents a trend and isn't just a short-term chance fluctuation. . . . We feel that it's more likely that these colder average temperatures in the northern hemisphere will continue for twenty or thirty years, and therefore we consider it a significant climate effect that the world will probably have to contend with for a long time."

Unless, of course, the problem was not that the world was cooling off, but that it was drying up. A meeting of world climate experts sponsored by the Rockefeller Brothers Foundation in 1974 observed with alarm that the Sahara Desert was advancing southward at a rate of about thirty miles a year, threatening the people of the grasslands of the Sahel. This conference also was reported on the front page of the *Times*. Desertification, it was called, and soon the television sets of the western world were beaming heart-rending pictures of nomads leading their cattle southward as the dust blew and the grass dried up.

Then again, it could equally be that world was neither cooling, nor drying, but warming up. At the meeting of the American Geophysical Union in June 1977, a series of papers argued that the world's temperature was rising and that *this* was the real danger. The Carter Administration was sufficiently impressed to create an Office of Carbon Dioxide Environmental Effects. Stephen Schneider jumped on this new bandwagon. The most-quoted Ice Age alarmist of the 1970s became, in a neat public-relations pivot, one of the most quoted Global Warming alarmists of the 1990s.

The Lord High Executioner in the *Mikado* announced that it really didn't matter which names were put upon his little list, and in that same cheerful spirit it was less important to the new apocalyptics to know *which* catastrophe was going to ravage the world than to agree that *some* catastrophe was sure to do so.

PART IV

DESIRE

ARE WE HAVING FUN YET?

*"He always passed through Sayville with a lingering regret for
its big white houses and friendly front yards with picket fences
and climbing roses. . . . 'Isn't this beautiful?' Malone would ex-
claim as we drove past the girl doing handstands on the lawn,
a young woman walking a flock of children down a dabbled
sidewalk. 'Why don't we take a house here next summer instead?' But he knew we wouldn't, and he knew he wouldn't, for
even now the drums were in our blood, we sat forward almost
hearing them across the bay, and the van raced through the
streets so that the driver could hustle back for another load of
pleasure-seekers, so bent on pleasure they were driving right
through Happiness . . . "*

—*Andrew Holleran,*
Dancer from the Dance[1]

NOTHING, ABSOLUTELY NOTHING, MADE THE THIRTYISH GRADUATES OF THE
class of 1982 feel quite so middle-aged as the eruption of seventies nostalgia among undergraduates and high-school students at the end of the
nineties. If the members of my generation agreed on one thing as we entered adulthood, it was our disdain for the decade in which we had come
of age. My more leftish contemporaries looked backward to the heroic
1960s; those of more conservative outlook exulted in the Reagan 1980s. All
of us agreed that the 1970s were a slum of a decade. Right or left, we delighted in the narrowing of neckties, the demise of disco, the restyling of
the Camaro, the extinction of the fern bar. Imagine our dismay when only
two decades later it all came roaring back: happy-face buttons and the Bee
Gees, bellbottoms and glitter balls, pet rocks and platform shoes. In our

accelerated era, the most halicious styles can zoom through the cycle of chic-outré-retrouvé in scarcely twenty years.

Don't tell the kids they have bad taste. We rediscover old things because they speak to the present in some unanticipated way. When old-stock Americans suddenly went gaga for colonial artifacts in the 1930s—hanging battered pewter tankards over the mantles of their Park Avenue apartments and placing rickety old spinning wheels in the living rooms of their country homes—they were reasserting their connection to the country's history for a reason, and we can learn important things about the culture of the 1930s by inquiring into what that reason was. The same is true of the strange nexus between our time and the Mood Ring decade.

From the point of view of the young, the 1970s must look like a time in which people had more fun than anybody is permitted to have today. The high school students and university undergraduates of the 1990s and 2000s live in a zero-tolerance world in which smoking is prohibited and seatbelt use is mandatory. Possession of a couple of grams of marijuana can send them to prison. The fear of AIDS or accusations of rape hover over every date. The legal drinking age has been hiked back to twenty-one. They cannot bicycle without a helmet, cannot paddle a canoe without signing a disclaimer, cannot safely neck without a blood test and a formal grant of permission, cannot wear grandmother's old fur stole without risking an unpleasant confrontation with animal-rights activists. They imagine the 1970s as a glorious moment of guiltless hedonism, and they yearn for the strobe lights of the discotheques as nostalgically as Talleyrand yearned for the courtliness of *ancien régime* France: "Nobody who was born after the Revolution," the wicked old nobleman once sighed, "will ever know the sweetness of life."

Imagine a club like Studio 54 opening in Rudy Giuliani's New York—a dance parlor in which nearly naked bartenders offered themselves to male and female customers alike, while the owners and their friends snorted cocaine in public view, heroin was pumped in the bathroom stalls, and unusual sex acts were consummated in the alcoves overhead. In 1995, the place would have been permanently shuttered within the first twenty-four hours under a barrage of drug, prostitution, public hygiene, liquor licensing, and traffic violation charges. Imagine a movie like Lina Wertmuller's 1975 *Swept Away*—which treats rape as a deserved and comical comeuppance for a bossy woman—being released now. Or compare a year's worth of *New York* magazines from 1975 and 1995. The 1975 volume contains 209 photographs and drawings of scantily clad or naked or provocatively posed women; 1995 contains fewer than thirty—and even the most lurid of those was far less lubricious than the earlier crop. The typical image from 1975: an ad for Scotch whisky in which a sultry redhead in a bikini gazes smokily into the reader's eyes; the typical 1995 image: an ad for a gym featuring an unsmiling, muscled woman in a tight leotard. In the 1979 film *Manhattan*, Woody Allen quips that he is relaxing by reading the lingerie ads in the *New York Times* magazine, a joke incomprehensible to anyone who began reading the magazine in the next decade. Hollywood movies were likewise toned down. Roger Moore's James Bond enjoyed at least half a dozen sexual encounters per film; Pierce Brosnan's was allowed only one. In the 1970s, the laws that require milk stores to display only the titles of *Playboy* and *Penthouse* had not yet been passed, and women grabbing a late-night half-gallon had to walk past the bare breasts of the Pet of the Month on their way to the register.

College authorities winked at the discreet smoking of marijuana on campus. President Carter's adviser on drug policy, Dr. Peter Bourne, attended parties at the home of the head of the National Organization for Reform of the Marijuana Laws. (Bourne got into trouble when it was discovered that cocaine had been consumed at the party, but, incredibly by contemporary standards, he survived, resigning only after he was caught signing a prescription for sedatives to a White House colleague who asked that Bourne insert a fictitious name in place of the user's real identity.) Men who wanted to hint at their sophistication wore sterling silver cocaine spoons on chains around their necks. Harold Robbins published mass-market paperbacks in which men drive women wild by sprinkling powdered cocaine on their penises before sex. *Variety* reported that the Cheech and Chong stoner comedy *Up in Smoke* sold more tickets than any other movie in the United States and Canada in the week ending October 4, 1978. Twenty years later Hollywood would release a movie about two fun-loving Klansmen before daring to make light of the dangers of drugs. The 1978 release of *Animal House* inspired boozy toga parties at fraternities across the country, at which the girls who attended arrived expecting to be groped and mauled. In 1999, Dartmouth, the alma mater of the film's writer, Chris Miller, banned fraternities and sororities for good. President Ford was routinely photographed smoking a pipe, and nobody thought much of it. Twenty years later, First Lady Hillary Rodham Clinton declared the entire White House—even her husband's office—a smoke-free zone and awkwardly had to be begged to make exceptions when leaders from unenlightened countries like France came to visit.

It's possible to see the recent history as the story of a once-Puritanical country going on a bender in the 1970s, sobering up in the 1980s, and then returning to its moralistic ways in the 1990s. That is in fact how recent history usually *is* seen, which is why it is understandable that undergraduates bent on naughtiness would idealize the years of the debauch, much as the undergraduates of the serious-minded 1950s liked to mimic the styles of the Roaring Twenties. But this version of recent history misses the mark. The debauchery of the 1970s is analogous to the frivolity and drunkenness with which we welcome a new century. In the morning, we put a compress on our head and wash up the glasses. That does not mean the clock has been turned back. The new era has arrived for keeps.

Drugs, for instance. Yes, the enforcement of the drug laws has stiffened since the 1970s; yes too, young people must listen to much more scolding on the subject. (Arcade video games now flash antidrug messages between rounds.) This unpermissive stance has achieved some good results. Marijuana smoking by high-school students tumbled by some two-thirds between 1980 and 1992. Cocaine and heroin addiction dropped off in all age groups. But even when the "war on drugs" goes relatively well, millions of American young people smoke marijuana, swallow tranquilizers, and snort paint thinner. And since 1992, the war has not been going well. Half the progress made during the Reagan-Bush years was lost in the five years 1993–97.[2] A social evil that scarcely existed in 1960 became a chronic source of anxiety and grief in almost every industrial society, and new criminal enterprises made billions of dollars out of doping the Western world's youth.

Sex followed a trajectory very similar to that of drug use. The compulsive promiscuity of the 1970s has subsided. But it is very wrong to think of the sexual history of the past forty years as the swinging of the pendulum from restraint to license and then back to restraint again. The 1970s blew to smithereens an entire structure of sexual morality. Revolutions like that do not last forever. They cannot. But the ending of a revolution is not the same thing as the restoration of the old order. It is the institutionalization of a new one.

OUR BODIES, OURSELVES

HUFFA-PUFFA-HUFFA-PUFFA. DOWN THE SIDEWALK THEY COME, POUNDING THE cement with their $75 waffle-soled shoes. Huffa-puffa-huffa-puffa. First hundreds, then thousands, soon millions of Americans were tying on lurid plastic shoes, stripping down to nylon shorts and sleeveless athletic shirts, and jogging (or running, as its devotees always preferred to call it). It was a mass migration of people to rival the Crusades—minus only a destination. The Gallup polling company estimated in 1978 that 15 million American men and women jogged regularly. Between 1976 and 1978, membership in the New York City Road Runners club, an association of the city's most dedicated joggers, tripled, from two thousand to six thousand. Paid circulation of *Runner's World*, the premier joggers' magazine, rocketed from 76,000 in May 1977 to 250,000 in May 1978.[3]

America had been gripped by fitness crazes before. The jogging boom followed immediately upon the great tennis mania of the early 1970s. The Bancroft sporting goods company, the oldest maker of tennis rackets in the United States, reported that its sales of rackets more than doubled between 1971 and 1973.[4] But unlike previous fads, which gripped only segments of society (the Midwest bowled, the Northeast skied; men hunted, women practiced yoga), jogging appealed to almost everybody. That same 1978 Gallup survey found that joggers were divided almost precisely equally between those who had attended college and those who had not, and nearly evenly between men and women. Previous crazes had offered either amusement (golf) or a more attractive body (calisthenics). Nobody would ever describe jogging as fun, and its aesthetic benefits are minimal. Yet, strangely enough, those very negatives constituted the essence of jogging's attraction. That it strengthened the heart and lungs *without* building a man's biceps or shrinking a woman's thighs proved that jogging was something one did, not to please the opposite sex, but *for oneself.* Likewise, jogging's very dreariness proved that it was not some childish game, but a serious, even spiritual, act, like meditation. James Fixx's 1978 *Complete Book of Running* suggested that if one ran long enough and hard enough, one would experience a "trance-like state, a mental plateau where they feel miraculously purified and at peace with themselves and the world."[5] Even if one never quite attained Fixx's sublime state, the fact that one was seeking it marked one as a person of elevated consciousness. Exercise was the first sacrament of the new religion of the self, as Fixx himself perceived. "Having lost faith in much of our society—government, business, marriage, the church and so on—we seem to have turned to ourselves, putting what faith we can muster in our own minds and bodies."[6] The knee-injuries runners were always suffering were the equivalent of the bump on the forehead of a devout Muslim: an external sign of fidelity to the duties of one's creed. The lowered pulse rate of the long-distance runner signified more than a promise of longer life (actually not a very reliable promise: Fixx dropped dead at age fifty-two). It was what a theologian might describe as the outward sign of inward grace. "Runners," the author of *The Joy of Running* told a magazine interviewer, "seek each other out. They regard other runners as good and trustworthy, particularly the marathon runner, and look down on other people, thinking of them as bad, lazy, indolent, immoral."[7]

If runners were superior, bicyclists were downright smug. Before 1970, bicycles were children's toys. Some 6.9 million bicycles were sold in the United States in 1970, down slightly from the 1968 peak, and nineteen out of twenty of them were bought for children. Some adults did ride—most famously, Paul Dudley White, a Boston cardiologist who made himself a prominent local character by pedaling to and from his hospital in the car-crazy 1950s and early 1960s—but there was a strong whiff of carrot-juice drinking and sandal-wearing about them. Then, in 1971, college students discovered in ecology a substitute for the passions roused by the fading Vietnam War. What better way to prove your dedication to the earth than by abandoning the car? In the first four months of 1971, a bicycle clip on one's right pant leg became *the* sign of commitment to the environmental cause. Since the best bikes were all imported—Raleigh and Dawes from Britain, Peugeot from France—the bicyclist could strike a second symbolic blow against the cloddishness and junkiness of American industry. By the end of the third year of the bicycle boom, 1973, the industry had doubled its sales to 15.2 million bikes a year, more than half of them to adults.[8] When the *New York Times* magazine profiled Robert Nozick, Harvard's libertarian philosopher in 1978, the professor had himself photographed toting his ultra-light bike on his shoulder as he walked down the steps from his lecture hall, a perfect semiotic cue that this advocate of free markets was no chamber of commerce stooge.

The new religion had its own garb: the track suits that fashion-conscious Americans now permitted themselves to wear in public; the tight shirts and pants that displayed a taut and trained body. It had its own hourly rituals: the little neck and hamstring stretches that runners would perform, not too discreetly, in movie lines. Above all, it had its special dietary laws. "Harvey had got to know Marlene," wrote the author of *The Serial*, the best comic novel of the 1970s, "as she checked out his groceries, expressing horror at the 'the garbage,' he put in 'his one and only body.' 'Do you know what white flour does to you?' she asked him, handing the loaf of bread he'd picked out to a stockboy to go back on the shelf. '*It kills your enzymes*.'"[9] Between 1968 and 1972, the number of health-food stores in the United States more than doubled, from 1,200 to 2,600. Beef consumption, 54 pounds per person per year in 1952, peaked in 1972 at 116 pounds per person, and then commenced a decline that continues to this day. That same year, 1972, Pepperidge Farm introduced an additive-free bread and Sears, Roebuck added an all-natural food and cosmetics section to its catalog. "We don't know if health food is a trend or a fad, but Sears, Roebuck can't afford to overlook any business that grosses $2 billion a year," explained the department store's health and beauty merchandise manager.[10] That was merely the beginning. Just as early Christianity progressed from celebrating its sacraments with battered cups and tin salvers to the gorgeous ornamentation of chalice, surplice, and salver in the High Middle Ages, so the sacraments of the cult of beauty were elaborated and beautified.

It was a young New Jerseyite named Alice Waters who determined to make the natural foods of the 1960s into food human beings would cheerfully eat. In 1971, she opened in Berkeley, California, one of the most influential institutions of the 1970s, Chez Panisse. It insisted on local and organic ingredients, minimized the number of red-meat offerings, and became one of the first American restaurants to serve three-star meals in a room where nobody was expected to wear a necktie. At Chez Panisse the horrible dandelion salad eaten by the hippies evolved into the deliciously bitter mesclun salad now served by ambitious eateries from Boise, Idaho, to Tampa, Florida. Chez Panisse pioneered the custom of listing virtually every ingredient in a dish, so that food-fearful customers could be sure of precisely what they were eating: "Sautéed black sea bass with olive and fennel sauce on a bed of young spinach, etc." What was happening at Chez Panisse was often compared in the 1970s to the nouvelle cuisine of French chefs like the Troisgros brothers, Jean and Pierre. The cuisines may sometimes have tasted similar, but their conceptions could not have begun further apart. Nouvelle cuisine attempted to renovate and modernize French cooking, to make tasty food healthier. The new cooking of California attempted to make palatable the hippie diet, to make healthy food tastier.

Although the new French and American cooking of the 1970s originated on opposite sides of the dial, they tended naturally to converge.

Yumminess—which the all-natural cooks at first only cared about as a way to induce people to eat what was good for them—gradually became an end in itself. The people who bought exquisite flourless chocolate cakes at the elegant new patisseries that sprang up in medium-sized cities in the 1980s were very often the same people who had bought mealy carob brownies at the all-natural bakeries that had opened in the 1970s. And the people who *sold* the cakes were even more surprisingly often the same people who had sold the carob brownies. Why not? Your body deserved the best. One rejected tap water in favor of Perrier not because one was showing off one's ability to pay two dollars for a drink that had traditionally arrived free, not because one wanted to impress a date that one knew how to pronounce the French brand name, but because one was the sort of person who cared about his or her body. (Perrier's consumers remained contentedly ignorant for years that the drink's carbonation was actually artificially infused and that the purity standards for American tap water were usually stricter than those for the bottled waters of Europe.) Understanding that the cult of exercise and the cult of food began as moral imperatives—the sacraments of the cult of the body—makes it possible to resolve the otherwise puzzling mystery of how the fitness-mad 1970s could also be so obsessed with fine food and drink. Name a fine American wine, and odds are it first went into production between 1968 and 1980: Diamond Creek in 1968; Clos du Val, Stag's Leap, Jordan, and Caymus in 1972; Trefethen in 1973; Joseph Phelps in 1974; Edna Valley in 1980. Nor were Americans neglecting the wines of Europe. Between 1968 and 1982, imports of French wine into the United States quadrupled.[11] The 1970s were also the heroic age of American restauranting. Mark Miller stepped out of the Chez Panisse kitchen to move to the Southwest and open the Coyote Café, the restaurant that first taught Americans that a great cuisine could be founded upon American regional specialties. Down the coastal highway from Alice Waters, Austrian immigrant Wolfgang Puck's Ma Maison and Spago belatedly liberated Hollywood cuisine from its long thralldom to the delicatessen traditions of vaudeville and Broadway. (Pre-Spago, the movie industry's favorite restaurant was Chasen's, with specialties including such swift tickets to thrombosis as pork-shoulder chili, braised short ribs, and "hobo steak" fried in one full pound of butter.) Along the way Puck transferred the gastronomic capital of America from New York City to Los Angeles.

To which we can only say huzzah—right? Who wants to return to the days when dreary restaurants like The Colony and "21" were the best even New York City had to offer? Or when American cooking meant vichyssoise, chop suey, and manicotti, to name three of the pseudo-foreign dishes invented on these shores? It must gratify patriots that Nancy Reagan could confidently replace French wines with Californian at White House dinners. It's painful today even to read a pre–1965 recipe, never mind eat one. *The Alice B. Toklas Cookbook*, first published in 1954, contains a recipe for turkey with truffles that begins, "For a turkey weighing 6 to 7 lbs., you will require 3 lbs. of the fat that surrounds pork kidneys."[12]

So progress has been made. But grateful as we are for the herb-crusted olive bread and the duck enchiladas, it is worth asking whether we are proud of ourselves for thinking as much about food and wine as we do. C.S. Lewis shrewdly observed that the sin of gluttony consists not of overeating but of awarding food too central a place in one's life. The anorexic is just as much a glutton as the fat man, the picky eater as much as the greedy eater. Gluttony of the greedy type is of course as American as overstuffed apple pie; gluttony of the persnickety type has had a harder time gaining a foothold in American culture. Historically, Americans were not fussy eaters. Raymond Chandler memorably complained that they would swallow anything "if you put it between two slices of bread with lettuce and mayonnaise." To show overmuch concern with one's creature comforts, to be "dainty at one's feeding," as the scornful old-fashioned phrase has it, used to seem absurd and unmanly.

The dispelling of that prejudice is a cultural transformation of enormous proportions—enormous, too, in a literal square-footage sense. In a house built before 1970, the largest room will usually be the living room. The second biggest will probably be the dining room, which is normally sharply demarked from the kitchen. In the 1970s, the kitchen started to grow. People who could afford it built "two-chef" kitchens, with room for husband and wife to potter about together. Living-room space began to spread around the cooking area, so that guests could watch—or participate in—the cooking of the meal. The kitchen grew and grew until finally it had metamorphosed into the family room or great room of the 1990s, in which the children play, grown-ups watch television, and all but the very most formal dinner parties are held. The old living room and dining room, meanwhile, are atrophying into invisibility, in exactly the same process that shrank the Great Hall of the Middle Ages into the humble front hall of today. Of course, it's not just food-consciousness that explains the growth of the kitchen. Social and sexual changes played a part, too. No longer was the wife prepared to work alone while her family and guests waited to be served, and not since the war had middle-class families been able to afford to hire cooks. On the other hand, the emancipation of women and the disappearance of servants from middle-class life might have equally plausibly caused the kitchen to shrink into a glorified airline galley, containing only a microwave and a dishwasher. In 1969, futurists often predicted that this is exactly what would happen—and maybe there would not even be a dishwasher, because everyone would be eating off disposable plates. Instead, at the very moment that cooking ceased to be women's work, food became a middle-class obsession: The monster kitchen is the consequence.

If pre-1965 Americans hesitated to seem sensitive to comfort, they positively disdained safety. They lit rockets in their backyards on the Fourth of July. They bought their steak marbled with fat. They smoked. They bought cars without seatbelts. They gave boys .22-caliber rifles for their eleventh birthdays. How they would gape and stare at a contemporary playground, with its rubber matting underneath the swings, safety belts on the teetertotters, and three-year-olds strapped into crash helmets before they can mount their tricycles. How they would snicker at grown men girding themselves like test pilots to pedal through the park, at a Post Office that airbrushes the cigarette out of Humphrey Bogart's hand lest some impressionable stamp-collector get the wrong idea about smoking, at the massive Range Rovers we buy so that we can commute to the office without fear. Back then, one did not show so much concern for one's carcass. When Jacques Plante of the Montreal Canadiens became the first goaltender in the National Hockey League to adopt a face mask, it was only his extremely aggressive style—he moved farther out onto the ice than any goalie had ever done, stealing the puck before the opposing team had a chance to fire off an aimed shot—that protected him from insinuations of cowardice. "My face is my mask," boasted the New York Rangers' Gump Worsley, who by the end of his career had collected some 800 stitches. Worsley lost the argument. By the end of the 1970s, every goaltender, and most forward players, wore protective headgear.

The 1970s were the decade when governments took up the job of extirpating physical danger. The Occupational Safety and Health Administration and the Environmental Protection Agency came into existence in 1970, the Consumer Product Safety Commission in 1972. The wind could roar through Peter Fonda's hair in *Easy Rider* in 1969, but he'd be paying many hundreds of dollars in fines if he tried the same stunt in 1979: Helmets had been compulsory on interstate highways since 1973. (California took the next logical step and imposed the first compulsory bicycle helmet regulation in 1987.) The federal Department of Transportation issued orders in 1971 requiring lap-and-shoulder belts in all new cars by the summer of 1972. The following year, the Food and Drug Administration ordered that foods be labeled with percentage-of-daily requirements of a series of vitamins and minerals. In the same spirit of caution, the FDA was waiting longer to approve new drugs. In the mid-1970s, thirteen of the fourteen new drugs whose approval the FDA itself regarded as most important had become available in other countries before they could be sold in the United States.

Smokers and non-smokers were segregated on airplanes in 1973. The Interstate Commerce Commission confined smokers to the symbolically loaded back 20 percent of the bus that same year. Airboard cigars and pipes were banned in 1977. The following year, Health Secretary Joseph Califano declared himself in favor of a total ban on airplane smoking, although it took until 1990 for him to get his wish. In 1973, Arizona became the first state to ban smoking in public buildings, although it did permit ventilated areas to be designated for smokers. The federal government instituted its first set of restrictions on smoking in federal buildings in 1978. Discomfiting smokers did indeed discourage smoking. The Agriculture Department reported in 1980 that America's adults consumed less tobacco per person in 1979 than at any time since 1898. Per-person cigarette consumption in 1980 had tumbled to its lowest levels since 1957.

The fewer the number of smokers, the more politically feasible it was to impose ferocious rules upon them. Smokers began to be seen less as adults exercising their right to opt for a less than perfectly healthy lifestyle, but as pitiful addicts (at best) and as transmitters of filth and disease (at worst). Public-service announcements blared at them from television, their children came home from school to lecture them about the perils of tobacco, strangers felt free to approach and harangue them. It might be thought ironic that the decade in which Americans were most stridently told to quit being judgmental was the same decade in which the political authorities launched their most comprehensive and longest-lasting campaign for the suppression of a vice since the repeal of Prohibition. The urge to chide and admonish our neighbors is one of the most deeply engrained of human drives. As it was denied and thwarted in one realm of life after another, it accumulated in the one or two realms remaining to it with ever-intensifying force. The Americans of the 1970s had no more tolerance than their Victorian predecessors for pleasures they deemed dangerous. They might tolerate—even applaud—fornication, gambling, gluttony, and dandyism. But smokers were knowingly poisoning themselves. They were consciously violating the commandment to care for their bodies. They were something worse than dissidents. They were heretics whose every puff blasphemed against the new religion of the self.

ME AND MY CALVINS

"NOTHING GETS BETWEEN ME AND MY CALVINS." ON A THOUSAND BILLBOARDS across the country, this line appeared over model Brooke Shields, provocatively posed closing the first (or was it opening the last?) button on her shirt. It was a taboo-busting ad, and not just because it invited us to imagine the still underage Shields minus her briefs. It was taboo-busting because it was inviting American women to spend $50 on jeans at a time when a pair of Levi's could be had for less than $25.

Blue jeans were adopted as the uniform of the young in the late 1960s, a time when young collegians felt—or felt that they ought to feel—solidarity with the oppressed and toiling masses who (they imagined) wore these pants to work in fields and foundries. "The unvarying style of Yale today," wrote Tom Wolfe in 1968, "is best described as Late Army Surplus. . . . Visible at Elm and York are more olive-green ponchos, clodhoppers, and parachute boots, more leaky-dye blue turtlenecks, pea jackets, ski hats, long-distance truck warms, sheepherder's coats, fisherman's slickers, down-home tenant-farmer bib overalls, coal-stoker strap undershirts, fringed cowpoke jerkins, strike-hall blue workshirts, lumberjack plaids, forest-ranger mackinaws, Australian bushrider mackintoshes, Cong sandals, bike leathers, and more jeans, jeans, jeans, jeans, jeans, more prole gear of every description than you ever saw or read of in a hundred novels by Jack London, Jack Conroy, Maxim Gorky, Clara Weatherwax, and any who came before or after."[13]

Wolfe, naturally, took a deeply cynical view of the message these socially concerned young Yalies were trying to send. Was it entirely a coincidence that they chose to dress like a member of the working class of half a century rather than like the real poor a few blocks away? "They did it *wrong*! They did it *lame*! They never bothered to look at what the brothers on the streets were actually wearing! . . . A lot of the college boys, for example, would go for those checked lumberjack shirts that are so heavy and wooly that you can wear them like a jacket. It was as if all the little Lord Byrons had a hopeless nostalgia for the proletariat of 1910, the Miners with Dirty Faces era, and never mind the realities—because the realities were that by 1968 the real hard-core street youth in the slums were not into lumberjack shirts, Can't Bust 'Ems, and Army surplus socks. They were into the James Brown look. They were into ruffled shirts and black-belted leather pieces and bell-cuff herringbones, all that stuff, macking around, getting over, looking sharp . . . . If you tried to put one of those lumpy mildew mothball lumberjack shirts on them—those aces . . . they'd *vomit.*"[14]

So when Calvin Klein hiked his prices, he was only admitting what everybody had quietly known all along: Jeans were not poor man's clothing. They were worn by the middle class not because they were cheap and durable, but because they were sexy. And the conclusion that Klein—and Gloria Vanderbilt and all the other designers of designer jeans—drew was that if they could be made sexier still, they did not have to be cheap at all. So Klein cut his jeans to flatter a woman's hips and reintroduced the leggier stovepipe pant in place of the leg-hiding flare. The oldies who had never liked jeans in the first place and the young radicals who saw them as a political statement grumbled—when the Andy Rooney style of curmudgeonly humorist wanted to complain about money losing its value, designer jeans were always Exhibit B, right after the notorious $5 novelty "pet rock"—but the women of America quickly made Calvin Klein a very rich man.

Klein flourished because he spotted an important trend early. A generation earlier, the coveted objects of upper-middle-market desire had been cheaper versions of things only the very rich could have: silver tea services and pink-and-white Wedgwood teacups; Buicks with plastic dashboards printed to look like burled elm; antiqued brass front-door knockers copied in two-thirds original size from English country homes. Since the 1970s, the upper middle of the market has hankered instead after costly versions of things that everybody has: leather-upholstered trucks; $200 hiking boots; gigantic digital television sets with stereophonic speakers; coffee brewed from fine beans; white-truffle pizza. Once the upper middle aspired to look like the very rich, only on a more modest scale. Since the 1970s, it has aspired to look like everybody else—only much more lavishly.

Of all the absurdities in the history of the Law of Unintended Consequences, this must be the grossest. The upheaval of the 1960s aimed—insofar as they had an aim at all—at democratizing social life. Every time a boss gets his own coffee instead of asking his secretary for it, or a professor chats chummily with a student, or a child calls an adult by her first name, or a client wears an open-necked shirt to meet his banker, or a teacher overlooks spelling mistakes in her students' work, the egalitarian spirit of those heady days wins a small retrospective victory. The great rebellion against stuffiness and snobbery was supposed to have finished off the absurd middle-class infatuation with the demarcations of status, the gradations and striations that supposedly distinguished them from the common herd. Bye-bye to the pink-rosed Wedgwood. Good riddance to the plastic burled elm. Off come the doorknockers. The bum's rush to the relentless pursuit of *gentility*. Yet, barely a decade later, here was the Bronx-born son of Leo Klein and Flore née Stern, reinventing gentility for the New Age.

One had to be subtle about it of course. To the undiscerning eye, the only difference between a pair of Calvins and a cheaper brand was the tiny white-and-black tag on the right-rear pocket where the red-and-white Levi's insignia would otherwise have been sewn. As upper-middle-class Americans opened their wallets to purchase the trappings of the new gentility, they explained to themselves and their friends that what they were seeking was not status, but *quality*.

The wonderful thing about quality is its invisibility. Hand-roasted and home-ground $30-a-pound Jamaican Blue Mountain coffee beans yielded a drink that looks exactly like Maxwell House. Nobody could accuse the couple who drank it of preening. It was an expenditure known only to themselves—and the small circle of their friends who could taste the difference and understood how much that difference cost. Ditto for the greenish Tuscan extra-virgin olive oil and the crusty loaves of Eli Zabar's bread. Ditto for the Timberland boots.

Better still, investing one's surplus dollars in quality rather than in status avoided the need to keep up those uncomfortable old-fashioned appearances. One of the standard comic bits of mid-century was the plight of the ordinary Joe suddenly come into money. "Between ourselves," an anguished wife in a P. G. Wodehouse novel laments of her husband, "Mr. Steptoe is a hick. . . . He hates dressing for dinner. He says collars scratch his neck and he can't stand the way stiff-bosomed shirts go pop when he breathes. . . . I wouldn't put it past Mr. Steptoe, if left to his own unbridled instincts, to show up in a turtleneck sweater."[15] But cast aside the ideal of gentility, and a man who came to dinner in a turtleneck was a positive Beau Brummel. No more stiff entertainments in what previous generations of anglophile Americans would bite their lips to remind themselves to call the "*drawing* room." No more cajoling disgruntled immigrant girls into trying a little harder to emulate milady's maid. No more fumbling with black bowties for a night at the local symphony.

Perhaps the most striking thing about the home life of upper-middle Americans at the end of the century, as compared to fifty years before, is how very much more emphasis it puts on effortlessness. One reason for the shrinkage of the formal living room, architects explain, is that clients demand that their homes be arranged so that they don't have to feel bad about shlumping around in their sweats—and who wants to shlump in sweats atop a Louis Quinze sidechair? Sipping beer out of the bottle, munching popcorn out of the microwave bag, and watching golf on a 72-inch screen: That's luxury, yes, but it's a very democratic luxury, one that imposes on its beneficiary none of the irksome obligations to act his part that were shouldered by the well-to-do half a century ago.

Maybe not so coincidentally, at exactly the moment when the upper-middle was modeling its behavior on those below, the lower-middle was being extended the perquisites of the classes above. What bank regulators call "revolving credit" remained very much a rich man's privilege through the 1960s. As of January 1968, commercial banks carried only about $1.4 billion worth of credit-card debt on their books—about one-twentieth of the value of the U.S. auto-loan market. Between January 1968 and January 1982, consumers' credit-card debt skyrocketed by almost *5000 percent*, to $63.4 billion. (It's now $576 billion, or about 25 percent bigger than the auto-loan market.)[16] By 1980, there were more than three and a half cards in circulation for every adult in the United States.[17]

Moralists have been scolding Americans for over-borrowing since the days of Benjamin Franklin. But Americans figured out equally long ago that borrowing made good sense in their bustling country. Britain's Industrial Revolution was financed with retained earnings. A cotton mill circa 1820 cost relatively little to start and in good years yielded such fabulous profits as to pay for itself in months. The industrial growth of the United States, however, was financed by credit on a scale never seen before, and not for nothing did the man who managed the flow of that credit into the United States from Europe, J. P. Morgan, become the most famous businessman of his day.[18] Almost every great American fortune was earned by men who could borrow the equivalent of hundreds of millions of nineties dollars without a pang: Andrew Carnegie, John D. Rockefeller, Thomas Edison. One of the rare exceptions, John Jacob Astor, is said to have regretted on his deathbed that his aversion to debt had prevented him from buying even more of Manhattan Island than he actually did.

Borrowing is a means by which the future's wealth is shifted into the present, and people's willingness to borrow is an indicator of their faith in their prospects. As urban living standards bolted upward during the boom of the 1920s, the first form of consumer credit—buying on the installment plan—was introduced. The shock of depression taught an entire generation of Americans how dangerous borrowing could be, but as the long postwar boom rolled on and on, the specter of depression frightened them less and less. The Franklin National Bank in New York introduced the first credit card in 1951. The Bank of America unveiled the ancestor of today's Visa card in 1958; a consortium of smaller banks rolled out the ancestor of MasterCard in 1966. Suddenly, you too could be a Carnegie, Rockefeller, or Edison—and with inflation every year repealing between 5 and 12 percent of the value of your debt, indebtedness to purchase furniture or other hard goods made sense even for the least well off. Self-denial was becoming downright irrational.

With demand for credit growing, it seemed more and more intolerable for the federal government to be choking off the supply. Since 1934, federal regulators had set a maximum permissible interest rate on consumer bank deposits. (In the summer of 1974, with inflation in double-digits, that maximum was 7.9 percent on a four-year deposit of a minimum of $1,000. Short-term and small depositors were paid even less.) This was the famous Regulation Q, and its effect in inflationary times was to prod depositors to withdraw their funds, forcing banks to squeeze credit, thus touching off a recession and, in theory, ending the inflation. But the politics of Regulation

Q in a consumer-credit economy were unsustainable. Imagine telling millions of credit card borrowers that their maximum balance was being slashed because depositors were withdrawing their funds to protest low returns. Regulation Q was repealed in 1980; from then on, bankers could pay their depositors whatever the market would bear.

A new kind of consumer was creating a new kind of credit market, and that new credit market in turn was reshaping American society and law. American bankruptcy law has always been one of the world's most forgiving, but the substantial revision of the law in 1978 pushed it so far in a pro-debtor direction that it was sometimes hard to figure out why any American paid his bills at all. (The law soon redounded on the left-of-center Democrats who had written it. Corporate managers figured out in the early 1980s that by declaring bankruptcy they could wriggle out of the generous contracts they had unwisely negotiated with their unions in the inflationary 1970s, without being obliged—as they would in Britain or Canada—to surrender control of their company to a receiver.) Bankruptcy law is one of those subjects whose colossal importance is disguised by its unbearable dullness. But the terms and conditions by which people can escape their debts shape an economy more totally than almost anything else does. The super-lenient terms adopted in 1978 go far to explain both the fantastic spurt of enterprise that enriched the United States in the final two decades of the twentieth century—because nothing so encourages people to take risks as the assurance that failure will not destroy them forever—and also the often-low character of American commercial morality. Why not make glib promises of repayment? If you fulfill them, you're a hero. If not, you're always entitled to a second, or third, chance. It seems an unresolvable dilemma: You cannot empower the creative without emboldening the hustlers, and you cannot constrain the hustlers without stunting the creative. The United States chose the first option, and though it may have cost bank shareholders' tens of billions in bad loans, it ignited the most convulsive explosion of entrepreneurial innovation seen on this continent since the Roaring Twenties. As tradeoffs go, this was a grand winner. And thanks to it, nothing, not even being flat broke, need stand between you and *your* Calvins.

AL JOLSON'S *JAZZ SINGER* IT WAS NOT, BUT IN 1978 THE OTHERWISE OBSCURE production company Satori Films achieved a motion-picture breakthrough all the same. It released a movie titled *Secrets*, in which Jacqueline Bissett enacted a graphic five-minute sex scene entirely nude. Before *Secrets*, name actresses in American feature films did not strip for the camera. (Virna Lisi tore up a contract with United Artists in 1968 rather than appear in the skimpy costumes designed for *Barbarella*—and risqué as that movie was, in its big sex scene Jane Fonda was exposed only from the neck up.) So strong was the taboo, in fact, that Satori hesitated for seven years after the 1971 shooting of *Secrets* before letting it out the door.

By then, the producers must have had difficulty remembering what they'd been afraid of. On-screen grappling and grasping had become as familiar a theatrical convention as the tenor aria was 150 years ago. Suddenly the pop stations on the radio pulsed to the copulatory rhythms of disco: "Push, push in the bush"; "Voulez-vous coucher avec moi, ce soir"; "That's the way, *uh-hunnh uh-hunnh*, I like it, *uh-hunnh uh-hunnh*." On middle-of-the-road stations, Tenille crooned "Do that to me one more time" to her piano-playing Captain. Respectable bookstores stocked items that would have been hauled off by the vice squad half a dozen years earlier. Dell's paperback edition of *The Happy Hooker* sold 6.6 million copies by mid-1973, one hundred thousand copies more than the year's best-selling non-smut paperback, *Jonathan Livingston Seagull*. Bob Guccione's *Penthouse* eclipsed the sales of *Playboy* by publishing graphic pictures of female genitalia and lesbian sex; Larry Flynt's *Hustler* carved out a niche for more obscene stuff still. Manhattan office workers could stroll over on their lunch hour to the theaters where Noel Coward's tinkling comedies used to play and watch live sex shows. Soft-core films like *Flesh Gordon* were screening on Main Street in Chattanooga, Tennessee, and Topeka,

Kansas. A central figure in the Watergate scandal was given the title of a triple-x movie about fellatio as a nickname, and the ambitious production values and sustained story line of 1973's *The Devil in Miss Jones* prompted *Variety* to comment that hardcore pornography was becoming an art form that critics "may have a hard time ignoring."[19]

By century's end, more than 20 million U.S. households were connected to cable or dish television systems that offer the soft-core Playboy Channel.[20] Hard-core pornographic movies were available at the flick of a switch in almost 1 million of the nation's hotel rooms.[21] Daytime soaps have sex scenes that once would have earned movies an "R" rating while evening situation comedies string one salacious remark after another. The Internet puts high-quality photographs of sex with children, animals, and people in wheelchairs in easy reach of anyone with a credit card. In the 1970s, Donna Summer became nationally notorious for simulating orgasm in her disco hits; many stations simply banned her music outright, for fear of what their listeners and the Federal Communications Commission might say. A quarter-century later, Madonna simulated masturbation in a musical number at the Grammy awards, and nobody thought much of it.

Virtually nobody expected anything like this back in 1966, when the Supreme Court effectively voided America's obscenity laws. It's positively quaint to reread the words of Justice Tom Clark's dissent in that case. "I have 'stomached' past cases for almost ten years without much outcry. Though I am not known to be a purist—or a shrinking violet—this book is too much even for me." [22] And what was that intolerable book that drove Clark over the edge? John Cleland's *Fanny Hill*! Compared to what was coming next, *Fanny Hill* looks like a high-school English text. Clark, a stolid and conventional Democratic politician born in 1899, could not possibly have glimpsed the future. On the other hand, neither could the judges who ruled in favor of *Fanny Hill*. Their mental image of the sort of book endangered by obscenity prosecutions seems to have been set sometime about 1930: *Ulysses* maybe or possibly *Lady Chatterley's Lover*.

Over the next few years, the Court discovered otherwise, and frantically attempted to resurrect the old smashed standards in a series of cases that gave states the power to proscribe materials deemed obscene by local communities. But the flow of obscenity that commenced in 1966 had by then done its work: Local standards were no longer what they used to be.

A very great many Americans, too, had absorbed the notion that (in the words of a Unitarian clergyman quoted in Justice Douglas's opinion in the crucial 1966 obscenity case) "self-control and self-expression are at opposite ends of the continuum. . . . If we want people to behave in a structured and predictable manner, then the ideal of creativity cannot have meaning." The notion that self-discipline stifles creativity, anathema to artists but dear to the artistic, held unusual sway in the late 1960s. In the name of creativity, aesthetic standards were junked and rules of speech and conduct jettisoned. Words that men once were supposed never to utter in front of a woman were delightedly seized by women writers like Erica Jong, who sprinkled them across her best-selling pages like paprika upon a goulash. The release of the obscenity-strewn Nixon Watergate tapes had shocked the president's small-town supporters (some Republicans believe, in fact, that the deleted expletives were the most damaging of all the Watergate revelations). It was an appropriate irony that in 1976 *All the President's Men* achieved the distinction of becoming the first movie to use the word "fuck" and not be slapped with an "X" rating.

The great sex party of the 1970s was *on!* Here's Richard Avedon's May 1974 photo spread in *Vogue*, in which a beautiful woman has collapsed into exhaustion atop two sleepy, satiated men; here again is Helmut Newton's May 1975 shoot, in which a luscious blonde looks demurely downward as the man behind her reaches two hands around to unclasp her bra. When readers expressed shock, *Vogue*'s editor, Grace Mirabella, affected total puzzlement. We were only looking for a picture, she demurely explained, that conveyed the information that the bra in question opened from the front.

It was Mirabella, not her shocked readers, who was in touch with the times. For centuries—for millennia—the job of saying "no" had been the woman's responsibility. As late as 1972, when the National Opinion Research Center first began probing male and female sexual attitudes, a solid majority of American women condemned premarital sex as immoral. The

NORC survey offered four alternative answers: Premarital sex was "always wrong," "almost always wrong," "wrong only sometimes," or "not wrong at all." In 1972, only 20 percent of women said that premarital sex was "not wrong at all"; almost twice as many men, 35 percent, did so. While 60 percent of men gave one or the other of the two permissive answers, 56 percent of women gave one or the other of the restrictive ones.

Between 1970 and 1980, those lingering inhibitions flew straight out the window. Feminists like Germaine Greer championed promiscuity as a means to break women's "doglike" devotion to men,[23] and the young women of the 1970s listened and obeyed. More than two-thirds of the women who turned eighteen between the end of the Korean War and the Kennedy inauguration acknowledged sleeping with only one man as of their thirtieth birthday—their fiancé or husband, presumably. Only 2 percent of the women who turned eighteen between 1971 and 1980 could say the same thing on their thirtieth birthdays. Only slightly more than 2 percent of the women who came of age in the 1950s had slept with five or more men by their thirtieth birthday; 22.5 percent of the post-Vietnam group had carved that many notches in their bedpost.[24] "I remember feeling really weird because I hadn't slept with more guys than were on my two hands," said one of the characters in Naomi Wolf's memoir of her 1970s adolescence. Wolf continued, "The women agreed that girls we knew expected to have slept with anywhere from ten to thirty guys by the time we were in college. If you hadn't at least made a start, you were repressed or geeky or 'inexperienced,' a real pejorative."[25]

"Nice girls do!" proclaimed a 1980 bestseller.[26] Between 1972 and 1982, the proportion of American women who fully or conditionally endorsed premarital sex jumped by nearly twenty percentage points, to 58 percent, with fully 36 percent of women now espousing the ultra-permissive view that premarital sex was "not wrong at all." Tentatively at first, but with rising confidence, women were claiming unrestricted erotic freedom. Their parents sighed and shrugged their shoulders. In 1967, 85 percent of the parents of college-age young people condemned premarital sex as morally wrong; by 1979, only 37 percent of parents still held out against the trend of the times.[27]

As women experimented sexually, they came to regard men in new ways. Gore Vidal remarks that until the middle 1960s, when you looked at a man, you saw a loose suit, a shirt and tie, a shoeshine, and a hat. The male costume neatly identified a man's position in society, but it concealed him as a sexual creature. Not any more. The 1970s saw the greatest revolution in men's clothing since swallowtail coats and knee breeches passed out of fashion almost two centuries ago. Supertight double-knit crotch-hugging pants, ripped-open shirts with a medallion between the pectorals, platform shoes for height, moussed and blow-dried hair—the whole panoply of discowear leapt across the lines of class, race, and sexual orientation to become the evening garb of Midwestern college boys. Before 1965, women tended to judge potential mates in much the same way that a steel company might assess a new blast furnace: Will it throw off sufficient income to justify the trouble of acquiring and maintaining it? The clothes a man put on for a date were chosen to broadcast a simple but powerful message: I am a steady, reliable fellow, who will be able to provide for you and yours. As women acquired economic independence, they also acquired the means to look at men in a new way—they were "just desserts," as a 1983 bestseller nicely phrased it. In 1973, three quarters of the young women surveyed by Daniel Yankelovich identified concern for a woman's sexual satisfaction as "one of the most important" qualities in a man. "Being a good provider" followed well behind.[28]

Alex Comfort, the British pacifist who published *The Joy of Sex* in 1972, speculated hopefully, "The day may come when we regard chastity as no more a virtue than malnutrition." One good vantage point from which to watch the coming of that day is the historical romance novel, a theater for the fantasies of millions of women. Before 1970, this "pornography for women" was sexual only by implication. Its dominating presence was Dame Barbara Cartland, whose heroines invariably preserved their purity unspotted to their wedding day. The blushing conventions of the genre were blown to smithereens in 1972 by a previously unknown writer named Kathleen E. Woodiwiss. Her novel, *The Flame and the Flower*, was discovered in the slush pile by the chief editor at Avon, Nancy Coffey, who somehow managed to struggle through the mauve prose of the first chapter to reach page 28, where the rakish hero, Captain Brandon Birmingham, strips and rapes the beautiful orphan, Heather Simmons. "She stood fixed to the floor until he stepped forward and with a frightened squeak she turned to flee but found her arm squeezed in a grip that was gentle yet as unyielding as a band of steel." Helplessly she is forced onto a bunk: "She felt his hardness searching, probing between her thighs . . ."[29] This was something new. Despite the misgivings of Coffey's superiors—did women really want to read about hardness probing them?—*The Flame and the Flower* was pushed into paperback, where it sold 4.5 million copies over the next six years. It continues in print to this day.

Shortly afterward, a manuscript appeared in that same Avon slush pile from a Rosemary Rogers, addressed only to "the editor of Kathleen Woodiwiss." The book would be published in 1974 as *Sweet Savage Love*. Unlike the victimized Heather Simmons, nobody needed to rape the heroine of *Sweet Savage Love*. It is *she* who makes the decision to surrender her virginity to the forceful stranger who has dragged her underneath a Conestoga wagon. Kidnapped and dragged across the southwestern United States and into the middle of the war between Benito Juarez and the Emperor Maximilian, she happily carries on with three men at once before ending for good in the arms of the Conestoga man. *Sweet Savage Love* sold 10 million copies in the first three years after publication. It too remained in print a quarter-century later.[30] *Sweet Savage Love* convinced American publishers that a grand national trend had been born, and they scrambled to market ever-racier stories to women. Rogers followed with a second novel, *Wicked, Loving Lies*, in which the impetuous, self-sufficient heroine sleeps with half a dozen men in 483 pages. "Jennifer Wilde" (actually the pseudonym of a male author) produced *Love's Tender Fury*, in which the heroine is sold into slavery and serves in a brothel. More than 2 million copies were bought. Here's a 1976 ad in *Publishers Weekly* for *Savage Eden* by Constance Gluys. "For the huge and growing market for women's historical fiction, a big new blockbuster from NAL. It's the story of beautiful Caroline Fane, unjustly accused of adultery and murder, flogged naked in public ... and Justin Lawrence, the daring, flamboyant highwayman whose lust for Caroline was irresistible. Together, they escape to the New

World, only to be recaptured and sold into slavery. In the untamed, violent world of the notorious plantation known as Montrose, they fight for survival against a brutal master and a sadistic mistress with monstrous erotic appetites—and, in spite of every obstacle, fulfill their fierce and tender love for each other." In Barbara Riefe's 1977 book, *Far Beyond Desire*, the heroine is abducted and repeatedly gang-raped. One might have thought this rather extreme for the romance market, but *Far Beyond Desire* sold nearly 2 million copies in a year.

Unlike male stroke literature, books like *Sweet Savage Love* and *Love's Tender Fury* were not read furtively. They were reviewed in newspapers ("a deeply romantic love story" was the verdict on *Sweet Savage Love* from the *New Orleans Time-Picayune*) and opened on the bus. Their success encouraged midmarket writers like Danielle Steele and Judith Krantz, whose books cost $10.95 in hardcover and were sold in bookstores, to jettison old inhibitions and pack their fantasies with sex, sex, sex.[31] For two hundred years, writers used the alleged depravity of the wealthy to conceal sex inside a tale of moral uplift. (Virtue is rewarded, but only after lots of exciting scenes in which the virtuous maiden wriggles deliciously in the evil hands of the bad baronet.) Steele and Krantz junked that tradition. For them, the careless sexual abandon they attributed to the rich was just one more fabulous lifestyle detail, like private jets and ski chalets. They served up the trash heroine, with her own wealth and her skillfully juggled lovers, as a model for independent-minded young women. *This is how it's done. She feels no shame. Why should you?*

When Edith Wharton's Newland Archer expostulates "Women ought to be free—as free as we are," Wharton allows him to puff his cigar for only a moment before tartly commenting that "he was too irritated to measure the terrific consequences" of his words.[32] High on the list of those consequences was the disappearance of the old male entitlement to sexual exclusivity. Only fifteen years before Wharton published *The Age of Innocence*, Pittsburgh millionaire Harry K. Thaw had jolted New York by murdering the great architect Stanford White on the roof of Madison Square Garden because White had seduced the then sixteen-year-old Evelyn Nesbitt, Thaw's future wife. Three separate (all-male of course) juries refused to convict Thaw. If Thaw had wanted, he could have piled his precedents as high as the courtroom's elevated ceiling: In Choderlos de Laclos' savage portrayal of the depravity of the pre-Revolutionary French aristocracy, *Les Liaisons Dangereuses,* a boy who discovers that the girl he loves has been tampered with by an older man discards her and then kills him—and as the interloper lies dying, he forgives the boy and agrees that his death is just.

The sudden and total disappearance of the ideal of bridal virginity has to be reckoned one of the more astonishing psychological developments in recent American history. Here was something that men once killed and died over—and *poof!* it's gone. It did not quite go without a pang: The reading and television-watching public had to be barraged with warnings about the unacceptability of old-fangled male possessiveness. "Most people learn to live comfortably with 'ghosts of loves past,'" one advice book reassuringly cooed.[33] Not only that, but "in many societies around the world, including the Eskimo, the Marquesans, the Lobi of West Africa, the Siriono of Bolivia, and others, jealousy is at a minimum; and in still others, such as the Toda of India, it is almost completely absent."[34] Let your husband read your old love letters, suggested a book by a pseudonymous couple who claimed to lead a particularly active sex life. "It might please him to know that other men loved and desired you before he met you, but that he got you."[35] If not, then he could salve the sting by talking out his feelings, meditating, or reading some classic works of wisdom like the I Ching or the Desiderata.[36] The Desiderata! Imagine Thaw cheering himself up with that!

> *O who can hold a fire in his hand by thinking on the frosty Caucasus?*
> *Or cloy the hungry edge of appetite by bare imagination of a feast?*
> *Or wallow naked in December's snow by thinking on fantastic summer's heat?*[37]

But guess what? It worked. Whatever hesitations and doubts the elder generation might feel about the new rules, the young adapted to them cheerfully. A 1972 poll of boys aged sixteen to nineteen found that only 23 percent professed an unwillingness to marry a non-virgin.[38] At midnight screenings of the 1975 cult comedy *The Rocky Horror Picture Show*, audiences hooted and jeered when a newly engaged woman mistakes in the dark the transvestite Dr. Frankenfurter for her fiancé. "And to think I was saving myself," she sobs afterward. "For what—a rainy day?" the audience would howl in reply. In the span of a little more than a decade, a male emotion that had once seemed as primordial as lust or rage had been brusquely erased, leaving only the faintest chalk outline behind. Wharton, it turned out, had got men wrong.

Or had she? Perhaps the male enthusiasm for female sexual freedom in the 1970s was just as self-interested as Newland Archer's. "One recent Sunday morning," a female California journalist observed in 1976, "I happened . . . to be sitting in the kitchen of a Redondo Beach house inhabited by four young computer engineers. Good, tennis-playing, semi-jock fellows they were, in tracksuits, running shoes of advanced design, and pulsar watches. They were talking about a party they'd all been to the night before, and one seemed to have been taken with a girl he'd met there. He'd given her his phone number, and was plainly impatient for bells to ring. I said maybe she wouldn't think it inexcusably pushy if he called her. He muttered something about cigarettes and left the room, while the others all looked at their fancy feet as if I'd said something particularly dumb. . . . I began to question them, and after a little prevarication they all said that they liked being asked out for dates by women, that they would often sweat it out for days rather than make the first move themselves. Being invited was the greatest thing since transistorized calculators; it made them feel good and saved a lot of hassle, not to mention rejection. . . . They all agreed that a date initiated by a woman was likely to be a more relaxed and promising occasion—you'd hardly be there if she found you repulsive. I was startled, and suspicious. But they didn't seem to be exaggerating or showing off—it was as though they were researchers describing an interesting discovery they'd just made."[39]

The same demographics that had favored men over women in divorce favored young men over young women in courtship. Flick on a movie from the 1960s and it's hard to miss the moviemakers' giddy awareness of being surrounded by hordes of twenty-something girls. Of course this was mostly pornographic fantasy. But it was not *all* pornographic fantasy. For every four boys born in 1945, there were five girls born in 1950, and while the discrepancy shrank for the later boomers, it persisted as long as the boom did. In 1955, when a 26-year-old man born in 1929 met an attractive 22-year-old woman born in 1933, he silently understood that he'd better *act*: She was likely to have an easier time finding another plausible suitor than he was to find an equally appealing alternative. A silent mathematical undertow tugged him to do things her way. That usually meant early engagement and marriage. The baby boom reversed the undertow's current. As Naomi Wolf sadly acknowledged in retrospect. "'Become a woman,' in our culture, does not mean: show us you can weave, as it did in Melanesia, or even show us you can embroider samplers, direct the servants, and play a harpsichord, as it did in 'refined' society in the nineteenth century in the West. No, in our culture, the cliché exclamation to an adolescent girl—'My, how you've grown'—has no cultural echoes whatsoever. The reference is purely physical. In our world, 'Demonstrate that you are a woman' means simply 'Take off your clothes.'"[40]

Although the sexual revolution emancipated female desire and freed women from traditional moral scrutiny, it simultaneously upped the sexual ante for them. Chanel advertised a new perfume for the youth market, Number 19, with an image of a gorgeous model gripping a grinning man's head in a hammer lock and pulling him toward her for a passionate kiss. The cheaper fragrances adopted an even more aggressive tone. Tabu, fearing that its old trademark image of a romantic violinist sweeping his accompanist into his arms had fallen out of style, switched the male and female roles in its 1974 ad campaign: It was the woman who played the violin and grabbed the man. Enjoli produced a notorious commercial in which a sexy career woman performed a bump-and-grind in her kitchen: "I can bring home the bacon, cook it up in a pan, and never ever let him forget he's a man—'cause I'm a *wo*-man, W-O-M-A-N."

Susan Faludi has argued that we must distinguish between '70s feminism and '70s advertising. "Madison Avenue and Hollywood and the fashion industry and mass media all saw a marketing opportunity in 'women's lib' and they ran with it."[41] It's certainly true that Chanel, Revlon, and countless other companies saw marketing opportunities in women's lib. They saw them *because they were there*. Women intuited that they had better pick up the phone or pay the check or do more in bed because they knew that if they did not, there was some other woman who would. In the dark days before feminism, no respectable woman ever sat at a bar, even in the company of a bevy of girlfriends. Feminism ejected that wearisome old taboo. One of the storied moments of the feminist rebellion was the sit-in at McSorley's, an old-fashioned sawdust-on-the-floor saloon near New York University, whose doors were closed to women before 1969. Emancipated from antiquated Victorian restrictions on where women could and could not consume alcohol, women were freed to mingle with men in the new "singles bars" that sprang up in every American city. (The first one is thought to have opened in Washington, D.C., in 1965.) A newly divorced woman described with amazement her first visit to one of the new bars: "the place was a meat store. People sitting around being looked over like pork chops on a tray. Only nobody was selling. They were giving themselves away."[42]

Many feminist intellectuals at first enthusiastically applauded the next sexual order. Lenin hated the passivity of the proletariat much more fiercely than the villainy of the bourgeoisie, and like him Germaine Greer was angrier with the women she wanted to liberate than the men she thought oppressed them. "Part of the battle will be won," Greer wrote, "if [women] can change their attitude towards sex, and embrace and stimulate the penis instead of *taking* it."[43]

"J," the author of the 1969 hit *The Sensuous Woman*, assumes that her (female) readers will regard fellatio as an exotic and faintly disgusting practice. In the years since then, according to the most authoritative study of American sex practices, oral sex has become as American as lo mein. While fewer than 40 percent of the women born before World II had ever given or received oral sex, almost 80 percent of those born since the war have at least tried it.[44] "I am not brilliant and I don't have a magnetic personality," remarks "J." "[But] through intelligence and hard work, I have become a Sensuous Woman. And that's what almost every man wants. More than beauty. More than brilliance. More than great housekeeping abilities. More than a model mother to his children. He wants a Sensuous Woman . . . "[45]

The pressure to be a Sensuous Woman was being felt in the most conservative quadrants of American society. Compare two marital advice books aimed at evangelical Christian women: Helen Andelin's *Fascinating Womanhood* of 1963 and Marabel Morgan's *The Total Woman*, published in 1973. Andelin and Morgan agree that a woman can best retain and intensify her husband's love by appealing to his protectiveness and masculine pride and making a show of her own femininity. Morgan suggests that women murmur baby talk and pretend to be unable to open jars. Both authors call for submission to the husband's will (the more worldly Morgan cagily promises that by submitting the wife will in the end extract more goodies from her husband). They differ, really, on only one subject: sex. Andelin offers no sexual advice at all, aside from a blunt warning that most men will want more of it than their wives will care to give, and that women should feel no more obligation to assent to these demands than to their children's requests for candy. She recommends exercise, hard work, and medicinal herbs to bring a husband's excessive appetites under control. Morgan, on the other hand, understands that under the conditions of 1973, a husband's unsated appetites constitute a coiled menace to hearth and home. "A mistress seduces," Morgan wrote, "a hausfrau submits," and Morgan's book bulges with often alarming seduction plans. She did not, as legend has it, suggest that a wife meet her husband at the front door wrapped in Saran Wrap, but she does propose wearing exotic costumes— cheerleader outfits, high heels, an apron, and nothing else—to perk up the jaded husband, and she reminisces excitedly about the night she put the kids to bed early, cooked a romantic dinner for two, and then slid under the dining room table to please her husband. It's all rather sad and desperate: *The Stepford Wives* crossed with *9 1/2 Weeks*.[46] But it spoke to *somebody*. *The Total Woman* outsold *All the President's Men* in hardcover, and went on to sell another 3 million copies in paperback by the end of 1976.

Today, the freeing of the American id is almost invariably described as a victory for human freedom as grand as the Declaration of Independence or the fall of the Berlin Wall. But this upheaval had its victims—and the middle-aged women prancing around the kitchens nude but for their polyester lace aprons, grimly hoping to defend their homes, were the most comic and the most poignant of them all.

For all their wildness, the 1970s were not (sorry, kids) a frivolous era. Despite the binge, America had not been transformed into a nation of good-time girls and boys. "No, they are not gay. They are sober; they are even severe. They are of a pensive cast; they take things hard," one of Henry James's European characters observes of his American relatives,[47] and the description still holds true.

Americans in the 1970s were shedding old moral inhibitions for a serious reason. They were bringing an entire new pattern of family life into being, rejecting one sexual regime and groping their way toward another. This pattern is so familiar now that it's hard to recall how vast a chasm separates it from the pattern that prevailed fifty years ago. Instead of flirtation, courtship, and marriage, modern Americans proceed through a series of "relationships." Judith Martin, the columnist better known as Miss Manners, calls this new pattern "commit and switch." Open a supermarket tabloid and you'll see a headline about an actress furious that her beau of the moment is cheating on her. The actress and her beau are not married to each other. How therefore can he be cheating? Because as the institution of marriage has contracted—as we marry later, more briefly, more carelessly—the definition of adultery has expanded. The relationships Americans consummate beginning around the time of their sixteenth birthday are serious affairs: miniature marriages, from which they expect all the exclusivity and intimacy of the real thing, minus only the real thing's permanency. For two weeks or two months or two years, we act like husband and wife. But we always retain our freedom to cancel at a moment's notice and start all over again with somebody else. Indeed, as Miss Manners complains, the concept of "dating"—keeping company with a large number of people of the opposite sex in the period before one has selected one to marry—is seen by young people nowadays as the nadir of immorality, because it entails "cheating" on one's "relationship." "Relationships" are not trips to the moon on gossamer wings: They are, as the thousands of relationship books warn us, hard, unremitting toil. "Show me a relationship without conflict and issues and I'll show you a couple that is either dead or in denial," one relationship guru, Barbara De Angelis, tells her television audiences. The rebels who sparked the sexual revolution promised the country more joy, more delight, more pleasure. But, as so often happens after a revolution, the promised joy, delight, and pleasure appear only on hortatory billboards erected by the revolutionary leaders—in this case, the purveyors of jeans, underwear, and perfume.

GENDER BENDERS

ALL TWENTIETH-CENTURY REVOLUTIONARY MOVEMENTS HAVE DREAMT OF CREating a "new man." Only in the United States has one done it.

That's him, changing a baby on the changing tables now found in both men's and women's public restrooms. That's him too, sitting on the bus staring past the pregnant woman standing in front of him. For a quarter of a century he's been poked and prodded, screamed at and scolded. He must do more of the housework. He must express his feelings more articulately. He must hug more. He should take pride in knowing how to cook. He should let his wife drive, quit feeling obliged to hurl a punch every time he's insulted, stop dominating and bullying, and get in touch with his feminine side. He will be better for it. Really.

A new baby is born, lamented a 1974 book by a self-described male liberationist. "A cursory examination of the pubic area reveals the presence of a penis, and the exhausted mother and nail-biting father are informed that they have a son. From that moment, the cultural indoctrination begins. The blue blanket, the miniature boxing gloves, the blue Superman tights with accompanying cape, subtly inform this newly hatched amorphous bit of protoplasm of the great and impossible expectations which constitute the essence of his recently acquired humanity. He is to become the embodiment of heroism and courage, aggressivity and aptitude, an amalgamation of the fantasies of Hemingway and Mailer. The roughhouse play with adults, the injunction that 'little boys don't cry,' the 'did you win?' when he returns home after his first pugilistic encounter with the boy next door, nose bloodied and tears only barely contained: the message is received, the boy is trained to be a 'man.' Vulnerability is a vice, emotionality is odious, and stoicism connotes strength."[48] That's how it had been in the bad old days. But it would be that way no longer.

"As men," the publisher Michael Korda observed in an early dispatch from the sex wars, "we don't see the way our behavior is *oppressive* . . . . I *think* of my wife, C., as an equal—no question about it in my mind as we dine with a mutual woman friend in London. I try not to make decisions for C., try to ask what she wants to do, try not to impose, but the old urge to dominate, the simple crass desire to have my own way, still marks the male chauvinist's power erection, so linked to the sexual one, that it is sometimes hard to separate sex from power." And then he told the following story.

"Across from us, at a banquette, a group of noisy gentlemen on the verge of drunkenness are staring at us—at C., to be exact, who is beautiful and tanned and has her back turned to them. I, on the other hand, am facing them. Ponderously and inaccurately, they toss a few pieces of bread in C.'s direction to attract her attention. She ignores them. A few minutes later the waiter appears with a silver platter bearing a card, accompanied by the expectant giggles of our neighbors. Before C. can reach it, I pick it up and turn it over. It is one of those thick printed cards you can buy at fun fairs or in novelty shops: *I want to sleep with you! Tick off your favorite love position from the list below, and return this card with your telephone number* . . . .

"I tear the card up. Then suddenly transfixed by the stupid, sniggering stare of the man who sent the card, I pick up the ashtray from our table and hurl it straight at his face. Instant scene: the crash of breaking glass, both of us on our feet, the headwaiter and my two companions pulling me away, the old instincts lurking there as strong as ever. '*Kill* the bastard . . . '

"Well, it's a scene—we've lived through them before—but outside on the street I find C. in tears, as furious as she is miserable. What did I expect? That she'd be *grateful*? That she'd thank me for defending her honor? I had made her into an object, *my* object. . . . 'I don't mind being hassled by some drunk, I can take that, but to be treated like a chattel, to be robbed of any right to decide for myself whether I'd been insulted, or how badly, to have you react for me because I'm *your* woman—"Hands off her, or I'll kill you"—that's really *sickening*, it's like being a *slave*.'"[49] The magazine that printed Korda's vignette followed it with a symposium. Had Korda done the wrong thing? The contributors' opinions were evenly divided.

The 1970s were the decade in which the word "macho" entered the American language. It immediately acquired two meanings: positive in the gay subculture ("Macho, macho man," sang the Village People, "I want to be a macho man"), fiercely negative just about everywhere else. "Must you be so *macho?*" hissed put-upon wives and girlfriends. The 1970s witnessed a revolution in the understanding of what it meant to be a man, in which courage, hardihood, and the defense of one's own were all devalued, and expressiveness and emotionalism upvalued. The New Man had a face, that of the actor Alan Alda, who first on *M*A*S*H* (the top comedy of the 1970s) and then in a series of movies represented to American men what the sensitive man should look like. The New Man had a voice, the throaty baritone of the lecturer Leo Buscaglia, who became a very rich man by traveling around the country expressing his feelings. Singers like James Taylor, Jackson Browne, Dan Fogelberg, Dan Hill crooned their music with the quaver of tears in their throats. At the movies, heroes were no longer permitted to rescue heroines. Beginning with the first Indiana Jones movie and continuing to the present day, the heroine must punch the menacing villain *herself* before the hero is allowed to rescue her. Better still if she rescues him. It's suggestive, I think, that of the eighteen Oscars awarded for Best Actress or Best Supporting Actress between 1974 and 1982, only three went to women playing romantic leads. The rest went to actresses in undomestic, unromantic roles: Faye Dunaway as a hard-charging executive who used and disposed of men in *Network,* Sally Field for playing a union organizer in *Norma Rae,* Meryl Streep for playing a concentration camp inmate in *Sophie's Choice.*[50]

Middle-class boys and girls were handed non-sex-specific toys and dressed identically. The old idea that fathers and mothers each had their distinct roles flew out the window. Indeed it was in the 1970s that "parent" began to be used as a verb, formally signifying the erasing of the line between the work of mothers and that of fathers.

Nobody probably worried less about the merits and demerits of a unisex utopia than the men who gathered to drink and dance at the now world-famous Stonewall Inn on Christopher Street in Greenwich Village, but in years to come, nobody would get more credit for bringing it about. The Stonewall was a pretty dubious venue even by the standards of 1960s gay bars, a Mafia-controlled enterprise that dispensed watered drinks in none-too-clean glasses. The New York City police took bribes to avert their eyes from the joint, but apparently under pressure from federal authorities—who suspected the owners of the Stonewall of selling untaxed liquor—the cops unexpectedly showed up in the hot early morning hours of June 28, 1969.[51] As the policemen entered, the Stonewall bartenders flashed white lights as a warning to stop dancing, dancing with a person of the same sex then being a crime in New York State. The police ordered most of the patrons out and arrested a couple of employees and also some of the more luridly dressed transvestites—wearing the clothing of the opposite sex was also a crime. As the police exited the bar, the rousted drinkers and a crowd of onlookers pelted them with coins, bottles, rocks, and, famously, a size-11 lady's pump. The cops retreated inside the building and bolted the door. Some rioters tried to smash it open with an uprooted parking meter. One tossed lighter fluid inside the building and tried, unsuccessfully, to ignite it. Others formed a chorus line and performed a high-step kick while chanting to the tune of "Tra-la-la-boom-dee-ay,"

> *We are the Stonewall girls*
> *We wear our hair in curls*
> *We wear no underwear*

We show our pubic hair
We wear our dungarees
Above our nelly knees.

Reinforcements arrived and, after a little more yelling, the crowd was dispersed.

Drag queens hurling high-heeled shoes at cops and chanting campy songs? Who would have thought of this as a world-historical event? But the suddenly energized gay-rights movement seized on Stonewall as its storming of the Bastille. When the first gay pride marches were organized the following year, the anniversary of Stonewall was unanimously acclaimed as the only possible date.

Some skepticism is in order as to exactly how significant Stonewall was. The radicalism of the 1960s celebrated spontaneous, violent, popular insurrections against oppression, and with only a little judicious editing (passing lightly over the bit about the unlicensed liquor, for instance), the Stonewall riot accorded splendidly with the favorite myths of the age. The name helped too. Had the bar on Christopher Street been known as the Flamingo Lounge, it's possible that June 28 would have continued to be best known to the world for the assassination of the Archduke Franz Ferdinand in Sarajevo in 1914. And in the end, insurrections, spontaneous or otherwise, contributed little to the many successes of the gay rights movement over the next thirty years. Homosexuality's victories would be won from the courts, in the universities, in the marketplace, on the stage, and at the movies—everywhere but in the streets. It would be more accurate, if less transgressive, to cite as the real commencement of the gay liberation movement 1948 (the year of the publication of the Kinsey Report, *Sexual Behavior in the Human Male*), 1957 (the year a British royal commission called for decriminalizing all sex acts between consenting adults), 1962 (the year Illinois became the first American state to repeal its sodomy laws), 1968 (the year the play *The Boys in the Band* opened in New York and Phil Donahue welcomed his first homosexual guest), or 1971 (when the Florida Supreme Court overturned the state's law that declared homosexuality a felony).

Whichever date one selects, sometime between 1970 and 1980 the gay rights movement succeeded in promoting homosexuality in the minds of millions of liberal Americans to a civil-rights category analogous to race or religion. Between 1971 and 1980, twenty-two states repealed their sodomy laws,[52] forty cities—including Seattle, Detroit, and Minneapolis—enacted ordinances forbidding discrimination on grounds of sexual orientation, and more than a hundred U. S. corporations extended their internal equal-employment codes to cover homosexuals. E. M. Forster's *Maurice*, a candidly homoerotic novel by one of the acknowledged masters of twentieth-century English prose, was posthumously published in 1971. The 1972 Democratic convention adopted a platform plank endorsing freedom of "lifestyle and private habits without being subject to discrimination or persecution" and invited two homosexual delegates to address it. That September, Pennsylvania certified the first openly homosexual teacher in the nation. In December 1973, the trustees of the American Psychiatric Association deleted homosexuality from their diagnostic manual of mental illnesses; in April 1974, a vote of the membership ratified the trustees' decision.

A state court in Seattle ruled in 1974 that two lesbian divorcées were not bound by a family court order that they live "separate and apart." They could live together and retain custody of their children by their marriages. In February 1975, the Defense Department for the first time granted a security clearance to a declared homosexual. In July, the Civil Service Commission ruled that homosexuals would no longer be ineligible for government service. At its 1977 synod, the United Church of Christ, the inheritor of the old Puritan churches of New England, deplored "the use of scripture to generate hatred and the violation of the civil rights of gay and bisexual persons"—the strongest gay-rights language yet heard from an American religious authority. In 1977, a homosexual delegation was received for the first time at the White House—albeit while President Carter was visiting Camp David. The United Methodist Church's highest court ruled in November 1979 that open homosexuals could serve as pastors, the first major religious denomination to do so. "On the tenth anniversary of Stonewall, seventeen-year-old Randy Rohl took twenty-year-old Grady

Quinn to the senior prom in Sioux Falls, South Dakota. The National Gay Task Force announced that this was the first time two acknowledged homosexuals had attended a high school prom together in America."[53]

Even the one big setback suffered by the gay-rights cause ended up strengthening it. In 1977, the county commissioners of Dade County, Florida, voted to amend the local antidiscrimination ordinance to cover homosexuals. Dade encompasses the Miami metropolitan area, making it the largest jurisdiction to recognize sexual orientation as a forbidden ground of discrimination, and the first in a Republican-trending state. Conservative Floridians were jolted and forced a measure to repeal the commissioners' decision onto the county's ballot. Led by singer Anita Bryant, the "Save Our Children" initiative won by a crushing 71-percent to 29-percent margin. Flushed with that success, Bryant went on to win two more repeal votes: one in St. Paul, Minnesota, the other in Eugene, Oregon. But her crusade soon fizzled. Seattle voters voted "no" in 1978 to a repeal of their city's gay-rights law, and Californians rejected a ballot measure forbidding the employment of open homosexuals as school teachers. Bryant paid a heavy personal price for her outspokenness. Under pressure from a gay-organized boycott, the Florida orange-juice growers canceled her contract as their spokeswoman. Bryant was suddenly unbookable as a singer. Her marriage collapsed under the strain. The implosion of Bryant's career taught a dramatic lesson: While it could be dangerous for a public figure to speak in favor of homosexual rights, it was positively lethal to oppose them. A majority of Americans would continue to disapprove of homosexuality until the end of the century—in 1982, only 34 percent regarded homosexuality as an "acceptable" lifestyle and as late as 1999, 43 percent thought homosexual conduct should be illegal[54]—but that disapproval was quiet and largely ineffective. The disapprovers tended to be drawn from the least influential segments of American society, the less affluent, the less educated, the less white. As early as 1969, a majority of college-educated Americans had come to accept homosexual relations between consenting adults as "not wrong."[55]

Arriving at that opinion required special broadmindedness in the 1970s, because in the dozen years between Stonewall and the onset of AIDS, a large and flamboyant minority of homosexuals seemed bent on casting aside the secrecy of the past to test the outermost limits of sexuality. Surveys conducted in the mid-1970s by Alfred Kinsey's Institute for Sex Research at Indiana University found that 75 percent of then-active white homosexual men claimed to have had more than one hundred partners in their lifetime; 28 percent claimed more than one thousand. Black homosexual men claimed significantly fewer (the Kinsey Institute published no aggregate numbers for all races). Of the whites, 73 percent claimed to have felt no affection at all for the majority of their sex partners; black homosexuals reported a slightly higher degree of emotional involvement with the men with whom they had sex.[56] It's not clear whether this hyperpromiscuity represented any sort of departure from the past. What was a departure was the visibility and fearlessness of hyperpromiscuity. Rather than meeting furtively in darkened parks or alleyways (Charles Kaiser in the *Gay Metropolis* reminds us that the streetlighting of New York City was much dimmer in the 1960s than it is now) or in clandestine bars, homosexuals, both men and women, boldly declared their existence to the public. They created a conspicuous new sexual culture, first in New York and San Francisco, then throughout the country.

Most of the bathhouses of the 1970s were shut in the 1980s by the public health authorities to combat AIDS. In his acclaimed book, *And the Band Played On*, the late Randy Shilts accused bathhouse owners and gay political leaders of fatal passivity in the face of the AIDS epidemic. But the preponderant tone in accounts of those orgiastic days is nostalgia.

There was a loft on New York's Fourteenth Street, one writer recalls, where "you would check your clothes in a bag. And you would wear boots and you'd put the little check in your boot and you would walk around naked. And there were like four hundred guys in a loft. This happened a lot. Marijuana, poppers, wine, and I think the beginning of cocaine and the beginning of those exotic drugs, MDMA and MDMMA and all." Party places like that came and went, but one bar that endured for almost the whole of the decade was New York's Anvil, near the old docks on the lower Hudson. "There was a ledge that ran the length of the back room. . . . I remember this particular night, there I was lying on the ledge, my underpants and my jeans cradled in my armpit beside me. . . . I could feel [men] one at a time inside me, even though I never saw them. Either I was truly liberated or truly psychotic."[57] Jack Fritscher fondly recalled San Francisco's Folsom Street Barracks in his novel/memoir of the 1970s: "Men lay on sheeted bunks, arms across their pecs, teasing their own tits, surrounded by huge latex dildoes. . . . In four-poster beds made of heavy lumber, men with chinstrap beards and crewcuts hung cradled in black leather slings, their booted feet spread high in stirrups ... waiting for the right man propelled by the right drug to shove his fist [into them] .. . . [I]n other rooms, men . . . straddled chairs under the acid-red glow of the naked lightbulbs ... turning on and turning down most of the hungry men stopping at their door, waiting for the right man to come along to be tied up spreadeagled, whipped, tortured.... In darkened toilets, men lay back in long urinal troughs, jerking off, wet by hot streams.... In the orgy rooms men stood four deep around the central bed ... not knowing whom they tongued, not knowing who in the pigpile below them sucked on [them] . . . [then retreating to] the juice bar in the lobby, to catch a second wind, to smoke a joint . . . to watch the newly arriving meat being buzzed in at the door."[58] One amateur historian of the San Francisco gay scene has counted a dozen such sex clubs near the city's waterfront warehouse district, with many others spread through the city. (There was a second dense congregation near Castro Street, where the pleasure-seeking was somewhat tamer.)[59]

The scene intoxicated the French philosopher Michel Foucault—for better or worse, the most influential thinker on sex and gender since Sigmund Freud—on his first visit to California in 1975. Foucault argued for the abolition of all conceptions of normality, in all areas of life. His first book, *The Birth of the Prison*, attacked eighteenth-century advocates of humane treatment of criminals. Better, Foucault said, to toss a man into a dank dungeon and chain him there forever, than to label him "bad" and to seek to rehabilitate him, for that invaded man's sacred right to be himself. This improbable line of argument was extended by Foucault through books on insanity and sexuality, until his death from AIDS in 1984.

Foucault insisted that the sadomasochistic delights he witnessed in the

United States constituted a genuinely new form of sexuality, something that had not existed before the gay-liberation movement conjured them into being. "I don't think that this movement of sexual practices has anything to do with the disclosure or understanding of S/M [sado-masochistic] tendencies deep within our unconscious," he said in a 1982 interview with the Toronto homosexual magazine, *Body Politic*, after a month spent in exploration of the Canadian city's sado-masochistic subculture. "I think that S/M is much more than that: It's the real creation of new possibilities of pleasure."[60] "It is," he further explained, "the body made totally plastic by pleasure: something that opens itself, that tightens, that throbs, that beats, that gapes.'"[61]

In the minds of many men, however, this pleasure was not an end in itself, but a means to a higher end. The pleasures they pursued had long been forbidden and condemned by law and morality. By indulging flagrantly and compulsively in the forbidden, they were challenging society either to punish them or to rethink its old taboos. It was, in its own way, an act of civil disobedience, the assertion of a right to lead an entirely new kind of life. The lesbian feminists could at least invoke the pseudo-scientific myth of a Stone Age goddess-culture as a precedent for the society they dreamt of.[62] The men of San Francisco could take refuge in no such illusion. Tom Stoddard, the executive director of the Lambda Legal Defense Fund, later explained that the astonishing goings-on in San Francisco and New York were no ordinary debauch. "It was in the largest sense exploratory," he said. "That's really the key to understanding it. For me it was an exploration of sex, but it was also an exploration of relationships: casual relationships, friendships, and deeply felt romantic relationships."[63] The Village People, less intellectual than Stoddard, phrased his thought more economically. In their anthem to the gay life of San Francisco, "City by the Bay," the refrain consisted of two words, repeated over and over: "Freedom. Pleasure. Freedom. Pleasure."

This pleasure and this freedom in the end exacted a terrible price from those who pursued it. The HIV virus infected some 40 percent of a randomly selected sample of homosexual men in San Francisco by 1984.[64]

The virus probably began its spread in the mid-1970s. But even in the very first year of the plague—before the AIDS virus was identified and named—Foucault glimpsed and welcomed the destination to which his life was tending. The pleasure he sought, he insisted in his 1982 Toronto interview, was a pleasure that would transcend all limits and annihilate consciousness—in other words, death. "I think that the kind of pleasure I would consider as *the* real pleasure would be so deep, so intense, so overwhelming that I couldn't survive it. I would die."[65] Foucault's Toronto companion later told his biographer, "My sense is that his obsession with death—and there is no doubt but that he was obsessed with it—had something to do with death as a kind of presentation of self, death as an indication of self, death as a distancing of self."[66]

These sophistications were largely lost on the larger society. It was stumped by a much more basic challenge. If nonmarital sex between consenting adults was okay, as a majority of Americans was coming to believe, how did it become wrong if those adults happened both to be women or both to be men? If it was praiseworthy for heterosexual men and women to abandon the oppressive sexual roles of the past, how did it become blameworthy for homosexual men and women to do so? Indeed, if smashing stereotypes was liberating, then who was contributing more to liberation than men and women who defied those stereotypes in the most radical possible way? Homosexuals, it could now reasonably be argued, ought to be seen as pathfinders, heroes, harbingers. "How can we rear male infants to bisexuality?" wondered Phyllis Chesler in her influential 1972 book, *Women and Madness.*[67] One popular feminist lecturer, Barbara Seaman, exhorted women who disavowed lesbianism "'not to knock it unless you've tried it.'" Seaman ruefully acknowledged that she herself had not yet tried it. Nevertheless, as she told an interviewer, "she's more or less persuaded that she ought to like it: 'I used to feel a lot of fear and contempt coming from straight women about lesbians. Now the question I'm hearing from a lot of my friends is 'Why can't we be like them?'"[68] The bisexual had transcended the mire of sexual identity to become a pure monad, capable of loving other monads, regardless of their plumbing. "The fall was from some primeval division into two sexes," contended the les-bian activist Jill Johnston. "I think any bio-analytically oriented person knows we were originally one sex."[69]

The Fall: What is it but a prelude to Redemption? Karl Marx imagined Redemption as a return to the "primitive communism" of early man, and he convinced himself that the industrial proletariat would bring about that Redemption. The proletariat, as Marx saw it, was the only universal class, the only class whose interests were identical to the interests of all mankind. When the proletariat overthrew capitalism, it would be acting for the good of all. In the early 1970s, feminist and gay intellectuals adapted this Marxian scheme to the sexual revolution. Lost in the mists of ancient time lay the golden age of androgyny and bisexuality. The appearance of patriarchy destroyed this blissful state. But humanity could return to it by an act of revolution. And who was the proletariat in this scheme, the universal class? Who else but the homosexuals?

That sense that homosexuals somehow incarnated a more equitable, more pleasurable future may explain the extraordinary explosion of gay cultural influence in the 1970s. From Perrier to sandblasted Victorian row-houses, from Quaaludes to anthologies of women's literature, gay society set the tone for the rest of America. To see this pace-setting come to life, one needed only to pay a visit to the top tourist attraction of late 1970s New York: the Studio 54 discotheque. There on West Fifty-fourth Street, in-side an abandoned television studio theater, two young entrepreneurs, Steve Rubell and Ian Schrager (one gay, one straight), had created the most talked-about nightclub in the city's history.[70] Beautiful young men and women gyrated nearly naked on the floor—half in male-female cou-ples, half in male-male—under dazzling decorations that changed almost nightly. In the banquettes that surrounded the dance floor sat the planet's most famous celebrities, served drinks by handsome waiters wearing nothing but boxer trunks and snorting drugs provided by the open-handed Rubell. Overlooking the floor was the old mezzanine, its chairs still bolted in place, now given over to the discotheque's clients for hasty assignations. Beyond the floor were the famous unisex bathrooms; in the basement, the VIP room, where Mick Jagger held court. On the street outside, there massed a huge throng of ordinary young men and women. Above them, on little stepladders from which they could monitor the crowd, Rubell's young men played St. Peter, picking out "you and you and you—but not you." Straight America was pushing its way into a new world of pleasure and freedom. And it was gays who manned the ropeline between that world and the old one.

PART V

DAM YANKEES

> *"But because people in the West are not threatened by concentration camps and are free to say and write what they want, the more the fight for human rights gains in popularity, the more it loses in concrete content, becoming a kind of universal stance of everyone toward everything, a kind of energy that turns all human desires into rights. The world has become man's right and everything in it has become a right: the desire for love the right to love, the desire for rest the right to rest, the desire for friendship the right to friendship, the desire to exceed the speed limit the right to exceed the speed limit, the desire for happiness the right to happiness, the desire to publish a book the right to publish a book, the desire to shout in the street in the middle of the night the right to shout in the street."*

> —*Milan Kundera*
> Immortality[1]

AN EARLY FLAG OF THE AMERICAN REVOLUTION DISPLAYED A COILED RATtlesnake (and the fierce motto "Don't Tread on Me") to symbolize the country's fierce determination to rule itself. Two hundred years later, the animal with the best claim to represent the American character was not the rattler but a small freshwater fish: the snail darter.

The snail darter owes this distinction not to any merit of its own, but to the intricacies of pork-barrel politics in the state of Tennessee. During its first thirty-five years in the dam-building business, the Tennessee Valley Authority had more or less ignored the Republican-voting hilly up–country of eastern Tennessee. But the state was trending Republican, and in 1970 the TVA produced a plan for a dam on the Little Tennessee River near Knoxville, to be called Tellico, after an ancient Indian settlement nearby.

Everything was going smoothly. Then, in the summer of 1973, a naturalist named David Etnier discovered a previously unknown species of perch in the Little Tennessee's waters.

The fish might not have been much to look at, but it had a sure sense of timing. Had it been found even eighteen months earlier, the TVA would have annihilated its home without so much as a backward glance. But in 1973, Congress had enacted the Endangered Species Act, which prohibited spending any federal money on any project that might extinguish a species of animal. Construction of the Tellico dam was halted, and the snail darter became the central figure in a complex nexus of regulation, legislation, and litigation that went all the way to the Supreme Court.[2] President Carter had to personally broker a compromise that relocated the snail darters to new homes. A dam originally proposed before the marines waded ashore at Danang at last opened its gates nine days after Iranian militants seized the American hostages in Tehran. That's an interval three times as long as it took Depression America to build the gigantic Hoover Dam in bleak Nevada. An impressive achievement for a little fish, especially since it had never really been endangered at all. In the summer of 1984, naturalists discovered snail darters in two other southeastern rivers.

The snail darter's dam-busting was far from unique. Its tastier cousin, the Hudson River striped bass, delayed a freeway for almost a quarter of a century. In December 1973, the weight of a heavy truck caused a sixty-foot section of the elevated West Side highway over Manhattan's Hudson River waterfront to collapse. Fortunately, nobody was seriously hurt, but the accident convinced the city that the much-hated First World War vintage road needed to be replaced. The section of the road below Fifty-ninth Street was demolished and planning began in earnest for construction of the up-to-date federally funded interstate highway along the Hudson that Governor Rockefeller had begun calling for in the mid-1960s. After four years of wrangling, the new road, Westway, was given what was supposed to have been its final approval in March 1975 by Governor Hugh Carey and Mayor Abe Beame. After a further six years of environmental, structural, and traffic studies, the final permits were issued in the summer of 1981.

Then the bass bit. Westway was to have been built upon landfill, just like the East Side's FDR Drive. In early 1982, a federal judge, Thomas Griesa, ordered the project halted, because the Army Corps of Engineers had not adequately considered the impact of the landfill upon the bass. If fifteen years of study was not enough, it was hard to know how much *would* be, but the Corps dutifully trundled off for three more years of assessments. In 1985 the army returned with the news that at the very worst, no more than one-third of the bass in the lower Hudson were at risk, but Judge Griesa was unimpressed and ordered the Corps to start all over again. The message was unmistakable. In 1986 the city and state surrendered and returned the federal highway money. After ten more years of wrangling, the city began work on a much more modest boulevard.

Who says the pace of life is accelerating? In all, New York's new westside road will have taken thirty-five years from planning to opening. Half a century before, the George Washington Bridge over the Hudson had been built in thirty-nine *months.*

Mid-century American government had been organized in such a way as to *get things done*: to fight wars, build colossal public works, regulate giant industries, stabilize the economy. Looking back on the accomplishments of those years, modern-day Americans must feel like a seventy-year-old former athlete browsing through his college scrapbooks. Did we really spend the equivalent of $500 billion a year on foreign aid during the Marshall Plan? Did it only take us eight years from start to finish to land a man on the moon? Did urban school systems really manage to deliver a perfectly adequate education to hundreds of thousands of slum-dwellers? *How?* And then another thought follows almost instantly—*What is wrong with us that we can no longer do this now?* The last important addition to New York City's transportation system, the Verrazano-Narrows Bridge, opened in 1964. The city's most recent attempt to modernize itself, by opening a direct rail link from Manhattan to John F. Kennedy Airport, collapsed in humiliating failure—the train to the plane will terminate in Jamaica, Queens, instead. Nor is this dilatoriness a uniquely East Coast problem. Los Angeles International Airport did not manage to build a single new runway between 1970 and 2000, despite repeated tries.

Before succumbing too completely to nostalgia, think of this. The energy and effectiveness of mid-century government was far from the normal state of affairs in the United States. For almost all of the century and a quarter from the Declaration of Independence to the accession of Theodore Roosevelt to the presidency, American government—federal, state, and local—was notorious for its incapacity. By 1900, Imperial Germany had a modest welfare state and Britain had a functioning income tax and a professional civil service. America, meanwhile, was run by patronage hacks on an agricultural schedule. Most of the country's paper money was issued by privately owned banks. These banks frequently miscalculated how much money was needed, triggering financial panics at regular intervals: in 1893, in 1907, and again in 1913. When a recession struck, the federal government could not even count the unemployed, much less aid them. Late nineteenth-century American cities were filthy and mismanaged compared to English, Dutch, or German cities of similar size, their roads and ports a mess. James Bryce, who served as British ambassador to the United States in the 1880s, observed when he got home, "No impression regarding American politics is more generally diffused in Europe than that contained in the question which the traveler who has returned from the United States becomes so weary of being asked, 'Isn't everybody corrupt there?'"[3]

Beginning in the 1880s, reformers began inveighing against the feebleness and venality of America's governments—a feebleness and venality that they did not hesitate to blame on the defects of the Constitution. In 1885, the young Woodrow Wilson complained in the first, and less tactful, edition of his book *Congressional Government*: "The Constitution was adopted when it was six days hard traveling from New York to Boston; when to cross the East River was to venture a perilous voyage; when men were thankful for weekly mails; when the extent of the country's commerce was reckoned not in millions but in thousands of dollars; when the country knew few cities, and had but begun manufactures; when Indians were pressing upon near frontiers; when there were no telegraph lines and no monster corporations." To adapt, the Constitution either had to be formally amended or else "wrest[ed] to strange and as yet unimagined uses."[4]

The great spasm of political reform we call Progressivism was an attempt to do that wresting. The publication of Wilson's book is as good a date as any for the movement's intellectual beginnings. 1913—the year of the first income tax and the creation of the Federal Reserve, and the ratification of the constitutional amendment providing for the direct election of senators—was its climax. The New Deal was its apotheosis. The people we lump together as Progressives disagreed with each other about almost everything. Woodrow Wilson and Theodore Roosevelt both accepted the designation "Progressive" (Roosevelt ran as the candidate of the party of that name in the 1912 election), and yet hated each other as heartily as any two rival politicians in American history. But almost all Progressives were inspired by the shared conviction that the country's institutions had failed to keep pace with the times. Too much power, they said, lay in the hands of politicians accountable only to small slices of the electorate: aldermen rather than mayors, state legislators rather than governors, congressmen rather than presidents. "The New Nationalism," Roosevelt said in a 1910 speech, "puts the national need before sectional or personal advantage. It is impatient of the utter confusion that results from local legislatures attempting to treat national issues as local issues. It is still more impatient of the impotence that springs from overdivision of governmental powers, the impotence that makes it possible for local selfishness or for legal cunning, hired by wealthy special interests, to bring national activities to a deadlock. This New Nationalism regards the executive power as the steward of the public welfare. It demands of the judiciary that it shall be interested primarily in human welfare rather than in property, just as it demands that the representative body shall represent all the people rather than any one class or section of the people." Progressives worried that too much of the routine work of government was being done by elected officials worried about the next election. As the Progressives saw it, the big decisions ought to be made by leaders elected in ways that gave them a mandate strong enough to crush the objections of entrenched interests, while the routine tasks of administration were executed not by small-time pols, but by a professional civil service, chosen for its expertise and protected from political interference.

This defense of concentrated political power and professional administration was a new thing in American intellectual life. The Constitution had artfully separated the powers of government with an eye to protecting "entrenched interests" from the whims of temporary majorities. On the rare occasions that strong personalities, like Andrew Jackson, seized political power in the name of a national majority, nineteenth-century Americans recoiled in fright. Jackson's vigorous, even brutal, presidency united his opponents in a new political party, the Whigs, who agreed only that the dangerous powers of the presidency should be curtailed. (The Whigs took their name from the British political party that had insisted that Parliament, not the monarch, should rule.) The Whigs won few elections, but their ideas prevailed. For the three-quarters of a century after Jackson, virtually no president—not even the strongest of them all, Abraham Lincoln—regarded it as his role to propose legislation. The president could advocate the broad general ideas about public policy, but actually drafting laws—that was Congress's job. The presidents of the twentieth century did not accept such modest roles, and from Theodore Roosevelt to Lyndon Johnson, the story of the presidency is a story of steadily expanding power. Even the most unambitious man in the series, Warren Harding, contributed to the presidency's enlargement: He created the Bureau of the Budget, and thus became the first president to assert a role in determining overall federal expenditures.

The Progressives' distaste for legislators and small-scale politics has provoked some later critics to accuse them of contempt for democracy. The Progressives, however, believed they were *enhancing* the power of the vote by concentrating decision-making in the hands of a few highly visible elected officials. Since we began by talking about dams and rivers, perhaps an aquatic metaphor would help illuminate the difference between Progressivism and what went before. Think of political power as flowing water. The framers of the 1787 Constitution keenly perceived water's potential dangerousness. They worried about floods and whirlpools and torrential rain. The system of political hydraulics they designed was intended to ensure that water was collected in discrete, small ponds where it would never harm anyone. This same system of hydraulics, however, equally prevented the water of power from generating any substantial benefit. And not only were these minute pools of water unusable, the smaller of them had a nasty tendency to become brackish and polluted. The Progressives wished for a system of political hydraulics that gathered water within gigantic reservoirs under the control of a few visible and accountable leaders whose corps of expert underlings would then sluice it to irrigate the deserts and power the motors of industry.

Perhaps some intuitive appreciation of this aquatic metaphor explains why so many of the twentieth century's modernizers seized on dams and hydroelectric power as the symbols of progress. And no mid-century American responded more heartfully to the allure of waterpower than Franklin Delano Roosevelt. Arthur Schlesinger Jr. reverently describes the visit President-elect Roosevelt paid to the federally owned Muscle Shoals Dam in northern Alabama in January 1933. The Republicans had wanted to sell the dam. Roosevelt watched as "thousand of gallons of water, white and turbulent, plunge through the spillways. Now, at least, the rushing water might light homes, turn wheels, replenish the [Tennessee] Valley. . . . In a few days, seated before the Little White House at Warm Springs, he unfolded before a group of newspaper reporters a broad vision of multi-purpose development throughout the Tennessee Valley, linking waterpower, flood control, forestry, conservation, reclamation, agriculture, and industry in one vast experiment. 'I think,' he said, 'the development will be the forerunner of similar projects in other parts of the country, such as in the watersheds of the Ohio, Missouri and Arkansas rivers and the Columbia river in the Northwest.'"[5] A vast experiment in central direction and control, all of it intended to develop the country and uplift the common man—it was a vision to make the pulse race.

Once set in motion, however, the experiment quickly revealed some disturbing side effects. Those giant projects often turned out to be excessively costly and environmentally ruinous. Perhaps the single most notorious example was the flooding of Glen Canyon in southern Utah. Glen Canyon on the Colorado River was regarded by naturalists as second in its awesome beauty only to the Grand Canyon itself. But the waters of the Colorado were coveted by farmers and hydroelectric utilities, and in 1956

Congress authorized the construction of a great dam just below Glen Canyon. The Colorado's flow was stopped, and the backed-up river waters inundated the canyon, transforming it into today's Lake Powell. The loss of the canyon galvanized what was then still called the conservation movement, which began to raise haunting questions about the laws that gave the Reclamation Bureau the power to proceed with its pet projects heedless of all opposition.

"You can't fight City Hall" was the bitter lesson of the conservation fights of the 1950s and 1960s, and nobody taught that lesson more brutally than Robert Moses, the master builder of New York, who controlled the commissions responsible for state and city parks, highways, bridges, and public housing from the days of Herbert Hoover to those of Richard Nixon. Governor Rockefeller finally forced Moses out at the end of the 1960s, and in 1974 Robert Caro published a searing indictment of the man's career, *The Power Broker.* Caro's painstakingly researched and elegantly written book deservedly soared onto the best-seller lists. But it suffered from a strange internal contradiction in its argument. Moses was a man willing to smash eggs to make an omelet. Caro's postwar generation grew up amidst great mounds of Moses's shattered eggshells, and decided that the shards were beginning to stink. The trouble was that while liberal-minded people in Caro's generation disapproved of egg-smashing, they still enjoyed the omelets. Caro did not object to Moses's trampling on the property rights of Long Island's great estate-owners to build parkways to the new state parks, but he was horrified by Moses's trampling on the occupancy rights of South Bronx tenement-dwellers to build the Cross-Bronx Expressway. To reconcile these two conflicting emotions, Caro proposed a distinction between a good early Moses, who wanted to serve the people, and a bad late Moses, driven mad by his own lust for power. And this distinction was not very convincing.

There was only one Moses, and he was the same man when he brushed aside the arrogance of the rich as when he shrugged off the pleas of the poor. Moses's Progressivism—he was a Theodore Roosevelt Bull Mooser till the end—postulated the existence of a general good, larger than the interests of any single class. If the general good called for parks, too bad for the selfish rich. If it called for expressways through the slums, too bad for the inconveniently domiciled poor. And who got to define this general good? Cynics will say: Moses himself. But Moses could wield his power only because he was the appointed agent of representatives of the political majority. The Progressives are often derided as snooty elitists, but the truth is that they greatly increased the number of decisions made on the principle of majority-rule. That is fine so long as you are in sympathy with the majority, as liberal-minded people generally were in the 1930s. It is not so fine when you find yourselves in the minority, as liberal-minded people so often did in the later 1960s and 1970s. Thirty years of economic progress had transmuted the labor-farmer Roosevelt majorities into the rural-suburban Nixon majorities. And this shift in American politics is the ultimate source of the foaming rage that gripped so many of the era's liberal-minded writers as they contemplated their fellow citizens. "Reentering America [after a trip abroad]," observed the writer of *The Pursuit of Loneliness*, a much-quoted 1970 book, "one is struck first of all by the grim monotony of American facial expressions—hard, surly, and bitter—and by the aura of deprivation that informs them."[6] In *The Greening of America*, Charles Reich could barely contain himself on the subject of blue-collar white people and "their sullen boredom, their unchanging routines, their minds closed to new ideas and new feelings, their bodies slumped in front of television to watch the ballgame Sunday."[7]

In her 1962 attack on Moses-style urban planning, *The Death and Life of Great American Cities*, Jane Jacobs tells a story about a Greenwich Village bakery that gives a wonderfully revealing glimpse of the post-Progressive liberal political ideal. The bakery was located on a low-rise street of small shops and apartments. One day it filed with the city-planning department an application to expand its operations. The residents objected, but they faced a quandary. The surest way to stop the bakery, under the prevailing zoning rules, was to have the street zoned residential. This could easily have been done—but it would also have put the street's small shops, which the neighbors liked, out of business. Jacobs argued from this little parable that what New York needed was zoning not by "use"—residential, commercial, industrial—but by "scale"—some things were just too big for some places. Jacobs proposed that each block in the vast metropolis of New York be governed by its unique set of rules about how big a use could be. This scheme would require more than fifty sets of zoning rules simply to govern the small section of Greenwich Village that lies between Sixth and Seventh Avenues from Waverly Place to West Houston Street, but Jacobs had an answer for that: Cities should be divided into self-governing zoning districts, none larger than "about a mile and a half square," and most of them smaller.[8] In 1898, Progressives had merged the five boroughs of New York into one city because they regarded Manhattan and Brooklyn as inefficiently small. Jacobs regarded even the boroughs as monstrously large. This mile-and-a-half standard would imply at least *nine* distinct planning authorities simply for that fraction of Manhattan Island south of Central Park. Each of those authorities would be governed, not by some so-called expert appointed by the mayor, but democratically, ideally by "a kind of legislature of two hundred elected representatives from smaller organizations and street neighborhoods."[9] Think of it. *Eighteen hundred* planning legislators south of Fifty-ninth Street charged with writing a unique set of rules for every single city block. Another eighteen hundred more above. Then Brooklyn, then Queens, then the Bronx, then Staten Island. . . .

Jacobs and people like her were driven to such absurd extremes because, while they begrudged the old Progressive means, they still willed the old Progressive ends: political control of private economic activity. Jacobs found the idea of letting Manhattan grow freely as repugnant as Robert Moses ever had. She wanted its growth controlled—but controlled by neighborhood activists like herself rather than by the bureaucrats and engineers unto whom Moses had delivered the city.

Jacobs was a utopian, but utopians sometimes get their way. Through the 1970s, political power in the United States was transferred in exactly the way Jacobs had hoped. Even her pet project of municipal district government was realized. The Lindsay administration acquiesced in the division of New York City into community boards that gave an opportunity for activist citizens to comment on, criticize, and even halt real-estate developments. State and federal courts, which had traditionally refused to let third parties intervene in lawsuits, took a welcoming new attitude toward lawyers who claimed to represent the public interest. Federal and state regulatory agencies opened their doors to a much broader public. With a bit of political luck, activists could do better still. In Jimmy Carter's Washington and Jerry Brown's California, radicals who in 1971 had been struggling to gain a hearing were by 1977 holding the gavel.

In 1980, Lloyd Cutler, a Washington lawyer and adviser to Democratic presidents, published a much-cited article warning that America was becoming "ungovernable."[10] Presidents from FDR through Nixon had commanded the deference of Congress. But Congress was splitting up into factions, beyond the control of any leader. Even the executive branch had spun out of presidential control, as an "iron triangle" of bureaucrats, tiny congressional subcommittees, and interest groups made the real decisions. Carter had come to office intending to create a vast, comprehensive system of federal energy controls; instead he was forced grumblingly to accept gradual deregulation. Carter's top international priority had been a grand arms-control deal with the Soviets. Threatened with certain defeat in the Senate, he had to withdraw his SALT-II treaty and preside instead over an arms buildup. Carter was, up to a point, a victim of his own incompetence. (During an August 1980 interview, Dan Rather of CBS asked Carter, "Mr. President you recently directed your staff to make report cards on their employees. Now, in specific areas, I'm going to ask you to grade yourself A through F. Foreign policy?" Carter's reply: "You put me on the spot. I would say maybe a B or a C-plus . . . Let's say B-minus." "Overall domestic policy?" "Under the circumstances, I think about a B . . . maybe a C." "And on leadership?" "Maybe a B." Honest enough. But dumb.) But it was also true that by 1980 the president's policy-making power had badly corroded. The collapse of party discipline in Congress crippled his ability to get legislation passed, and tightening judicial scrutiny made it harder for him to act by executive order. What Cutler failed to perceive, however, was that the power ebbing out of the presidency was not being lost—it was dissipating. The United States was not ungovernable; it was, rather, being governed by new institutions, in new ways, and for the benefit of new interests.

SEE YOU IN COURT

AT THE END OF HIS LONG CAREER, SUPREME COURT JUSTICE WILLIAM BRENNAN was asked which of his opinions he regarded as his most important. Brennan had served on the high court for thirty-five years, masterminding its liberal majority until the mid-1980s, and then leading the opposition to its more conservative decisions. He might very understandably have been expected to hesitate. He didn't. He replied straightway: *Goldberg* v. *Kelly*.[11] It might seem strange that a case few non-lawyers have ever heard of should be rated by its author as outweighing his opinions outlawing school prayer, requiring states to provide indigent defendants with free lawyers, or smashing the ancient political power of farmers by mandating that all state senate districts contain roughly the same number of people. But Brennan was quite right.

The Goldberg in *Goldberg* v. *Kelly* was Jack R. Goldberg, New York City's commissioner of social services. Since the 1930s, New York had prided itself on its generous municipal welfare state. It's not clear that the city was ever really able to afford these benefits, but by the mid-1960s the financial undergirding of the municipal welfare state was visibly crumbling. Middle-income taxpayers left for the suburbs. The city paid its bills by ever more desperate financial jiggery-pokery. Because benefit cuts were politically unpalatable to the liberal city government, city officials responded to the gathering crisis with a series of crackdowns on welfare fraud. This outraged the city's litigious political left, who mounted a suit in the name of twenty of the most sympathetic individuals purged from the rolls.

Under prevailing law, the plaintiffs would not seem to have had much of a case. There is no constitutional right to welfare, much less a right to receive welfare fraudulently. The plaintiffs conceded that New York might be entitled to deny welfare to Juan De Jesus—one of the lead plaintiffs in *Goldberg*—if he were (as the city maintained) a drug addict. What they denied was that the city was entitled to decide for itself whether De Jesus *was* an addict. It was this latter contention that Justice Brennan inscribed into American law. The Fifth Amendment to the Constitution says that no American can be deprived of "life, liberty, or property" without "due process of law." Before stopping De Jesus's check, Brennan decreed, the City of New York owed him a formal evidentiary hearing where he could argue his side of the case. That may not sound like a revolutionary statement. But it was. It meant that every individual instance of welfare fraud would have to be litigated, with appeals available to the federal judiciary, at immense cost in both money and time. *Goldberg* was a decisive milestone en route to New York City's 1975 financial collapse.

William Brennan, like Mao Zedong, was one of those unusual men who get more radical as they age. In his early years on the Supreme Court, he distinguished himself by devising ingeniously plausible legal arguments for liberal policies. But as the liberal majority on the court expanded in the middle 1960s, his opinions simultaneously became bolder and less convincing. He took less trouble to wrap his personal preferences in the tissue and ribbon of constitutional law. In *Goldberg*, Brennan faced a conundrum. He wanted to grant the legal protections of property to welfare payments, which he himself acknowledged were *not* property. His solution: Instead of the old stark binary distinction between property and not-property, Brennan proposed a vast intermediate range of "property interests" that deserved some blurry, intermediate, to-be-figured-out-later measure of legal protection. This was typical of Brennan's jurisprudence. For him, the law was never a clear-cut set of rules by which citizens could ascertain their rights and officials govern their conduct. It was an unpredictable and continually shifting set of standards. When Brennan was new to the court, Americans delighted in sonorous invocations of the majesty of the law.

Think of the great speech Robert Bolt gave Thomas More in his 1962 play, *A Man for All Seasons*:

> MORE: What would you do? Cut a great road through the law to get after the Devil?
>
> ROPER: I'd cut down every law in England to do that!
>
> MORE: Oh? And when the last law was down, and the Devil turned round on you—where would you hide, Roper, the laws all being flat? The country's planted thick with laws from coast to coast–man's laws, not God's—and if you cut them down—and you're just the man to do it—d'you really think you could stand upright in the winds that would blow then? Yes, I'd give the Devil benefit of law, for my own safety's sake.

Almost nobody talks like that any more. The sacredness of the law was a pretty illusion blown to the winds by the chilly power of the zeal of Brennan's liberal majority to have its own way, regardless of precedent or logic. In person, Brennan was the gentlest, mildest, and most considerate of men. Many of the ideals he manipulated the law to uphold were admirable. But the ideal of ideals that ought to have guided his judging—that no result is admirable enough to justify illegitimate methods—that was as alien to the mind of this kindly, unscrupulous man as an uncharitable act or an uncivil word.

America has always been a legalistic society, but it has not always found it necessary to settle every dispute in court. In mid-century, actually, Americans seemed to be taking unusual pains to *avoid* submitting problems to the courts. The law is slow; judges are inexpert. For an era interested in comprehensive solutions to large-scale social problems, law and lawyers seemed inadequate. The judges themselves felt their inadequacy. In their articles and books, the leading jurists of the era declared their willingness to defer in almost all things to the judgment of legislators and their bureaucratic deputies. "[I]t certainly does not accord with the underlying presumptions of popular government," Judge Learned Hand said in his famous lectures on the Bill of Rights, "to vest in a chamber, unaccountable to anyone but itself, the power to suppress social experiments which it does not approve."[12]

What changed the minds—first of the jurists, then of the larger society—were the school desegregation decisions of 1954, *Brown* v. *Board of Education* and *Bolling* v. *Sharpe*, decided on the same day. With very flimsy legal justification (Chief Justice Earl Warren's own law clerk described the court's reasoning as "gibberish"[13]), the justices boldly overturned a social institution supported, to their shame, by the majority population of seventeen states.[14] It was by no means certain that the court would prevail over the opposition of the Southern governors and the Southern bloc in Congress. But it *did* prevail, and that success inspired the bold self-confidence that was such a striking feature of American courts in the 1960s and of American lawyers in the 1960s and 1970s. Lawyers then were like doctors in the two decades after the discovery of antibiotics. There was nothing they could not do, no problem they could not solve. Whatever ailed the country, more law was the answer. When Justice Brennan wrote *Goldberg* v. *Kelly*, he did not pretend to know better than the social service commissioner *how* an effective welfare program should be run. What he believed, however, was that the appropriate place in which to decide the matter was a courtroom, and that the right way to decide it was as a question of justiciable rights, in an adversarial proceeding under the supervision of a judge. Indeed, that was the right place and the right way to decide almost everything.

Such as: How to run the schools. In January 1975, the Supreme Court ruled that public school pupils suspended for disciplinary reasons also had a right to a hearing. "Young people do not shed their rights at the schoolroom door," wrote Justice Byron White in *Goss* v. *Lopez*. The constitution of Ohio guaranteed its residents an education and that right could not be taken away "absent fundamentally fair procedures." The Supreme Court had laid down what might be called the Bad Kid's Magna Carta—a set of rights that would grease the public schools' slide into ungovernability.

Such as: Who qualifies to practice medicine. When Charlotte Horowitz flunked out of the University of Missouri Medical School, she decided that her constitutional rights had been violated and sued. Although Horowitz had attended class irregularly and failed her examinations, she believed she was entitled to a miniature trial before the school could legally bounce her. The Eighth Circuit Court of Appeals agreed, and so did four of the nine justices of the Supreme Court. Only one vote prevented *Board of Curators* v. *Horowitz* from becoming the Dumb Doctor's Magna Carta.

Such as: Which foreign nationals might be dangerous to the United States. After a spate of pro-Khomeini demonstrations by Iranian students in the United States during the 1979 hostage crisis, the Immigration and Naturalization Service decided to look into the status of the demonstrators. It found that fully 10 percent of them were in the United States unlawfully, but in December 1979 U.S. District Judge Joyce Green ruled that the INS investigation was impermissibly arbitrary and must halt: "There is at best a dubious relationship between the presence of Iranian students in this country, whether legally or otherwise, and the safety and freedom of the hostages in the U.S. Embassy in Tehran."

Such as: What equipment could be used in athletic competitions. Disabled would-be marathoners obtained a judgment in 1979 that the New York City's Road Runners Club must drop its rules forbidding racers to use wheelchairs. The club argued that it ought to be allowed to set its own rules for its own events, and it warned that on some of the steep downhill portions of the race, speeding wheelchairs could pose a hazard to other runners. The court waved away both arguments.

Like the mix of two volatile chemicals, the due-process revolution mingled with the ambitious new environmental protection laws of the 1970s to ensure that virtually every road, dam, airport, sewage plant, harbor, or levée built by any federal, state or local agency—and a big chunk of private-enterprise activity as well—could be second-guessed by a court. Was an environmental impact statement filed? Was it detailed enough? Had the appropriate federal agency reviewed it in the manner required by the latest federal regulations?

If the law could save the environment, protect students from intolerant teachers, and safeguard the rights of wheelchair-bound athletes, surely it could do something for victims of defective lawnmowers and industrial pollution as well? Multimillion-dollar mass tort actions are a phenomenon of the 1980s and 1990s, but it was in the 1970s that the legal foundations of the supersuits were laid. The Supreme Court of California ruled in 1978 that in product liability cases, the burden of proof belonged to the defendant: If your machine injured a user, it was up to you to prove that the machine was *not* unsafe.[15] The rules governing class actions were relaxed by state courts, New Jersey and California typically leading the way. Punitive damage awards skyrocketed. "Theodore Olson of Gibson, Dunn & Crutcher found that the California record on punitive damages upheld on appeal rose from $10,000 in the period between 1922 and 1959 to $250,000 in the 1960s, $740,000 in the 1970s and $3 million in 1986."[16] The obstacles to contingency fees—the devices that would lead to the truly colossal payouts of the late 1980s and 1990s—were bulldozed one by one.

The old Progressive regulators were systemizers. They believed in institutions and rules, rather than individual hard cases. "Early in his professorship at Harvard," observes a study of James Landis, often thought of as the single most intellectually brilliant of the young lawyers who made the New Deal, "Landis had become fascinated by the obvious gap between legislation and administration that characterized modern American government. Studying the lack of connection, he tried to puzzle out the resulting paradox—so common in regulation—between admirable intentions of legislation and perverse results of administration. . . . What was needed . . . was a way of institutionalizing the linkages between ends and means, between legislation and administration."[17] Tort law as it evolved through the 1970s was determinedly unsystematic. It did not worry about inconsistent or even counterproductive results. It cared not about rules, but about the plight of one particular individual demanding his rights.

The Progressives had glorified science. The new tort law was often willfully anti-scientific, allowing the testimony of even the most eccentric and discredited "experts" to be presented to the jury as if it were just one opinion among many. (One of the first great mass tort cases of the 1980s involved a morning-sickness drug called Bendectin. Juries awarded women who used Bendectin, and then gave birth to deformed children, verdicts of up to $95 million, despite the near-unanimous scientific consensus that Bendectin did not cause the injuries.[18]) The Progressives had reposed their trust in the dispassionate, qualified civil service professionals; the new tort law put the work of defending society into the hands of freelance lawyers, skilled at emotionally appealing to juries, motivated by personal gain.

The due-process revolution in the public sector and the tort revolution in the private sector had been launched to protect citizens against the potential arbitrariness of bureaucrats and the selfishness of corporations. But asking judges to second-guess bureaucrats and businessmen seldom yielded, the fairness that Justice Brennan had promised. Quite the opposite. The harder judges tried to mete out equal justice to all, the more capricious and whimsical the legal system looked.

Telling a welfare agency or housing authority that it must administer "due process" before cutting off a fraudster or evicting a hoodlum raises more questions than it resolves. What sort of process, exactly, *is* due? Might some bureaucratic decisions require more process and others less? There is an argument, after all, that we want to make it easier to evict a bad tenant from public housing (where he might threaten the safety of the other tenants) than to cut off his welfare check (which merely wastes money). On the other hand, there's an equally good argument that we might want to make it harder to evict a tenant (this is the man' s *home* we are talking about after all) than to stop his check. The deeper the courts plunged into this thicket of confusion, the more unsatisfactory, even ludicrous, the results. And unfortunately, the area of law that they made the worst mess of also happened to be one of the most political explosive: religion.

American local government has long struggled with the problem of how much aid can and should be given to religious schools. From the 1920s until the mid-1960s, federal courts had tended to take a permissive attitude, allowing (for example) states to donate textbooks and provide school transportation. The Warren Court cast aside this easy-going attitude. Richard Nixon scored political points in 1968 by promising to appoint judges who would treat religious schools more indulgently; in 1971 that promise was put to the test in the case of *Lemon* v. *Kurtzman*.[19]

Lemon challenged the constitutionality of two state programs, one in Rhode Island, which subsidized the salaries of religious school teachers who taught secular subjects, and another in Pennsylvania, which reimbursed religious schools for purchases of instructional materials from the state's public school system. Chief Justice Warren Burger used the case to lay down some principles of law. State aid to religious institutions was permitted, he said, provided it met three conditions: (1) It was provided for a secular purpose; (2) it neither aided nor inhibited religion; and (3) it did not "excessively" entangle church and state. On that basis, the court struck down both the Rhode Island and Pennsylvania programs.

The new rules did not pack anything like the clarity that Warren Burger thought they did. By striking down the Pennsylvania law without explicitly over-ruling either the Court's older, laxer, precedents or its newer, stricter ones, the Burger Court had blundered its way to the conclusion that the Constitution permitted states to give schools geography textbooks but not the maps that illustrated them. Worse, the key section of *Lemon*—the part prohibiting "excessive entanglement"—simply restated the problem it was supposed to solve. How much entanglement is excessive? Only more litigation could provide the answer. The vagueness of the *Lemon* test ensured that the constitutionality of almost every contact between church and state would henceforward be determined by a judge's seat-of-the-pants determination. The civil status of the religion that illuminates the lives of tens of millions of Americans was plunged into perpetual murk.

Not that the judges of the 1970s could not be decisive when they really wanted to. The deinstitutionalization of the mentally ill was a public policy on which judges never wavered. The availability of antipsychotic drugs after 1954 prompted some states to test whether the insane could be released under a doctor's supervision. The states' motives were mostly economic. The cost of caring for the more than half-million state mental patients of the mid–1950s was threatening to overwhelm state budgets, especially in those states—New York and California—which tried hardest to treat the mentally ill rather than indifferently warehouse them.

Deinstitutionalization was not an entirely wild idea, if carefully put into effect. The new drugs held out hope that many of the insane could be restored to liberty. But the seriously mentally ill cannot simply be released into the community with a jar of pills. To protect the community, they must be carefully monitored by doctors who can have them recommitted if they relapse. Alas, that is just what America's judges decided the Constitution forbade, creating the misery that we have all learned to step over on our sidewalks and to look away from as it searches through trash cans for food.

Judges are not all-knowing wise men. They are human beings like anyone else, in thrall to the ideas of their times. If anything, the lawyers chosen for the bench are probably among the most conventionally minded members of a profession itself notorious for conventionality. And one conventional notion whizzing around in the air of the 1960s and 1970s was that insanity was a medically meaningless category that stigmatized people whose only offense was a refusal to conform to the rituals of a corrupt society. It sounds pretty funny when you put it like that, but in the middle 1960s the refusal to believe in insanity was the very acme of chic. R. D. Laing, a radical British psychoanalyst, achieved an almost-Beatles' level of celebrity by arguing that schizophrenics were actually reacting rationally to intolerable situations—that indeed they were saner in many ways than the people who had "adjusted" to a society that could, for instance, build hydrogen bombs and wage war in Vietnam. Michel Foucault made his reputation with a dissertation, translated into English as *Madness and Civilization* in 1965, that argued that the very attempt to help the mentally ill was a form of oppression, by denying them their human difference. "[T]he asylum becomes . . . an instrument of moral uniformity and social denunciation" that imposes "a social segregation that would guarantee bourgeois morality a universality of fact and permit it to be imposed as a law upon all forms of insanity."[20] The meaninglessness—even the goodness—of madness became something of a 1960s literary trope. It inspired the 1966 cult film *King of Hearts*, in which a British soldier cut off from his unit during one of the battles of the First World War stumbles into a French insane asylum and finds the residents eccentric, yes, but charming, and in the end far less mad than the blood-crazed world around them. Ken Kesey's 1962 novel, *One Flew Over the Cuckoo's Nest* (and the movie of the same name, which won the Academy Award for Best Picture in 1975), made the same point. The people who run insane asylums are not only crazy, but also dangerous.

Of all the anti-psychiatric writers of the 1960s, the one who had the most impact on American society was the Hungarian-born libertarian Thomas Szasz, at least if the number of citations in judicial opinions is any guide.[21] In a series of books beginning with *The Myth of Mental Illness* in 1961, Szasz charged that the concept of mental illness served only to enlarge the power of the state to lock up people who might be troublesome and offensive, but who had broken no laws. Szasz's suggestion that treatment for mental illness be analogized to incarceration for a crime made tremendous sense to a society increasingly inclined to interpret every issue in terms derived from civil rights and civil liberties law. His disdain for the alleged expertise of psychiatrists was given a tremendous boost by a notorious experiment by a Stanford professor of psychology named David Rosenhan published in the journal *Science* in 1973.

"Rosenhan sent eight pseudopatients (among them were three psychologists, a pediatrician, a psychiatrist, a painter, and a housewife) to gain admission to twelve different hospitals in five states on the East and West Coasts. Each pseudopatient was to come to the hospital admission office complaining that he had been hearing voices. Asked what the voices said, the 'patient' was to say they were unclear, but seemed to be saying 'empty,' 'hollow,' and 'thud.' Apart from falsifying name, occupation, and employment, the patient was to report his life history truthfully. Immediately upon admission, the patient was to cease simulating any symptoms of abnormality."[22] All eight patients were diagnosed as schizophrenic; all were admitted to the hospital; they were held for an average of nineteen days before being released. Then the experiment was performed in reverse. Rosenham told a major teaching hospital that he would be sending pseudopatients their way over the next three months. The hospital asked its receiving staff to identify which of the applicants seemed likeliest to be acting. Of the 193 patients who presented themselves over the test period, twenty-three were considered suspect by at least one psychiatrist. In fact, all 193 were genuine. Rosenhan had sent no pseudopatients at all.

Now, as two wise observers put it, while "this was scarcely psychiatry's finest hour," it also proved far less than Rosenhan implied that it did. "The study shed light on the limitations of hospitals and psychiatrists, but none on the nature or reality of insanity. Rosenhan sent no patients feigning symptoms of heart disease or muscular dystrophy or epilepsy to internists; would he have concluded, had they been fooled, that this proved the nonexistence of these diseases?"[23]

But if Rosenhan's experiment had dubious scientific meaning, it had large legal implications. In the deferential 1950s, psychiatrists had broad power in most states to commit patients to hospital against their will; in the 1970s that power was snatched away. In June 1975, the Supreme Court delivered its ruling in the important case of *O'Connor* v. *Donaldson*[24]: The mentally ill could not be detained unless they could be shown to constitute a danger to others or were incapable of living on their own. Potter Stewart's opinion might well have been scalped from Thomas Szasz. "May the state fence in the harmless mentally ill solely to save its citizens from exposure to those whose ways are different?" One might as well ask, Stewart continued, "if the state, to avoid public unease, could incarcerate all who are physically unattractive or socially eccentric. Mere public intolerance or animosity cannot constitutionally justify the deprivation of a person's physical liberty." Who is to say which of the mentally ill are harmless? The Supreme Court settled that question in 1979. Frank Addington, a mental patient, disputed the right of Texas to confine him against his will. Chief Justice Burger decided for the court that the relevant standard for deciding the question ought to be far more stringent than a doctor's opinion alone. The insane also had their due-process rights, and unless the state's medical experts could prove to the satisfaction of a court by "clear, unequivocal and convincing" evidence that a mental patient represented a danger to society or to himself, he or she could not be detained against his wishes.[25] One reason the court dared go this far was that the state supreme courts were going further. Indeed the Massachusetts, New Hampshire, District of Columbia, Minnesota, New Jersey, and Kentucky courts had imposed on the mental health authorities the same "beyond-a-reasonable-doubt" standard that prosecutors had to meet for the jailing of a criminal.[26]

Cases like Addington's accelerated the emptying out of the state mental hospitals. Between 1955 and 1970, the number of patients in state hospitals declined from 559,000 to 339,000. Between 1970 and 1980, the number of patients fell from 339,000 to 130,000.[27] (The figure for 1995 is approximately 70,000.) What happened to these people? At first, thanks to the sluggish urban real-estate market of the 1970s, they found shelter in deteriorating old buildings converted to slum hotels. They paid the rent, often, with the help of a new federal program, the Supplemental Security Income program created in 1974, which recognized schizophrenia and other severe mental illnesses as disabilities and paid pensions to those suffering from them. (This created a very stark set of financial incentives for states. Because the federal government had refused to extend Medicare or Medicaid to mental hospitals in 1965, states had to pay the full cost of treating the mentally ill if they kept patients institutionalized. If they released them to the streets, however, Medicaid would cover their treatment at a nursing home or community health center, and SSI would pay their living expenses.)

But as the urban housing market warmed up in the 1980s, the old slum hotels were demolished to make way for apartment buildings and condominiums. By then, the new legal standards were ensuring that younger generations of mentally ill people were never institutionalized in the first place. California, which admitted 42,000 people to its mental hospitals in 1970, admitted only 19,000 in 1980; Massachusetts had admitted 13,000 at the beginning of the 1970s but only 6,000 at the end. Obviously disturbed people began to appear on America's streets, pushing stolen supermarket shopping carts filled with their forlorn possessions, their hair grown to their back, their feet bare and scarred, sleeping on sewer grates, cursing passersby or attacking them, sometimes fatally.

And when local officials tried to do something for these troubled people, the courts hastily interposed themselves. A landmark 1972 Supreme Court decision declared laws against vagrancy unconstitutional.[28] In December 1973, the Court affirmed an appellate decision that had struck down a New York State law prohibiting loitering "without apparent reason and under circumstances which justify suspicion that [the loiterer] may be engaged in a crime." In the 1980s, a federal judge in New York declared begging a constitutional right. Another forbade the town of Morristown,

New Jersey, to order an unwashed, foul-smelling man who stared menacingly at single women to leave its library. Individuals like Larry Hogue, the "Madman of Ninety-sixth Street," who assaulted women and children and smashed parked cars, and "Billy Boggs," the alias of a woman who shrieked obscenities at black men and defecated on street corners, became local celebrities, protected in their right to haunt the streets by the New York Civil Liberties Association. And because this final collapse of the old state mental health system happened to coincide with the controversial first months of the Reagan administration, few local governments were really *eager* to remove people like Hogue and Boggs. After all, by reimagining the deinstitutionalized mentally ill as merely "homeless," the Democrats who typically controlled city governments acquired a powerful new weapon with which to rebuke the Republican-controlled federal government for cutting its spending on public housing and rent subsidies.

Not all the homeless were mentally ill. Some were drunks or addicts, and others were ex-cons unable to make the transition to conventional life. Some had been thrown out of work in the recessions of 1979–82 and never managed to clamber back in. Some were mothers who had heard that by arriving at a city shelter with children they could jump to the head of the queue for subsidized housing. But many—at least 40 percent, and by the end of the 1980s probably closer to two-thirds[29]—*were* seriously mentally ill. The best estimates of the number of homeless in the United States ranged between 300,000 and 600,000, or rather fewer than the number of mental patients the country would have if the 1955 number had kept up with increases in population.

It had once been thought society's duty to care for the insane. Even Calvin Coolidge, that famously frugal Yankee, pushed through substantial increases in spending for state mental hospitals as governor of Massachusetts. In the 1970s, in the name of civil liberties, that duty to care was rescinded. Advocates for the homeless insisted that the people they claimed to speak for could be entirely self-reliant, if only society paid their rent for them. They were not sick. They were victims. And so they were—not of a housing shortage, but of an institutional failure: the attempt to stretch law far beyond its rightful limits.

THE GORGEOUS MOSAIC

POLITE PEOPLE DID NOT ACKNOWLEDGE THE EXISTENCE OF ANY SUCH THING AS an Asian in the 1960s. There were Chinese restaurant owners in small towns across the country and Syrian grocers selling olives on Atlantic Avenue in Brooklyn, Japanese students in medical school in southern California and Filipinos counting ammunition at naval bases. But the idea that one broad racial category might stretch to include all the populations from the sands of Sinai to the breadfruit trees of the South Pacific would have seemed—well, it would have seemed like a throwback to the worst days of imperialism, when topee-wearing sahibs sipped gin on the verandah while talking condescendingly of the "Asiatics." It was the civil rights laws of the 1960s that reintroduced "Asiatics," suitably renamed, into American discourse, to take their place alongside the four other great categories familiar to anyone who has ever filled out a census form or applied to a university: white, black, Hispanic, native American.

The civil rights movement altered the way Americans perceived themselves and their society as much as it altered the law of the land. It taught Americans to look at each other in radically new ways: to see, for example, those Syrian olive-sellers in Atlantic Avenue as having much more in common with the sharecroppers of Mississippi than with the Italian tomato-sellers five blocks south. Both the Syrian and the sharecroppers were "nonwhites" and thus entitled to the special protection of the law; as for the Italian, legally speaking his family might as well have sailed into Massachusetts Bay on the *Arabella*.

Even more significantly, the civil-rights movement taught Americans to think in new ways about the workings of society. Before 1965, it would have seemed incredibly odd to describe the disabled, say, as victims of discrimination. No question that the disabled suffered an incredible array of hardships. But those hardships inhered in the disability itself, in being blind or deaf or lacking the use of the arms or legs. They did not arise, as the hardships of southern blacks did, from bias in the law. Indeed, the disabled were entitled to a broad array of benefits from government. If they had been injured in war, they drew veteran's benefits; if they had been railway employees, the government had a special fund for that; and if they had not served either in the armed forces or on the rails, they still qualified for a Social Security disability pension. And again unlike southern blacks, who faced the disdain and hostility of their neighbors, the disabled could often count on the sympathy of their fellow citizens. Before they could see themselves as maltreated by the law, they—and the rest of society—had to reach a new understanding of what fair treatment meant.

President Johnson introduced the American public to that new understanding in his justly famous 1965 commencement address at Howard University. "You do not take a person who, for years, has been hobbled by chains and liberate him, bringing him up to the starting line of a race, and then say, 'you are free to compete with all the others,' and still justly believe that you have been completely fair. . . . This is the next and the more profound stage of the battle for civil rights. We seek not just legal equity but human ability, not just equality as a right and a theory but equality as a fact and equality as a result." Within weeks of his speech, the Duke Power Company of North Carolina offered the administration and the courts an opportunity to live up to Johnson's pledge. Duke Power had for many years excluded blacks from all but the most menial of employments. On July 2, 1965, the day the Civil Rights Act of 1964 came into effect, Duke Power swept away its old frankly discriminatory hiring policy and replaced it with a new, ostensibly neutral one: All applicants for non-menial jobs had to have a high-school diploma or achieve a certain minimum mark on an IQ test. In rural North Carolina in the mid-1960s, this new policy reserved the best jobs for whites very nearly as effectively as the straightforward racial bias. The NAACP Legal Defense Fund, with the Department of Justice's support, sued Duke Power. In March 1971, the NAACP and the U.S. government won the verdict they had sought. "[P]ractices, procedures, or tests neutral on their face and even neutral in terms of intent," the Supreme Court declared in *Griggs* v. *Duke Power,* "cannot be maintained if they operate to 'freeze' the status quo of prior discriminatory employment practices."[30] It was Duke Power's responsibility to figure out a test for promotion that blacks would pass in the same proportions as whites, and if that test turned out to be less convenient or effective than high-school promotion, too bad.

Griggs redefined discrimination from an *intentional* to an *unintentional* wrong. Before that lawsuit was filed, most employers could feel reasonably sure that so long as they treated black and white applicants and employees equally, judging all by the same standard, they were acting fairly. *Griggs* served notice that equal treatment no longer sufficed. Employers—and everybody else with benefits to dispense—must make allowances for the special circumstances of black Americans if they hoped to avoid accusations of discrimination. In itself, this was not an unreasonable proposition. The world after all was not created in 1965. The gap between the attainments of blacks as a group and whites as a group did not arise from the mysterious workings of fate, but from three centuries of deliberate oppression by the white majority. On the other hand, the gaps were there, and even conscientious employers could hardly avoid noticing them.

Federal civil rights agencies had begun promoting quotas as an emergency remedy to extreme discrimination in 1969, when Secretary of Labor George Shultz wearied of negotiating with the militantly antiblack construction unions of Philadelphia and finally ordered them simply to enroll a certain number of blacks in each of their locals, or else. Soon the Labor Department was forcing quotas on unions from Long Island to California. After the Duke Power case, the lower courts were emboldened to order up quota plans too. Bridgeport, Connecticut, got one of the first, in January 1973, when a federal judge decreed that half the new hires by the city's police department must be black or Puerto Rican. In April 1974, the Department of Justice and the United Steelworkers of America agreed to the biggest quota plan to date, governing all of the country's 350,000 unionized steel-making jobs. By then, employers had got the message. Why wait to be sued by your employees or the government? A quota plan provided the best possible—the only reliable—insurance against an accusation of discrimination. True, a badly divided Supreme Court declared in its 1978 *Bakke* case[31] that public institutions like universities could not make use of rigid numerical targets, but it also said that "goals" and "timetables" for the sake of "diversity" were acceptable. Promptly, every law school, medical school, graduate school, and college began developing goals and timetables. The very next year, in the *Weber* v. *United Steelworkers* case, the court announced that private employers *could* use rigid numerical targets, so long as they did so voluntarily.[32] The year after that, 1980, the court declared an explicit 10-percent racial quota in federal contracting to be OK.[33] Those three cases left civil-rights law in such a gnarled and tangled state that nobody could quite be sure what was legal and what was not—and (more important in the end) who was demanding and enforcing these plans. *Bakke* and *Weber* together created powerful incentives for public institutions and private corporations to lie: to pretend that they were not maintaining quotas when in fact they were, to pretend that those quotas were voluntary when in fact they had been surrendered to under the threat of a federal lawsuit. By the end of the 1970s, the country was governed by an elaborate undeclared law enforced by nobody knew whom. Presidents, cabinet officers, congressmen, even the justices of the Supreme Court denounced quotas—and yet with every passing year they spread and grew.

The white resentment provoked by quotas may explain the strong mood of racial pessimism that gripped blacks in the 1970s, even as the black middle class flourished and the number of black college graduates doubled.[34] Sixty percent of surveyed blacks said there had been "real change" in their position in 1964; by 1976, only 32 percent of blacks answered that question affirmatively. Only 8 percent of a sample of black leaders surveyed by the Harris poll in 1978 agreed that racism in the United States was declining. Between 1968 and 1978, the percentage of blacks who felt they had experienced discrimination at work consistently rose.[35]

Large as black-white differences loomed in the 1970s, they were adventitious and fated to disappear. But there were other differences that were never going to disappear: between men and women, between adults and children, between the able-bodied and the disabled. "Disparate impact" was the weapon that would be used to attack them all. During the legislative battle over what would become the Civil Rights Act of 1964, the bill's wiliest opponent—Representative Howard W. Smith of Virginia, chairman of the House Rules Committee—sought to sabotage it by proposing to include the word "sex" after "race, religion, creed, and national origin" on its list of prohibited grounds of discrimination. Smith knew that Republicans would have to vote in favor of his amendment. Their party's envelopes were stuffed, its doorbells rung, and its voters driven to the polls by middle-class Protestant at-home mothers who would have been alienated and offended by any hint of backsliding on women's rights. (The Republican National Convention endorsed an equal-rights-for-women amendment to the Constitution in 1944, and reaffirmed that commitment every four years until 1980.) Banning discrimination on grounds of sex, however, was poison to northern Democrats. Their mostly blue-collar constituents saw the equal rights for women campaign as an attack on the restrictive practices of their trade unions, which ensured that the best-paying jobs went to men with families to support. (The Democratic National Convention would not endorse the ERA until 1972.) So Smith plotted an obstructionist two-step. First: Trap feminist Republicans into voting with mischief-making southern Democrats to add the killer amendment. Second: The unpalatable amendment then forces labor-oriented northern Democrats to vote with segregationist southern Democrats to defeat the bill as a whole. Very clever, but in the end not clever enough. The act passed.

At first, the sex provisions of the 1964 act worked in exactly the equal-opportunity way that their moderate Republican proponents had hoped. In January 1971, the Supreme Court delivered its first ruling on the sex provisions of the 1964 act, declaring it a violation of the law for companies to refuse to hire women with preschool children unless they also refused to hire equally situated men. The act, the Court said, prohibits firms from maintaining "one hiring policy for women and another for men." In March 1971, a federal judge in Ohio told General Electric that it was no longer bound by a state law that barred women from jobs that required the lifting of objects weighing more than twenty-five pounds. The section of the law that required lunchbreaks for women but not men was voided as well. That same month, a state judge in Pittsburgh told the city's newspapers that the venerable practice of printing separate job listings for men and women was illegal, and within a few more months a newspaper convention older than the headline had vanished from the country's press. In May, the U.S. Civil Service Commission ordered the federal government to drop "men only" and "women only" designations for public-sector jobs.

The spirit of equality quickly moved beyond the job market. In November 1971, the Supreme Court invoked the due-process clause of the Fourteenth Amendment to strike down for the first time a state law that discriminated against women: an Idaho statute that favored male relatives over female relatives in deciding who should administer the estates of those who died without a will. The U.S. House of Representatives passed the Equal Rights Amendment in October 1971; the Senate voted eighty-four to eight in favor of the amendment in March 1972, after first defeating by a large margin provisions suggested by Senator Sam Ervin of North Carolina to exempt women from the draft. President Nixon endorsed the ERA at once and by the end of the year it was speeding through the state legislatures. In February 1972, the Government Printing Office approved use of the new feminist honorific "Ms." in government documents; in the spring of 1978, the Census Bureau announced that the 1980 census would eliminate the line asking for the name of the head of the household. The Weather Service decided in 1978 that henceforward it would give hurricanes both male and female names.

It didn't take long, however, for Americans to begin noticing that the attempt to eradicate male-female differences was not going to be quite so morally straightforward as the elimination of Jim Crow. In June 1975, federal civil rights officials warned the public schools of Scottsdale, Arizona, that their end-of-term, father-son, mother-daughter baseball games and picnics were prohibited by the 1964 act. President Gerald Ford quickly intervened, and the incident got laughed off as a bit of over-zealous officiousness. But applying the civil rights model to the sexes threw up one such eyebrow-raising result after another. In September 1974, the first female corrections officer went to work in a men's maximum-security prison. Melissa Ludtke, a reporter with *Sports Illustrated*, won a court order before the 1978 World Series commanding professional baseball to open its clubhouse lockerrooms to female reporters; professional basketball, football, and hockey quickly fell into step. In January 1978, a federal judge in Dayton, Ohio, ruled that it was unconstitutional for high schools to deny qualified girls a place on boys' athletic teams, even when they maintained girls' teams in the same sports.

Few of the cautious but fair-minded Americans who had nervously welcomed "women's lib" at the beginning of the decade could have imagined that the campaign for equal rights for women would treat an all-boy Little League team or a men's lunch club as the functional equivalent of Little Rock High School. As it became clear that that's *exactly* how the campaigners for female equality saw these institutions, the popular enthusiasm for the campaign perceptibly subsided. By the end of 1974, the most visible symbol of that campaign, the Equal Rights Amendment, was faltering politically. The ERA had been badly injured by the Supreme Court's *Roe* v. *Wade* decision in January 1973. It is telling that of the thirty-five states that ultimately ratified the ERA, twenty-two did so in the ten months before *Roe* v. *Wade*, and only thirteen in the ten years after. It didn't help either that the leaders of the ERA campaign seemed so indifferent to the anxieties of middle-aged, middle-class women worried that the amendment could be used to outlaw alimony and end the bias in favor of maternal custody in divorce proceedings.[36] But what really finished the amendment off was the constant flow of stories like the one about the Scottsdale picnics. North Dakota ratified the ERA in January 1975. It was the amendment's last victory. Seven states—Arizona, Georgia, Louisiana, Nevada, Oklahoma, Utah, and Virginia—rejected the ERA in the next six weeks. Idaho and Kentucky voted to join Nebraska and Tennessee and rescind their ratification. As the time limit dribbled away, the battle for the ERA closed in on Illinois, the only large industrial state not to have ratified. Illinois happened to be the home of Phyllis Schlafly. Schlafly was not the sort of person feminists found it easy to take seriously. A devout

Catholic, a mother of six, a self-described housewife, she wore her hair in a bouffant, wore pastel suits with large buttons, pumps, and pink lipstick, and began speeches by thanking her husband, Dr. John Schlafly, for giving her permission to be away from home that day. In other words, she incarnated in her own person everything that the advocates of the ERA found retrograde, stupid, and maddening. Unfortunately for them, she also happened to be something none of them were: a genius grass-roots political organizer who had devoted twenty years to intrastate politicking. And she had filing cabinets full of Scottsdale-like bureaucratic absurdities.

Still, in the end Schlafly could have saved her breath. The ERA was defeated, but the federal courts proceeded to decide cases as if it had won. In 1976, the Supreme Court by a seven-to-two majority struck down an Oklahoma law that permitted women to buy 3.2 percent alcohol beer when they turned eighteen while requiring men to wait to age twenty-one.[37] Justice Brennan used the case to declare for the majority that from now on, any law that treated men and women differently would be squinted at suspiciously by the courts. "[C]lassifications by gender must serve important government objectives and must be substantially related to achievement of those objectives." Brennan described this new squinting as an "intermediate" scrutiny—not as strict as the scrutiny the court gave to laws that made distinctions between blacks and whites, but much stricter than the scrutiny given to, say, laws that made distinctions between the steel industry and the aluminum industry. For all practical purposes Brennan's intermediate scrutiny was every bit as lethal to prefeminist laws as the ERA itself would have been. After all, the Oklahoma law sought to reduce male traffic fatalities, an important objective, and banning drinking by college-age boys was certainly "related" to the achievement of that objective. If so elementary a sex-based distinction could not survive "intermediate" scrutiny, then no sex-based distinction could.

Delaying beer-drinking by Oklahoma girls until their twenty-first birthday was, however, an awfully circuitous route to the unisex utopia. Unlike the racial divide, the sexual divide corresponded to something deep and real about men and women. "Feminists have to question, not just all of *Western* culture, but the organization of culture itself, and further, even the

very organization of nature," the radical feminist Shulamith Firestone au-
daciously argued in 1970.[38] And questioning nature was exactly what the
new civil rights law of disparate impact did.

Americans over a certain age are often surprised to see diminutive
women patrolling their city's meanest streets. The policemen of their
childhood were tall, commanding figures. Have the cops shrunk? Well, yes.
In March 1973, the federal Law Enforcement Assistance Administration issued an order forbidding any local police department that received federal
funds (that is, all of them) to maintain minimum height requirements—the
rules disqualified too many women. In 1977, the Supreme Court seconded
LEAA by striking down Alabama's minimum height requirement as a violation of the 1964 act. The federal government lived up to its own principles.
In 1971 it waived size and strength requirements for its own police forces.
In 1977, New York City acceded to a judicial order and permitted women
to apply for fire-fighting jobs. None of the applicants passed the department's strength test so the judge ordered the strength test made easier until sufficient numbers of women could pass. In July 1978, Judge John Sirica
of Watergate fame struck down as unconstitutional the law that barred
women from serving on any naval vessel except hospital and transport
ships. The first female seadogs shipped out on the USS *Vulcan* in September. Of the fifty-five women aboard the *Vulcan*, ten became pregnant
within their first four months aboard.

When sexual tension could not be ignored, it had to be blamed on male
brutishness. That too, however, required a lot of wishful thinking. In February 1980, five female soldiers from Fort Meade, Maryland, described to a
congressional subcommittee their harassment by the men on base.
Twenty-three-year old Private First-Class Sarah Tolaro told the subcommittee, "I have suffered nothing but sexual harassment. It is widespread in
the army, but Fort Meade is the worst." When asked whether the men's reaction to her might have anything to do with her moonlighting as a nude
go-go dancer in a Baltimore club, Tolaro and her supporters indignantly
replied that they could not see any connection between the two.

It was women's role as mothers, however, that was hardest to reconcile
with their new destiny as co-men. Linda Eaton, the first female firefighter

in Iowa City, Iowa, brought suit against her department in 1979. Iowa City expected firefighters to spend twenty-four-hour shifts at the firehouse, waiting for the firebell to ring. Regular visits by family members during those shifts were forbidden as too distracting. Eaton complained that this policy impermissibly burdened female firefighters by preventing her from nursing her son while she was on duty. After a year of litigation, she won $2,000, plus lawyer's fees, plus permission for all future women firefighters to keep their babies with them at the station.

By any objective measure, the 1970s were a decade of stunning progress for American women. In 1971, only 4 percent of America's lawyers and judges were women; 14 percent were by 1981. Only 9 percent of America's doctors were women in 1971; 22 percent were by 1981. Only 10 percent of America's Ph.D. holders were women in 1971; 30 percent were by 1981.[39] And yet, while in 1962 two-thirds of women said they had never been victims of discrimination, and as late as 1970 only half said they had, by 1974 two-thirds said they had been treated unfairly on account of their sex. It may be that as more women worked, more had a chance to suffer a bad experience. Or alternatively, women's heightened consciousness may have led them to resent remarks or behavior that they would have shrugged off in the early 1960s. Either way, this harsh discovery of the limits of legal guarantees of equality may explain why women, like blacks, came to feel themselves increasingly wronged as they increasingly succeeded.

Equal opportunity was an opportunity, nothing more, and for millions of people that was not enough. It took a dozen years for the civil-rights movement to move from "I have a dream" to quotas. It took barely half that time for the women's movement to progress from arguing that women could do any job that men could do to arguing that any job women could not do would have to be changed so that women could. In the wake of the women's movement came the new disability-rights movement—whose equivalent of Stonewall was the occupation of a federal office building in San Francisco in April 1977. A Disability Rights and Education Defense Fund was founded in 1979 to litigate for ever-expanding federal regulation of private business. What the advocates of the disabled wanted was almost exactly the opposite of what their inspirations at the NAACP Legal Defense Fund had sought: not the elimination of laws that denied equality, but the enactment of laws to require companies to pay the costs of remaking the world so that inequality would no longer matter. The civil-rights laws that had once modestly tried to protect people from irrational hatreds had been inflated into an audacious guarantee that the state would eliminate any obstacle between the citizen and the fulfillment of his dreams. That the modern world possesses the money and know-how to overcome the worst effects of many forms of disability is a fantastic achievement. But the insistence that these effects exist only because of malign and discriminatory attitudes constitutes an equally fantastic—and dangerously embittering—delusion.

A HARVARD PLAN FOR THE WORKING-CLASS MAN

WHEN IT CAME TIME TO BUILD DAMS OR FIX ROADS, THE PUBLIC AUTHORITIES OF the 1970s dithered and quavered. But when there was something they wanted to do, they could muster surprising determination. In the sixteen years after 1964, the racial caste system that had so long governed American life was dynamited. But the near-total disregard of public opinion during the dynamiting left behind ever-mounting anger, resentment, and resistance in the people on the receiving end of the endless stream of orders emitted by an adamant and aloof federal government.

In the debate over the 1964 Civil Rights Act, Representative Emanuel Celler of New York, the act's floor manager in the House, forthrightly addressed one of the most damaging arguments of the bill's opponents: that it would be interpreted to require the moving around of schoolchildren to attain a mathematical racial balance. Celler insisted, "There is no authorization for either the Attorney General or the Commissioner of Education to work toward achieving racial balance in the schools." In the Senate, Thomas Kuchel of California insisted that the bill specifically provided that "'desegregation' shall not mean the assignment of students to public schools in order to overcome racial imbalance. Let that be thoroughly understood." And just in case it wasn't thoroughly understood, the act's leading sponsor, Senator Hubert Humphrey, wrote two amendments designed to allay all honest fears of busing. One amendment declared, "Nothing in this title shall prohibit classification and assignment for reasons other than race, color, religion or national origin." Thus, Humphrey triumphantly pronounced, "Classification along bona fide neighborhood school lines, or for any other legitimate reason which local school boards might see fit to adopt, would not be affected . . . "

In his speeches on the act, Humphrey repeatedly cited the most recent school desegregation court case, the 1963 judgment in *Bell* v. *School City of Gary, Indiana.* In *Bell*, the Court of Appeal for the Seventh Circuit ruled, "Desegregation does not mean that there must be intermingling of races in all school districts. It means only that they may not be prevented from intermingling or going to school together because of race or color." *Bell*, Humphrey said, "makes it quite clear that while the Constitution prohibits segregation, it does not require integration. The busing of children to achieve racial balance would be an act to effect the integration of schools. In fact, if the bill were to compel it, it would be a violation [of the Constitution], because it would be handling the matter on the basis of race and we would be transporting children because of race. The bill does not attempt to integrate the schools, but it does attempt to eliminate segregation in the school systems."

Jacob Javits, the liberal Republican senator from New York who led the fight for the act on the minority side of the aisle, offered his own personal assurance to his fellow Republicans that fears of forced busing were "negated expressly in the bill." Any government official who sought to use the law to require school-by-school racial balance would be "making a fool of himself."

It took the federal government all of twenty-four months to rubbish every one of these solemn guarantees. In April 1966, in the face of all this legislative history and without any judicial authority to support it, the Office of Education in the Department of Health, Education, and Welfare issued regulations stipulating that desegregation should no longer be understood to mean what Humphrey, Kuchel, Javits, and the Seventh Circuit had said it would mean. From now on, school boards in the South would be held accountable for by-the-numbers integration. That regulation was approved later in the year by a federal appeals court and, in 1968, by the Supreme Court.[40]

The Office of Education now threw away all caution. From using enrollment figures as evidence that deliberate segregation might be occurring, it quickly progressed to using enrollment numbers as evidence that deliberate segregation almost certainly was occurring, and then finally to using enrollment numbers as evidence of segregation no matter how strong the evidence that deliberate segregation was *not* occurring. After 1968, the education office hurriedly imposed or negotiated busing agreements first with cities across the South, and then in the North and West, beginning with Denver. In 1972, the Supreme Court disregarded the promises by the authors of the 1964 Act, and in *Swann* v. *Charlotte-Mecklenburg Board of Education* gave the federal government permission to proceed with virtually any busing scheme it liked.[41]

The government liked them all. The public did not. A Gallup poll taken in September 1973 found that large majorities of both blacks and whites favored integrated schools and were prepared to accept ambitious methods to get the job done: shifting the boundaries of school districts and building low-income housing in middle-income areas. But only 9 percent of blacks and 4 percent of whites favored busing children outside of their own neighborhoods. Busing was truly a revolution imposed from above, and as expected, it met violent resistance from below. The antiwar demonstrations of the 1960s were just a handful of pickets compared to the mass, spontaneous outbursts of protest sparked by the busing plans of the 1970s.

One bad, but not atypical, example. Busing was ordered for the city of Louisville, Kentucky, for the 1975–76 school year. Kentucky was a border state, one in which Jim Crow had been dismantled relatively quietly and in which racial tensions were on the whole low. But because many whites had left the city of Louisville for the blue-collar suburbs of Jefferson County, desegregation—as usual—failed to bring about full integration. So Louisville became one of the list of cities in which federal judges ordered busing across municipal lines. Almost 23,000 pupils were to be shuttled between downtown and the suburbs. On the first two days of busing, the protests were large, but relatively orderly. Thousands of blue-collar workers stayed home from their jobs; about one thousand of them showed up to picket at the area's 165 schools. The serious trouble began on the evening of September 5, 1975. Between 8,000 and 10,000 Jefferson County whites, many of them teenagers, converged by car on Valley High School, honking horns and shouting slogans denouncing busing. They were met by police, and the crowd turned ugly. They pelted the police with abuse—calling them "pigs," just like the protesters on television—and then throwing rocks and bottles at them. News of the riot spread through the county. Soon crowds were forming at other schools. One thousand people showed up at another poor-white school, Southern High, where they vandalized thirty-nine school buses and a police car. Two hundred people were arrested that night, and thirty-five were hurt. The next day, the mayor of Louisville banned further demonstrations. He was ignored. Pickets went up around Jefferson County's schools on the morning of the sixth. Governor Julian Carroll ordered 800 armed National Guardsmen to Louisville and stationed armed guards on every school bus. The troops restored order, but mounting tension between black and white students provoked the most violent protests of all. On the evening of September 26, 1977, 400 demonstrators gathered again at Southern High School. They threw rocks and bottles at police, who dispersed them with tear gas. Infuriated by these tough tactics, 8,000 townspeople gathered the next day in central Louisville, in a march led by a woman in a wheelchair who would—the marchers hoped—deter the police so long as the cameras were running.

In the end, the Louisville protesters lost. The busing plan went unamended and the demonstrations gradually subsided. Parents expressed their anger in a more effective way: by removing their children from public schools. Between the end of World War II and 1970, the proportion of

American children enrolled in private schools had steadily dwindled— largely because Catholics were having fewer children and were becoming more willing to send them to the state's schools. In 1970, that trend abruptly reversed itself. Over the next decade, the proportion of the nation's elementary pupils in private schools would edge up from one out of nine to more than one out of eight.

Private education is expensive. A more common response to busing was, therefore, to move beyond the reach of the court order into the suburbs or exurbs. Between 1972 and 1980, despite busing, the percentage of black students who attended predominantly minority schools barely budged: 63.6 percent vs. 63.3 percent. By 1980, only four of the nation's fifteen largest school systems had an enrollment that was more than half made up of non-Hispanic whites.[42] In the Northeast, the racial isolation of blacks actually increased under busing: 67 percent of northeastern black students were enrolled in black-majority schools in 1968, 80 percent were in 1980—more than in 1954.

In 1978, a Rand Corporation study of white attitudes to busing tried to understand the hostility of American whites to busing. Were they bigots? Rand concluded that they were not. Whites, the study's authors said, did not believe busing helped race relations, but they felt certain that it wrecked neighborhood schools and aggravated discipline problems. "Thus most white parents believe they are being forced to give up something they value—the neighborhood school—in return for a policy that benefits no one and may even be harmful."

Parents voted with their feet because it was the only vote they were permitted. One often hears it said that the 1960s introduced a new style of politics to America, one more participatory, more open than the old. Reading through the decrees and decisions of the courts and commissioners that ordered busing, one has to wonder whether that's true. The judge who drew up the 1970 busing plan for Detroit and its suburbs—a plan encompassing fifty-three distinct and independent school districts in Wayne, Macomb, and Oakland counties—dismissed all objections with a contempt as lofty as any ever exuded by any king or cardinal. "Within appropriate time limits," he wrote, busing "is a considerably safer, more reliable, healthful and efficient means of getting children to school than either car pools or walking, and this is especially true for younger children." Therefore, "for school authorities or private citizens now to object to such transportation practices" would raise "the inference not of hostility to pupil transportation but rather racially motivated hostility to the desegregated school at the end of the ride." And this applied not just to ten- and eleven-year-old children, but to children in kindergarten too. "Transportation of kindergarten children for upwards of forty-five minutes, one-way, does not appear unreasonable, harmful, or unsafe in any way. In the absence of some compelling justification, which does not yet appear, kindergarten children should be included in the final plan of desegregation."[43]

This overweening judgment was quickly over-ruled. In fact, the Detroit litigation, which came to be known as *Milliken* v. *Bradley*,[44] in the end imposed sharp new limits on the power of the lower courts to impose busing. In *Milliken*, the Nixon appointees to the Supreme Court (Warren Burger, William Rehnquist, and Harry Blackmun) joined with Eisenhower's Potter Stewart and Ford's first appointment, Lewis Powell, to rule that in all but the most exceptional cases, busing orders must halt at municipal boundaries. Children could lawfully be bused *within* Detroit, but not *between* Detroit and the surrounding suburbs. That ruling doomed the more ambitious busing plans, but it also sounded the death knell of the industrial cities of the Northeast and Midwest. Parents who resided within city limits confronted a very real risk of loading their children onto buses to schools they regarded as unacceptable; parents who headed out to the suburbs did not. The moral was obvious: Sell the house and move. The civil rights bureaucracy was not, however, daunted by this failure of nerve at the Supreme Court. It barreled ahead, unchastened and unrepentant, to the biggest fight of all: Boston.

As in most cities, the history of the school desegregation litigation in Boston is mind-numbingly complex. Underneath it all was a stark geographic fact. Boston was a city whose neighborhoods had historically been demarked by ethnicity more distinctly than almost anywhere else. The Irish lived in Charlestown and South Boston, Italians lived in the North End, blacks lived in Roxbury, and so on. Because the city was so ethnically segmented, its schools were ethnically segmented as well. The democrati-cally elected school board had acquiesced in this situation. Inevitably, it was sued, and a federal judge, W. Arthur Garrity Jr., a Harvard Law gradu-ate and a close political associate of the Kennedy family, found himself in control of the destiny of close to one hundred thousand students and their parents. If he ever felt a moment of self-doubt in this autocratic role, the record is silent about it. On June 21, 1974, Judge Garrity issued his original order in the case of *Morgan* v. *Hennigan.* He would not issue his last un-til 1988, having in the interim assumed greater control over his school sys-tem than any judge in American history.

South Boston High became Ground Zero for Judge Garrity's integration plan. Boston is actually a very small city in the center of a large urban area. It is surrounded by wealthy towns: Brookline, Newton, Wellesley, all of them founded by New England Yankees who persuaded the state to pre-vent the Irish majority in Boston from annexing them. As a result, even be-fore the white flight from busing, more than half the students in the Boston public schools came from families at or below the poverty level. And one of the poorest schools in the whole system was also one of the whitest: South Boston High.

To outsiders, South Boston is best known as the neighborhood in which the John F. Kennedy presidential library is located. But the I. M. Pei-designed structure on the Atlantic, with its sweeping view of the urban coastline stretching to downtown Boston, four miles away, has little con-nection with the neighborhood of wood-frame dwellings, corner bars, and small groceries that abutted it back in the early 1970s. Overwhelmingly Irish and Catholic, South Boston was the sort of place for which contem-porary writers about urban community profess great nostalgia: compact, homogenous, built around common rituals of religion and work. Back in 1970, communities like that were regarded rather differently—as outposts of white privilege and prejudice. Garrity chose to pair the high school in South Boston with Roxbury High, in the heart of the black ghetto. The en-tire South Boston junior class would be bused to Roxbury. Sophomores from the two schools would be mixed, and seniors would be allowed to choose which school to attend. "It was like the hostage system of the Middle Ages whereby the princes of opposing crowns were kept in rival kings' courts as a preventive against war," observed William Reid, South Boston High's headmaster.[45] Roxbury and South Boston were generally regarded as the two worst schools in Boston, and it was never clear what educational purpose was to be served by jumbling them.

For the next three years, state troopers were stationed at South Boston High to keep order. Attendance in the Boston system over those years hovered between 40,000 and 60,000 of the 80,000 previously enrolled. By the time the Great Experiment came to an end, the Boston school system had shrunk to some 57,000 students, of whom only 15,000 were white. Almost all of the undeparted whites were enrolled in elementary schools, where busing had dwindled away, or else in East Boston High (which had never been subject to a busing order) or selective Boston Latin. Sixty percent of the families remaining in the public schools when Garrity handed them back to local control in 1985 earned less than $15,000 a year. By 1988, when racial busing was finally halted, nearly 40 percent of the system's ninth graders were dropping out before graduation.

The confrontation between Boston and Garrity began on the first day of school, September 12, 1974. Only about one hundred of the 1,300 students expected at South Boston showed up. The black pupils bused from Roxbury had to drive across a terrifying picket line of South Boston whites, who taunted them, throwing stones and holding up bananas. Of the 550 South Boston juniors expected at Roxbury, only thirteen showed up. In the first twenty-six days of school in 1974, there were dozens of injuries, hundreds of arrests, countless incidents of racial harassment. Ione Malloy, an English teacher at South Boston High, kept a diary of the desegregation of the school. It makes horrifying reading. The students at South Boston lived with constant low-level racial tension that periodically exploded into outright rioting. Malloy tells of a white girl who came to typing class carrying a handful of her own hair pulled out in a fight with black girls. In early October, the cafeteria erupted in violence when a white boy kicked over a black boy's tray. Fists flew, trays full of spaghetti were thrown all over the room, and one hundred fifty state troopers were called in. Nearly every day, South Boston parents staged protests, big and small. The football season, the center of South Boston life, had to be canceled. By November, whites and blacks were entering the school by different doors. On December 11, 1974, a white boy, Michael Faith, was stabbed as he walked through the halls of the school. The school closed for a month. When it reopened, South Boston High had installed metal detectors, one of the first high schools in the United States to do so. By then, 400 students were attending South Boston High on a typical day—guarded by 500 police.

South Boston High was the most troubled high school in Boston, but it was not unique. Hyde Park High was disrupted by riots, and the city's junior high schools also seethed with tension.

The troubles convinced Judge Garrity that he had not gone nearly far enough. On May 10, 1975, he released a revised busing plan for the 1975–76 school year even more radical than the plan for 1974–75. It called for busing 21,000 students, 4,000 more than those (theoretically) bused in the 1974–75 school year. Busing was to be extended all the way down to the first grade.

The more sternly Garrity issued decrees, however, the more rapidly the school system dissolved. Polls found that 60 percent of Boston parents, black and white, agreed that discipline had collapsed in the schools. In spring 1975, South Boston High was exempted from fire drills, for fear for the safety of black students if they left the school building. White Bostonians of high school age used addresses of aunts and uncles to enroll in suburban schools. An aide at South Boston High School came upon a black fifteen-year-old girl "sobbing in the lobby, who pleaded with the woman to ask her mother to allow her to quit school. The youngster had not eaten lunch since the start of the school year because she feared going into the cafeteria, scene of numerous fights."[46] The seven-year-old daughter of a white legal secretary came home from school with bruises all over her legs and arms, reporting that gangs of second- and third-grade black boys and girls were hitting, punching, pinching, and pulling the hair of white pupils.

The black pupils bused into South Boston faced the threat of organized violence every day—howling, cursing, spitting mobs of adults. The whites bused out faced seemly endless violence from their classmates. A father wrote to Judge Garrity telling him of a black student "in jest" pulling a knife on his son, and of a black teaching aide's refusing to reprimand him, telling him just to put the knife away. That same man complained that his son and two of his friends were mugged by black students during a fire drill. Another father wrote to complain that his daughter came home needing three stitches on the back of her head. A father from the comfortable neighborhood of Roslindale said that white children at Philbrick elementary school were afraid to use the bathrooms, and that black pupils threatened violence to bar whites from the playground. The same man said that the seven Hyde Park High tenth-graders with the best grades had been attacked and beaten by a large gang of black classmates; they all left the school.

Judge Garrity was unmoved. But his determination to impose his will struck again and again upon the unyielding resistance of the Boston Irish. In September 1975, the teachers walked out on an illegal weeklong strike. In October, 200 students marched out of Charlestown High in protest. That same month, there was more violence in South Boston after an all-white South Boston football team played the all-black Dorchester squad. The game ended in an eight-eight tie, and the angry Dorchester fans hurled bottles at the South Boston team. The next day, word of the attack spread through South Boston High, and white students started fights with blacks. Eight blacks and seven whites were arrested, and eighteen students were suspended. Three days later, on October 26, 1975, 6,000 South Bostonians marched through the streets of the neighborhood. Of the 785 whites enrolled at the school, 782 boycotted classes. All but twenty-six of the 595 whites enrolled at Charlestown joined the boycott. The students returned to class the next week, and fighting erupted again on November 4, 1975, this time leading to eight arrests. In December, Judge Garrity ejected the headmaster of South Boston High and took the school under his own personal control.

By spring of the second year, racial incidents were spreading through the whole city of Boston, claiming both white and black victims. At a protest at City Hall, whites from South Boston attacked a black lawyer, stabbing him with the point of a flagpole, seriously wounding him. The next day, in apparent retaliation, black youths in Roxbury stoned the car of a white motorist, causing him to crash. They dragged him out of his car, and crushed his skull with paving stones. Police arrived to find the victim lying in the street surrounded by a mob of as many as one hundred people, chanting "Let him die." He never recovered from a coma.

The third year of integration at South Boston High opened in September 1976. Five people were sent to hospital and several others arrested during the first month of classes. Interracial violence was reported almost every day. In the first eighteen days of school, 196 students were suspended. Boston motorcycle police escorted buses to and from the school, state troopers patrolled the corridors inside.

A reporter from a local paper, the *Herald Advertiser*, spent a day in the school in September 1976. It was a typical day, without any unusual flare-ups. He kept a minute-by-minute notebook of what he saw.

8:12 A.M. White students slow on entering; black male student arrested for assaulting a teacher.

8:45 A.M. One-on-one fighting in lobby and on second floor during first period filing.

10:25 A.M. Black male students and white male students involved in confrontations on second floor; suspensions reported; four white males and two black males, five days for fighting; one white male, two black males and one black female, three days for fighting.

11:20 A.M. Suspensions reported: one white male, three days for fighting; one white male, five days for refusing to go to class; one black male, five days for possession of a weapon (nail).

1:05 P.M. Disruption in cafeteria during study period; books thrown but no injuries; some students sent to holding rooms.

3:00 P.M. Suspensions reported: three black males and one white male, three days for book throwing; one white male, three days for fighting.

3:10 P.M. Follow-upon on fight this morning; teacher was taken to City Hospital for broken wrist.[47]

The situation never improved. One of the biggest racial brawls at South Boston High occurred as late as October 1980, when white neighborhood toughs tried once again to prevent buses carrying black students from entering the school grounds. The school was obliged to cancel classes for the day.

Boston's story was the worst in the nation, but similar stories could be told in almost every major American city outside the South. Nancy St. John, a proponent of desegregation who had begun her work in the late 1940s, published in 1975 a review of more than one hundred studies of busing in the urban North. To her consternation, she found that integration made little difference to students' academic performance. It did, however, have an immediately and sharply negative effect on interracial attitudes. Whites and blacks in an integrated school were more hostile to people of the opposite race than whites and blacks who had not been integrated. David Armour, another early advocate of school integration, came to similarly depressing conclusions. Studying a group of black students bused into a predominantly white school in the early 1970s, he found that "the bused students reported less friendliness from whites, more free time spent with members of their own race, more incidents of prejudice, and less frequent dating with white students" than black students who lived in the school's neighborhood. "The data suggest that, under the circumstances obtaining in these studies, integration heightens racial identity and consciousness, enhances ideologies that promote racial segregation, and reduces opportunities for actual contact between the races."[48]

By the late 1970s, overwhelming majorities of whites—up to 95 percent—opposed racial segregation. But majorities of up to 91 percent opposed busing, and 70 percent of whites said they opposed it "strongly." Among blacks, support for desegregation dropped from 78 percent in 1964 to 55 percent in 1978. A 1977 National Opinion Research Center poll confirmed the growing unpopularity of administered integration. Only 53 percent of blacks, and only 36 percent of Hispanics, endorsed busing for desegregation. Minorities, it turns out, care every bit as much as whites do about being able to drop by their child's school if she has forgotten her lunch. And they found themselves resenting bitterly the fact that it was much more often their children than white children who had to ride the bus. It's simple arithmetic—if you are going to equalize the distribution of a minority and a majority population, a larger proportion of the minority will have to move. But knowing the math didn't make it any easier to rouse a seven-year-old child before sunrise so that he could eat breakfast and get dressed in time for an hour-long bus ride. "It's abusive to our children, who need to be in their own neighborhood," said a black St. Louis mother interviewed by the *New York Times* in 1983. "Why uproot our babies? The Caucasians stay in their own neighborhood until they go to college. It's unfair. It's unsafe. It's a damn shame."[49]

Busing triggered a whole new perception among ordinary middle-class people of the malignity of public authority. On the first day of school in 1975—the same day that Bostonians were loading their kids onto buses for a second year away from their neighborhoods—Massachusetts governor Michael Dukakis was photographed walking his children to school. Dukakis lived in Brookline, an elegant suburb just minutes away from downtown Boston. He didn't have to load his children onto a bus and send them miles away. Judge Garrity's children did not ride the bus either. The Garritys lived in genteel Wellesley. The main author of the second Boston busing plan, Robert Dentler, the then-dean of the Boston University School of Education, lived in the leafy suburb of Lexington. No wonder the Bostonians called busing "a Harvard plan for the working-class man." J. Anthony Lukas, who wrote a classic book on the Boston schools battle, describes how a community meeting to explain busing to the people of South Boston "erupted into shouting and jeering from the audience when it was discovered during the question and answer period at the end that none of the four panelists, two blacks and two whites, lived in the city of Boston." "How can it be the law of the land, as we are told," a mother in the working-class Irish neighborhood of Charlestown asked in a bitter letter to Judge Garrity, "when you can move less than one mile away and be out from under this law?"

The television show *60 Minutes* reported in 1971 that many of Washington's leading advocates of busing sent their own children to private schools. Senator Edward Kennedy sent his sons to St. Alban's. George Mc-Govern, although a District of Columbia resident, paid $1450-a-year in tuition to enroll his daughter in the Bethesda public schools—a school system then 3 percent black. Thurgood Marshall had two sons in Georgetown Day School. Kenneth Clark, the sociologist whose work was the main authority cited in the Supreme Court's *Brown* v. *Board of Education* decision, sent his children to private school as well. "My children," he said, "have only one life and I could not risk that." Arvonne Fraser, the wife of Donald Fraser, the most vociferously liberal member of the Minnesota congressional delegation, struck a similar note. "Your children get educated only once." The judge who ordered the integration of the school systems of Richmond, Virginia, and its suburbs, Robert Merhige, likewise sent his children to private school. "When I'm on the bench I'm a judge," he said, "and when at home, I'm a father." Frank Mankiewicz, McGovern's campaign manager; Benjamin Bradlee, editor of the *Washington Post*; and Senator Phil Hart, the very liberal senator from Michigan: all Georgetown Day parents. Senator Birch Bayh and ultra-liberal newspaper columnists Tom Wicker of the *New York Times* and Philip Geyelin of the *Washington Post* sent their boys to mingle with Senator Kennedy's at St. Alban's.

In their now-classic study of the failure of the U.S. Army in Vietnam, *Crisis in Command*, Richard Gabriel and Paul Savage scathingly point out that American senior officers in Vietnam were about half as likely to be killed as American senior officers in World War II. "[T]he leaders who formulated the rules of the game—duty, honor, country—did not live up to them . . ."[50] The American military in Vietnam was, Gabriel and Savage charged, disfigured by officers' disloyalty to their subordinates. The fathers of the South Boston public school students of 1977 were the sort of men who served in Vietnam. They had first glimpsed this disloyalty on the Indochinese battlefields of the 1960s. Now they were confronted with it in the courtrooms and legislative chambers of the 1970s.

At bottom, the American system is founded on the belief that government ought to respond to the wishes of the majority of the people. Here, however, was an issue in which crushing, 90-percent majorities were ferociously opposed to the decisions of the political authorities. In 1968, 1972, and 1976, the voters elected presidents pledged to halt busing. Congress likewise repeatedly voted to curb busing. Yet, the courts, the federal bureaucracy, and increasingly the state bureaucracies and local school boards all enforced the busing the people despised. The government had been hijacked, and there was almost nothing an unhappy citizenry could do about it. A remarkably frank book by one of busing's staunchest academic defenders, the Yale sociologist Jennifer Hochschild, expressed the haughty attitude of the busing advocates: "[I]f we follow popular wishes, we will not desegregate successfully. To desegregate successfully, authorities must find the will to ignore (temporarily, one hopes) popular opposition."[51] Disregarding public opinion was justified, because "[p]eople learn to accept and even support what they cannot change; if they see hope for avoiding an undesirable future, they will struggle to do so."[52]

Hochschild misjudged her fellow citizens. The American people were never reconciled to busing. But they did learn its lesson. The power of government had moved from the elected branches to the unelected, had moved to regions beyond the citizens' power to control.

AMERICANISM, 100%

THE HOUSE COMMITTEE ON UN-AMERICAN ACTIVITIES, SENILE FOR YEARS, WAS at last put to sleep in January 1975. A huge Democratic congressional majority had been elected in November 1974, and as far as it was concerned, anticommunism was nothing more than an excuse for wiretapping Martin Luther King and plunging the country into disastrous foreign wars. Worse even than the committee's work was its name. The crusading liberals of the new majority were offended and appalled by the notion that there existed such a thing as activities that were more or less "American" in any sense other than a geographic one. High on the list of rights endorsed by the 1972 Democratic campaign platform was "the right to be different," and although the Democrats lost the 1972 election, they interpreted the 1974 landslide as an acknowledgment by the American public that they had been right all along. There would be no more compulsory Americanism while they were in charge. Take that, J. Edgar Hoover! Good riddance, Roy Cohn! But J. Edgar Hoover and Roy Cohn did not originate the ideal of Americanism. Its roots sank far deeper into native soil, a hundred years deep, and in uprooting it, the Americans of the 1970s tore up much more than the work of the tormenters of the Hollywood Ten.

The United States entered the twentieth century about as badly divided as a great nation could be. The trees planted around the Civil War graves in Arlington Cemetery were still young in the 1890s. An eighteen-year-old who joined the blue or gray in 1861 would have been fifty-four when President William McKinley, himself a veteran of Antietam, took the oath of office. In 1898, when McKinley sent the army south to Florida for the invasion of Cuba, he worried that there might be sabotage or harassment of the railway lines that ran through the old Confederacy. And across the old dividing lines of North and South, new fractures had cracked. The races were segregated by Jim Crow. The classes glared at each other across the picket lines of America's uniquely bloody strikes. City dwellers who had access to electricity, central heating, telephones, running water, public libraries, streetcars, and theaters were resented by western and southern farmers who lived barely more comfortably than Daniel Boone a century before. The farmers in turn terrified the city dwellers with their mad demands for Prohibition and monetary inflation. Frightening stories about bizarre and dangerous foreign ideologies filled the new daily newspapers. An adherent of one of those creeds, a Polish anarchist, had murdered President McKinley in April 1901, the third president to die violently in thirty-six years. More than 20 million immigrants steamed into the United States between 1881 and 1914. Towns erupted into cities, cities into metropolises, and the streets of those metropolises were jammed with uncouth strangers in bizarre clothing, jabbering away in Czech, Magyar, Greek, Italian, Slovene, Ruthenian, Yiddish, and Romanian and Lord knows what else.

In the sepia photographs in our family albums, in the herky-jerky motion pictures we see in television documentaries, life in 1900 looks very quaint and picturesque. But at the time it was alarming. How could a self-governing republic be sustained in a society whose people could not communicate with each other? Where some lived in the marble palaces of Fifth Avenue while others starved? Where the president could not take for granted the loyalty of southerners or immigrants if the country had to go to war? In a speech given after the United States entered the First World War, former ambassador to Germany James Gerard told an ominous story. "The Foreign Minister of Germany once said to me your country does not dare do anything against Germany, because we have in your country five hundred thousand German reservists who will rise in arms against your government if you dare to make a move against Germany. Well, I told him that that might be so, but that we had five hundred thousand *and one* lamp posts in this country, and that that was where the reservists would be hanging the day after they tried to rise."[53] The only way to sustain American democracy, the Americans of a century ago believed, was by forging a stronger sense of American nationhood. "We must Americanize [immigrants] in every way," Theodore Roosevelt declared in an 1894 magazine article, "in speech, in political ideas and principles, and in their way of looking at relations between church and state. We welcome the German and the Irishman who becomes an American. We have no use for the German or Irishman who remains such. We do not wish German-Americans and Irish-Americans who figure as such in our social and political life; we want only Americans. . . . There are certain ideals he must give up. . . . He must revere only our flag, not only must it come first, but no other flag should even come second."[54] Immigrant absorption was only the beginning of nation-building. North and South had to be reconciled, the classes brought together by a "square deal," responsibility for regulating the emerging national economy transferred from the states to Washington, D.C., racial violence in the South curbed, and alien ideologies banished. It was this program that made Theodore Roosevelt the most popular president of the entire century from Andrew Jackson to FDR.

The memory of the elder Roosevelt's accomplishments has faded over the years. He succeeded so completely that it is difficult now to remember the problems he set out to solve. From his day until the middle 1960s, the United States moved steadily and peacefully toward the unity and power he dreamt of. Labor relations were soothed, and the extremes of wealth and poverty narrowed. The racial caste system was overthrown. Hollywood, television, higher education, the interstate highways, and, most important of them all, two world wars and the peacetime draft fused the country together culturally. Prosperity relegated anarchism, socialism, and communism to the margins of national life, leaving the center to a powerful consensus in favor of a moderated and regulated free-market capitalism. The First World War and the restrictive laws of the 1920s ended the great immigration. By the middle 1960s, the United States was a more uniformly English-speaking country than it had been at any time since the 1840s and steadily becoming more uniformly so. The percentage of foreign born in the population bottomed out at 5 percent in 1970.[55] One still heard foreign languages spoken only in poorer urban neighborhoods, in remote coal-mining towns, at the old-folks' homes. Americanization had worked so stupendously well that social critics of the 1950s fretted that their country was in danger of becoming *too* homogeneous.

No fear of that. With not a word of apology to Theodore Roosevelt's unquiet ghost, the country's leaders began snipping one by one at the fibers of national unity after 1965.

That year, Senator Edward Kennedy introduced a package of reforms to the immigration laws intended, he said, to purge them of their bias in favor of Europeans. In those days, immigration was one of those subjects whose very mention conjured up memories of a bygone era (like League of Nations mandates, white slavery, or railroad-rate regulation), and Kennedy's bill moseyed through Congress without arousing much controversy or even interest. Fewer than 250,000 immigrants arrived in the United States in 1965. Kennedy solemnly promised that his bill would not cause the total to rise. Nor would it, he answered the Senate, much alter the ethnic composition of the country.

The pre–1965 immigration law held overall numbers down because it offered almost all the available visas to European countries and to Canada, where population growth and unemployment rates were low. In fact, in 1965, many countries' allotted quotas went unfilled: Few West Germans felt the need to bid family adieu and learn a new language in order to settle in a country where wages were rising more slowly than they were at home. Kennedy's bill reallocated those unused quotas to poorer countries with higher population-growth rates, and then reinforced the pro-Third World tendency of the new law by giving first preference for all future visas to the extended families of the most recent arrivals. The annual intake of legal immigrants doubled between 1965 and 1970, and then doubled again between 1970 and 1990. Between 1964 and 1978, the number of illegal immigrants apprehended in or on their way to the United States jumped from 75,000 to more than 1 million. Between 1968 and 1999, counting both legals and illegals, some 30 million newcomers settled in the United States. Almost half of those people came from just one region of the world, Latin America and the Caribbean, and 20 percent of them from Mexico alone.[56] (More than 90 percent of the illegals were Mexican; the next largest group was Haitian.) In the 1976 movie *Taxi Driver*, Robert de Niro plays a character who is unusual in a lot of ways, but the one that may make the strongest impression on a twenty-first century audience is the one that the filmmakers probably considered least: He's white. Who ever sees a white cabbie in New York City any more? The new immigration transformed the American working class, darkening its skin and—by virtue of its immense numbers—deeply depressing its wages.

So huge and so sudden was the movement of people that the state of California—the home of the Beach Boys' golden "California girls"—became in 1999 the first American mainland state to have a non-white majority. If immigration continues at its 1990s pace, and barring some unlooked-for upsurge in white birthrates, the *whole* United States, whose white population peaked at 90 percent of the total in 1940, will have a non-white majority by the year 2050.

Relative to the size of the American population, the 1968–1999 immigration, huge as it was, was still smaller than that of 1881–1913. But unlike that early immigration, the post–1965 immigrants arrived in a country seemingly implacably determined *not* to assimilate them. That right to be different, the Democratic platform of 1972 had said, included the right "to maintain a cultural or ethnic heritage or lifestyle, without being forced into a compelled homogeneity," and though the Democrats lost the election, that part of their platform carried the day. Twenty-seven years later, presidential candidates were giving speeches in Spanish, in order to be understood by the country's growing non-English-speaking minority. Many of the members of this minority had been born and educated in the United States. They retained their ancestral language because their new country had consciously chosen to instruct them in it.

Bilingual classrooms had been pioneered in Arizona in the 1960s. Children were to be taught academic subjects in their own language while their English was hastily brought up to par. What this tended to mean, given that the number of school hours is finite, was that the students began each day with thirty or sixty minutes of English instruction, and then proceeded to math, history, science, and so on, in their native tongue. Bilingual instruction spread rapidly across the country after the Supreme Court ruled in 1974 that the school board of San Francisco had violated the 1964 Civil Rights Act by plunging non-English speaking children into the same public-school classes as everyone else. The court ordered San Francisco to make special accommodations for non-English speakers and suggested it take a look at bilingual education.[57] The same mood of ethnic self-assertion that inspired the Chicanos of Arizona enflamed Spanish-language immigrants across the country. Money played its part. Bilingual education raised the demand for Hispanic teachers—and their pay too, since bilingual teachers usually received higher wages than their monoglot colleagues. The New York Board of Education acceded in August 1974 to the demands of Puerto Rican activists and instituted a plan immediately to put 200,000 students into bilingual classes. By the mid-1990s, almost one-third of California schoolchildren were enrolled in bilingual classes, despite periodic reminders from the lower federal courts that bilingualism had been mentioned by the Supreme Court only as one alternative out of many.[58] Federal spending on bilingual education jumped from $7.5 million in 1968 to $150 million by 1979. The states, of course, spent much more.

It quickly became obvious that "bilingual education" was a misnomer. Not even California could guarantee children a place in a Tamil, Khmer, Armenian, Russian, Malay, or Eritrean language classroom. Instead, those Tamil, Khmer, Armenian, Russian, Malay, and Eritrean kids were placed in a Spanish-language classrooms. Worse, almost from the beginning, it was apparent that bilingual education did not work very well. Spanish-speakers emerged from high school barely more fluent in English than when they entered kindergarten. But if bilingual classes did not teach English, they very effectively immersed their students in foreign nationalism, principally Mexican. On May 5, the anniversary of the 1862 Battle of Puebla, the great Mexican patriotic day, bilingual classrooms filled up with enough green-and-white flags and bunting to gladden the heart of Benito Juarez.

The unwillingness to compel assimilation extended to adults as well as children. Over the 1970s, courts and bureaucracies step by step enlarged the political rights of non-citizens. In November 1971, a three-judge panel ruled that New York State's law restricting civil service jobs to citizens violated the equal protection clause of the Fourteenth Amendment.[59] In 1973, the Supreme Court declared that aliens had a constitutional right to practice law.[60] Nor, the Court added in 1976, could they be barred from the federal civil service.[61] (The Court did inexplicably rule in 1979 that New York State could require high-school teachers to be American citizens.[62]) By then, even the insistence that immigrants enter the country legally had come to seem unduly onerous. The phrase "undocumented alien" replaced the harsher "illegal immigrant" in official speech. President Carter, campaigning in California on the Cinco de Mayo holiday in 1979, personally committed himself "to making sure that all people within our borders, no matter how they may have gotten here, are treated with dignity and justice. I am committed to protecting the basic human rights of every person in this country, whatever their legal status." On November 26, 1979, Attorney General Benjamin Civiletti announced that the Immigration and Naturalization Service would cease to raid residences it suspected of harboring illegals—searches would be confined to workplaces. The Supreme Court decided in 1982 that young illegal aliens have a constitutional right to a free public education.[63]

The collapse of the assimilationist project in some ways touched the native-born even more deeply than the new arrivals. The turn from integrationism to separatism that had convulsed civil rights organizations like the Congress on Racial Equality in the mid–1960s began to influence the broad mainstream of black opinion in the 1970s. Separate black dormitories, pioneered at Cornell University in 1969, spread from university campus to another. Half-remembered, half-invented bits of Africanicity, like the Kwanzaa holiday and the kente cloth, began to show up in middle-class black homes. New school curricula were drawn up, teaching that black Africans invented the smallpox vaccine and the telephone, and sailed across the Atlantic Ocean fifteen hundred years before Columbus.[64]

Unfortunately, ethnic pride can all too easily boil over into chauvinism and xenophobia. The *Los Angeles Times* reported an increasing number of racially motivated assaults on servicemen in Hawaii by locals: 110 in the first nine months of 1979, resulting in at least two deaths. Four soldiers were mobbed and beaten by Hawaiian natives when they tried to come to the aid of a tourist whose purse had been snatched; two army sentries were wounded by sniper fire from six teenage assailants.[65] The violent American Indian Movement provoked a prolonged standoff at Wounded Knee, site of the 1890 massacre by the U.S. Cavalry, that ended in a chain of shootouts with the FBI in May 1973. In 1981, the American Jewish Committee conducted a large survey of the prevalence of antisemitic attitudes in the U.S. population, the first such survey in seventeen years. It found a gratifying dropoff in prejudice among whites, but reported with alarm that "the level of antisemitism among blacks has remained unchanged since 1964." More alarming still, while anti-semitic feeling declined among whites the better-educated they were, well-educated blacks were every bit as prone to anti-semitism as the less-educated.[66] These poisonous prejudices were abruptly exposed to public view in 1979, after President Carter fired U.N. Ambassador Andrew Young, the first black American to hold that office, for conducting secret and unauthorized meetings with members of the Palestine Liberation Organization. Only one of the nine major Jewish organizations in the United States had called for Young's firing, but the incident snapped something in Young's spirit and that of his old friends in the civil-rights organizations. They were sick to the eyeteeth of being reminded of how grateful they should be. Appearing on *Meet the Press* on August 19, 1979, Young condemned Israel as "stubborn and intransigent." Two days later, Joseph Lowery, head of the Southern Christian Leadership Conference, met in New York City with representatives of the PLO and emerged to endorse Palestinian self-determination and to urge the PLO to give "consideration" to recognizing Israel. On a trip to the Middle East that summer, Jesse Jackson called Israeli Prime Minister Menachem Begin a "terrorist" and Israel a "theocracy." Returning home, he met with an Arab-American group and told them, "I can help your cause, but you have to help my cause by putting your efforts behind the civil-rights movement." They immediately gave him $10,000, with the promise of more.

Non-black Americans, meanwhile, were also jettisoning the old Rooseveltian ideals. The grandchildren of the great immigration reacted to the fading of the assimilationist idea with a defiant, if often hazy, new ethnic consciousness of their own: "Kiss Me, I'm Irish" T-shirts, gold crucifixes worn around the neck in defiance of America's Protestant sensibilities, gold Hebrew "chai" (life) symbols worn in defiance of the crucifixes. Often this new ethnic self-assertion was a hardheaded response to the new incentives created by affirmative action. Italian-American faculty pressured the City University of New York into recognizing them as an affirmative-action category for purposes of hiring and promotion in December 1976. More often the rewards for staking out claims of victimhood and separateness were psychic rather than material. They were, paradoxically, a way of finding a place for oneself in an increasingly balkanized America. One belonged by complaining that one had never belonged. As for those who could not make the complaint—who could not excuse themselves as black, or female, or disabled, or gay, or the descendents of immigrants— they had two choices: Either accept the role of villain or else start apologizing for all the dreadful things their ancestors had done during the course of building America.

The identity politics of the 1970s sprouted into a rococo mass of tendrils, shoots, and curlicues. Accusations of racism were followed by charges of sexism, then of homophobia, then of age-ism, able-ism, lookism, and finally—inevitably one supposes—of species-ism. (Yes, really. The Australian philosopher Peter Singer coined the word in his bizarre but important 1975 book, *Animal Liberation*. Ironically enough, Singer now holds Princeton University's DeCamp Professorship at the University Center for Human Values.) The demand for equality is getting mighty exacting when human beings are told not to feel superior to chickens. But these movements were not about equality. The new identity politics was yet another late-twentieth-century-throwback to the ideas and prejudices of the late nineteenth century—in this case, to Social Darwinism. Social Darwinists envisioned nations and peoples as constantly struggling for their existence against other groups. According to the more radical Social Darwinists, there were no universal truths, only the unique experiences of particular groups. "[L]anguage," the ultra-nationalist German historian Heinrich von Treitschke declared, "is directly given to consciousness in association with reason . . . the concept cannot be detached from the word, and . . . *differences of language inevitably imply differing outlooks on the world.*"[67] The feminist theorist Catherine A. MacKinnon endorsed a similar point of view a century later: "[T]he white man's standard for equality is: Are you equal *to him?* That is hardly a neutral standard. It is a racist, sexist standard. . . . But if you present yourself as affirmatively and self-respectingly a member of your own culture or sex . . . if you insist that *your* cultural diversity be affirmatively accommodated and recognized in ways equal to the way *theirs* has been, that's not seen to be an equality challenge at all."[68] MacKinnon believes that members of each "culture"—her word for what Treitschke would call each "*volk*"—have their own distinct moral and intellectual norms. If in an essay she claims that 13 percent of all American women, or more than 18 million people, have at one time or another in their lives worked as prostitutes, and if she cites as her only authority for this improbable claim an article in a student newspaper,[69] then while she may be guilty of flouting white, male standards of evidence, she has not fallen short of standards of evidence in general, because there are no such things. Just as there were once German physics, in which atoms behaved in certain ways, and Jewish physics, in which they behaved in other ways, so there are white, male standards of evidence—which rely on

FBI reports and police blotters—and . . . what? White female standards of evidence? Apparently so.

"The entire project of building a new kind of left-wing movement had begun with a moral worry about being privileged in a world of suffering," Paul Berman explains in his history of the generation of 1968. "The idea had been to take privileged young people and put them on the side of the oppressed. On someone else's side, not their own. On the side of people who needed help. But the argument for feminism and gay liberation said, in effect, that in the student world everybody was not, on closer inspection, so wonderfully privileged. On the contrary!"[70] They would, thank you very much, take their own side, and militantly so. Their words may have been borrowed from Marx, but their feelings came straight from Commodore Decatur: "My sex/race/orientation! May it always be right—but my sex/race/orientation, right or wrong!"

THE PEOPLE'S HOUSE

AT TWO O'CLOCK IN THE MORNING ON OCTOBER 9, 1974, FEDERAL PARK police spotted a sedan weaving boozily across the lanes of Independence Avenue, on its way to Capitol Hill from downtown Washington. They pulled the car over. As it drew to a stop, the passenger door was flung open and a woman hurled herself out of the car, lurched toward the Mall, stumbled, and flung herself into the Tidal Basin to make a swim for it. The police fished her out. The next morning all Washington knew who she was: an Argentine-born stripper named Fanne Fox. With rather more surprise, it also learned who the driver of the car was: Representative Wilbur Mills of Arkansas, chairman of the House Ways and Means Committee, the tax-writing committee of the House of Representatives. As if that were not enough excitement, Mills flew to Boston a couple of months later and held a drunken press conference in the dressing room of Fox's strip-club.

Mills is not well-remembered any more. More famous Arkansans have since had more celebrated trouble with women. But in 1974, he ranked as one of the half-dozen most powerful economic policymakers in Washington. The foundation of Mills's power was the arcane procedures of the U.S. Congress. Nineteenth-century congresses were jumbles of strangers, yoked together by party feeling and ruled, to the extent they were ruled at all, by high-handed Speakers of the House.[71] In the early years of the twentieth century, the hubbub and fractiousness of Congress calmed down and regularized itself. Members served longer and longer. The committees became more powerful. A quiet oligarchy of long-serving chairmen came to rule Capitol Hill, and Mills was paramount among those men. He ruled his committee like a tyrant—the committee staff, for example, was hired by and reported to him personally—and his committee ruled the Congress. His committee (meaning Mills himself) wrote American tax law. Mills's tax bills invariably went to the floor under a "closed rule"—meaning no amendments were permitted, Congress could only vote straight up or straight down.

Mills controlled the larger Congress too. In those days, the Ways and Means Committee, again meaning Mills himself, also functioned as the Committee on Committees, and assigned all committee House memberships. It was Mills who decided whether the eager young freshman from Kansas was assigned to the agriculture committee—or else to the committee on the fisheries.

Mills was the strongest of the congressional old bulls, but there were a half-dozen other men to be reckoned with: the chairman of the rules committee, which determined when and how a bill would get voted on; the chairman of armed services, who presided over the defense budget; and so on. These men got their original assignments when they were comparative striplings, and then—if they lived and their party held onto power—ascended into the chairmanship by unshakable rights of seniority. Not even visible and palpable senility could dislodge a chairman so long as his constituents kept returning him to Congress.

As might be expected of a legislature ruled by old men, the mid-century House of Representatives was a conservative institution. Between the pas-

sage of the Fair Labor Standards Act in 1938 and Lyndon Johnson's whirl-
wind of legislation in 1964, Congress passed only a single major new domestic program, the interstate highways. To liberals, it was maddening.
Every other November, the New Deal coalition worked like a charm, elect-
ing big Democratic majorities from farm and factory. Then for the remaining 729 days of the biennium, the committee chairmen balked and stymied
all the New Dealers' best work.

How could this happen? Look at the shape of the Congress elected in
one of those New Deal coalition elections, 1954, the election in which the
Democrats recaptured the House after the Eisenhower sweep of 1952. On
paper, the Democrats enjoyed a comfortable majority in the 1955–1956
House: 232 to 203. But ninety-two of those 232 Democrats came from
eleven segregated states: Alabama, Arkansas, Florida, Louisiana, Mississippi, North Carolina, Oklahoma, South Carolina, Tennessee, Texas, and
Virginia. As a result, the real working majority of most of the Congresses
from 1938 to 1974 was a coalition of ninety or so Southern Democrats and
the 125 most conservative Republicans.

The congressional system of mid-century gets a bad press nowadays.
The racial attitudes of its barons were unappetizing and they did not always worry quite as hard as they ought about ethics. Congress cared more
about paying down the country's World War II and Korean war debts than
about creating anything new. Its leadership was dismayingly unrepresentative of the country: all white, all male, mostly southern, mostly elderly,
mostly rural. But the old unrepresentative Congress was also capable of
surprisingly decisive action. When a president wanted something from the
House, there were usually only about three or four men he needed to dis-
cuss it with—and they were almost invariably men for whom deference to
the president, especially on national security and foreign affairs, was a
central doctrine of their creed. It was the old unrepresentative barons who
delivered the votes for the Marshall Plan, who agreed to dismantle cen-
tury-old American tariffs to promote European and Japanese recovery,
who stuck by John Kennedy without a whisper of doubt as he brought the
world to the brink of nuclear war first over Berlin and then over Cuba. In

other words, the system had its points—so long as Americans were willing to trade representativeness for effectiveness. By the mid-1960s that willingness was running out.

Lyndon Johnson's 1964 landslide—he swept 295 Democrats into the House with him, the most smashing Democratic congressional victory since 1936—freed him from dependency on the southern Democrats. For two magic years, Johnson led the liberal coalition that FDR had dreamt of. It was this new coalition that passed the mighty Voting Rights Act of 1965, which pressed the plunger on the dynamite charges that would destroy the Bourbon Democracy of the South. There had been only five black members of the U.S. House of Representatives in 1965, all from the North.[72] There were already ten in 1970, and by 1975 there would be eighteen. Between 1965 and 1973, the number of black elected officials in the eleven southern states jumped by a factor of ten, culminating in the election of Maynard Jackson as mayor of Atlanta, the most important city of the South, on October 16, 1973. The northern liberals, white and black, now greased their guns, filled their ammo boxes, and readied themselves to hunt down the last of the great white chairmen.

The hunting party was led by Phillip Burton, a labor-backed congressman from San Francisco and the real leader of the House in the middle and late 1970s. Burton's premature death in 1983 crimped his fame. He is now remembered, when he is remembered, as the name over the door of the federal building in downtown San Francisco. It seems a paltry acknowledgment of the man who created the modern Congress. If only he had not been so abrasive, difficult, tyrannical, ruthless—or possibly if that modern Congress were a more attractive and appealing thing—then perhaps the Capitol dome would have been named after him. Burton set to work to make himself speaker and to break the chairmen, and he steadily made converts among the ever-more liberal Democrats sent to Congress in 1970, 1972, and 1974. The old bulls sensed the crumbling of their position and vainly tried to placate the reformers. In February 1973, Mills agreed "as an experiment" to let a tax bill go to the floor unprotected by a closed rule— the first time that had occurred since the 1920s.

Mills's "experiment" triggered an explosion in the number of lobbyists employed in Washington. Although statistics on lobbying are hard to come by, one of the few solid ones shows that some 3,000 people were registered as lobbyists of the Senate in 1976, the first year that body kept count. By 1987, that figure had tripled to 9,000.[73] Before 1973, a corporation seeking a tax favor need worry only about convincing a single man or, at most, a few party leaders. After 1973, any one of the 435 members of the House or the one hundred members of the Senate could write an amendment containing the favor and have a fair change of negotiating it into law.

Burton seized on the disgrace of Mills as an opportunity to break the power of the old southern congressional barons, but he really needed no excuse. Within days of the November 1974 election, which sent a huge class of reform-minded liberals to Washington, Burton transferred the power to name committee members from Ways and Means to a new steering committee. The Democratic caucus had already voted to put an end to committee secrecy. All committee meetings would be open unless the committee affirmatively voted to close it. Burton and the 1974 freshmen next pressured the party's old leadership to permit a secret ballot on any chairmanship if half the members of the Democratic caucus would sign their names to a request for a vote. The leaders acceded. They felt the ground shifting under their feet, and the Burton request seemed relatively moderate. After all, the old leaders figured, unless a chairman was glaringly past-it, what caucus member would dare risk his retaliation by publicly coming out in opposition to him? Burton, however, had outsmarted them. He immediately rallied the liberals in the Democratic caucus to sign papers calling for secret ballots on *all* committee chairmen. By calling for a vote on every chairman, Burton enabled his liberal followers to explain to the sputtering Old Bulls that his signature was nothing personal—"I wasn't voting against you; I like you. I was voting against the *system.*" And because the actual selection ballot would be secret, Burton freed his followers to promise their support to the existing committee chairmen that they would support them on the final vote. Burton showed up at the end of December with his signatures. As soon as the Christmas holidays ended, the aged grandees of the party were hauled before the baying liberals of the caucus and quizzed for hours about their worthiness to retain their posts. Not all took kindly to the interrogation. F. Edward Herbert, the 74-year-old Louisiana chairman of the Armed Services Committee, a member of the House for thirty-four years, sarcastically addressed his questioners as "boys and girls." Herbert was one of the three chairmen and two sub-committee chairmen deposed that January.

True, the great majority of the old bulls survived the post-revolutionary guillotine. Their power, however, had been stripped. Nothing humbles an autocrat quite like the need to grub for votes. The old chairmen used to ascend to their gavels by longevity. They did not have to be nice to anybody. Suddenly, they had to be nice to the Democratic caucus. So, like the skilled politicians they were, they went to work to ascertain what their new constituents wanted—and to deliver it. Did Democratic caucus members want chairmanships of their own? And without waiting thirty or forty years? No problem. Like owners of grand Edwardian homes in an age of shrinking families, the grandees promptly set about chopping up their draughty committees into dozens of subcommittees, dozens of them, each surmounted by a happy new subcommittee chairman. Burton's reforms leveled power within Congress. Instead of a mighty few surrounded by the obedient many, Congress was now made up of a somewhat mighty many able to compel no obedience at all.

Burton had promised that weakening the big shots would heighten the accountability and responsiveness of Congress. No question, Congress became more responsive. But it simultaneously became dramatically *less* effective and accountable. Under the old system, only a comparative handful of members had any power. If they abused that power, it would be noticed—if not by the press, then by their colleagues, and if noticed, then punished. But now dozens, maybe even hundreds, of congressmen controlled the fates of firms, industries, whole nations. Hundreds of special interests soon buzzed round those dozens, pressing money into their hands, lobbying, cajoling, persuading. The ambitious new subcommittee chairmen, hungry for campaign contributions to stave off the electorate's post–1978 Republican trend, all too eagerly responded to their donors' concerns. But since their most active constituents simultaneously expected them to flay those donors in the name of anticorporate liberalism, that responsiveness had to be disguised and concealed. The chairmen coped with their dilemma by evasion: by voting one way on procedural votes and then another on the merits of the bill, or voting "no" on laws they really favored after first establishing that the thing had the support to pass even without their vote. In this deliberately created muddle, nobody—often not even the congressmen themselves—could ever quite discern why things happened, who had made things happen, or even frequently what had happened. It was hopeless to imagine that an ordinary citizen could force his way through the buzzing cloud, much less exert any real influence. Very much to the surprise of the reform members, this new, more responsive, less hierarchical Congress got less done than the old oligarchy had. "The day is gone," said new Ways and Means chairman Al Ullman of Washington State, "when a chairman can wrap a neat little package in his back room. The open hearings and open markups, in which all members, not just a few, have a say, is the way this committee must work." The old unreformed Congress had enacted the Supplemental Security Income program in 1971. The new reformed Congress could never quite organize itself to enact anything on such a large scale ever again.

Besides, it did not have the money. The old bulls had maintained a reasonable grip on the finances of the United States, indulging themselves every other year with a big hike in Social Security payments. The reformed Congress let that grip slip. It could not even complete its budgets on time. In a desperate attempt to get back on schedule, it voted in 1974 to shift the end of its fiscal year three months forward—from March 30 to June 30, effective in 1976. The gambit failed: Congress missed the June 30 deadline the very next year. After that it gave up and relied instead on "continuing resolutions"—resolutions telling government agencies to carry on what they were doing until they were told otherwise. These CRs were blank checks to the bureaucracy. In the first six months of 1974, spending jumped by $30 billion, this at a time when $30 billion was still real money. Over the seven fiscal years from 1974 through 1980, non-defense and foreign-assistance spending jumped from $174 billion to $444 billion.

Not only did the reformed Congress accomplish less than the unreformed Congress, it was, despite its endless preoccupations with ethics,

quickly perceived as more corrupt. Congress enacted a comprehensive reform of campaign finance in 1974, legislating strict limits on how much political campaigns could spend and political donors could give: $1,000 for
individuals, $5,000 for political action committees. The Supreme Court de-
clared the spending limits unconstitutional in 1976, but the donor limits
stayed. Raising the money to fight a modern political campaign in $1,000
increments, however, is, as politicians complain, like filling a bathtub with
a tablespoon. In the 1990s, it costs at least $1 million to run a professional
House race in an urban district. That means that even a member of Congress willing to raise all his money from political action committees needs
to receive a minimum of two hundred contributions in two years. All that
schnorring makes even an honest man look crooked.

In the 1950s and early 1960s, only about a quarter of Americans said
"yes" to the question, "I don't think public officials care much what people
like me think." That sad response rose to about one-third by the
mid–1960s, to more than 40 percent in 1968, and to an outright majority of
the population in 1976. By the mid–1970s, two-thirds of the public said
they felt "what they think does not really count."[74] Sociologists would
spend years puzzling over those numbers, but one ought not too quickly to
reject the hypothesis that people felt that their views did not much count
because in fact *their views did not much count.*

The schools children attend, the curriculum they will study, and the
way in which those schools are financed, even the language of instruction,
have in hundreds of communities been decided not by an elected school
board but by a federal judge. The highways follow not the route preferred
by local elected officials, but one that emerged from a negotiation between
local environmental groups and the federal environmental bureaucracy,
again brokered by a judge. Offices are designed not for beauty or comfort,
but to conform to the minute regulations of the Americans with Disabilities Act and the Energy Department's fuel-efficiency standards. Whether
there is sufficient electricity to power a town's air conditioners depends on
whether the Environmental Protection Agency, the Department of Energy,
state officials, and the federal judiciary could reach a deal on the local util-
ity's latest expansion plan. An executive's chances of promotion depend

rather less on his merits than on his employer's need to ensure that upper management conform to the Equal Employment Opportunity Commission's assessment of how many blacks, women, Hispanics, Native Americans, disabled persons, and foreign-born are appropriate for a firm in its region and its industry. A similar story could be told in almost every advanced industrial country. In Europe, decision-making power is shifting from elected legislatures to an unelected European commission with vast regulatory power. In Canada, New Zealand, and Australia, parliaments are being displaced by the judiciary and appointed commissioners.

The South Bostonians tried and tried again to stop busing at the ballot box. They never came close to succeeding, and they raged bitterly at the representatives who could not or would not help them. "We're the poor sunavabees who pay our taxes and sweat tuitions, sweat mortgages and car payments and the cost of groceries and fuel, get no handouts, give our blood, take our turn in line, volunteer for charities, and work two jobs, sometimes three," wrote a columnist in the *West Roxbury Transcript* at the fiercest moment of the busing struggle. But none of it mattered. His people were entitled to nothing. "Praise Angela Davis! Hurrah for Ellsberg! Feel sorry for poor Patricia Hearst! But the poor, battered, bruised white Bostonians. Forget them."[75] In 1960, the ward of Boston that encompasses Southie gave 88 percent of its vote to Kennedy. It forgave Lyndon Johnson for not being Irish, and gave him 90 percent in 1964. But the Democratic vote in this most Democratic of districts slipped in 1968, and then collapsed. In 1980, South Boston voted 53 percent for Reagan, in 1984, 60 percent.

If it was not busing, then it was something else. In 1964, when Barry Goldwater ran for president, his warnings against overweening government struck most Americans as hyperbolic. Only 30 percent agreed with Goldwater that government had grown too powerful. He was only slightly ahead of his time. Four years later, in 1968, 40 percent had come to agree that government was too powerful, and between 1968 and 1980, that 40-percent plurality became an absolute majority of the American people. The attempt to make government responsive had instead stoked voters' fears and dulled their sense of connection to government.

Americans withdrew from civic life in the 1970s. In every presidential election from 1940 through 1968, except 1948, participation approached or exceeded 60 percent; off-year turnout between 1950 and 1970 bounced between 40 and 45 percent. After 1976, voter turnout plunged to a consistent 50 percent in presidential years and barely 33 percent in off-years. This unwillingness to vote corresponded to an even more drastic unwillingness to read about or pay attention to politics. Between 1972 and 1980, the proportion of Americans who said they followed public affairs "hardly at all" or "only now and then" jumped from 27 to 38 percent, while the proportion who paid attention to public affairs "most of the time" dropped from 36 percent to 26 percent.[76] There was much handwringing over these statistics. But sensitive nostrils could not help sniffing the aroma of hypocrisy. In 1973, the Yankelovich poll found that 60 percent of Americans now believed the country to be a democracy "in name only." This was supposed to be a very bad thing, the ultimate manifestation of the people's lack of confidence in their government. But was it really so surprising? For a decade, power had been massively and systematically transferred from the elective branches of government, where it could be controlled, to non-elective branches, where it could not. Power flowed from prominent and visible officials to a multiplicity of the obscure and invisible. Was it surprising that a country whose government had decided to treat its people like subjects should find that those same people no longer felt themselves to be citizens?

PART VI

REGENERATION

TIME OF TROUBLES

"I have begun to think that the '70s are the very worst years since the history of life began on earth . . . "

—*Joseph Alsop*, January 3, 1974.[1]

"IT IS THIS THAT CAUSES THE VARYING SUCCESS OF A MAN: THE TIMES CHANGE, BUT he does not. The ruin of states is caused in like manner."[2] So observed Niccolo Machiavelli five hundred years ago, and the more successful the man, or the society, the more true that observation is. Americans in 1960 had every reason to esteem their society as more wholly successful than any society anywhere, anytime. A man who grew up with the century had seen America shoulder one great load after another, heft them all without stumbling, and grow stronger with every weight heaped upon it. "In his lifetime," wrote Allen Drury in his 1959 novel *Advise and Consent*, "he had seen America rise and rise and rise, some sort of golden legend to her own people, some sort of fantasy to others." Sometimes it seemed that every third book published between 1945 and 1965 carried a title like *America Comes of Age*. The country had grown up, put aside its nineteenth-century boisterousness and brashness, and turned itself into a sober and capable great power, blessed with a carefully managed economy, a sophisticated military, a clear sense of its rule in the world, and a disciplined and loyal people. The extremes of the nineteenth century had been curbed: The robber barons had been brought to heel, their empires bureaucratized, an adequate but not overgenerous cushion put underneath the working man. Political passions had subsided. It had all worked. And then, as things so often do, it all stopped working.

The details of the 1970s that most captivate us in retrospect are the ridiculous ones: the clothes, the hair, the psychobabble. Over the long haul, however, what probably will matter most about the era is the grand ascent that the world then began to tread toward democracy, freedom, and the information age. The last noncommunist dictatorships in Europe—in Greece, Portugal, and Spain—were all replaced by democratic governments. Communist coups were thwarted in Portugal and Chile. Open dissidence erupted in Communist central Europe. A pro-democracy movement was born in China. The personal computer and the precursor of the Internet were developed. The tangle of economic regulations left behind by two world wars and a depression began to be cleared.

But *at the time* these hopeful signs were not easy to see. For those who lived through them, the 1970s felt like an era of endless disasters. If anything, these disasters touched the United States rather more lightly than the other advanced countries: more lightly than Britain, which was spiraling toward ever-greater impoverishment, class conflict, provincialism, and backwardness; or than Italy, collapsing into civil war between a weak state and the ruthless Red Brigades; or than Germany, plunging into an abyss of random terrorist violence; or than Canada, teetering toward the secession of the French-speaking province of Quebec and the division of Confederation.

Perspectives always shift with time. But in the case of the 1970s, the perspective of the past and the perspective of the present diverge unusually acutely. In 1980, Felix Rohatyn, a Manhattan financier and economic adviser to Democratic presidents, contrasted in gasping alarm the $90 billion a year the United States then spent on imported oil and the $1 trillion total valuation of the stocks listed on the New York Exchange. At this rate, he warned, the United States would "ship abroad in a decade or two the accumulated wealth Americans had built over 300 years—in exchange for a few more years of carefree driving."[3] Pretty scary. But at the very moment that Rohatyn wrote those words, Paul Volcker was curbing the great inflation and Bill Gates was inventing his first operating systems: breakthroughs that would help push the total valuation of the stocks on the New York Exchange to nearly *$13 trillion* by mid–1999.[4] In 1976, three years before Rohatyn wrote his gloomy words, Americans won every single Nobel Prize awarded—in medicine, chemistry, physics, literature, and economics—the first time in the history of the awards that one country swept them all.[5]

Yet Rohatyn and his contemporaries were not wrong to complain of danger and weakness where a later generation would perceive the first sprouts of future triumphs. The achievements of the 1980s and 1990s were not easily scooped up. America won the cold war, pioneered the computer revolution, squelched inflation, and suppressed crime, yes, but only because it first underwent a decade and a half of disappointment and humiliation. The 1970s were daunting and frightening because habits and institutions that had succeeded brilliantly for half a century suddenly sputtered. At first, Americans refused to accept that their old ways had failed. They redoubled their obsolete efforts, and then redoubled them again, unable to comprehend, or unwilling to accept that the harder they pushed, the worse things got. But within a remarkably short span of time, they did comprehend and they took the tough decision to junk the out-of-date and stumble forward, without any guarantees of success, toward the new.

The 1970s were America's low tide. Not since the Depression had the country been so wracked with woe. *Never*—not even during the Depression—had American pride and self-confidence plunged deeper. But the decade was also, paradoxically, in some ways America's finest hour. America was afflicted in the 1970s by a systemic crisis analogous to the one that struck Imperial Rome in the middle of the third century A.D.: "At the beginning, the problems to be solved seemed and were familiar. No one could be blamed for not predicting their consequences or for not understanding as one whole the layers of difficulty that were subsequently to unfold."[6] But unlike the Romans, Americans staggered only briefly before the crisis. They took the blow. For a short time they behaved foolishly, and on one or two occasions, even disgracefully. Then they recouped. They rethought. They reinvented. They rediscovered in their own past the governing principles of their future. Out of the failure and trauma of the 1970s they emerged stronger, richer, and—if it is not overdramatic to say so—greater than ever.

SOUND AS A DOLLAR

TAKE A HARD LOOK AT THAT DOLLAR BILL IN YOUR WALLET. PHYSICALLY, IT HAS not much altered since 1928. But in purchasing power, it's actually a 1956 dime. Forty years ago, twenty-five dollars a week was a typical starting wage for a white-collar job, and a man earning $10,000 a year could decently house, feed, and clothe a family. A new Chevrolet cost $1,500; a candy bar cost a nickel; the *New York Times* cost three cents. If you saw a penny glinting on the sidewalk, you stooped to pick it up. The Americans of the 1950s knew all about inflation. They knew about the wheelbarrow-fuls of money it took to buy a loaf of bread in Germany in 1923. They knew about the Italian lire and the Brazilian cruzeiro. Weak and unstable countries suffered from weak and unstable currencies. But the dollar! It was an imperishable fact, like U.S. Steel, or the Latin Mass, or the supremacy of the New York Yankees. In the late 1940s, when Americans were plagued by postwar inflation, they persistently described the problem as one of rising prices. Like medieval peasants watching the sun orbit the earth, Americans imagined it was the dollar that stood still and the cost of a pound of coffee or steak that moved.

Money is a series of promises. You give me something I want now—an hour of work, a pound of hamburger, a new dress—and I give you this piece of paper, which you'll in turn be able to use to get the things you want. When the value of money drops, promises are broken and expectations are shattered. You took a job in January because you were told you would be given enough dollars to buy this amount of food and that amount of clothing, and you discover in December that the dollars have somehow *shrunk*. You acted in good faith. You did what you said you would do. But your reward has been tampered with. How? By whom? The American Republic prints up pieces of paper, emblazons them with the symbols of its power and permanence, and on its "full faith and credit" declares them to be worth a certain amount. Inflation slyly and surreptitiously diminishes their value. It is an act of betrayal.

If you had the nerve to borrow a lot of soggy cash, and then use it to buy hard assets—land, grain, metals, art, silver candlesticks, a book of Austro-Hungarian postage stamps—you could make a killing in the 1970s. *Forbes* magazine published its first list of the 400 richest Americans in 1982; 153 of them owed their fortunes to real estate or oil. (On the 1998 list, by contrast, only fifty-seven fortunes derived from real estate or oil.) Ordinary people could score an inflation windfall of their own simply by buying a house. Hundreds of thousands of California and Florida bungalows, bought in the early 1960s for less than $35,000 on 5-percent mortgages, were suddenly tripling and quadrupling in value. "What sellers are asking," gasped a California magazine writer, "is sometimes staggering. A one-bedroom wooden shack in Benedict Canyon with only 22-by–26 feet of living space goes for $71,000. Why? It's located in the fashionable Beverly Hills post office district."[7] Over the three years 1972–1975, the median price of a new home in the United States jumped by nearly 50 percent. Worse than the rise in housing prices was the rise in interest rates. Baby boomers who had grown up in homes financed at 4.5 percent were by 1975 facing mortgage rates that had passed 9 percent. In 1950, seven out of ten American families could afford the monthly payments on a median-priced new home; by the end of 1975, only about four of ten families could.[8]

Working Americans were also being squeezed by surging prices of food, clothing, and fuel. The cost of meat, poultry, and fish rose by more than 40 percent between August 1972 and August 1973, so fast that steakhouse menus arrived with stacks of little white handwritten stickers over their printed prices. I remember being taken out to dinner as a boy of twelve and scraping off a little mountain of superimposed surcharges to gaze at the primordial price at the very bottom. I felt like Heinrich Schliemann, digging through the fragments of forgotten centuries to gaze at a lost world, where a ribeye with baked potato at a restaurant with red-leather banquettes cost $5.95.

Only twice in the twentieth century, 1930–1939, and 1970–79, did Americans end a decade poorer, on average, than they began it. The two slumps could not, however, have resembled each other less. Depressions induce despair; inflations fog the atmosphere with paranoia. Depressions usually originate in the disorder of private finance; inflations are produced by governments. Depressions strengthen the state; inflations discredit it.

In January 1980, consumer prices were rising at a 17-percent annual clip. The prime interest rate would touch 20 percent in April, drop, and then return and pass 20 percent in December. President Carter conceded in February 1980 that inflation was indeed reaching the "crisis stage." *Business Week*, of all publications, editorialized that the time had come for semi-permanent wage and price controls. "The U.S.," it warned, "is in danger of becoming another Brazil, with an intolerably high rate of inflation institutionalized. The result will be an end to the democratic system." Institutionalized inflation, an end to the democratic system—it all seemed sickeningly plausible. No eye could penetrate to the bottom of the 1970s economic slump. The dollar seemed to be *melting away*. It took only thirty-five of them to buy an ounce of gold in 1970, but 875 to buy an ounce in 1980. One dollar commanded more than 4 German marks and fully 360 Japanese yen in 1970. It could be exchanged for fewer than 2 German marks and barely 200 yen in 1980.

Disaster followed disaster, and the authorities stood slack-jawed, baffled, and apparently helpless. In fact, they were not nearly as helpless as they looked. The United States had consciously *chosen* to inflate its currency. It made that choice because of the political ideology and personal weakness of the men entrusted with the job of managing the American economy: their utopianism, their arrogance, and then finally their cowardice, dating back to the day that John Kennedy was elected president of the United States on a promise to "get the country moving again."

It might seem incredible now that anyone could think the country had been standing still in the 1950s, an era the Americans of the 1970s would wistfully remember as a time of almost perfect economic felicity. But the country had endured three recessions in the 1950s; the last of them, 1958–60, was the first severe and prolonged slump since the Great Depression. Making matters worse was the fear that the Soviet Union was overtaking the United States economically. That too seems incredible now. Yet the Soviets were reporting fantastic economic statistics, 10-pecent annual growth and more, and the economists of the day, who found it perfectly plausible that a centrally planned economy could function well, were impressed and frightened. Richard Crossman, the British Labour MP who edited *The God That Failed*, spoke for the Kennedy coterie when he described his anxiety over "the terrifying contrast between the drive and missionary energy of the Communist bloc and the lethargic, comfortable indolence of the Western democracies. . . . Judged in terms of national security, scientific and technological development, popular education, and, finally, even of mass living standards, free enterprise is losing out in the peaceful competition between East and West."[9] The solution, Kennedy and his advisers concluded, was to dash for faster growth by forcing U.S. interest rates down almost to zero and holding them there. "We Democrats," the party's 1960 campaign platform declared, "believe that the economy can and must grow at an average rate of 5 percent annually, almost twice as fast as our average rate since 1953. . . . As the first step in speeding economic growth, a Democratic president will put an end to the present high-interest rate, tight-money policy."[10]

Five percent growth! That is the speed of growth recorded in Third World "catch-up" countries that can import technologies and techniques from abroad, not in an industrial leader like the United States. By promising to force march the economy at a double-time pace, the Kennedy Democrats were courting trouble. Low interest rates are very pleasant, but they can also stimulate inflation. Ideally, the Federal Reserve acts like a thermostat. It lowers interest rates and injects cash into the economy during recessions, and it raises interest rates and removes cash during booms, thus preserving a stable, steady price level. But if the Federal Reserve were to continue lowering interest rates and injecting cash during a boom, cash would soon become ridiculously over-plentiful and its value would begin to tumble. The Kennedy economists foresaw this price, and were prepared to pay it. Two of the economists closest to President Kennedy, the future Nobel laureates Paul Samuelson and Robert Solow, argued in a

1960 essay that the United States should willingly accept higher inflation to accelerate growth and push unemployment toward zero. "In order to achieve the nonperfectionist's goal of high enough output to give us no more than 3 percent unemployment, the price index might have to rise by as much as 4 to 5 percent a year. That much price rise would seem to be the necessary cost of high employment and production in the years immediately ahead."[11] Samuelson and Solow believed that inflation and unemployment were opposites, like sheep and cattle. The more you had of one, the less you can have of the other. As late as 1974, when consumer prices varoomed upward by 12.2 percent while unemployment shot past 7 percent, James Tobin, another Kennedy adviser and future Nobel laureate, continued to insist that each precluded the other and that of the two, unemployment was by far the greater evil. "Our economy, like all others of the modern world, has an inflationary bias. When it operates without socially intolerable levels of unemployment and surplus capacity, prices will drift steadily upward. . . . As consolation, I can only offer my opinion that inflation is greatly exaggerated as a social evil."[12]

So the Best and the Brightest invited the inflation monster into the house. At first, he behaved himself, and unemployment dropped as promised. But by the middle 1960s, he was testing his claws on the furniture: 2 percent inflation in 1965 rose to almost 3 percent in 1966 and to more than 3 percent in 1967. Then the monster began to snarl and bite: 4 percent in 1968 and 1969. Still, the leading economic thinkers of the sixties pooh-poohed the beast's mounting rage. Unemployment had been driven down to 3.5 percent in 1969, and President Johnson, already in desperate trouble because of Vietnam and the urban race riots, refused to countenance a recession. The newly elected President Nixon felt exactly the same way. He was urged by the more conservative members of his economic team to cool off the economy before it was too late. "I remember '58," he replied. "We cooled off the economy and cooled off fifteen Senators and sixty Congressmen at the same time."[13] The president refused to act, and the monster began to smash up the house in earnest.

In the 1950s and 1960s, almost every currency in the world, with the interesting exception of the Canadian dollar, was anchored to the U.S. buck. At a rambly old resort hotel in Bretton Woods, New Hampshire, teams of economists and treasury officials from the United States and its allies had devised a new financial constitution for the planet in 1944. The currencies of the industrial democracies would be defined in terms of U.S. dollars. A Japanese yen would be worth 1/360 of a dollar, there would be 4.37 Swiss francs to the dollar, and so on. The dollar, in turn, was anchored to gold, at the rate of thirty-five dollars to the ounce. The hope of the framers of this economic constitution was to retain the best elements of the old gold standard while avoiding the panics and depressions the gold standard had so often engendered.

Bretton Woods constructed the financial equivalent of a school system without examinations. In hope of squelching the destructive speculation of the 1920s and 1930s, currencies were carefully protected from the shock of reality, from ever being forced to confront their real standing. Under the pre-1914 gold standard, an inflation in the United States would cause dollar-holders to dump dollars for gold. Under the post–1973 system of floating exchange rates, an inflation in the United States would cause the dollar to depreciate against other currencies. But under Bretton Woods, if the United States inflated, other countries were forced to choose: Either inflate at roughly the same pace as the United States, preserving the relative value of the dollar and other currencies, or else blow up an international monetary system from which they benefited much more than the United States. The Bretton Woods system rested on the unflinching willingness of the United States to uphold the integrity of the dollar. But it simultaneously created attractive incentives for American politicians not to do their duty. If those politicians inflated just a little, they could enjoy a nice (if temporary) burst of prosperity without having to worry about any slippage in the dollar on world money markets. The central bankers of Europe would all be compelled to depreciate their currencies at the same rate. As for the depreciation against gold, that too would be disguised for some time because the people who owned most of the world's dollars, America's citizens, had since 1934 been forbidden to sell those dollars to buy gold.

President Eisenhower understood Bretton Woods' temptations and sternly resisted them. He accepted three recessions over his presidency to wring out the last of the wartime inflation. In 1961, Eisenhower handed over to Kennedy a stable but sluggish economy. The national debt was under control, inflation was virtually zero, and all stood ready for sustained, noninflationary growth. Instead, Kennedy and his team reversed the old joke about the central banker "taking away the punch bowl before the party gets rowdy." Kennedy's central bankers saw it as their job to slip a couple of tablets of LSD into the punch bowl. What followed was one of the gaudiest, splashiest economic parties in American history—and one of the worst spells in the detox clinic. By 1970, the United States was clearly heading toward some kind of financial crisis. The country's gold reserves were being depleted as foreign central banks wearied of blotting up excess U.S. dollars on international markets and started demanding that the Federal Reserve buy them back. The stock market was slumping; long-term interest rates were rising. In early 1970, the Federal Reserve, now led by Nixon's friend Arthur Burns, decided that action could no longer be postponed. Burns hoisted short-term interest rates to 8.5 percent and pushed the economy into its first slump in nine years. He was trying to brake gently, to slow the inflation and defend the currency without triggering an election-losing recession. He failed.

Although the recession of 1970 was one of the mildest in history, it cost the Republicans dearly in November, just as Nixon had feared. With his own re-election campaign now only two years away, Nixon decided there could be no more recessions. Inflation would have to be contained in some other way. At the beginning of 1971, President Nixon granted a television interview to four network correspondents to announce a formal surrender. "What we're going to do first is have an expansionary budget. . . . We also, according to Dr. Arthur Burns, will have an expansionary monetary policy, and that will, of course, be a monetary policy adequate to meet the needs of an expanding economy." The complaisant Burns was good as his word. White-haired, fond of pipes and tweeds, Burns looked just the way a central banker should look. Perhaps it would have been better for the country if he had dyed his hair pink, fastened a safety pin to his nose, and come to work in black leather. In April 1971, Burns forswore any repeat of his 1970 policy, informing the Senate Banking Committee that another rise in interest rates to defend the dollar "would not meet our lasting needs at home or abroad." Still, something would have to be done. Despite the recession, consumer prices had risen at a pace of 5.9 percent in 1970. The inflation monster was now raging out of control, punching holes in the walls, ripping apart the banisters, dangling the baby out of the second-story window. With higher interest rates precluded, Burns proposed to fight inflation with wage, price, and investment controls.

Eleven years of unwillingness by Americans to discharge their Bretton Woods responsibilities had vexed and maddened all the system's members, but nobody more than inflation-chary West Germany. In May 1971, with U.S. prices rising at a rapid 7.2 percent annual rate, the West Germans announced that they had had enough, and quit the Bretton Woods system. Their government would no longer sell marks to prop up the dollar, no longer subject its people to a made-in-America inflation. The dollar must now sink to its own level. It promptly did. Over the next three months, it dropped 7.5 percent against the deutsche mark. With prices zooming, American trade unions demanded tremendous wage increases to protect their membership, and employers, counting on inflation to bail them out, amiably acceded in a series of deals announced over the summer of 1971. Copperworkers extracted 28 percent over the next three years. Aluminum and steelworkers each secured a 31-percent raise over three years. Railworkers won 42 percent over three and a half years.

In July 1971 testimony to Congress, Burns ruefully admitted that he had been working the printing presses like a New York tabloid editor with exclusive photographs of a topless starlet. The money supply had bloated by a disturbing 10 percent in the first half of the year. Quizzed by hostile Democrats, Burns conceded that perhaps he had been a little slack. But he and his master had learned their lesson in 1970. They were not interested in quieting inflation by vote-losing means. At a press conference on August 4, 1971, President Nixon mused that he had an open mind about the wage and price controls Burns was now aggressively touting. Three days later, the Bretton Woods system—badly battered by West Germany's defection—began to crack apart. On August 7, the Joint Economic Committee of Congress released a report recommending a devaluation of the dollar. On August 9, speculators blasted the Swiss franc loose from its Bretton Woods level. It climbed to 4.06 to the dollar, and the Swiss declared that they too were seceding from Bretton Woods. The dollar plunged against even the sick currencies of Europe, the Italian lire, the French franc, the British pound. Gold climbed on August 9 to $43.95 an ounce on the free London market. The Swiss traded $50 million for gold in July. The French demanded $191 million worth of gold in August. U.S. gold reserves fell to the lowest level since 1938.

The American public did not monitor the gold market, but it knew what a pound of hamburger cost. On August 9, 1971, the Harris poll reported that disapproval of Nixon's economic policies had reached a new high, 73 percent. If the election were held that day, Nixon would lose to the Democratic front-runner, Senator Ed Muskie of Maine. It was time for a bold stroke. Nixon helicoptered off to Camp David. He descended from his mountaintop on Sunday, August 15, to unveil before a national television audience the most startling change in U.S. financial policy since the Hundred Days of 1933. Prices and wages would be frozen for ninety days. Foreign governments would no longer be permitted to trade dollars for gold at thirty-five to the ounce. Foreign imports would be slapped with a 10-percent surcharge. The postwar economic order was dead. From the point of view of 2000, Nixon's grand gesture fell somewhere between folly and madness. Twenty-first century Americans believe in the free movement of prices in the way that medieval man believed in the efficacy of prayer. But the Americans of 1971 reacted to Nixon's controls ecstatically. The notion that government could control inflation not by *ending* the inflation, but by forbidding businesses and workers to notice that it existed, made good sense to them. In one of the most dramatic somersaults in polling history, the 70-plus percent disapproval rating for Nixon's economic policies of early August upended itself into a 70-plus percent approval rating in September. Left-wing economists Arthur Okun, Paul Samuelson, and John Kenneth Galbraith applauded. So, eye-openingly, did business groups like the National Association of Manufacturers, the Chamber of Commerce, and the DuPont and General Motors companies. The Dow Jones average rallied a then-appreciable thirty-three points.

The wage-and-price freeze ended in October. There followed a prolonged period of controls, which the Nixon administration called "Phase II." Companies were forbidden to raise prices and workers were denied raises unless they could convince the bureaucrats at the Cost of Living Council that the increases and raises were justified. Photographs of earnest price-controllers suddenly filled the newspapers, their youthful faces dwarfed by the five-inch collars charging south from their necklines, their pallor accentuated by the lurid orange and purple of their neckties. They spent their days in Talmudic inquiry: If a union negotiated a price or wage increase in May to go into effect in November, when did the "transaction" occur? If General Motors made a standard piece of equipment an option, had it raised the price of a car? Was honey a raw material or was it processed by bees? (Answer: a raw food.) What about popcorn? (Answer: processed.)

Controls only made sense if one believed that companies had freedom to set whatever prices they liked. The controllers soon discovered how false that assumption was. They targeted the 1,500 biggest U.S. corporations for especially vigilant supervision. Every request for an increase by those companies was carefully scrutinized to ensure that it was motivated by genuine surges in costs rather than lip-smacking greed. The flinty-eyed controllers were mostly devotees of the John Kenneth Galbraith theory of corporate wickedness. Yet of the 4,741 requests for price increases from big companies during the controls, 93 percent were approved. Baffled, Nixon resorted to another wage-price freeze, this one for sixty days, in the summer of 1973. It failed even more dismally than that of 1971.

People believe what they have seen, or, as magicians understand, what they *think* they have seen. The generation of World War II *thought* they had seen price controls work in the 1940s, and so believed in them. Those who experienced the controls of 1971 and 1973—and the oil price controls that lasted until 1981—saw them fail. And thus they learned to disbelieve.

If controls did not work, what would? The inflation hidden by the 1971 controls resurfaced in 1972. An election-minded Federal Reserve goosed the money supply faster than in any year since 1944. The extra cash was needed to finance, among other things, the huge increase in Social Security payments Nixon signed ("with very great pleasure") on October 30, eight days before the presidential ballot. The conservative economist Beryl Sprinkel, a future member of Reagan's Council on Economic Advisers, warned that Americans ought to get used to "perpetual, sizeable inflation on the order of 5 percent." Walter Heller, the chairman of John Kennedy's economic council, predicted permanent inflation in the vicinity of 4 percent. Paul Samuelson said he would be happy if inflation could be reduced to 4 percent by the end of the 1970s, but doubted that this would be possible. And all of this was *before* the oil shock of 1973.

The inflation of the 1970s is often blamed—especially by the people who happened to be on duty at the time—on Arab oil sheikhs. It is much closer to the truth to say that the oil shocks of 1973 and 1979 were themselves caused by the inflation of the 1970s. Oil prices rose in the 1970s for the same reason that the price of gold and houses and coffee rose: because the value of paper money relative to commodities was plunging. As Milton Friedman tirelessly pointed out throughout the decade, a sudden spike in the price of any single commodity will not by itself trigger inflation. If the commodity is sufficiently important, as oil is, a price spike may trigger a recession, as consumers are forced to cut back sharply on other purchases. To turn a commodity shock into a decade of inflation demands the all-out, full-time effort of dozens of hardworking public officials.

Politicians in the 1970s were usually puzzled by inflation, but they all agreed on one thing—it was somebody else's fault. President Ford believed that inflation was caused by individual over-consumption. In his "Whip Inflation Now" addresses of October 1974, he urged families to shop more wisely and spend less. To those gluttons who could not spare a morsel, he appealed, "If you can't spare a penny from your food budget, surely you can cut the food you waste by 5 percent." To discourage overeating, he asked Congress to impose a 5-percent surtax on families earning more than $15,000. Ford summoned twenty-two citizens to form a national Whip Inflation Now committee, under the chairmanship of Sylvia Porter, the personal finance columnist. Porter's committee crafted a weird reprise of the ill-fated National Recovery Act of 1934, in which private citizens pledged to stop spending their money so recklessly.

"For business people: I pledge to my customers that to the very best of my ability I will hold or reduce prices and will buy whenever possible from those who have pledged to do the same. I also pledge to be an energy saver. This signed pledge is evidence of my participation in, and support of, the WIN program.

"For consumers: I pledge to my fellow citizens that I will buy, whenever possible, only those products or services priced at or below present levels. I also promise to conserve energy and I urge others to sign the pledge.

"For workers: I pledge that I—through my union—will join with my fellow workers and my employer in seeking ways to conserve energy and eliminate waste on the job. I also promise to urge others to sign this pledge."

The quadrupling of the price of oil in 1973-74 pushed the whole world into the most severe recession since the Second World War. That would normally have sufficed to stop the inflation, and even in the 1970s it did manage to slow it. Not for long: The governments of the West chose immediate reflation. In May 1975, Arthur Burns announced that he would "err on the side of ease" in his monetary policy for 1976, as if he had not already been easy enough.[14]

Burns reignited American inflation too late to save his friend Gerald Ford. Ford's challenger, Georgia Governor James Earl Carter, campaigned as a new, sobered-up sort of Democrat. (His running mate, Walter Mondale, was a cheerfully unreconstructed liberal. In his acceptance speech at the 1976 convention Mondale disregarded the printed text, which reproduced John Kennedy's exhortation to get the country moving again, and blurted out instead what he really thought: "Let's get this *government* moving again!") In office, Carter reverted to type, spending wildly and then trying to control the inevitable inflation with price controls. He asked

Congress to enact new controls on consumer prices, on energy, and on medicine. The Democratic Congress eagerly accepted his spending proposals, but rebuffed his controls.

If American maturity was the favorite cliché of the writers of the 1950s, W. B. Yeats's "Second Coming" was the favorite of the 1970s. "Things fall apart; the center cannot hold; Mere anarchy is loosed upon the world . . ." In the first year of Carter's presidency, the dollar plunged by more than 25 percent against the Swiss franc and more than 13 percent against the German mark. In July 1977, gold passed the $200-an-ounce level for the first time. Still the dollar plunged.

1978. Consumer prices were now rising at 12 percent a year—as fast as during the first oil shock.

1979. Gold broke $300 in July and ended the year at $524. Consumer prices rose by 13 percent in twelve months; after-tax, after-inflation wages dropped by an average of 5 percent in 1979. The general price level had doubled in only eight years. The United States dropped to eighth place in income per-capita among the countries of the Organization for Economic Cooperation and Development, behind Norway.

1980. Gold passed $600 on January 3; $700 on January 15; $750 on January 17; $800 on January 18; $875 on January 21. That month, consumer prices rose at an annualized rate of 16 percent.

The decade was ending in what looked and felt like economic apocalypse. It was no excitable hysteric, but the reserved Alan Greenspan, then chairman of the Council of Economic Advisers, who told Congress at the decade's midpoint, "Capitalism is in crisis." The United States, Greenspan said, had arrived at "the point of discontinuity," a point at which it was obliged to choose either to turn back toward the principles of a market economy or to proceed forward toward something ominous and unprecedented.

"OUR INORDINATE FEAR OF COMMUNISM"

FOR A BRIEF MOMENT, IT LOOKED AS IF AMERICA MIGHT ACTUALLY HAVE WON its war in Vietnam. The moment was April 1972, sixty days before the Watergate break-in.

In the month of terrible fighting in January 1968 known as the Tet Offensive, the Viet Cong guerillas had learned for themselves the fearful lesson learned by the Chinese and North Koreans fifteen years before: It is not a smart move for Third World peasants to hurl themselves at the machine guns and helicopters of the U.S. Army. Even fierce critics of the war, like Neil Sheehan of the *New York Times*, conceded that after Tet, "[l]arge sections of the [Mekong] Delta acquired a tranquility that was spoiled only once in a while by shooting. Bridges were repaired and long-closed roads and canals reopened. The farmers who had stayed on the land or returned to it thrived. . . . [T]elevision antennas [were] appearing on the roofs of the bigger farmhouses."[15] But while the guerillas had been shattered, the regular North Vietnamese Army preserved itself intact and formidable, just beyond America's reach. And America's reach was receding. By spring 1972, only some 95,000 Americans were left in Vietnam, down from more than half a million when Richard Nixon took office. More than a thousand of those remaining troops were departing for home each week. If the North Vietnamese attacked, America would fight from the air, but the job of meeting the enemy on the ground would have to be shouldered by the Army of the Republic of Vietnam. Whether South Vietnam could survive under those circumstances had been an open question. The fighting of April 1972 closed it.

On March 30, 1972, the North Vietnamese Army struck. This was no guerilla operation. This was real war, with tanks, Soviet-supplied anti-aircraft missiles, and carefully coordinated infantry formations, all aimed at the supposedly hopelessly corrupt and inept army of the south. But even men led by rotten officers will do heroic things in defense of their homes, so long as they hold some hope of winning. Equipped by the departing Americans with vast stores of equipment, ammunition, food, and fuel, the Southern army gave ground but did not break. In the open field, the North Vietnamese Army made an easy target for American warplanes and their new "smart" bombs. The campaign turned into a gigantic trap, with the south's army as the bait and American B-52s the snapping bar. A B-52 attack killed men by the hundreds; those it did not kill were buried under thirty feet of dirt; and those who somehow escaped burial staggered out of their craters dazed, deaf, and helpless. "[S]lowly, despairingly, the Communist soldiers had to give way and withdraw, leaving thousands of their comrades on the battlefield. . . . "[16]

The April 1972 offensive proved that South Vietnam could defend its independence without American ground troops—which was more than could have been said at the time for, say, West Germany—*if* it could count on American aid and airpower. When Henry Kissinger initialed the U.S.-North Vietnam peace agreement of January 1973, he promised South Vietnam that the aid would be forthcoming and warned the North that so too would the airpower if the North should violate its commitment to pursue reunification with the South only by "peaceful means."

Those promises and threats did not count for much for long. In March 1973, the arrested Watergate burglars, menaced with decades-long prison sentences by Judge John Sirica, agreed to finger their higher-ups. In April, John Dean testified to the Senate Watergate Committee, and Nixon's two top aides, H. R. Haldeman and John Ehrlichman, resigned. A Gallup poll at the end of April found that Nixon's popularity had slipped below 50 percent for the first time in two years. The antiwar faction in Congress had long before made up its mind to seek peace in Indochina at any price. At last it could force that policy on the Nixon administration. "The so-called peace movement," Kissinger acidly comments in his memoirs, "had evolved from seeking an end of the war to treating America's frustrations in Indochina as symptoms of a moral degeneration that needed to be eradicated root and branch. . . . The total collapse of non-communist Indochina, which three American administrations had striven to prevent in the name of national security and honor, was, for this group, nothing less than a desirable national catharsis."[17] In June 1973, Senators Frank Church of Idaho and Clifford Case of New Jersey wrote into the fiscal 1974 budget an amendment forbidding the use of any American forces "in or over" Indochina, stripping away the guarantee of American air support if South Vietnam were attacked again.

By late 1973, North Vietnam was visibly preparing to attack again. Some 70,000 men and 400 tanks were being smuggled into the South; satellites detected the construction of a new military supply road from the North. Despite that ominous news, Congress chopped military aid to South Vietnam from $2.1 billion in fiscal 1973 to $1.1 billion in 1974 and $700 million in 1975—this while the price of petroleum was quadrupling. Commanders had to ration bullets. Artillery stopped firing. Trucks ceased moving. The South Vietnamese air force was grounded. When the Pentagon's accountants tried to use a couple of hundred million dollars of unused appropriations left over from 1972 and 1973 to aid the South Vietnamese, Edward Kennedy mobilized a 43–38 Senate vote to forbid the expenditure. Giving South Vietnam the money it needed to survive, he said, "would perpetuate an involvement that should have ended long ago."

Defense Secretary James Schlesinger plaintively argued that South Vietnam deserved something better than "a retroactive punishment for our having gotten involved in the war on their side. If we continue to give them support and they fail to survive, that's a different issue than pulling the support out from under them. It is unworthy of us, in my judgment, to behave on this issue in such a niggling manner."[18] But the House was more persuaded by the argument of Representative Bob Giaimo of Connecticut that cutting the South's aid budget would force it to quit provoking the North.

In August 1974, the month of Nixon's resignation, the North Vietnamese had begun tentatively to test South Vietnamese defenses around Danang and near Saigon. This time, they encountered comparatively feeble resistance from the weakened forces of the South. In January, President Ford pleaded with Congress to grant an extra $300 million in emergency aid for South Vietnam. He made a specially eloquent personal appeal for an extra $222 million for Cambodia: "Are we to deliberately abandon a small country in the midst of its life-and-death struggle? Is the United States, which so far has consistently stood by its friends throughout the most difficult of times, now to condemn, in effect, a small Asian nation totally dependent upon us?" The short answer to that question was yes. In a hearing before the House Foreign Affairs Committee, Acting Secretary of State Robert Ingersoll asked Representative Donald Fraser of Minnesota if he were really demanding that the Lon Nol government surrender to the Khmer Rouge. "Yes," replied Fraser, "under controlled circumstances to minimize the loss of life."[19]

By now, the South Vietnamese army was staggering. Forces that had been trained for a decade by American advisers to move rapidly, to defend themselves with overwhelming firepower, and never to advance without air support now found themselves meting out a few dozen bullets per man per day, putting a gallon or two of gas in their Jeeps, and fighting blind because their airplanes had been grounded by lack of fuel. On March 20, 1975, the day the exhausted South Vietnamese army evacuated the central highlands, Senators Adlai Stevenson III of Illinois and Charles McC. Mathias of Maryland introduced legislation requiring termination of all aid to South Vietnam by June 30. American aid, they warned, was encouraging South Vietnam to stretch out the fighting.

Terrified Cambodians fled toward Phnom Penh from the homicidal lunatics of the Khmer Rouge. Tens of thousands of South Vietnamese poured Saigon-wards. Ford appeared before a joint session of Congress on April 10 to beg for a last infusion of the arms and fuel needed at least to mount a defense of the refugee-swollen capitals. Phillip Burton blasted Ford's request as "an outrage" and stomped out in the middle of his speech. Other Democrats made the same point less flamboyantly. No further help could be expected from the United States. On April 12, 1975, the eighty-two Americans remaining in Phnom Penh were airlifted out. The ambassador, John Gunther Dean, offered to evacuate the leading figures in the Cambodian government as well. "To our astonishment and shame," recalls Henry Kissinger, "the vast majority refused, including Lon Nol's brother, Lon Non, and Premier Long Boret, both of whom were on the Khmer Rouge's published death list." Sirik Matak, a former Cambodian prime minister, sent his refusal in a note "handwritten in elegant French":

"Dear Excellency and Friend:

"I thank you very sincerely for your letter and for your offer to transport me towards freedom. I cannot, alas, leave in such a cowardly fashion. As for you, and in particular for your great country, I never believed for a moment that you would have this sentiment of abandoning a people which has chosen liberty. You have refused us your protection, and we can do nothing about it.

"You leave, and my wish is that you and your country will find happiness under this sky. But, mark it well, that if I shall die here on this spot and in my country that I love, it is no matter, because we all are born and must die. I have only committed this mistake of believing in you.

"Please accept, Excellency and dear friend, my faithful and friendly sentiments." Matak, Kissinger tersely notes, was shot in the stomach and left without medical care. It took him three days to die.[20]

Hawks in the late 1960s wore T-shirts printed with the Stars and Stripes and underneath the motto "This flag doesn't run." But if it did not run on April 30, 1975, it was folded, tucked underneath the arm of U.S. Ambassador Graham Martin, and evacuated. Great nations sometimes lose wars. But to deny a one-time ally arms and fuel for fear that it might keep on fighting; to insist, not just on disentanglement, which was reasonable, but on actively throttling that ally, this went beyond defeat, to disgrace. "The South Vietnamese can blame only themselves for their present situation," G. V. "Sonny" Montgomery, representative from Mississippi and one of the last of the Democratic hawks, declared on the floor of the House on April 7, 1975. His words would have rung less false had the United States in fact continued to give the South Vietnamese the tools they needed to do the job. Even warlike Israel would have lost its war in 1973 had it not been resupplied after the first week of fighting. But there would be no airlift for South Vietnam. Americans had decided that the country's demise was foreordained and therefore the faster it died, the better. It mattered not at all that the South Vietnamese might feel differently.

Over the more than twenty years from the death of FDR to Tet, American politics had been governed by a strong consensus on foreign policy. That consensus did not preclude rancorous disagreement and vicious partisan battle, but the scuffles were fought over a remarkably narrow terrain. Vietnam destroyed that consensus, throwing the American political system open to ideas and ideologies until then barred from power: William F. Buckley's crusading anticommunism, George McGovern's fellow-traveling appeasement. (At a meeting on June 28, 1972, with South Carolina's delegation to the Democratic national convention, McGovern was incredulously asked, "You want us to do all they demand and then beg them to give back our boys?" He replied, "I'll accept that. Begging is better than bombing.")

Not since the 1930s had such wildly disparate factions struggled for intellectual power. Depression-vintage communism was rehabilitated. Two of the decade's most bankable film stars, Barbra Streisand and Robert Redford, co-starred in 1973's *The Way We Were*, the story of a grand passion between a liberal screenwriter and his Communist girlfriend, and how it was severed by the terrors of McCarthyism. The hauntingly sentimental title song won an Academy Award. Academy Awards went to sentimentalists about contemporary Communism too. Three weeks before Saigon fell, the Oscar for best documentary was awarded to *Hearts and Minds*, an account of the Vietnam War so sympathetic to the North Vietnamese point of view that directors Peter Davis and Bert Schneider read a telegram of greeting from the Viet Cong in lieu of an acceptance speech. (Frank Sinatra later stepped out to disassociate the Academy from their remarks.) Lillian Hellman published her memoir of the anticommunist investigations of the 1950s, *Scoundrel Time*, in which she described how the committee room exploded into applause when she uttered her immortal words, "I cannot and will not cut my conscience to suit this year's fashion." Both remark and the applause were wholly fictitious, as were the stories of her heroics inside Nazi Germany that she described in her novel *Julia*. *Julia* was nonetheless filmed and nominated for Best Picture in 1978. Hellman got the tap to appear in an ad for mink coats over the manufacturer's trademark headline, "What becomes a legend most?" A new generation of historians vindicated Stalin's American apologists. In a 1977 book, *The Romance of American Communism,* Vivian Gornick used the methods of oral history to present American Communists as regular folks, well within the bounds of political normality. Gornick's work inspired a battery of imitators. Even spies and traitors were rehabilitated. The Massachusetts Supreme Court ordered Alger Hiss readmitted to the bar in 1975, the first debarred lawyer to be readmitted in the history of the Bay State. The court said Hiss had demonstrated his "moral and intellectual fitness."

The upper reaches of the Democratic party concluded in the 1970s that ideological anticommunism had led the country to disaster: "[W]e are now free of that inordinate fear of Communism which once led us to embrace any dictator who joined us in our fear," President Carter declared in a 1977 Notre Dame commencement address, and his party and his administration gave life to these words by refusing to react to the rapidly growing reach of Soviet power. Mozambique, Angola, and Ethiopia in Africa all slid under Marxist, pro-Soviet rule in the year 1975, and a Democratic Congress prevented the Ford administration from intervening to stop it. The American-built base at Cam Ranh Bay in Vietnam was taken over by the Soviet navy. So was the old British base in South Yemen, the best port in the vicinity of the Persian Gulf. East German advisers and Cuban soldiers were airlifted into Ethiopia to win that country's 1977 war against Somalia, and there they stayed, just across the Red Sea from Saudi Arabia. A pro-Cuban guerrilla force blasted its way into power in Nicaragua in 1979; another nearly conquered El Salvador in 1980. In 1979, a Soviet army swooped into Afghanistan, the most blatant Soviet aggression since the invasion of Finland in 1940. The Soviets began deploying a highly accurate mobile missile, the SS-20, in the mid-1970s, for the first time credibly threatening the cities of Western Europe with nuclear annihilation. The Ford administration, like a man in a nightmare, had tried to react, but could not move through the congressional goo. The Carter administration disdained even to try.

Instead, Carter set out to win Soviet goodwill by allaying Soviet fears. In June 1977 he announced that he was scrapping the B–1 bomber program without asking for any reciprocal Soviet concession. Two weeks later, Carter stepped to the president's rostrum to tell the assembled press that the neutron bomb program he had been pressing upon the NATO allies would also be cancelled. (He had given German chancellor Helmut Schmidt no advance warning of this sudden about-face, the origin of Schmidt's later-to-be-conspicuous contempt for him.) Carter confessed himself to be surprised by the continuing "unfriendly rhetoric" emanating from Moscow despite all his efforts to placate the Kremlin. He could only guess, he said, that the "Soviets perhaps have some political reasons for spelling out or exaggerating the disagreements." Nevertheless, he promised, "Calm and persistent and fair negotiations with the Soviet Union will ultimately lead to increased relationships with them." Carter's eagerness to befriend the Soviets did produce at least one positive result, although a completely unintended one. The outcome of the 1973 Arab-Israel war had convinced Anwar Sadat that, as he told a Kuwaiti newspaper in September 1975, the existence of Israel was "an established fact." In 1974 Sadat broke with the Arab world's thirty-year prohibition on face-to-face talks with Israel, chucked his Soviet military advisers out of his country, and opened American-brokered negotiations. Carter, however, insisted on including the Soviets in the talks. This so alarmed Sadat that he seized the initiative himself. Thus began the breathtaking diplomacy that led to Sadat's historic flight to Jerusalem and the Camp David deal of 1978.

Carter did not disdain ideology in general. His administration's commitment to toppling the governments of South Africa and Rhodesia was a much *more* ideological policy than Ronald Reagan's anticommunism, which was directed only against regimes that posed a threat to the United States. What Carter did set his face against, however, was any ideology that prodded the United States to take a harder line against its enemies. In February 1979, at the very moment at which the Ayatollah Khomeini was solidifying his rule over Iran, President Carter deplored "the temptation to see all changes as inevitably against the interests of the United States, as a kind of loss for us or a victory for 'them.' . . . We need to see what is happening not in terms of simplistic colors of black and white, but in more subtle shades."

But sometimes black and white are the colors of truth. As Aleksandr Solzhenitsyn lamented in his Nobel address, belatedly published in Stockholm in August 1972, the "civilized world has found nothing with which to oppose the onslaught of a sudden revival of barefaced barbarity, other than concessions and smiles." Europe and America were gripped by a "sickness of the will." Those afflicted in this way "elect passivity and retreat, just so as their accustomed life might drag on a bit longer, just so as not to step over the threshold of hardship today—and tomorrow, you'll see, it will be all right. (But it will never be all right! The price of cowardice will only be evil.)" Another gallant Soviet dissident, Andrei Sakharov, won the Nobel Peace Prize in 1975. His defiance of the police and prisons of the Soviet regime cast a rather squalid light on those Americans who insisted in the press and the corridors of power that the regime was too powerful to be confronted and must therefore be accommodated. The first volume of Solzhenitsyn's *Gulag Archipelago* was translated into English in 1974, and the continuing truth of its terrible message was horrifyingly confirmed by the postwar agonies of Indochina. Between 1975 and 1978, at least half a million people fled Vietnam. What happened in Cambodia the entire world now knows. Back in 1975, George McGovern had proposed that the United States pay the passage of any Vietnamese who wanted to return to his country: Once things settled down, McGovern predicted, almost 90 percent of the boat people would opt to go back. By 1978, McGovern was calling for a U.S. invasion of Cambodia to overthrow the Khmer Rouge.

Liberal anticommunism expired in Vietnam. Liberal anti-anticommunism was drowned in the South China Sea and hacked to death in the slaughter pits of Cambodia. The Democrats who had led the country into the Vietnam War, and then finished South Vietnam off in 1975, lost the presidency in 1968 and went on to lose four of the five next presidential elections.

THE MORAL EQUIVALENT OF WAR

THE MODERN WORLD IS FUELED BY DECAYED SEA SCUM. FOR HALF A BILLION years before man first walked, plankton died and sank to the bottom of ancient oceans, to be covered by shifting sand and decomposed into gunky sludge. The mysterious processes of geology encased the sludge in underground cavities, preserving it as a viscous liquid: oil. There it waited, quadrillions and quadrillions of tons of goo, for men to find it, imagine uses for it, and then—through the even more mysterious processes of mass hysteria—terrify themselves that they were running out of it.

Sixty years almost to the day that Woodrow Wilson asked Congress for a declaration of war against Germany, April 18, 1977, another southern Democrat appeared on the nation's television screens to declare the energy crisis "the moral equivalent of war." The stark fact, President Carter intoned, was that "the oil and natural gas we rely on for 75 percent of our energy are simply running out." "Each new inventory of world oil reserves has been more disturbing than the last. World oil production can probably keep going up for another six or eight years. But some time in the 1980s it can't go up any more. Demand will overtake production. We have no choice about that." And things were only going to get worse. "If we do not act, then by 1985 we will be using 33 percent more energy than today. Within ten years, we would not be able to import enough oil—from any country, at any acceptable price."

Carter intended to act. The new president was sending to Congress a comprehensive plan for taxing foreign oil, regulating the price of domestic oil and natural gas, subsidizing alternative energy, rationing fuel, and regulating the wattage of toaster-ovens and the temperatures of office buildings. Carter understood that his plan would be controversial. But unless Congress accepted it, he warned, "We will face an economic, social, and political crisis that will threaten our free institutions."

Who could doubt him? By the end of the 1970s the jig seemed more or less up for the American way of life. The number one nonfiction best-seller on the *New York Times*'s list in the fall of 1978 was Barbara Tuchman's book about the calamitous fourteenth century, *A Distant Mirror*, which offered readers the grim consolation that things had been even worse during the Black Death. "The era of growth is over and the era of limits is upon us," a prominent economist told readers of the *Times*. "It means the whole politics of the country has changed. All problems have become distributional. We already see it in a whole set of divisive tendencies: blacks versus Jews, men versus women, and the whole debate over energy policy . . . "[21] What Americans worried about, energy producers gloated over. "The industrial world will have to realize that the era of their terrific progress and even more terrific income and wealth based on cheap fuel is finished," the Shah of Iran said in December 1974. "They will have to find new sources of energy and tighten their belts."

The oil and gas shortages of the 1970s inspired a vast collective end-of-the-universe feeling among Americans and Europeans, a certainty that the good times were over, that the Last Trump had truly sounded. In 1972, a conclave of economists and businessmen led by an Italian social scientist published *The Limits to Growth*, a book whose title would give a slogan to the decade. The book itself was silly. It simply plotted the inflation-driven upward trend in the price of raw materials of the previous few years and extrapolated it unthinkingly into the future.[22] What was brilliant was the byline the publishers chose for themselves: the Club of Rome. Rome! With its triple associations of the ruin of a great republic, mystery and infallibility, and revelation and apocalypse, *Rome* was a word that resonated in the American mind. Had the publishers of *The Limits to Growth* called themselves "the Club of Glasgow" or "the Club of Hamburg," it's doubtful they would have achieved equal success. The Clubmen of Rome avoided that blooper, and when gasoline ran short at American filling stations in the summer of 1972, millions of ordinary Americans began to wonder whether those conclaved anonymous wise men in the Eternal City might not know something.

They didn't. The energy shortage was not inflicted on man by nature, but by his own illusions and mistakes. It had nothing to do with geology, and everything to do with economics. It was created by government interference with the marketplace, prolonged by government's attempts to alleviate it, and vanished the very instant government stopped trying to cure it. As M. A. Adelman, an oil economist who in the hysterical 1970s correctly predicted the energy bust of the mid-1980s, has elegantly put it, oil reserves are "no gift of nature. They [are] a growth of knowledge, paid for by heavy investment." The world's oil is not like the world's supply of an old master's paintings: There are precisely thirty-three of them and if one were to be destroyed, only thirty-two would remain. The world's supply of oil is more like a supermarket's supply of canned tomatoes. At any given moment, there may be a dozen cases in the store, but that inventory is constantly being replenished with the money the customers pay for the cans they remove—and the more tomatoes that customers buy, the bigger an inventory the store will carry.

That may seem to fly utterly in the face of common sense, but it corresponds to the facts. In 1930, the United States possessed proven reserves of some 13 billion barrels of oil. Those 13 billion barrels were the stock with which the country fought World War II, energized the postwar consumer boom, and fueled all those cars idling in traffic jams in high-school documentaries about the energy shortage. Sixty years later, how much of that 13-billion-barrel reserve do you suppose was left? The answer: In 1990, the lower forty-eight American states, omitting Alaska and Hawaii, had proven reserves of 17 billion barrels of oil, 25 percent *more* than in 1930. The same calculation can be performed for the Persian Gulf. In 1975, in the darkest days of the energy crisis, the Persian Gulf was authoritatively reported to contain some 74 billion barrels of oil. This was, Americans were ominously told, "only" enough to fuel the world for a few more decades, whereupon everyone would freeze in the dark. After two decades of frantic pumping, how much of that 74 billion was still there? Answer, as of 1993: 663 billion barrels, *nine* times as much as twenty years before.

But for oil supplies to keep pace with demand, prices must be permitted to move freely. This the American leaders of the 1970s could not bring themselves to tolerate. When the Arab oil embargo struck in October 1973,

President Nixon quickly named William Simon, a New York financier, as his "energy czar."[23] As Simon recalled in his memoirs, Nixon granted him absolute authority: "I was to decide everything and to decide it rapidly. He equated our energy crisis to the kind of problem one has in wartime, and he likened the job he was giving me to that of Albert Speer in the Third Reich when he was put in charge of German armaments. Nixon told the Cabinet that if not for the power that Hitler had given Speer to override the German bureaucracy, Germany would have been defeated far earlier."[24] That might seem a rather unnerving parallel, but in 1973 it came quite naturally. A conservative like Nixon might praise free markets to the Republican faithful, meaning that he disliked excessive taxation and interference in business. In an emergency, however, even conservatives reverted to the tools and techniques of the 1940s: rationing, controls, planning. As a sign of the times, the national debate topic set for the country's high-school students in 1976 was "Resolved: An international organization ought to allocate all scarce resources."

Nixon's 1971 price controls had almost immediately been imitated by other industrial countries like Britain, France, and Italy. While most of those controls were soon lifted or relaxed, controls on the price of oil were not. Controls never work well, and controls on the price of internationally traded raw materials function especially badly. Unfortunately, the Americans of the early 1970s had a hard time recognizing oil as an internationally traded commodity. Even in 1970, the United States still produced more oil than any other country: 87 percent of the oil Americans burned was drawn from American wells. Maybe the price of oil pumped in Saudi Arabia and sold in Italy lay beyond the reach of the U.S. president, Americans thought. But surely the price of oil pumped in Texas and sold in California could be set in Washington?

As we now know, no, it cannot. Queues began appearing at American gasoline stations in the summer of 1972, as Nixon's controls dampened production and discouraged people from figuring out ways to use the stuff more efficiently. The queues stretched even farther in the summer of 1973.

Controls were the main reason that the Persian Gulf, which had provided less than 20 percent of the world's oil in 1960, was providing 36 percent by 1973. With the price of gasoline held artificially low, it made short-term narrow sense simply to pump from the fields already in production. If controls made the oil cartel of the 1970s possible, Vietnam made it thinkable. Until the late 1960s, oil-producing governments had good reason to worry about how the Western countries might react to any attempt to put a thumb on their energy windpipe. The CIA in 1953 toppled an Iranian prime minister who had attempted to nationalize that country's oil industry. Mexico had nationalized its oil industry in 1938 and had been cut off from foreign technology and capital. A British fleet still patrolled the Persian Gulf. More immediately, the oil-producing countries did not have their hands on the oil switch. They *owned* the oil, yes, but they had leased the right to pump it to foreign multinational companies. If they ordered the companies to halt pumping, it was by no means certain that the companies would obey.

After 1970, however, both those anxieties troubled the oil producers a lot less. The 1970s were the heyday of Third World state ownership. Zambia, the world's second-most important copper exporter, nationalized its mines in 1969; first-place Chile followed after Salvador Allende took power. In his 1975 year-end television interview, Canadian Prime Minister Pierre Trudeau—a man who so admired the Third World that he apparently aspired to have his country join it—announced that the "free enterprise system" has not worked "in more than thirty years." A report by the Organization of American States on the tenth anniversary of the Alliance for Progress recommended that the United States reconcile itself to a socialist path for Latin America. Why should oil producers feel bashful about imitating these distinguished precedents?

There would be much moaning in the 1970s by Arab governments and their many paid and unpaid sympathizers in the West about the supposed injustice inflicted by the oil multinationals upon the oil-producing countries. It is hard to see much merit to the case. In 1970, about 80 percent of the difference between the cost of producing Middle Eastern oil and its contractual price was pocketed by local governments.[25] It was the oil companies that found the oil, the oil companies that invented the technology that brought the oil to the surface, oil companies that preserved and extended the useful lives of the fields, the oil companies that built the pipelines, refineries, and docks that brought the oil to market. The only contribution of the locals was to have had the good luck to have parked their tents atop a raw material that Western ingenuity had found uses for. Still, few human delusions are quite as universal as the conviction that one is underpaid, and when the opportunity arose to correct the situation the oil producers pounced.

In February 1971, Algeria nationalized 51 percent of the French oil concessions in the former French colony. It seized the gas pipelines as well. Compensation was promised, at a rate to be determined by the Algerians. A nervous pause—but France did not retaliate. Libya expropriated the British Petroleum concession in December 1971, again with compensation to be settled unilaterally. Another pause—but again no retaliation. Audacious Iraq was the first to tweak the United States. It seized a U.S.-owned concession in June 1972. A *very* nervous pause this time—but once more, no retaliation.

Well, then! It was safe. In a March 1971 interview with the columnist C. L. Sulzberger, President Nixon said, "I seriously doubt if we will ever have another war. This [Vietnam] is probably the very last one."[26] Between 1968 and 1973, the proportion of college-age youth who described themselves as willing to fight to defend America's national interests dropped from 54 percent to 34 percent; the proportion willing to fight to maintain America's power in the world dropped from 35 percent to 23 percent.[27] In July 1971, the Senate voted to repeal the resolution passed in 1955 authorizing the president to use force to defend Taiwan from aggression. American power was ebbing especially quickly in and around the eastern Mediterranean. Libya's new dictator, Muammar al-Qaddafi, ordered the American air force base in his country closed in 1969. Malta expelled NATO naval forces from its magnificent harbor in the summer of 1971. The British fleet in the Persian Gulf was called home at the end of that year.

At dawn on October 6, 1973, the Jewish religious holiday of Yom Kippur, the armies of Egypt and Syria invaded Israel. Taken by surprise, Israel's armies retreated, and for a few days it seemed possible that the Arabs might make good their perennial threat to snuff out the Jewish state.

But the tide of war quickly turned: Within two weeks, Israeli tanks were nearing the suburbs of Damascus and Cairo, and an entire Egyptian army was surrounded in the Sinai desert, dependent on Israeli mercy even for its water.

Indignant, Egypt and Syria's oil-rich patrons announced an oil embargo of the United States and the Netherlands and sharp reductions in their total production. Frenzy, pandemonium, hysteria gripped the oil markets for the next ninety days. The price of oil rocketed from $3 a barrel to $12. State governments across the country asked consumers not to put up Christmas lights to save fuel. The state of Oregon banned decorative and commercial lighting altogether. Mike Mansfield, the leader of the Democratic majority in the U.S. Senate, and David Rockefeller, chairman of the Chase Manhattan Bank, called for a national gasoline-rationing program. Senator William Proxmire of Wisconsin explained in a near-hysterical national television address: "We need it [rationing] now. It would provide some gas at present prices to everyone with a car and enough heating oil to keep from freezing in every home."

Nixon rejected that advice, but in an address to the nation on November 25, 1973, he proposed the next closest thing. He announced that he would ask Congress for authority to control all fuel shipments. In the meantime, he was asking refiners voluntarily to concentrate on producing heating fuel and filling stations to refrain from selling gasoline on Saturday nights or on Sundays. More than 90 percent of the nation's 220,000 gas stations patriotically honored the president's request, provoking massive weekday lineups. Congress granted Nixon complete control over the nation's fuel supply on November 27.

At this, the United States was escaping lightly. Britain, Germany, Switzerland, Denmark, and Norway banned driving, boating, and flying on Sundays. Street lamps were dimmed across the European continent, factories slowed, fuel deliveries to private homes slashed. Sweden rationed heating oil as well as gasoline. The Dutch voted prison penalties for anyone who defied the restrictions on the use of electricity. Britain's trade unions chipped in in their inimitable way: As the country reeled from the oil embargo, the coal miners went out on strike and the railway workers followed, disrupting fuel deliveries to demand higher wages. In a message to the British people, Prime Minister Edward Heath warned, "We shall have a harder Christmas than we have known since the war" and implored his fellow-citizens to heat only one room in their homes.

The shaken governments of Europe decided that the Arabs were the new masters of the earth, and anyone who wanted to keep driving had better truckle to them. In January 1977, French immigration officers intercepted a disembarking passenger on a Beirut-Paris flight. He had flown into Charles de Gaulle Airport on an Iraqi passport under an assumed name, but French police had been tipped off to his true identity: He was Abu Daoud, a close associate of Yasser Arafat and the author of one of the most horrifying of the decade's many terrorist outrages, the massacre of the Israeli Olympic team at Munich in September 1972. The arrest was a rare and welcome triumph for anti-terrorist law enforcement. But soon something disquieting occurred. Strange unsourced stories appeared in the newspapers under Paris datelines: The French government was furious at its police, who had, it was said, failed to inform the political authorities of their intention to arrest Daoud. Iraq, Libya, and the Palestine Liberation Organization protested the arrest, contending that Daoud had been traveling to a funeral of a PLO comrade and was therefore entitled to diplomatic immunity. The French hastily rebuffed a West German extradition request, claiming that the required forms had not been filled in properly. Then, before the Germans could amend their request, they slipped Daoud onto a plane bound for Algeria and whisked him out of the country. He had spent all of four days in jail. The message could not have been clearer: *France was scared.* One of the five nuclear powers of the world, a permanent member of the U.N. Security Council, dared not bring a killer to justice. France was not alone. Between January 1972 and January 1974, European police forces apprehended fifty suspected Arab terrorists. Of those fifty, only seven ever saw the inside of a prison. *Thirty-six* were released in response to threats, direct or implied.[28]

At the behest of the oil states, the PLO's leader, Yasser Arafat, was invited to speak from the U.N.'s rostrum in 1974—the first and only man to address the General Assembly with a holster on his hip, although frantic last-minute negotiations persuaded him to leave the gun it normally contained at home. In 1975 (on, as it happened, the thirty-seventh anniversary of the Nazi *Kristallnacht*), the U.N. General Assembly voted by a 70–35 margin in favor of Resolution 3375, declaring Zionism "a form of racism." Daniel Patrick Moynihan, America's representative at the U.N., resoundingly condemned the resolution. The United States, he said, "does not acknowledge, it will not abide by, it will never acquiesce in this infamous act." The chairmen of the oil companies, however, would from time to time deliver speeches suggesting that it would be wise to do so.

On the other hand, the country was not ready to take the alternative step of trusting its energy future to the market rather than the goodwill of the sheikhs. Instead, William Simon and his bureaucrats drew up comprehensive plans to allocate the nation's supply of price-controlled domestic oil among its millions of clamoring users. It was an impossible job, and in the end the controllers simply assigned each state the same proportion of the nation's total fuel supply that it had used in 1972, the last "normal" year. So, if Massachusetts consumed 4 percent of the nation's heating oil in February 1972, it got 4 percent of the smaller amount available in February 1974. In states where the population was stable or shrinking, the allocation was more or less adequate. Where the population was growing fast—California, New Jersey, Georgia, northern Virginia—motorists were obliged to line up for two and three hours to fill up. The American Automobile Association reported that 20 percent of the nation's gas stations had no fuel for sale in the final week of February 1974 (fuel ran shortest at the end of the month, when the allocations were drawn down) in the fast-growing Southeast, 36 percent of stations lacked supplies.

Violence erupted on the highways in December 1973, as truckers launched a two-day strike to protest what they regarded as an insufficient allotment for their industry. In Ohio and Pennsylvania, striking truckers fired guns at trucks that did not honor the strike. Non-striking trucks were blown up by bombs in Arkansas and vandalized at truck stops elsewhere in the country.

The more glaringly controls failed, the more truculently Congress demanded they be tightened. President Ford, a much more committed free-marketeer than Nixon, proposed one decontrol measure after another, but the enormous Democratic congressional majority swatted them down. At a joint press conference held in July 1975, three Democratic presidential aspirants—Senators Ernest Hollings of South Carolina, Edward Kennedy of Massachusetts, and Henry Jackson of Washington—savagely denounced Ford's attempt to free oil prices. Decontrol would inflict "economic chaos" and "catastrophe," warned Hollings. It would produce "no additional oil," Kennedy predicted, only higher prices, interest rates, and unemployment. By proposing decontrol, Jackson said, Ford was "working hand in hand with the major oil companies to push the price of oil up and up and up."[29]

But even as Hollings, Kennedy, and Jackson were speechifying, the oil crisis was subsiding. Higher prices, as they always do, curbed demand and called forth new supply. In 1970, the average car on the road got 13.5 miles per gallon. By 1985, average car mileage had risen to 17.4 miles per gallon.[30] The business pages filled up with reports of new finds: in Mexico, in the Spratly Islands, in the North Sea, in the oil sands of Alberta and in Wyoming. The inflation-adjusted price of oil arched back to earth: Between the beginning of 1974 and the end of 1978, the price of an ounce of gold more than doubled, from $75 to $200. The price of a barrel of oil, meanwhile, held constant at the $12 mark.

If the oil crisis was ebbing, however, the energy crisis was not. Not content with immobilizing Americans, the energy controllers were now freezing them. The price of natural gas in the interstate market had been regulated back in the 1950s, and the inflation of the 1970s had left it dangerously out of whack with reality. In fact, even to call it a "price" was wildly overoptimistic. Twenty years of hard bureaucratic toil had produced an awe-inspiring jumble of prices that ranged from 4 cents per thousand cubic feet to $1.50, depending on the vintage of the gas, the location from which it was extracted, and the market into which it was sold. This was not a regime calculated to encourage anyone to go out and find new gas, and by 1976 America was burning up natural gas faster than explorers were replacing it. The 237 trillion cubic feet of proven reserves on the country's books in 1974 shrank to only 203 trillion in 1978. As usual, the failure of one battery of controls only convinced the controllers that still stricter controls were needed. "Those now pressing to turn natural-gas price regulation over to OPEC, while arguing the rhetoric of so-called deregulation, must not prevail," the 1976 Democratic platform exhorted. During the 1976 campaign, Jimmy Carter condemned decontrol of either natural gas or oil as "disastrous" for the American economy. As president he repeatedly promised to veto any energy plan that did not include permanent controls on the price of natural gas.

Carter's certainty that the country's dwindling gas reserves had nothing to do with price controls on natural gas propelled the country into a fuel crisis worse, if possible, than that of 1973–74. The winter of 1976–77 was a cruel one throughout the Midwest and Northeast. After thirty-one consecutive days of below-freezing weather, Chicago was struck by vicious blizzard that ripped the windows out of high-rise buildings. Temperatures plunged to minus 100 in Minnesota. The governors of New York and New Jersey declared states of emergency; Ohio's Governor James Rhodes led a fifteen-minute service on January 29, 1977, to beseech God to relieve the storm. In the midst of the storm, the heat went off. Midwesterners cranked up the gas, and the gas did not come on. Schools shut. Homes went chilly. Ten thousand factories closed, adding 1.5 million to the rosters of the unemployed.

The next winter, 1977–78, was even harsher. New England was struck by the most devastating snowstorm in the region's recorded history in February 1978: fifty inches of snow, 110-mile-an-hour winds. New York City was whacked with the worst snowstorm in a decade, and then, three weeks later, with the worst since 1947. Meanwhile, another killer blizzard ravaged the Midwest, dumping thirty-one inches of snow on Ohio at the end of January, in what Governor Rhodes called "the greatest disaster in Ohio history." At least sixty people died in the Northeast from the weather; and more than one hundred died in the Midwest. Again the schools and factories closed and homes went cold. The situation was desperate—desperate enough for Americans to consider almost anything.

MAD AS HELL

FEW MAGAZINE ARTICLES GOT TO PRESS IN THE MID-1970S WITHOUT INVOKING the signature line of the 1975 movie *Network*: "I'm mad as hell and I'm not going to take it any more!" Americans had plenty to be mad about in the 1970s, but few things got them quite as riled as their taxes.

Before World War II, most Americans paid no income tax at all. World War II introduced the wage-earner to tax-withholding, but once peace returned, taxes subsided, if not to prewar levels, then still to quite bearable levels. Nominal tax rates may have looked high, but the personal exemptions for a family man were generous. In 1955, a married father of two earning the median income paid only about 5.6 percent of his income in federal income taxes, less if he had a mortgage.[31] Even with Social Security (a steal at 3 percent of income, split between employer and employee), state income taxes, property taxes, and sales taxes, American democracy still had to be rated the best bargain in town.

The very high tax rates faced by the rich functioned more as symbols than as real means of redistribution. The well-to-do had to soar very high into the earnings stratosphere before they faced a marginal rate of more than 22 percent in the 1950s, and even then generous loopholes relieved the pain. Companies could deduct the amenities of life for their executives, including club dues, cars, meals. Investors could take advantage of non-taxable state bonds and the low capital-gains rate. The truly wealthy could relocate to Bermuda, Monaco, or Canada, which in those days had neither a capital gains nor an inheritance tax. The people in most serious jeopardy from the tax system of the 1950s were the high-earning self-employed: lawyers, dentists, and . . . movie stars, like the very disgruntled Ronald Wilson Reagan. The low average-rate, high top-rate tax system of the 1950s worked brilliantly from a political point of view and none too badly economically. It threw off more than enough money to pay for America's costly defense programs, run the schools and retirement system, and pay down the debt from World War II, while encouraging robust, non-inflationary economic growth. What it did not do was throw off enough revenue to pay for John F. Kennedy's New Frontier and Lyndon Johnson's Great Society.

In fiscal 1945, a year that began immediately after D-Day and ended just before Hiroshima, the federal government spent $93 billion. By fiscal 1948, the Republican elected in 1946 had pared that expenditure to under $30 billion. Despite the Korean War, the construction of the interstate highways, and the Sputnik education boom, the Eisenhower administration never exceeded the $93 billion mark. President Kennedy laughed off the restraints of the past. He spent $98 billion in 1961, and in 1962 surpassed the $100 billion mark for the first time in the nation's history. The federal budget shot past the $200 billion mark in 1971, past $300 billion in 1975, past $400 billion in 1977, past $500 billion in 1979. The costs of Medicare, the grandest achievement of the Great Society, doubled every four years between 1966 and 1980.

How was this fabulous increase in expenditure to be financed? By economic growth, in part: The country did get richer between 1950 and 1973. By borrowing, in part: Kennedy's first budget proposed the country's first non-recession, non-war deficit; between 1961 and 1998, the country posted only one balanced budget, in 1969. But above all, the expenditure was paid for by inflation-generated tax increases. Between 1971 and 1977, for example, a period in which the consumer price index rose by 47 percent, the total tax take of the federal, state, and local governments jumped by 60 percent.

Remember our friend the average guy with the wife at home and two kids? Between 1955 and 1980, his income quintupled, but the value of his exemptions only doubled. As a result, by 1980, he was paying not 5.6 percent of his income in federal income taxes, but 11.4 percent. Meanwhile, the visible portion of his Social Security contribution had tripled, from less than 2 percent to 6.15 percent.[32]

The family man down the block who earned twice the median income—the not exactly princely sum of $48,664 in 1980—lost 10.76 percent of his income to the federal income tax when Eisenhower was president and 18.25 percent as he got ready to vote for Ronald Reagan.

And federal taxes were really the least of these two men's problems. State and local spending boomed much faster than federal spending in the 1970s, despite declining school enrollments, as states assumed brand new responsibilities and newly unionized teachers and other state employees forced through huge pay increases for themselves.

To the extent they could, Americans fled high-tax regions of the country for the booming Sunbelt. Between 1970 and 1980, the population of Massachusetts stagnated, and New York actually lost citizens, while low-tax states thrived: Georgia's population grew by 19 percent, Texas's by 27 percent, Florida's by 44 percent, Arizona's by 53 percent, and Nevada's by 64 percent. A state could join the boom even without sun, provided its taxes were low. The population of snowy but frugal New Hampshire jumped by 25 percent.

When they could not flee, Americans agitated. A crusty Orange County, California, businessman named Howard Jarvis collected tens of thousands of signatures to put a property-tax cut, Proposition 13, onto the state ballot. The national press flew out to watch Jarvis in bewildered fascination. California had pioneered the ultra-liberal policies of the 1960s: the country's most generous welfare system, the best-funded schools and universities, the first essays into environmentalism. Would Californians really turn their backs on all that? They wouldn't! They couldn't! . . . They did, and by a two-thirds margin. Two years later, the citizens of Massachusetts—the "Don't blame me, I voted for McGovern" state—enacted a similar cap, Proposition 2½.

"Tax and tax, spend and spend, elect and elect." That had been the political mantra of the New Deal. Taxes had been an unburdensome abstraction to the vast majority of Americans in the 1930s, while the benefits purchased by taxes were lively, immediate, and tangible. The hapless Republicans were left to sputter tediously about the harm done to the economy by the overtaxing of the wealthy. By the end of the 1970s, however, it was the taxes that were real, and the benefits that were abstract. Democrats were left to sputter tediously about the horrible unfairness of the undertaxing of the wealthy, and with the same dismal results.

HAYEK'S PRIZE

"THE INCREASING VENERATION FOR THE STATE, THE ADMIRATION OF POWER, and of bigness for bigness' sake, the enthusiasm for 'organization' of everything (we now call it 'planning') and that 'inability to leave anything to the simple power of organic growth' . . . are all scarcely less marked in England now than they were in Germany [before the Nazi seizure of power]."[33] How Friedrich Hayek despaired as he wrote those foreboding words in 1942 and 1943. He had fled his native Austria for Britain, homeland of the Gladstonian liberalism he revered, only to discover that nineteenth-century individualism was nearly as badly discredited in its birthplace as it was in the totalitarian Teutonic lands he had fled.

Live long enough, however, and everything returns to fashion: the Atkins diet, bellbottoms, and even economic liberty. Hayek was born in 1899. He died in 1992. A veteran of the armies of the Emperor Franz Josef II, he lived to witness the election of Margaret Thatcher and Ronald Reagan, the fall of communism, and the triumphant renaissance of the prestige of market economics in the 1990s. It is too bad he did not endure to his hundredth birthday. If he had, he would certainly have enjoyed seeing the heir to Clement Atlee campaigning for office by dropping nationalization from the British Labour party's charter and promising an audience of City of London financiers a cut in corporate taxation. "The presumption should be," Tony Blair declared a month before his 1997 election victory, "that economic activity is best left to the private sector."[34]

"The most important political event of the twentieth century is not the crisis of capitalism but the death of socialism."[35] It took a certain audacity for Irving Kristol to venture that cool claim in the middle of the 1970s, not one of the brighter moments in the annals of freedom. Yet the signs were there. Margaret Thatcher won the leadership of the British Conservatives in 1974, the same year that Friedrich Hayek won the Nobel Prize for economics. (The prize was sullied, but not spoiled, by the Swedish Academy of Science's decision to divide it between Hayek and Gunnar Myrdal, the theorist of Swedish socialism.) In 1976, those same Swedes hoofed the Social Democratic party out of office after forty-four uninterrupted years of power. Milton Friedman won the Economic Nobel that year. Deng Xiaoping took power in China in 1977 and steered his country onto the road to economic modernization.

Miners who have been trapped underground say that as they dig toward freedom, they can smell fresh air before they hear or see anything. So it was in the 1970s. Americans caught whiffs of a more competitive, bracing economy years before it materialized. The wacky 1967 comedy *The President's Analyst* jovially identified the phone company—in those days, there was only one—as the master conspiracy that ruled the world. The 1960s television series, *Rowan & Martin's Laugh-In*, featured a telephone operator who gleefully interrupted the calls of customers who displeased her. In 1970, a three-minute phone call from New York to London cost about $8 in 1990s money. A hissed "I'm calling *long distance*" would bring just about anyone to the phone, pronto. In 1982, AT&T settled the long-running antitrust suit against it on terms that put an end to the long-distance monopoly and opened the way to competition in local phone service as well, and the telecommunications revolution roared into life. Before the 1970s, antitrust law had been used to punish companies that outcompeted their rivals. Afterward, convinced by Yale Law Professor Robert Bork's 1978 book, *The Antitrust Paradox*, most courts insisted that the one and only purpose of the law was to protect the consumer from collusion.

Americans can wax nostalgic about the good old days of air travel, when leggy stewardesses settled trays of sizzling filet mignons before economy-class passengers. What they forget was how expensive air tickets then were, and how few people therefore flew. As of 1975, 80 percent of Americans had never traveled by air. "Between 1950 and 1974," future

Supreme Court Justice Stephen Breyer pointed out in 1982, "the Civil Aeronautics Board had received seventy-nine applications from companies wishing to enter the domestic scheduled airline industry; it granted none. Indeed, since 1960 only four (of thirty-two) such applications had been granted a hearing. Since 1965, less than 10 percent of all applications by existing airlines to serve new routes had been granted and between 1969 and 1974 fewer than 4 percent had been granted."[36] The airways were deregulated in 1978, bringing Americans the airport pandemonium they hate—and the $69 supersaver fares they would not do without.

Those Mexican plums on your Christmas table arrived courtesy of the deregulation of trucking in 1980, and that $14 Internet stock trade was made possible by the 1975 deregulation of brokerage commissions. In August 1974, President Ford signed legislation repealing the forty-year-old ban on private ownership of gold. In 1979, Congress removed from the comptroller of the currency the power to set maximum interest rates on bank deposits.

Deregulation liberated the American economy, bringing all the benefits that Hayek promised: dynamism, creativity, low inflation, low unemployment. But like all good things, those good things came at a price. The bursting of the carapace of the old economy shattered the power of trade unions, whose restrictive practices cannot survive wide-open competition.

Union membership continued to grow in the 1970s: The total number of unionized workers would peak in 1978. But the clout of unions had already begun to slip, because unions were failing to recruit as quickly as the labor force grew. Slightly fewer than 25 percent of American workers belonged to unions in 1970. By 1978, even before the Rustbowl Gotterdamerung of the late Carter and early Reagan years, that ratio had slipped to 22.5 percent. In 1970, the head of the AFL-CIO was one of the half-dozen most important people in the country. Politicians and business leaders took the same care to refer to "business *and labor*" when talking about the economy as their successors thirty years later did to say "he *and she*" when talking about anything else. Who refers to "business and labor" today? Who can so much as name the president of the AFL-CIO?

As the economy turned cooler toward unions, so did the U.S. government, their ally and protector for half a century. The Democrats elected in
1974, observes the biographer of Phillip Burton, "were younger, more reform-minded Democrats, many from marginal districts who defeated Republicans largely because of revulsion over Watergate. Traditional
Democratic constituencies, such as organized labor, meant little to
them."[37] The Democratic tide swept into office young, college-educated,
suburban reformers: passionately committed to affirmative action for
blacks, honesty in government, equality for women, a less confrontational
foreign policy, protecting the environment. It had not escaped their notice
that the big labor unions were not too keen on any of those things. Individualists themselves, they had little use for the subordination of the self
to the group that sustained unions. "Question authority!" their bumper
stickers said, and they did not pause to consider how many of society's authorities were bulwarks of the Democratic party. George McGovern had
run in 1972 not only against Franklin Roosevelt's policies—his foreign-pol-
icy hawkishness, his indifference to racial issues, his dislike of welfare—
but also against Roosevelt's political machine. McGovern pooh-poohed
labor's clout. The election would test, he said, "whether the union power
brokers are alive or dead. The question is whether governors can any
longer deliver their states. Can a mayor deliver his city? Can a union leader
deliver his union? Can a priest deliver his parish?"[38] Labor richly returned
McGovern's disdain. "I don't think this man is good material," AFL-CIO
President George Meany said as he delivered the news that his federation
could not endorse the Democratic nominee. Meany complained that a
"small elite of suburban types and students took over the apparatus of the
Democratic party." So in fact they had. What connection or sympathy
could a Tom Downey (Cornell '70), a Norman Mineta (U.C. Berkeley '53),
a Paul Tsongas (Dartmouth '62), a Tim Wirth (Harvard '61) feel for the
steelworkers and policemen, the mass-attending housewives and squirrel-
hunting farmers who hitherto had constituted the Democratic party? As
another of the 1974 freshmen, Senator-elect Gary Hart of Colorado (Yale,
J.D., '64) tersely put it, "We are not a bunch of little Hubert Humphreys."

The new liberals might *pity* the Democrats' traditional constituencies—it was in the 1970s that the word "compassion" came to dominate the political vocabulary of liberalism—but they had nothing much in common with them. Truth to tell, they did not pity them very much. The new Democrats were moved by the plight of people much more abject than a union carpenter or longshoreman: welfare mothers and farmworkers, the mentally retarded and unimmunized children, the illegal immigrant and the closeted homosexual. Jane Austen's Emma Woodhouse expressed their feelings well: "The yeomanry are precisely the order of people with whom I feel I can have nothing to do. A degree or two lower, and a creditable appearance might interest me; I might hope to be useful to their families in some way. But a farmer can need none of my help, and is therefore in one sense as much above my notice as in every other he is below it."[39]

So, at the very apogee of liberal Democratic political power, at a time when every plausible, semi-plausible, or even completely implausible victim group from Aleuts to Zoroastrians was collecting its bag of boodle from an open-handed Congress, organized labor, once so powerful, began to lose, and badly.

Nor could labor appeal from Congress to public opinion. Public faith in unions dropped as sharply as faith in all other institutions: Between 1965 and 1975, the percentage of Americans with "great confidence" in unions dropped by half; the percentage with "very little confidence" doubled. No union forfeited public confidence more grossly than John L. Lewis's United Mineworkers. On September 6, 1973, Tony Boyle, the longtime president of the UMW, was charged with the murder of an internal rival, Joseph Yablonski, along with Yablonski's wife and daughter. A UMW official, William Turnblazer, testified that Boyle had authorized him to pass $20,000 of union funds to a hired killer. Boyle was convicted of three counts of first-degree murder.

The decline of unions hastened the most marked of all changes between the American economy of mid-century and the American economy at century's end: the spreading divergence in income and wealth. From the imposition of the income tax until 1973, American society had been trending toward ever-greater economic equality. Very large fortunes became gradually more rare. J. Paul Getty, probably the richest American of the 1970s, was worth between $2 billion and $4 billion in 1974, or not much more than one-twentieth (adjusting for inflation) of what his fellow oil magnate, John D. Rockefeller, had been worth in 1914. The top 1 percent of American families earned 19 percent of the national income in 1929, but only 7.7 percent in 1946.[40] Nobody was rich in 1970 in the way that hundreds of families had been rich in 1900.

The upper middle's place in the scheme of things had slid too. In 1900, a "college professor on a salary of $2,000 to $3,000 . . . had to watch every penny and forego many satisfactions which he felt were the natural right of well-educated people, but he could afford a fair-sized house and at least one maid."[41] The family of a man earning around $8,000 a year, a moderately successful lawyer for instance, could in 1900 afford a house on the best street of Boston's Back Bay with "four stories above the basement [that] contained fifteen or twenty rooms, plus several bathrooms, and many ample-sized closets and storage rooms." That lawyer probably employed a staff of three: "a cook at perhaps $5 a week, a waitress at $3.50 a week, a laundress at $3.50 a week; the waitress and laundress shared the upstairs work. They could add the once-a-week services of a cleaning woman to come in at $1.50 a day, and also the very part-time muscle of a choreman who served several other houses . . . at a total annual cost of perhaps $800 a year."[42] To employ even a single full-time household worker in 1970 was, by contrast, a sign of real affluence, and a fifteen-room house was a luxury of the super-rich.

For the lower middle, by contrast, the middle years of this century were a golden age. A man born in 1920 in a rented apartment in a half-century old walkup tenement on Mulberry Street, with one toilet in the hallway for three or four families, and who joined the New York City Sanitation Department in 1945 at $1,800 a year could in 1950 afford to buy a semi-detached house in Bensonhurst with three bedrooms and a bath. His children would all be born in hospitals, and he could look forward to a pension of $20,000 on his retirement in 1980.[43]

Statistical measures of equality are unreliable in many ways. For what they are worth, however, they show 1972 to have been the most egalitarian year of the twentieth century. Adjusting for inflation, a New York City sanitation worker earns no more today than he did then. His *family* might be better off—his wife may work, he probably has fewer children to feed, school, and clothe—but his own individual wage has not increased. And he has only done as well as that because he holds a unionized public-sector job. A thirty-year-old high-school dropout in 1999 earned, on average, considerably less than his equivalent in 1969. A thirty-year-old high-school graduate earned, on average, no more. The changes in technology have enhanced the value of educated labor at the expense of the unskilled. The new immigration law tended to favor skilled labor too, flooding the American market with new arrivals to whom a job at the minimum wage felt like a dream come true.

The median income of married families in the 1990s, it should be said, has risen to a comfortable $50,000. But married families are becoming ever more atypical in America. Fewer than half of America's children will reach the age of eighteen with both their father and their mother continuously present in their home. At any given moment, one-third of American households are female-headed, either because of divorce or because the mother never got married in the first place.

Meanwhile, in the upper reaches of society, wealth is blooming like dandelions in summer. America in 1998 was graced by 239 billionaires. To make the *Forbes* 400 list of the richest Americans required a fortune of $75 million in 1982, but $425 million in 1998. Schools for butlers were reopened, although butlers now call themselves "household managers" and wear khakis and an earring rather than morning coats.

The upper middle, meanwhile, is again moving away from the middle and the lower middle. Eight million U.S. households earned incomes of more than $100,000 a year in 1998. Two million earned more than $200,000. For those families, vast fields of mansions have sprouted on the outer edges of American cities, each many times larger than the Back Bay mansions of 1900, and outfitted with three- and four-car garages, home movie theaters, and 2000-square-foot kitchens. The country that generated the world's first mass middle class in the middle of the twentieth century has spawned a mass upper class at that century's end.

THE NEW POVERTY

IF ALL IT TOOK TO CEASE BEING POOR WERE MONEY, THEN LYNDON JOHNSON could fairly claim to have won his war on poverty. In 1980, the federal government counted a family of three as poor if it had a cash income of less than $6,565, or approximately $20,000 in today's funds. On the eve of the Korean War, $20,000 in today's funds happened to be the *median* income of *all* American families. In other words, at the end of the 1970s a poor family could afford to buy about as much as a middle-class family could in 1950.

Does that sound incredible? It shouldn't. In 1950, more than one-third of all Americans lived in houses without a flush toilet and more than 15 percent lived in houses with more than one person to a room. As late as 1960, more than 20 percent of Americans lived in houses without a telephone anywhere near at hand. Comforts possessed only by the upper two-thirds of American society during the Truman administration were diffused to virtually everybody by the end of the Carter years. By 1980, electricity was so universal that only the Unabomber and vacationing Maine millionaires lacked it. More than 95 percent of American families possessed indoor plumbing and at least one room per person. Telephones, televisions and cars were owned by 93 percent of families.[44] Yet despite these cheerful statistics, the war on poverty had *not* been won. Material deprivation had given way to something arguably worse.

In 1982, *New York Times* columnist Russell Baker published a memoir of his hardscrabble boyhood in Virginia, *Growing Up*. Baker's book vaulted into best-sellerdom, and deservedly so. Still, there was something odd about the book's timing and success. 1982 was a bitter political year: the nadir of the inflation-squelching recession, the year of the Reagan budget cuts, and ketchup as a vegetable. Baker's own newspaper almost every day reported some some glaring datum that exemplified how the war on poverty had given way to a war on the poor. Yet, here was a *Times* columnist looking back on a poverty far more abject than the worst that Reagan-era America had to show and recollecting with a chuckle that it had not re-ally been so bad. Hundreds of thousands of people, many of whom had endured the same hardships as Baker or worse, plunked down $20 to chuckle along with him. How could that be?

Perhaps time had softened their memories. Or perhaps Baker and his contemporaries genuinely knew something. In the 1930s, families like Baker's led a middle-class life minus only a middle-class income. Their fa-thers' wages might be paltry, but at least they had fathers: Only 3.6 percent of the children born in America in 1940 were born out of wedlock. And those fathers *worked*, when there was work to be done. After the Depres-sion lifted virtually every able-bodied male over the age of eighteen partic-ipated in the labor force. The poor circa 1980 had food stamps, free food for pregnant women, free dental care, subsidized housing and any number of other social benefits for whose sake idealistic young people joined the Communist Party in the 1930s. True, inflation corroded the purchasing power of the cash welfare stipend in the early 1970s. Nonetheless, welfare remained much more generous in most places in 1980 than it had been in 1960, never mind 1940. But despite that generosity American poverty bit more savagely and cruelly than ever. To be poor in Baker's time did not im-ply that one lived in chaos, with mother out all day and children parked in front of the television, with dad replaced by a sequence of boyfriends, in a neighborhood where nobody worked and where fathers never lived with their families, where drugs were openly sold, bullets careened through the courtyards of the housing projects, and junk food was munched from morning to night. Tragically often, that was precisely what it meant to be poor in 1980.

In 1980, there were 27 million poor people in America, or about 12.4 percent of the population, approximately the same proportion as in 1965. The level of poverty in the United States had not much changed over those fifteen years, but its character had. Poverty, before 1960 mostly rural and white, became urban and nonwhite. Almost 70 percent of America's poor lived in metropolitan areas in 1980. The number of poor people living in ur-ban black-majority ghetto neighborhoods jumped by almost 30 percent between 1970 and 1980.[45] In the biggest cities, the increase in the number of inner city poor was even more arresting. Philadelphia was home to 50,000 in 1970 and 127,000 in 1980; Chicago to 74,000 in 1970 and 194,000 in 1980; New York to 134,000 in 1970 and 478,000 in 1980.[46] This "underclass"—a term originally coined by the Swedish economist Gunnar Myrdal and popularized in a 1982 book by journalist Ken Auletta—tallied perhaps 2.5 million souls nationwide, almost all of them black or Hispanic. Two and a half million people is a small proportion of the total American population. But this relatively minuscule population challenged the country's ideals of equal citizenship and equal human potential more radically than the tens of millions of unemployed in the 1930s had ever done.

The young men of the underclass were slaughtering themselves. In 1980, the United States suffered 10.7 murders per 100,000 residents—a horrible murder rate, the worst in the industrial world, and a rate almost exactly double that of 1965. In the same year that the country as a whole suffered those 10.7 per 100,000 murders, black males aged fifteen to twenty-four suffered some 84.3 homicides per 100,000, black males aged thirty-five to forty-four suffered 110.3, and black males aged twenty-five to thirty-four suffered more than 145.

Others among the black urban poor turned their rage outward. In 1971 and 1972, a group that called itself the Black Liberation Army shot and killed eight white police officers in and around New York City. Police in Illinois charged a gang of eight black Vietnam veterans with nine racially motivated murders of whites in October 1972. In a series of killings that the tabloids would dub the "zebra murders," four Black Muslims in San Francisco walked up to eighteen randomly chosen whites and shot them in the back of the head. A concert that attracted seven thousand white teenagers to Cobo Hall in downtown Detroit in August 1976 was surrounded and besieged by more than a hundred black gang-members. The concert was halted and the audience was evacuated. The teens were assaulted and robbed on their way out, and one was raped. During the 1980 Miami riot, the nation's worst since 1968, rioters were seen to target white victims. One white man had his ears and tongue cut off; rioters prevented an ambulance from reaching three dying white teenagers.

The young men of the underclass had dropped out of the labor force. In 1964, only 10 percent of nonwhite males in their early twenties were neither employed, nor in school, nor in the military. In 1980, more than 25 percent of nonwhite males in their early twenties were idle in this way.[47] Between 1959 and 1979, the percentage of black males who engaged in no paid employment at all doubled, from 8.2 percent to 16.4 percent.[48]

Poverty was exacerbated and entrenched by the shrinkage of marriage. In 1969, only 5 percent of white babies were born out of wedlock; 14.5 percent of white babies were born outside of marriage in 1986. Among blacks, married motherhood seemed to be disappearing. In 1969, 35 percent of black children were born to unmarried mothers; in 1986, 62.6 percent. Among black women who did not complete high school, the illegitimacy rate in 1986 was 83 percent.[49] By the end of the century, one out of every American babies would be born to an unmarried woman.

Illegitimacy perpetuated the cycle of misery. Children born out of wedlock, black and white, were 250 percent more likely to be abused than children born to married parents, the Centers for Disease Control reported in 1977. Illegitimacy subjected infant children to the temper of an overwhelmed and despairing mother and the predation of a series of resentful, insecure, and often violent boyfriends. As illegitimacy rates soared, so did injuries to children. Between 1950 and 1975, the homicide rate for children between ages one and four *tripled*; in 1975, murder was the leading cause of death of young children in the United States.

One prime article of faith of the optimistic 1960s had been the conviction that poor people acted and thought much like anyone else. This conviction inspired 1960s liberals like Robert Kennedy, who attacked the paternalistic bureaucracy of 1930s-era social work. The same conviction also animated 1960s conservatives like Richard Nixon, who proposed to replace the paternalistic welfare bureaucracy with his Family Assistance Plan, a subsidy delivered through the income tax system that would top up the earnings of the poor to a guaranteed annual minimum. The growth of the underclass shook this cheerful doctrine. The very poor seemed to lack something more than money: the basic skills necessary to make one's way in the modern world. As a vice president of a Chicago television station explained to two researchers sympathetic to the employment difficulties of the inner-city poor: "They go through the Chicago public schools or they dropped out when they were in the eighth grade. They can't read. They can't write. They can hardly talk."[50] So the poverty debate turned full circle, with some of the most radical of the 1960s reformers dusting off an updated version of 1930s paternalism. Hillary Clinton is the most famous advocate of early "intervention" in the families of the poor, but she is by no means unique.

In plenty of other countries, such interventionist policies would not be shocking. European societies have long been organized on the principle that only some people can be trusted to manage their own lives; the rest must be supervised and guided. Per Albin Hansson, the man who led the Swedish Social Democrats to power in 1932 and created the modern Swedish welfare state, habitually compared the relationship between the state and its citizens to the relationship between parent and child. "[W]e often speak of society—the state, the municipality—as our common home. . . . The good home knows no privileged and no disadvantaged, no favorites and no stepchildren."[51] Americans have until now adamantly rejected this concept of the citizen, or some set of citizens, as children of the state. Americans might agree that government should provide a hand up to people in momentary distress. But perpetual tutelage for a couple of million of their fellow-citizens—that dismayed and appalled them.

Yet tutelage for a considerable minority—"custodial democracy" as Charles Murray, who warns against it, has termed it—does seem to appeal to growing sections of the American elite. During the great welfare-reform debate of the 1990s, liberals and conservatives staked out positions that would have been indignantly dismissed as outrageously paternalistic thirty years ago. What the welfare poor needed was a firm guiding hand to find them jobs, all sides seemed to agree, compel them to show up at work, and baby-sit their children while they were there.

How had the country arrived at this unwanted destination? Students of poverty on the political left prefer to emphasize the bleak prospects the present-day American economy offers to the unskilled, and especially unskilled men. As manufacturing and mining jobs vanish, the gap between the best-paid and the least-paid widens. Unable to secure steady and decently paid work, unskilled men drop out of the job market entirely, turning to crime, drugs, and petty hustling. These devalued men make poor husband material. They could not support a family even if they wanted to, and the women who bear their children decide that the family can do better without a resentful and useless man. Male children grow up without a father, run wild, fail at school, and the whole fearful cycle repeats itself. More conservative analysts emphasize the fatal temptations of welfare, which lured women into single motherhood, and the disabling culture of the ghetto, which mocked work and education.

Perhaps both explanations are true, or partly true. Under pressure from immigration and automation, the wages of unskilled men did indeed dwindle after 1972 (although anyone inclined to romanticize the old blue-collar economy ought to remember that in 1960 more men worked as farm laborers than as assembly-line workers), just as the liberals say. And just as the conservatives say, at the same time as the economy was turning against the poor, so was American culture. The poor were bombarded with images of middle-class Americans avoiding marriage and scorning work. Barely half the college-educated young people of 1969, 57 percent, agreed that "hard work always pays off."[52] Cynical talk like that swiftly filtered through to the poor, who were perhaps disposed toward cynicism to start with. But the poor lack the margin of error that middle-class people take for granted. They cannot afford even one of the youthful mistakes that others can regret, or even chuckle over, in the security of middle age. Work and family: These are the two faint lightbulbs of hope in the life of the poor. Remove them and you smash the light, leaving the neediest of our fellow human beings groping for safety in the dark.

THE EMERGING REPUBLICAN MAJORITY

GLASS, GLASS EVERYWHERE: THAT'S WHAT TRAVELERS SAW WHEN THEY ENTERED Washington's new Dulles International Airport in 1959. Under a concrete roof that curved like the takeoff trajectory of a jet hung four vast windows without a retaining wall in sight. Beyond the glass, there was only the sky— the sky that America ruled in the way that Britain had once ruled the waves. It was from the air that America had dropped the atomic bombs that ended World War II. It was by air that America had sustained its hold on West Berlin during the darkest moment of the cold war. It was through the air that the Voice of America and Radio Free Europe subverted the enemy Soviet Union. And it was via air that millions of newly prosperous Americans, their wallets stuffed with their almighty dollars, were inflicting the new industry of mass tourism upon the unhappy residents of Paris and Rome.

You can still see the glass at Dulles. But you cannot see much of the sky. The vista overlooking the runways is now chopped off by a long wall, broken at intervals by doorways that lead to metal detectors and x-ray machines. It's incredible now, but within the memory of people now living air passengers routinely walked from the door of the airport to their seats on the plane without being searched, scanned, or interrogated. This was not seen as anything remarkable. It was the way things were expected to be. Despite, or maybe because of, the international tension of the 1950s and '60s, despite the Berlin and Cuban crises, the Eisenhower and Kennedy years were a time when Americans were secure from dangers much below the level of thermonuclear holocaust. Americans had reason to fear war, but they did not have to fear that some bomb-carrying fanatic might blow their airplane to smithereens.

The first task of government is to guarantee the safety of the citizen, and that was a task that after 1970 Western governments performed less and less well. Over the Labor Day weekend of 1970, teams of Arab commandos seeking the release of Sirhan Sirhan, the assassin of Robert Kennedy, performed the spectacular feat of simultaneously hijacking four jumbo jets, two of them the property of American airlines. Two of the hijacked jumbos were flown to Dawson's Field, near Amman, Jordan. Four hundred passengers, 150 or so of them Americans, were held hostage for three weeks until Jordan's King Hussein mobilized his army to force the release of the captives. The empty planes were blown up by the hijackers in a headline-grabbing act of destruction.

The first hijacking recorded by history occurred in Peru in 1930, when officers attempting a coup diverted a plane to drop leaflets over Lima. The United States suffered them intermittently in the 1950s, mostly by bank robbers commandeering planes to make good their exits. But so long as planes had relatively short flying ranges—and so long as there was nowhere within that range for a would-be hijacker to commandeer a plane *to*—hijacking's potential was severely limited. Then, on February 21, 1968, Lawrence Wilson Rhodes stepped aboard a Delta Airlines DC–8, pointed a pistol at a stewardess after takeoff, and demanded to be flown to Havana. Over the next two years, his example would inspire an assortment of crooks on the lam, lunatics, black nationalists, and Castroite radicals to hijack thirty-eight American planes, thirty-seven of them to Cuba. None of these hijackings resulted in any death or injury. The Cuban authorities behaved politely enough, feeding the abducted passengers roast beef dinners and selling them the famous local rum and cigars at duty-free prices before sending them home.

These early hijackings were not without their ludicrous aspects—"Take dees plane to Cooba!" became the punch-line of innumerable wearisome nightclub comedians—but their import was not funny at all. The United States was no longer able to protect its citizens from international anarchy. And through the 1970s, international anarchy obtruded itself ever more terrifyingly into American consciousness.

Between 1968 and 1981, terrorists murdered the American ambassadors to Guatemala, Sudan, Cyprus, and Lebanon, the prime minister of Jordan, the prime minister of Spain, the chairman of West Germany's second largest bank, the front-runner for the presidency of Italy, the uncle of the

Queen of England, the President of Egypt, and, very nearly, the commander of NATO and the Pope.[53] Thousands of perfectly ordinary people were
killed or maimed by international and domestic terrorism in Argentina,
France, West Germany, and Uruguay. The Irish Republican Army, an organization largely financed by money raised in the United States, murdered
2,261 English and Irish people between 1969 and 1982, was responsible for
7,500 bombings that claimed the lives of more than six hundred people,
and deliberately crippled more than one thousand journalists, businessmen, and ordinary fellow-Catholics who failed in the opinion of the IRA to
show insufficient enthusiasm for the cause.[54]

No grievance seemed too obscure to provoke terrorism. In May 1977,
gunmen demanding independence from Indonesian rule for South
Moluccua, a territory once known only to the clever eleven-year-olds in the
National Geographic Society's annual geography bee, seized 105 schoolchildren and their six teachers at a school in the small Dutch town of
Bovensmilde. Another South Moluccan band took hostage fifty adults
aboard a commuter train. After nearly a three-week standoff, Dutch
marines assaulted the train and the school. All the children were saved
alive; two adult hostages and all the terrorists were killed.

No portion of the earth's surface was too idyllic to escape. Black nationalists murdered the governor-general of Bermuda and his military aide
as the two men walked the governor's dog after dinner in March 1973. A
British diplomat and a French-Canadian cabinet minister were kidnapped
in October 1970 by terrorists demanding the independence of Quebec. The
diplomat survived, the minister was murdered.

No season of goodwill was too sacred to be sullied. A team of Palestinian terrorists attacked the Munich Olympics in September 1972 in an attempt to kidnap the Israeli Olympic team. The incident ended in the
violent death of all eleven athletes.

No taboo was too awesome to go unviolated. One leader of the German
Red Army Faction, usually known as the Baader-Meinhoff gang, drew up
plans to bomb the headquarters of what remained of Jewish communal
and religious life in West Berlin, "in order to get rid of this thing about

Jews that we've all had to have since the Nazi time."[55] He was caught before the plans could be carried out.

Terrorism *worked*, in the sense that it intimidated. In the summer of 1976, two German terrorists and five Arab hijackers seized an Air France jetliner en route to Tel Aviv and flew it to Uganda's Entebbe Airport. Ugandan dictator Idi Amin had food and supplies waiting and deployed troops around the perimeter of the airport as soon as the passengers were marched into it. On the ground, the Germans took command. They released the non-Jews and held the Jews. "Among the hostages at Entebbe," wrote a leading authority on the Baader-Meinhoff gang, "there were a few who had been in Hitler's concentration camps. Once again they found themselves being sorted out, Jews from non-Jews, the Jews selected to die. Once again they were ordered about by guards with guns, shouted at to move quickly—*Schnell!*—this time by a German woman hijacker, who also felt it was necessary to slap them. One of the captors went up to Bose [Wilfried Bose, the leader] and showed him a number indelibly branded on his arm. He told him that he had got it in a Nazi concentration camp. He said he had supposed that a new and different generation had grown up in Germany, but with this experience of Bose and his girl comrade, he found it difficult to believe that the Nazi movement had died. Bose replied that this was something quite different from Nazism. . . . "[56] Israeli commandos flew 2,000 miles and attacked the airfield in the middle of the night, scattered the Ugandans, killed the terrorists, and saved all but one of the hostages. The world's political leaders did not dare applaud. U.N. Secretary-General Kurt Waldheim condemned the Israeli raid on Entebbe as a violation of Ugandan sovereignty. The government of France, the owner of the hijacked plane, offered not a single word of thanks. The Ford administration managed to summon up only a milky expression of "satisfaction" that the lives of the passengers had been saved.

Supineness in the face of terrorist violence was such a distinctive trait of the 1970s that the phenomenon acquired a useful shorthand name: the Stockholm Syndrome, after an incident that occurred in the summer of 1973. Two ex-cons attempted to rob a bank in the Swedish capital. Police burst in on the robbery and, to protect themselves, the crooks grabbed four hostages and fled into the bank vault. The police besieged the robbers for five days, and finally flushed them out by drilling holes in the vault ceiling and dropping tear gas inside. Then a curious thing happened. One of the hostages emerged to announce that she had fallen in love with and intended to marry the lead crook. The syndrome entered ordinary speech a year later, when Patty Hearst, media heiress, threw in her lot with the political radicals who had kidnapped her. She denounced her family and fiancé on tape recordings. "I have changed—grown. I've become conscious and can never go back to the life we led before. . . . My love . . . has grown into an unselfish love of my comrades here, in prison and on the streets." Hearst even toted a gun alongside her captors in an April 1974 San Francisco bank robbery.

The Stockholm Syndrome seemed to grip the whole world. All too often, it was the targets of terrorism who endured the blame for the gunmen's crimes. The influential French newspaper *Le Monde* expressed this line of reasoning forcefully in a 1977 commentary on the outrages of the Baader-Meinhoff gang: "Only a society that is itself monstrous can produce monsters."

The Carter administration fell victim to the Stockholm syndrome too. In a speech given soon after the Iranians took fifty-two American diplomats in Tehran hostage, Secretary of State Cyrus Vance urged Americans not to get too upset over the incident. "Most Americans now recognize that we alone cannot dictate events. This recognition is not a sign of America's decline. It is a sign of growing American maturity in a complex world."[57] When Vance's boss, President Jimmy Carter warned a few weeks later that there was a limit to American maturity, Khomeini mocked him. "He [Carter] sometimes threatens us militarily and at other times economically, but he is aware himself that he is beating on an empty drum," Khomeini said. "Neither does Carter have the guts for military action, nor would anyone listen to him."[58] (When Carter finally attempted military action, which crashed and burned in the Iranian desert in April 1980, Vance resigned in protest.)

But America was not an empty drum. The Iran hostage-taking snapped the country out of its defeatist funk. Disc jockeys began playing a comic new song to the tune of "Barbara Ann": "Bomb, bomb, bomb; bomb, bomb Iran." A popular joke asked, "What's flat and glows in the dark?" The answer: "Iran, twenty-four hours after Ronald Reagan's inauguration." The Iranians must have heard the joke too. Before the twenty-four hours had elapsed, all the hostages were released.

The humiliations of the Carter years stiffened America's spine. A constellation of influential ex-Democrats—Paul Nitze, Irving Kristol, Eugene Rostow, and Norman Podhoretz—formed a Committee on the Present Danger, to rally the country for rearmament. In 1975, only 18 percent of Americans said the country was spending "too little" on defense. In 1978, still only 29 percent said the country was spending "too little." But by 1980, an overwhelming 60 percent worried the country was spending "too little."

Carter never managed to understand what the country was bothered about. He scorned Ronald Reagan's demand for firmness and resolve, telling reporters for the *Dayton Daily News* that Reagan's criticisms of his his policies reflected Reagan's "apparent inability" to understand the complexities of arms control. "If you've got just a strong military and you are jingoistic in spirit, and just show the macho of the United States," Carter explained to fifty Chicago suburbanites a month before the 1980 election, "that is an excellent way to lead our country toward war. . . . The Oval Office is not a place for simplistic answers. It is not a place for shooting from the hip. It is not a place for snap judgments that might have serious consequences." But if the choices were simplistic answers or Carter's answers, simplicity could look appealing. In September 1980, Leon Jaworski, a former Watergate special prosecutor, signed up as the honorary chairman of Democrats for Reagan. When reminded by a reporter of his earlier harsh assessment of the Republican nominee—not five months before Jaworski had described him as "an extremist whose over-the-counter simplistic remedies and shopworn platitudes trouble the open-minded and informed voter"—Jaworski replied, "I would rather have a competent extremist than an incompetent moderate."

American politics had been trending toward conservatism since the early 1960s. "A conservative," went a vintage joke of the 1960s, "is a liberal who has been mugged." If that definition is true, then it's surprising that the swing was not more overwhelming than it actually was. In 1962, a bare majority of Americans, 51 percent, described themselves as conservative. Twelve years later, 59 percent did so.[59] In the eight presidential elections between 1968 and 1996, the Democrats' best showing was 1976, when Jimmy Carter won 50.1 percent of the vote. In the Republicans' best showing, 1972, the Grand Old Party won 60.7 percent. More tellingly, over those eight elections, the Democrats averaged 43.7 percent of the vote to the Republicans' 49.1 percent.

A self-congratulatory liberal myth of the 1980s fixes the blame for this trend to the right on American racism. Liberalism faltered, this theory explains, because it heroically immolated itself for the cause of civil rights. But the self-congratulatory myth disregards the overwhelming popularity of the civil rights cause everywhere outside the white South in the years before 1964, and slights the millions of black votes added to the Democratic column by the 1965 Voting Rights Act. It was the collapse of social order at home and the ebbing of American prestige abroad—not the Civil Rights Act—that shattered Democratic liberalism. As anti-Vietnam protesters battled police outside the 1968 Democratic convention, a pollster asked the American public whether Chicago mayor Richard Daley had done right to unleash his cops to club and arrest unarmed students carrying "We are your children" placards. Sixty-six percent said yes, Mayor Daley was right; only 20 percent said no.[60] The Daley poll asked Americans to take sides, not between whites and blacks, but between the forces of order and the forces of disorder. By inventing excuses for riots, condoning crime, and cringing before terrorism, Democratic liberals convinced the public that only conservatives and Republicans could be trusted to defend American society. "Since 1960," observed Yale anthropologist Jonathan Rieder, "the Jews and Italians of Canarsie have embellished and modified the meaning of liberalism, associating it with profligacy, spinelessness, malevolence, masochism, elitism, fantasy, anarchy, idealism, softness, irresponsibility, and sanctimoniousness. The term *conservative* acquired connotations of pragmatism, character, reciprocity, truthfulness, stoicism, manliness, realism, hardness, vengeance, strictness, and responsibility."[61] In 1980, the Roosevelt Democrats of Canarsie voted overwhelmingly in favor of Ronald Reagan, the Jewish precincts nearly as heavily as the Italian ones.

Race obviously entered into this. It was race that embarrassed liberals into laxness on crime, for instance, and race that enticed them into dubious social experiments like busing. Race surely played some role in ending the mid-century infatuation with big and costly government. But even more damage to the cause of social welfare was done by those liberals who refused to accept that Americans could have any reason *except* racism for worrying about the growth of a dependent underclass. Hubert Humphrey roared in 1976 that those "candidates who make an attack on welfare are making an attack on government programs, on blacks, on minorities, on the cities. It's a disguised new form of racism, a disguised new form of conservatism."[62]

But Americans were not attacking government programs. By 1973, almost one-quarter of American young people thought they had a "right" to leisure. Almost one-half thought they had a "right" to a college education for their children. More than one-half thought they had a "right" to the best available medical care.[63] They were not even turning against social welfare. What they were doing was *rethinking* welfare—insisting that while individuals were entitled to help, they were also obliged to help themselves. Pollsters who asked "Should government do everything possible to aid the poor?" found a sharp drop in the number of people who strongly agreed, from 30 percent in 1975 to 18 percent in 1983. But when the question was turned around, "Or is it primarily each person's responsibility to take care of himself?" pollsters found *no increase* in the number of people who believed in strict personal responsibility.[64]

Americans were not returning to the era of *laissez faire*. Rugged individualism no longer swayed them. Neither, however, did the social-democratic ethos of the middle years of this century. Americans were moving on to something new, a creed that blended the antique ideal of self-reliance with a soft sense of entitlement for those who made some minimal effort on their own behalf. It was a fuzzy political idea—perfect for the fuzzy era to come—and the struggle to imbue it with meaning would define the politics of the post–Cold War era.

CONCLUSION

FOR HALF A CENTURY, AMERICANS HAVE BEEN ASKED TO CHOOSE BETWEEN two myths about their country's recent past. In one, the heroes are the parents; in the other, the children. In the parents' myth, the middle years of this century were a time of peace and prosperity, the well-deserved reward for enduring the Depression, defeating the Nazis, and resisting communism. In the children's, those same years were a dark epoch of racism, sexism, and homophobia, when Hollywood liberals flinched every time the doorbell rang, fearing it was the FBI come to tell them they couldn't write screenplays any more. In the children's myth, Americans huddled frozen and miserable (like Pepperland under the dominion of the Blue Meanies in the Beatles' *Yellow Submarine*) until the brave, joyous protesters of the 1960s liberated them. In the parents', a golden age of patriotism and duty was wrecked by draft-dodging, pot-smoking, hippie-turned-yuppie lowlifes. It is like the extinction of the dinosaurs: One minute giants are walking the earth, then suddenly—CRASH!—a comet smacks the planet and the giants are replaced overnight by tiny rat-like creatures.

In the 1990s, the stock of the parents' myth soared way above the children's. The scandals of the Clinton presidency touched off an explosion of baby-boomer self-disgust. Vice President Al Gore declared himself a candidate for the presidency in 1999 with a speech in which he distanced himself as far as possible from the experiences of his generation, recalling the pride with which he had worn his country's uniform in war, and describing "faith and family" as his deepest commitments. Former draft-evaders queued in bookstores to buy Tom Brokaw's valentine to their wartime parents, *The Greatest Generation*. Over on the political left, writers like Cornel West and Sylvia Hewitt rehabilitated the once-demonized 1950s as a time when a high-school graduate could adequately support a wife and family. The final blow to the children's myth: The millions of Americans born since 1970 seem to have collectively decided that the Boomers are absolutely the most boring generation of old-fogies ever to have inflicted their reminiscences on the young. The aging Sixties hipster who will not shut up is a figure of fun on television hits from Britain's "Absolutely Fabulous" to MTV's "Daria."

Liberation? The record of the years from 1965 to 1980 is blotted by the abandonment of a desperate ally to a ruthless enemy (South Vietnam to the communist North), the collapse of educational standards, the dissolution of the ideal of racial equality into rancorous arguments over special privileges, the discharge of hundreds of thousands of mentally ill people to fend for themselves on the sidewalks, rampant drug abuse, the shattering of millions of families by divorce, and the savaging of America's cities by crime and disorder. "The effect of liberty to individuals is," Edmund Burke wrote two centuries ago, "that they may do what they please: we ought to see what it will please them to do before we risk congratulations, which may be soon turned into complaints."[1]

The parents' myth is much more appealing than the other: Who would not be prouder of having fought through the mud of Guadalcanal than having fornicated in the mud at Woodstock? But a better myth is a myth all the same. It is as foolish to idealize the past as to condescend to it. The greatest generation was also the statist generation. Like them or loathe them, the middle decades of the twentieth century were an entirely anomalous period in American history. Never had the state been so strong, never had people submitted as uncomplainingly, never had the country been more economically equal, never had it been more ethnically homogeneous, seldom was its political consensus more overpowering. You can see now why people might pine for those days. But would they pine for them if they remembered more clearly that the top rate of federal income tax was 90 percent? Or that it was a very serious crime for a private citizen to own a gold coin? Or that the attorney general could wiretap more or less anybody he wanted to, without a warrant, if he attested he was doing so for national security purposes? The secretary of state could prevent any American he considered a security risk from traveling abroad by denying him a passport. When mayors and governors wanted to knock down existing neighborhoods to build highways, there was nothing much that anybody could do to stop them; they even got to decide for themselves without much second-guessing what constituted adequate compensation. To ship a crate of lettuce across the country, a trucker needed permission from a federal regulatory agency. Almost one-third of the country's best jobs were off-limits for anyone who refused to join a union. The story of the past must do justice to both its achievements and its destructiveness; equally to the obsolete and oppressive laws that have been uprooted and to the decent and valuable habits and institutions that were unnecessarily smashed. Justice must be done not solely for the sake of honesty, important as that is, but also for a very practical reason. Unless the people of the present day correctly understand the social convulsion of the 1970s, they will stumble into fatal errors of judgment about their own times and their own lives.

This danger is more than hypothetical. If the only way to stabilize the family and solidify the nation is by bringing the dead back to life, then the family will not be stabilized and the nation will not be solidified. Coming a close second to nostalgia in the pageant of uselessness is the sort of complacency that looks at the wreckage left by the rampages of the 1970s and shrugs it off as the price of progress. Progress can come at a lower price, and when it does, it is a better bargain.

Alexis de Tocqueville warned that thinkers in democratic societies will always be tempted by deterministic explanations of events. They "forge a close and enormous chain, which girds and binds the human race. To their minds it is not enough to show what events have occurred: they wish to show that events could not have occurred otherwise." This tendency denies individual choice and thus individual moral responsibility. "A cause sufficiently extensive to affect millions of men at once and sufficiently strong to bend them all together in the same direction may well seem irresistible. [H]aving seen that mankind do yield to it, the mind is close upon the inference that mankind cannot resist it."[2] If what happened to America in the 1970s was the product of some overwhelming global cause—if it was the inevitable consequence of the invention of the birth control pill, or the after-shocks of World War I, or something called "modernity"—why then, we are all excused, aren't we? What else could we have done but what we did? What else can we do but continue as we are, and hope that it will all somehow work out for the best?

While it may be true that grand historic forces beyond any man's or woman's control made the 1970s *possible*, what made the 1970s *happen* was individual choice. It was a person, not an impersonal social force, that mugged the old lady on the corner in order to buy heroin; and it was some other person or group of people who relaxed law enforcement and transformed mugging into a paying proposition. Identifiable people refused South Vietnam the bullets and fuel that might have turned the tide of war, other identifiable people decided that immigrants to the United States should be educated in Spanish, not English, and still further identifiable people opted to deal with the Arab oil embargo by extending price controls rather than abolishing them. Those were all choices, and they all had consequences. Other choices could have been made, and they would have had different consequences. And, what is more important, *other choices still can be made*. The cliché "you can't turn back the clock" is a truth that conceals a harmful falsehood. Time may move in only one direction, but it is never too late to lead a better life.

The first precondition of that better life is to identify where one went wrong. The turmoil of the 1970s should be understood not as some "great disruption" in which all of previous history is to be found on one side of a dateline and we ourselves on the other. It should be understood instead as the rebellion of an unmilitary people against institutions and laws formed by a century of war and the preparation for war. War, for the winners, is not always an unqualifiedly dreadful experience. It gives people a sense of purpose. Suicide rates fell in most combatant nations during World War II. War inspires faith in the political leaders who bring victory. With millions of able-bodied men removed from the work force, and the cooperation of union leaders absolutely indispensable to maintaining all-out production, the wages of labor rise, and the taxes that finance war constrain the wealth of the rich. War reinforces sex roles—men fight, women keep the home fires burning. War gives rise too to feelings of spiritual equality—the "we're all in this together" spirit that inspired former Labor party leader Michael Foot, when asked to give some idea of what his vision of the socialist Utopia would look like, to reply, simply, "1940." The America of the 1950s still enjoyed those benefits of war. And out of the colossal experience of 1941–1945 emerged a political consensus: However much Republicans and Democrats disagreed about the relatively petty issues of domestic politics, they were united on what then really mattered—the great issues of war and peace—and they trusted their leaders to resolve those issues correctly.

But war also has its demands. It demands taxation, regulation, and control; hierarchy, centralization, and secrecy; conscription, obedience, and authority—none of them easily reconciled with the American constitutional scheme or the American national character. The United States would not and could not endure as a garrison society. Sooner or later that midcentury discipline was bound to relax. The real conundrum to be explained is not why American loosened up, but why that loosening happened when it did. Why the 1970s, rather than the post–Cold War 1990s? Why did it take the abrupt, convulsive, and often hysterical form that it did, rather than proceeding slowly and gradually as the World War II generation cleared the scene? The answer can be summed up in three words: Vietnam, desegregation, and inflation.

Vietnam. "Americans hate a loser," George C. Scott announces at the beginning of the 1972 movie *Patton*, Richard Nixon's favorite. The Vietnam war did not merely discredit the government that chose to wage it; it discredited the habits of mind that made the war possible; it discredited the very style and sensibility of midcentury America, from Bob Hope's entertainment of the troops to the coats and ties in college dining lounges. It taught an entire generation the oppositional style that to this day so often substitutes for real politics.

Desegregation. The breezy self-confidence—the unthinking assumption of rectitude—that buttressed American life in the 1940s and 1950s was exploded by the civil rights movement. The United States had saved civilization from Nazism; the civil-rights movement charged that America bore a more than passing resemblance to Nazi Germany itself. It was a withering indictment, and one to which America's leading institutions, from its wealthiest corporations to its greatest universities, immediately pled guilty. If America could have been so terribly blind to justice in this one way, might there not be other ways in which it was equally blind? That was the bitter question that protest movement after protest movement would hurl at the country after 1965—and the country would never again feel entirely confident that the protesters were wrong.

Inflation. The statist economics of mid-century America generated the inflation of the 1970s and dismally failed to curb it. The controls and regulations meant to soften the ups and downs of the market acted instead like those breakwaters that beach towns build to stop the shifting of the sands: The longer the energy of the ocean is balked, the more terrible is the smash when it finally arrives.

Perhaps it might be well to add a fourth word: *technology.* Social democracy was born on the assembly-line and died with it. As companies grew huger and huger after 1880, it became natural to wonder why they could not grow larger still—until the entire economy merged into one enterprise, under one central management. The Germans seemed to have done exactly that with brilliant success during the First World War, creating what no less an authority than Lenin regarded as the world's first functioning socialist state. The great English jurist A.V. Dicey observed in 1905 that the dominant intellectual trend of his times had been the revolt against individualism in favor of collectivism.[3]

This trend arrived late in the United States, and provoked more resistance there than anywhere else. In the 1920s, Jeffersonian Democrats like New York Governor Franklin Delano Roosevelt fiercely condemned Commerce Secretary Herbert Hoover for trying to herd American industry into officially sanctioned cartels that would earn steady profits and could thus pay higher wages. But the Great Depression overcame individualist qualms, and by 1933 Roosevelt was adapting and expanding Hoover's cartels far beyond their unhappy author's wildest imaginings. The Supreme Court declared the cartels unconstitutional in 1935, but an even more sweeping system of collectivization was imposed during the war, and by the 1950s, left-leaning social theorists were confidently speculating that the United States and the Soviet Union might yet "converge" upon a system of democratic elections and socialized industry. The great wars of the twentieth century were fought by societies already predisposed to collectivism—indeed, as the unfashionable anticollectivists passionately argued, it was this bias toward collectivism that predisposed those societies toward war.

The stability of mid-century was the product of special and in some ways un-American circumstances: war and mobilization for war; the heyday of heavy industry; a depression that convinced normally individualistic Americans to submit to unprecedented direction and regimentation. A carapace of control had been locked upon the country as an emergency measure. But as the emergency dragged on for decade after decade, the carapace chafed and abraded. In the 1970s, the country at last burst through it.

In bursting through the carapace, Americans did not pause to distinguish between obsolete and unnecessary restrictions and good and wise ones. They smashed them all. A quarter-century later, as they sift through the shards and fragments of their grandparents' world, they have begun to feel regret. Suddenly, American society seems on the verge of a great turn away from the self-indulgence of the 1970s and toward . . . toward what?

Toward something more like the normal conditions of American life. The sprawling, garrulous, individualistic, fractious, unequal, polyglot republic of the early twenty-first century looks a very great deal like the republic of the beginning of the twentieth. Then as now, the United States was haunted by cares and doubts. Old certainties had collapsed and the new certainties—socialism, eugenics, imperialism, war—threatened traditional values and ideals. City streets jabbered in foreign tongues, racial tensions pervaded the country, the sudden agglomeration of wealth raised the ominous question of how democratic government could survive the arrogance of the rich and the envy of the poor. Family life seemed to be disintegrating, as the rise of great cities encouraged unhappy men to desert their families and the weakening of religion chipped away at traditional sexual norms.

The social stability of the 1950s was not inherited from some distant past. It was the self-conscious achievement of a society that had overcome its disorder, doubt, and disunity. And when that stability was lost, the disorder, the doubt, and the disunity returned.

Some have boldly suggested that American society is "walking back from the cultural abyss" it approached in the 1970s.[4] It's possible to imagine the cultural revolution of the 1970s as a kind of tidal wave that inundated homes and lives, but that is now receding, leaving the beach messy, but essentially unchanged. But is that really true?

Item: After losing a nasty custody battle for the three-year-old daughter she had deliberately conceived with a man she barely knew, pop star Sinead O'Connor concluded, "I wouldn't do it again. Not because it's immoral, but because it was stressful."[5] O'Connor is an oddball in many ways, but here for once she is perfectly conventional. Early twenty-first century is newly cautious society, not a remoralized one, and even that caution extends only so far. Americans born between 1963 and 1972, and who therefore came of age during the worst of the AIDS epidemic, are actually *more* sexually promiscuous even than their baby-boomer elders.[6]

But if remoralization is not yet a fact, it can still be an aspiration. Americans are a people of anxious conscience, and they do not seem very pleased with themselves these days. They see corruption in office, and their fellow-citizens apparently acquiescing in it; they see pervasive child-neglect, disrespect for legitimate authority, quotas in the workplace, gruesome crimes in the quietest towns, misspellings in the letters from their children's teachers, smut on the airwaves, the hardening misery of the poorest of the poor. They lack the vocabulary to express their misgivings: How can one judge if one has been taught all one's life that it is wicked to be judgmental? But rendering the misgivings inarticulate does not make them go away. So let's be articulate. It is not true that things in general were better half a century ago. Things in many respects were worse—more militaristic, less innovative, more statist, less tolerant, more unionized, less humane, more prejudiced. Nostalgia for the past would be misplaced, and even if it were not, nostalgia is the weakest and most useless of emotions, the narcotic of the defeated and the helpless. *But if things in general were not better, some things in particular were.* It was better when people showed more loyalty to family and country, better when they read more and talked about themselves less, better when they restrained their sexuality, better when professors and curators were unafraid to uphold high intellectual and artistic standards, better when immigrants were expected to Americanize promptly, better when not every sorrow begat a lawsuit.

And if things were better in these respects and others like them, if Americans really feel that way, then there is something healthier to do than pine for the lost days of the past. The very fact that so many people feel that all is not well is, surely, the best proof one could ask for of how much *is* well—that one's fellow-citizens and fellow-creatures are not morally numb, that they have consciences and memories. It is discontent, after all, that moves humanity: that invents the umbrella, the toothpick, the airplane, the microchip. It is discontent that moves us morally too—not backward, because the past never returns, no matter how lovely it was—but onward, away from the follies and triumphs of the 1970s and toward something new: new vices, new virtues, new sins—and new progress.

NOTES

INTRODUCTION

1. Daniel Boorstin, *The Americans: The National Experience* (Random House, 1965), p. 127.
2. Daniel Yankelovich, *The New Rules: Searching for Self-Fulfillment in a World Turned Upside Down* (Random House, 1981), pp. 98–99.
3. Stephen and Abigail Thernstrom, *America in Black and White: One Nation, Indivisible* (Simon & Schuster, 1997), pp. 174–75.
4. Richard N. Goodwin, *Remembering America: A Voice From the Sixties* (Harper Perennial, 1989), p. 8.
5. William Shannon, *New York Times*, Sept. 27, 1975, p. E–17.

PART I
TRUST

1. Jonathan Rieder, *Canarsie: The Jews and Italians of Brooklyn Against Liberalism* (Harvard University Press, 1985) p. 99.
2. National Opinion Research Center, *An American Profile: Opinions and Behaviors 1972–89* (Gale Research, 1990).
3. Quoted in Frederick F. Siegel, *Troubled Journey: America From Pearl Harbor to Ronald Reagan* (Hill & Wang 1984), pp. 182–83.
4. Ronald Inglehart, *Modernization and Postmodernization: Cultural, Economic and Political Change in 43 Societies* (Princeton University Press, 1997), p. 300.
5. Theodore Roosevelt was younger, forty-three, when an assassin's bullet elevated him to the presidency, but he was forty-six before he won election in his own right.
6. http://www.lbjlib.utexas.edu/johnson/archives.hom/speeches.hom/640522.htm

7. Daniel Patrick Moynihan, *Maximum Feasible Misunderstanding: Community Action in the War on Poverty* (Free Press, 1969), pp. xii-xiii.

8. *Canarsie*, pp. 75–76.

9. New York State Department of Corrections, *Annual Report of the Commissioner of Correction for the Year 1941*, p. 19.

10. *Ibid.*, p. 19.

11. I thank Michael Barone for drawing this fact to my attention.

12. Surveys by the American Institute of Public Opinion and the National Opinion Research Center, cited by Morris Janowitz, *The Last Half Century: Societal Change and Politics in America* (University of Chicago Press, 1978), p. 377.

13. *Maximum Feasible Misunderstanding*, p. 13.

14. *The Sourcebook of Criminal Justice Statistics*, www.albany.edu/sourcebook/1995/pdf/t256.pdf.

15. U.S. Bureau of the Census, *Statistical Abstract of the United States* (1989), p. 220.

16. *The Last Half Century*, p. 391.

17. Josh Sugarmann, *NRA: Money, Firepower and Fear* (National Press Books, 1992), pp. 37 and 54.

18. Judson Gooding, "Blue-Collar Blues in the Assembly Line," *Fortune* July 1970, pp. 112–113.

19. *Ibid.*, p. 70.

20. Robert S. Diamond, "What Business Thinks: The Fortune 500-Yankelovich Survey," *Fortune*, July 1970, p. 73.

21. The poll was taken by Opinion Research Corp. and released August 9, 1977.

22. Sears Tower, Chicago, 1973; One World Trade Center, New York, 1972; Two World Trade Center, New York, 1973; Empire State Building, New York, 1931; Amoco Tower, Chicago, 1973; John Hancock Center, Chicago, 1968; Chrysler Building, New York, 1930.

23. Oroville Dam, California, 1968; Cyprus Dam, Idaho, 1982; Hoover Dam, Nevada, 1936; Dworshak Dam, Idaho, 1973; Glen Canyon Dam,

Arizona, 1964; New Bullards Bar Dam, California, 1969; New Melones Dam, California, 1979; Shasta Dam, California, 1945; New Don Pedro Dam, California, 1971; Yankee Doodle Dam, Montana, 1972.

24. Verrazano-Narrows Bridge, 1964; Golden Gate Bridge, 1937; Mackinac Bridge, 1957; George Washington Bridge, 1931; Tacoma Narrows Bridge, 1950; San Francisco-Oakland Bridge, 1936; Bronx Whitestone Bridge, 1939; Delaware Memorial I Bridge, 1951; Delaware Memorial II Bridge, 1968; Seaway Skyway Bridge, 1960; Walt Whitman Bridge, 1957; Ambassador Bridge, 1929; Throgs Neck Bridge, 1961; Benjamin Franklin Bridge, 1926; Bear Mountain Bridge, 1924; William Preston Lane I Bridge, 1952; William Preston Lane II Bridge, 1973; Williamsburg Bridge, 1903; Newport Bridge, 1969; Chesapeake Bay Bridge, 1952.

25. J. Irwin Miller, quoted in Ralph Nader, Mark Green, and Joel Seligman, *Taming the Giant Corporation* (Norton, 1976), p. 77.

26. Robert Townsend, *Up the Organization* (Knopf, 1970), p. 114.

27. Richard J. Barnet & Ronald E. Muller, *Global Reach: The Power of the Multinational Corporations* (Simon & Schuster, 1974), p. 359.

28. Clyde Prestowitz, *Changing Places: How We Allowed the Japanese to Take the Lead* (Basic Books, 1988), p. 251.

29. Robert Reich, *The Work of Nations: Preparing Ourselves for 21st Century Capitalism* (Knopf, 1991), p. 72.

30. Quoted in Robert Caro, *The Years of Lyndon Johnson: Means of Ascent* (Knopf, 1990), p. 388.

31. Judith Exner, *My Story* (Grove Press, 1977).

32. *The Last Half Century*, p. 358.

33. William F. Buckley, *Stained Glass* (Doubleday & Co., 1978), pp. 231, 100.

34. A fascinating—if polemical—account of civil liberties abuses under Kennedy and Johnson can be found in Victor Lasky, *It Didn't Start With Watergate* (Dial, 1977). Department of Coincidences note: The literary agent for Lasky's book was one Lucianne Goldberg.

35. *West Virginia State Board of Education* v. *Barnette*.

36. *Chaplinsky* v. *New Hampshire.*
37. *Roth* v. *United States.*
38. *United States* v. *O'Brien.*

PART II
DUTY

1. Robert J. Ringer *Looking Out for Number One* (Funk & Wagnalls 1977), p. x.
2. Nena O'Neill and George O'Neill, *Open Marriage* (M. Evans & Co., 1972), p. 222.
3. See Robert Goldberg, *Barry Goldwater* (Yale University Press, 1995), pp. 170–72 and p. 194.
4. The main poll of American sexual attitudes, conducted by the National Opinion Research Center, extends back only to 1972. That year, 69 percent of Americans deemed adultery "always wrong"; by 1996 the "always wrong" figure had risen to 77 percent. Since the force driving this new implacability on the subject of adultery is the disappearance of the old double standard in favor of the occasionally wayward husband, it's very unlikely that the 1963 number would be higher than the number in 1973.
5. Derek Bok, *The State of the Nation: Government and the Quest for a Better Society* (Harvard University Press, 1996), p. 319.
6. Priscilla Tucker, "The New Boutique Bandits," *New York*, May 4, 1970, pp. 28–32.
7. *The State of the Nation*, p. 318.
8. John Stuart Mill, *On Liberty*, ed. Stefan Collini (Cambridge University Press, 1989), p. 67.
9. John B. Koffend, *A Letter to My Wife* (Saturday Review Press, 1972), p. 6.
10. Wayne Farrell, *The Liberated Man* (Random House, 1974), p. 91.
11. Television watching is not easily compared over the past few decades. Until the early 1980s, Neilson counted how many hours per week

were watched *per household* because the large majority of households contained only one set. As multiple televisions became the norm—51 percent of American households now own three or more—Neilson began clocking the hours watched *per person*. It does seem fair to say, however, that more television was being watched in the middle 1990s than in the middle 1970s.

12. Daniel Yankelovich, *The New Morality: A Profile of American Youth in the 1970s* (McGraw Hill, 1974), pp. 103–11.

13. Harvey Kaye, *Male Survival: Masculinity Without Myth* (Grossett & Dunlap, 1974), p. 20.

14. Daniel Yankelovich, *New Rules: Searching for Self-Fulfillment in a World Turned Upside Down* (Random House, 1981), p. 21.

15. William H. Whyte, *The Organization Man* (Simon & Schuster, 1956), p. 5.

16. Many economists think that the flood of women into the workforce was actually a *cause* of the productivity slowdown rather than a result. When the number of workers is rising rapidly, as it was in the 1970s, wage increases slow and employers can often raise output more cheaply by adding staff rather than by investing in new equipment. The biggest productivity jumps tend to occur in periods when the laborforce is growing slowly—the war years, for example—and productivity correspondingly tends to lag when the laborforce is growing fast.

17. Chinhui Juhn, Relative Wage Trends, *Women's Work and Family Income*, (AEI Press, 1996), p. 9.

18. *New Rules*, p. 5.

19. *New Rules*, p. 9.

20. Data on industrial accidents before the creation of the Occupational Safety and Health Administration in 1970 are sparse, but all experts agree that the trend has been sharply downward throughout the twentieth century.

21. See Michael Moritz, *The Little Kingdom: The Private Story of Apple Computer* (Morrow, 1984).

22. Robert Townsend, *Up the Organization* (Knopf, 1970), p. 124.

23. Labor force participation rate in 1970 for married men aged 45–64 was 91.2 percent; in 1980, it was 84.3 percent; in 1996, 83.2 percent. Rising longevity explains some of the shrinkage—there were a lot more 80-year-old married men about in 1996 than in 1970—but nowhere close to all of it.

24. Christopher Jencks, "Is the American Underclass Growing?" in *The Urban Underclass*, ed. Christopher Jencks and Paul E. Peterson (Brookings Institution, 1991) p. 59.

25. Betting at horse or dog races was, however, legal in almost all states.

26. *Legalized Gambling: For and Against*, eds. Rod. L. Evans and Mark Hance (Open Court Publishing, 1998), pp. 107–11.

27. *Open Marriage*, p. 219.

28. Kathleen Sheridan, *Living with Divorce* (Thomas More Press, 1976), p. 126.

29. Jennifer Skolnik, "Notes of a Recycled Housewife," *New York*, May 22 1972, p. 36.

30. Susan Gettleman and Janet Markowitz, *The Courage to Divorce* (Simon & Schuster, 1974), p. 45.

31. Charlotte Hold Clinebell, *Meet Me in the Middle* (Harper & Row, 1973), p. 11.

32. David L. Krantz, *Radical Career Change: Life Beyond Work*. Free Press, 1978, pp. 11–13.

33. Gail Sheehy, "The Men of Women's Liberation Have Learned Not to Laugh," *New York*, May 18, 1970, p. 30.

34. Frederick Lewis Allen, *The Big Change: America Transforms Itself 1900–1950* (Harper Brothers, 1952), p. 222.

35. See for example Barbara Ehrenreich, *The Hearts of Men: American Dreams and the Flight From Commitment* (Doubleday 1983) for a feminist argument that the divorce surge was driven by male preferences, and Cathy Young, *Ceasefire! Why Men and Women Must Join Forces to Achieve True Equality* (Free Press, 1999) for a neofeminist argument that it was women who were responsible.

36. Of all women of those ages, 2.5 percent were divorced and not remarried in 1950; 6.8 percent divorced and not remarried in 1975.

37. See Margaret Gallagher, *The Abolition of Marriage* (Regnery, 1996), for a brilliant analysis of the economic consequences of this legal change.

38. Erica Jong, *How To Save Your Own Life* (Holt, Rinehart, 1977), p. 45.

39. Ann Jones, *Women Who Kill* (Beacon Press, 1979), p. 14.

40. Gail Sheehy, *Passages: Predictable Crises of Adult Life* (E.P. Dutton 1976), p. 208.

41. *Living with Divorce*, p. 110.

42. Jessie Bernard, *The Future of Marriage* (World Publishing, 1972), p. 107.

43. *Ibid.*, p. 107.

44. *Living with Divorce*, p. 130.

45. *New York Times*, January 6, 1982, p. A–10.

46. Glenda Riley, *Divorce: An American Tradition* (Oxford University Press, 1991), p. 169.

47. *Courage to Divorce*, p. 105. Italics in original.

48. Martha McPhee, *Bright Angel Time* (Random House, 1997), pp. 19–20.

49. Quoted by Guenter Lewy, *America in Vietnam* (Oxford University Press, 1978) at 314–15.

50. Landon Y. Jones, *Great Expectations: America and the Baby Boom Generation* (Coward,McCann & Geoghegan, 1980), p. 94.

51. Edwards defeated Westmoreland by a 58–42 margin, and went on to serve as Secretary of Energy in the Reagan administration.

52. Morris Janowitz, *The Last Half Century: Societal Change and Politics in America* (University of Chicago Press, 1978), p. 214.

53. Thomas Conrad and Michael Marchino, "Disenchantment in the Ranks," *The Progressive* (February 1979), pp. 48–49.

54. See the Veterans' Administration website, www.va.gov/organization/Vahis.htm

55. Andrew J. Bacevich and Richard H. Kohn, "Grand Army of the Republicans," *The New Republic* (December 8, 1997), p. 24.

56. Jane Howard, *A Different Woman* (E.P. Dutton, 1973), p. 119.

57. *Sociology of Marriage and the Family*, p. 142.

58. Caroline Bird, *Born Female: The High Cost of Keeping Women Down* (David McKay Co., 1970), p. 246.

59. *New Rules*, p. 95.

60. *Great Expectations*, p. 258.

61. *The Sexually Aggressive Woman*, p. 138.

62. *Open Marriage*, pp. 84–85.

63. Robert Sorenson, *Adolescent Sexuality in Contemporary America* (World Publishing, 1973), p. 98.

64. *New Rules*, p. 96.

65. *Eisenstadt* v. *Baird*, 405 U.S. 438 (1972).

66. Alison Lurie, *The War Between the Tates* (Random House, 1974), p. 350.

67. Adrienne Rich, *Of Woman Born* (Norton, 1976), p. 127.

68. Howard M. Bahr, "Changes in Family Life in Middletown, 1924–77" in *Public Opinion Quarterly* (October 1980), p. 47.

69. *The New Morality*, p. 98.

70. *The Future of Marriage*, p. 90.

71. *How To Be Your Own Best Friend*, p. 52.

72. Wayne W. Dyer, *Your Erroneous Zones*, (Harper Perennial, 1991), pp. 154–55.

73. Quoted in Marsha Dubron, "Female Assertiveness: How a Pussycat Can Learn to be a Panther" in *New York* (July 28, 1975), p. 42.

74. *New Rules*, p. 81.

75. The International Olympic Committee barred Matthews and Collett from future competitions, but they retained their medals and their places of honor in the Olympic roster. Memory of the incident was almost instantly blotted out by the kidnapping and murder of the entire Israeli Olympic team bare hours later.

76. *Great Expectations*, p. 94.

77. *New Rules*, p. 93.

78. *New Morality*, p. 99.

79. Betty Rollins, "Motherhood: Who Needs It?" in *The Gender Reader*, ed. Evelyn Ashton-Jones and Gary Olson (Allyn & Bacon, 1991), p. 377.

80. Rosemary Radford Ruether, *New Woman, New Earth* (Seabury Press, 1975), p. 26.

81. Nancy Friday, *My Mother, My Self* (Delacorte Press, 1977), p. 24.

82. *Your Erroneous Zones*, pp. 191–92.

83. *New Rules*, p. 104.

84. Phyllis Chesler, *Women & Madness* (Doubleday, 1972), p. 280.

85. *Living with Divorce*, pp. 81–82.

86. Mary Mattis, *Sex and the Single Parent* (Holt, 1986), p. 294.

87. *Ibid.*, pp. 196–197.

88. *Courage to Divorce*, p. 139.

89. *My Mother/My Self*, p. xiii.

90. Elizabeth M. Landes and Richard A. Posner, "The Economics of the Baby Shortage," 7 J. Legal Studies 323 (1978).

PART III
REASON

1. Linda Francke "See Me, Feel Me, Touch Me, Heal Me: The Encounter Group Explosion," *New York* (May 25, 1970), p. 36. The estimate of 5,000 active groups cited by the author originated with the Manhattan Board of Mental Health.

2. Frederick Lewis Allen, *The Big Change* (Harper & Brothers, 1952), p. 164.

3. Bernard Berkowitz and Mildred Newman, *How To Be Your Own Best Friend* (Lark Publishing, 1971), p. 49.

4. Kurt Black, *Beyond Words* (Russell Sage Foundation, 1972), p. 31.

5. Harriett Mann, Miriam Siegler & Humphry Osmond, "Four Attitudes Toward Time," *Psychology Today* December 1972, p. 80.

6. Thomas J. Peters, *In Search of Excellence* (Harper & Row, 1984), p. 40.

7. Robert Pirsig, *Zen and the Art of Motorcycle Maintenance* (Morrow, 1974), p. 24.

8. George Leonard, "The Search for Health: From the Fountain of Youth to Today's Holistic Frontier," *New West*, January 3, 1977, p. 39.

9. I am indebted to an article by Michael Schaffer in the July 10, 1998 issue of *Washington City Paper* for its evocative descriptions and photographs of old Southwest.

10. F. A. Hayek, "'Conscious' Direction and the Growth of Reason" in *The Counter-Revolution of Science* (Liberty Press edition, 1979), p. 153.

11. I know someone who did it.

12. *Zen and the Art of Motorcycle Maintenance*, p. 102.

13. Barry Goldwater, *The Conscience of a Conservative* (Regnery Gateway edition, 1990), pp. 5–7.

14. David Krantz, *Radical Career Change* (Free Press, 1978), p. 64.

15. Norman Mailer, *Armies of the Night* (New American Library, 2nd ed., 1983), p. 62.

16. Gena Corea, *The Hidden Malpractice: How American Medicine Treats Women as Patients and Professionals* (William Morrow & Co., 1977), pp. 184–85.

17. Jerry Rubin, *Growing (Up) at 37* (M. Evans & Co., 1976), p. 20.

18. Landon Y. Jones, *Great Expectations: America and the Baby Boom Generation* (Coward, McCann & Geoghegan, 1980), p. 87.

19. A useful bibliography is appended to Larry Kusche, *The Bermuda Triangle Mystery—Solved* (Prometheus Books, 2nd ed., 1996).

20. "I suggest that the first in a series of devastating weather and seismic events has begun, and that it will reach its crescendo immediately after March 20, 1980, with a mighty wrench that will then be seen as the first supercolossal earthquake in modern times." Joseph Goodavage, *Our Threatened Planet* (Simon & Schuster, 1978), pp. 29–30.

21. Bill Henkin and Amy Wallace, *The Psychic Healing Book* (Delacorte, 1978), pp. 139–40.

22. See American Psychological Association, *The Rising Curve* (1998) for a discussion of the closing of the racial IQ gap over time.

23. Stephen L. Carter, *Reflections of an Affirmative Action Baby* (Basic Books, 1991), p. 12.

24. Charles A. Murray and Richard J. Herrinstein, "What's Behind the SAT-Score Decline?" *The Public Interest*, Winter 1992, p. 32.

25. *Great Expectations*, p. 124.

26. *Great Expectations*, p. 119.

27. Nicholas Zill and Marianne Winglee, *Who Reads Literature? The Future of the United States as a Nation of Readers* (Research Division, National Endowment for the Arts, 1990), p. 19.

28. *Publisher's Weekly*, September 27, 1976, p. 41.

29. *Great Expectations*, p. 126.

30. Norman Podhoretz, *Making It* (Random House, 1967), p. 241.

31. Stephen H. Balch and Glenn Ricketts, "The University of Chicago's Shrinking Core," *The Wall Street Journal*, June 3, 1999, p. A–26.

32. Robert Rosenblum, *Paintings in the Musee d'Orsay* (Stewart, Tabori & Chang, 1989), p. 15.

33. Edward Said, *Orientalism* (Vintage, 1994), p. 10.

34. Carroll, Jackson W.; Johnson, Douglas W.; Marty, Martin. *Religion in America: 1950 to the Present* (Harper & Row, 1979), p. 25.

35. Gregory Johnson, "Krishna Consciousness in San Francisco" in *The New Religious Consciousness*, ed. Charles Y. Glock and Robert N. Bellah (University of California Press, 1976), p. 39.

36. *Ibid.*, p. 38.

37. *Ibid.*, pp. 34–35.

38. The membership and attendance data in the previous two paragraphs are all taken from *Religion in America*.

39. *Publishers Weekly*, March 14, 1977, p. 30.

40. Paul Ehrlich, *The Population Bomb* (Sierra Club illustrated edition, 1969), p. 5.

41. *The Population Bomb*, pp. 67–69.

42. William and Paul Paddock, *Famine 1975!* (Little Brown, 1967).

43. Gerald O. Barney, *Entering the 21st Century* (Pergamon Press, 1980).

44. Julian Simon, *The Ultimate Resource* (Princeton University Press, 1981), p. 57.

45. See Colin McEvedy and Richard Jones, *Atlas of World Population History* (Penguin, 1978).

46. *Population Bomb*, pp. 124–50.

47. Stephen H. Schneider with Lynne E. Mesirow, *The Genesis Strategy: Climate and Global Survival* (Plenum Press, 1976), pp. 2–3.

PART IV
DESIRE

1. Andrew Holleran, *Dancer from the Dance* (William Morrow & Co., 1978), pp. 24–25.

2. The University of Michigan annually surveys drug use among high-school students. Their data can be found at the Office of Drug Control Policy's website, www.whitehousedrugpolicy.gov.

    In 1979, more than 35 percent of high-school seniors are estimated to have smoked marijuana within the previous thirty days. Between 1980 and 1992, that rate plunged to 12 percent; between 1993 and 1997 it rose back up to 25 percent, dipping slightly in 1998. The rate of increase was greatest among the very youngest adolescents. In 1992, only some 3.7 percent of eighth-graders had used marijuana within the previous twelve months; by 1997, 10.2 percent had done so.

3. Rinker Buck, "Reaping the Hidden Rewards of Fitness," *New York*, May 29, 1978, p. 41.

4. Judson Gooding, "The Tennis Industry," *Fortune*, June 1973, p. 126.

5. Jim Fixx, *The Complete Book of Running* (Random House, 1977), p. 34.

6. Quoted in John Van Doorn, "An Intimidating New Class: The Physical Elite," *New York*, May 29, 1978, p. 38.

7. Dr. Thaddeus Kostrubala, quoted in "An Intimidating New Class: The Physical Elite," p. 37.

8. Arthur Louis, "How the Customers Thrust Unexpected Prosperity on the Bicycle Industry," *Fortune* March 1974, p. 117.

9. Cyra McFadden, *The Serial* (Alfred A. Knopf, 1977), p. 22.

10. Mimi Sheraton, "A Skeptic's Guide to Health Food Stores," *New York*, May 8, 1972, p. 37.

11. Americans bought 17.2 million liters of still table wines from France in 1968 and 68.3 million in 1982. Data from the National Association of Beverage Importers.

12. *The Alice B. Toklas Cookbook* (Harper & Row, 1984), p. 153.

13. Tom Wolfe, *Mauve Gloves & Madmen, Clutter & Vine* (Farrar, Straus & Giroux, 1976), p. 206.

14. *Ibid.*, pp. 212–13.

15. P. G. Wodehouse, *Quick Service* (Penguin ed., 1954), pp. 53–54.

16. Credit card and auto-loan data can be found at the Federal Reserve's website, www.federalreserve.com.

17. *Credit Controls: An Evaluation,* Staff Report of the Subcommittee on Consumer Affairs of the House Committee on Banking and Finance (1980).

18. See Alfred Chandler, *The Visible Hand* (Belknap Press, 1977) for a discussion of the power of retained earnings in the early years of industrialization.

19. Softcore pornography simulated sex and did not show genitalia; hardcore pornography exposed the whole body to view and the on-camera sex was real.

20. See www.playboy.com/corporate/f.index.html.

21. See the website of the largest on-command movie programmer, www.oncommand.com.

22. *Memoirs* v. *Massachusetts,* 383 U.S. 413 (1966).

23. Germaine Greer, *The Female Eunuch* (MacGibbon & Kee, 1970) p. 59.

24. Edward O. Laumann, John H. Gagnon, Robert T. Michael, and Stuart Michaels, *The Social Organization of Sexuality: Sexual Practices in the United States* (University of Chicago Press, 1994), p. 201.

25. Naomi Wolf, *Promiscuities: The Secret Struggle for Womanhood* (Random House, 1997), p. 128.

26. Irene Kassorla, *Nice Girls Do* (Stratford Press, 1980).

27. Daniel Yankelovich, *New Rules: Searching for Self-Fullment in a World Turned Upside Down* (Random House, 1981), p. 99.

28. Daniel Yankelovich, *The New Morality: A Profile of American Youth in the 1970s* (McGraw-Hill, 1974), p. 98.

29. Kathleen E. Woodiwiss, *The Flame and the Flower* (Avon, 1972), p. 29.

30. For the Nancy Coffey story, see *Publisher's Weekly*, Jan. 31, 1977, p. 56.

31. Danielle Steele debuted with *The Ring* in 1980; Judith Krantz began her career with *Scruples* in 1978.

32. Edith Wharton, *The Age of Innocence* (Charles Scribner's Sons, 1968), p. 42.

33. Eugene Schoenfeld, *Jealousy: Taming the Green-Eyed Monster* (Holt, Rinehart & Winston: 1979), p. 162.

34. George and Nena O'Neill, *Open Marriage* (M. Evans & Co., 1972), p. 240.

35. "Jackie and Jeff Herrigan," *Loving Free* (Grosset & Dunlap, 1973), p. 45.

36. *Jealousy*, p. 9.

37. *Richard II*, Act I, Scene iii.

38. Robert C. Sorenson *Adolescent Sexuality in Contemporary America* (World Publishing, 1973), p. 122.

39. Jane Wilson, "The New California Man: Passive Conquistador?" *New West*, July 5, 1976, p. 33.

40. *Promiscuities*, p. 135.

41. www.slate.com, April 28, 1998.

42. Quoted in Adelaide Bry, *The Sexually Aggressive Woman* (Paul Ellek, 1974), p. 100.

43. *The Female Eunuch*, p. 33.

44. *The Social Organization of Sexuality*, p. 103.

45. "J," *The Sensuous Woman* (Lyle Stuart, 1969), pp. 10–11.

46. Two more products of the 1970s: *The Stepford Wives* was published in 1972; *9½ Weeks* in 1978.

47. Henry James, *The Europeans* (Library of America ed., 1983), p. 902.

48. Harvey Kaye, *Male Survival* (Grosset & Dunlap, 1974), p. 3.

49. Michael Korda, "Honor or Chauvinism? Test Yourself," *New West*, January 22, 1973, p. 32.

50. The drumroll: 1974 Best Actress: Ellen Burstyn for *Alice Doesn't Live Here Anymore*

    Supporting Actress: Ingrid Bergman for *Murder on the Orient Express*

    1975 Best Actress: Louise Fletcher for *One Flew Over the Cuckoo's Nest*

    Supporting Actress: Lee Grant for *Shampoo*

    1976 Best Actress: Faye Dunaway for *Network*

    Supporting Actress: Beatrice Straight for *Network*

    1977 Best Actress: Diane Keaton for *Annie Hall**

    Supporting Actress: Vanessa Redgrave for *Julia*

    1978 Best Actress: Jane Fonda for *Coming Home**

    Supporting Actress: Maggie Smith for *California Suite*

    1979 Best Actress: Sally Field for *Norma Rae*

    Supporting Actress: Meryl Streep for *Kramer vs. Kramer*

    1980 Best Actress: Sissy Spacek for *Coal Miner's Daughter*

    Supporting Actress: Mary Steenburgen for *Melvin and Howard*

    1981 Best Actress: Katharine Hepburn for *On Golden Pond*

    Supporting Actress: Maureen Stapleton for *Reds*

    1982 Best Actress: Meryl Streep for *Sophie's Choice*

    Supporting Actress: Jessica Lange for *Tootsie**

    Romantic roles marked with asterisks.

51. The canonical source on the Stonewall riot is Martin Duberman, *Stonewall* (E.P. Dutton, 1993).

52. Connecticut in 1971; Colorado and Oregon in 1972; Delaware, Hawaii and North Dakota in 1973; Ohio in 1974; New Hampshire and New Mexico in 1975; California, Maine, Vermont, Washington and West Virginia in 1976; Indiana, South Dakota, Vermont and Wyoming in 1977; Iowa and Nebraska in 1978; New Jersey in 1979; Alaska in 1980. Wisconsin followed in 1983; the District of Columbia in 1992; Rhode Island in 1998. Nevada, improbably enough, retained laws against oral and anal sex on its books until 1993. In the years since 1980, seven more states have had their sodomy laws invalidated by state courts:

New York and Pennsylvania in 1980, Kentucky in 1992, Tennessee in 1996, Montana in 1997, Georgia in 1998 and Maryland in 1999.

53. Charles Kaiser, *The Gay Metropolis* (Houghton Mifflin, 1997), p. 270.

54. Gallup poll results published at www.gallup.com/poll/releases/pr990301b.asp

55. *New Morality*, p. 93.

56. Alan P. Bell and Martin S. Weinberg, *Homosexualities: A Study of Diversity among Men and Women* (Simon & Schuster, 1978), pp. 308–309.

57. *Gay Metropolis*, pp. 245–46.

58. Jack Fritscher, *Some Dance to Remember* (Knights Press, 1990), pp. 158–161.

59. www.planetsoma.com/sf1970/index.shtml

60. Quoted in James Miller, *The Passion of Michel Foucault* (Simon & Schuster, 1993), p. 263.

61. *Ibid*, p. 274.

62. It was in the 1970s that the UCLA anthropologist Marija Gimbutas at last found an audience for her previously scorned theory that the Neolithic stone figurines of pregnant women that archaeologists have found across Europe were something more than fertility icons: They were relics of a lost matriarchal era.

63. Quoted in *Gay Metropolis*, p. 251.

64. Randy Shilts, *And the Band Played On: Politics, People and the AIDS Epidemic* (St. Martin's Press, 1987), p. 553.

65. *The Passion of Michel Foucault*, p. 280.

66. *Ibid.*, p. 306.

67. Phyllis Chesler, *Women and Madness* (Doubleday, 1972), p. 304.

68. Barbara Grizzuti Harrison, "Sexual Chic, Sexual Fascism, and Sexual Confusion," *New York* (April 1, 1974), p. 32.

69. Jill Johnston, *Lesbian Nation* (Simon & Schuster, 1973), p. 173.

70. Anthony Haden-Guest gives a thorough, if a little sugarcoated, description of the goings on in the place in his *The Last Party: The Life and Times of Studio 54* (Wm. Morrow & Co., 1997). Some of its jittery spirit is evoked in the extremely interesting collection of photographs

taken by Bobby Miller, *Fabulous! A Photographic Diary of Studio 54* (St. Martin's, 1998).

PART V
RIGHTS

1. Milan Kundera, *Immortality* (Grove, 1991), p. 136.
2. *Tennessee Valley Authority v. Hill* 437 U.S. 153 (1978).
3. James Bryce, *The American Commonwealth* (Macmillan, 2nd edition, 1914), Volume II, p. 156.
4. Woodrow Wilson, *Congressional Government* (Peter Smith reprint ed., 1973, pp. 54–55.)
5. Arthur Schlesinger Jr., *The Crisis of the Old Order* (American Heritage ed., 1988), pp. 454–55.
6. Philip Elliott Slater, *The Pursuit of Loneliness* (Beacon Press, 1970), xii.
7. Charles Reich, *The Greening of America* (Random House, 1970), p. 151.
8. Jane Jacobs, *The Death and Life of Great American Cities* (Random House, 1961), p. 410.
9. *Ibid.*, p. 298.
10. Lloyd Cutler, "To Form a Government, *Foreign Affairs*, Fall 1980, pp. 126–43.
11. 397 U.S. 254 (1970).
12. Learned Hand, *The Bill of Rights* (Atheneum, 1958), p. 73.
13. John Hart Ely, *Democracy and Distrust: A Theory of Judicial Review* (Harvard University Press, 1980), p. 32. Ely supported the results of the desegregation cases and that his book is dedicated to Earl Warren.
14. Alabama, Arkansas, Delaware, Florida, Georgia, Kentucky, Louisiana, Maryland, Mississippi, Missouri, North Carolina, Oklahoma, South Carolina, Tennessee, Texas, Virginia and West Virginia all had mandatory racial segregation. Arizona, Kansas, New Mexico, Wyoming all

had statutes permitting segregation at local option—an option no county in Wyoming ever used, it should be said.

15. *Barker v. Lull Engineering*, 573 P.2d 443 (1978).

16. Walter K. Olson, *The Litigation Explosion: What Happened When America Unleashed the Lawsuit* (E.P. Dutton, 1991), p. 283. Walter Olson is no relation to Theodore Olson.

17. Thomas K. McCraw, *Prophets of Regulation* (Harvard University Press, 1984), p. 174.

18. *See* Peter Huber, *Galileo's Revenge: Junk Science in the Court Room* (Basic, 1991) for discussions of this and other scientifically dubious litigation.

19. 403 U.S. 602.

20. Michel Foucault, *Madness and Civilization: A History of Insanity in the Age of Reason* (Vintage ed., 1988), p. 259.

21. See Rael Jean Isaac and Virginia C. Armat, *Madness in the Streets: How Psychiatry and Law Abandoned the Mentally Ill* (Free Press, 1990), for a brilliant summary of the intellectual history of the antipsychiatry movement and especially on the influence of Szasz.

22. *Ibid.*, pp. 54–55.

23. *Ibid.*, p. 57.

24. 422 U.S. 563 (1975).

25. *Addington v. Texas*, 441 U.S. 418 (1979).

26. *Ibid.*, see Footnote 5.

27. *Madness in the Streets*, p. 139.

28. *Papachristou v. City of Jacksonville*, 405 U.S. 156.

29. *Madness in the Streets*, pp. 4–5.

30. *Griggs v. Duke Power Co.*, 401 U.S. 424, 430 (1971).

31. *University of California Regents v. Bakke*, 438 U.S. 265 (1978).

32. *Steelworkers v. Weber*, 443 U.S. 193 (1979).

33. *Fullilove v. Klutznick*, 448 U.S. 448 (1980).

34. Lou Harris, "A Study of Attitudes Toward Racial and Religious Minorities and to Women" (Harris Associates 1978); Jennifer L. Hochschild, *The New American Dilemma: Liberal Democracy and*

School Desegregation (Yale University Press, 1984), pp. 22–23.

35. Stephen Thernstrom and Abigail Thernstrom, *America in Black and White: One Nation, Indivisible* (Simon & Schuster, 1997), p. 192.

36. See Jane Mansbridge, *Why We Lost the ERA* (University of Chicago, 1986).

37. *Craig v. Boren*, 429 U.S. 190 (1976).

38. Shulamith Firestone, *The Dialectic of Sex* (William Morrow, 1970), p. 12.

39. William H. Chafe, *The Paradox of Change: American Women in the 20th Century* (Oxford University Press, 1991), p. 222.

40. I am indebted to Lino Graglia's *Disaster by Decree* (Cornell University Press, 1977) for the quotations from the congressional debate over Titles IV and VI of the 1964 Civil Rights Act.

41. 402 U.S. 1 (1971).

42. Derek Bok, *The State of the Nation: Government and the Quest for a Better Society* (Harvard University Press, 1996), p. 104.

43. Quoted in *Disaster by Decree*, pp. 210–20.

44. 418 U.S. 717 (1974).

45. Ronald P. Formisano, *Boston Against Busing: Race, Class and Ethnicity in the 1960s and 1970s* (University of North Carolina Press, 1991), p. 70.

46. *Ibid.*, p. xiii.

47. Quoted in Emmett H. Buell Jr. and Richard A. Brisbin Jr., *School Desegregation and Defended Neighborhoods: The Boston Controversy* (Heath, 1982), p. 4

48. Quoted in Nancy St. John, *School Desegration: Outcomes for Children* (Wiley, 1975), p. 276.

49. Quoted in Jennifer L. Hochschild, *The New American Dilemma: Liberal Democracy and School Desegregation* (Yale University Press, 1984), p. 74.

50. Richard A. Gabriel and Paul L. Savage, *Crisis in Command: Mismanagement in the Army* (Hill & Wang, 1978), p. 68.

51. *New American Dilemma*, p. 191.

52. *New American Dilemma*, p. 180.

53. The speech, titled "Loyalty" can actually be heard at the Library of Congress' American Memory site.

54. Theodore Roosevelt, "What Americanism Means," *Forum* (April 1894), pp. 196–206.

55. Peter Brimelow, *Alien Nation* (Random House, 1995), p. 44.

56. *Ibid.*, p. 285.

57. *Lau v. Nichols*, 414 U.S. 563 (1974).

58. *Guadelupe v. Tempe*, 587 F.2d 1022 (1978).

59. *Dougal v. Sugarman*, 339 F. Supp. 906 (S.D.N.Y., 1971).

60. *In re Griffiths*, 413 U.S. 717 (1973).

61. *Hampton v. Mow Sun Wong*, 426 U.S. 88 (1976).

62. *Amvach v. Norwich*, 441 U.S. 68 (1979).

63. *Plyler v. Doe*, 457 U.S. 202 (1982).

64. Andrew Hacker, *Two Nations: Black and White, Separate, Hostile, Unequal* (Charles Scribner's Sons, 1992), pp. 173–74.

65. *Los Angeles Times*, September 21, 1979, p. 1.

66. American Jewish Committee, *Anti-Semitism in the United States* (July 1981), Vol. 1, p. 26.

67. Heinrich von Treitschke, *History of Germany in the Nineteenth Century*, ed. Gordon A. Craig (University of Chicago, 1975), p. 327. Italics added.

68. Catherine A. MacKinnon, "Whose Culture? A Case Note on *Martinez* v. *Santa Clara Pueblo*" in *Feminism Unmodified: Discourses on Life and Law* (Harvard University Press, 1987), p. 65. Italics in original.

69. Catherine A. MacKinnon, "Not by Law Alone," in *Feminism Unmodified: Discourses on Life and Law* (Harvard University Press, 1987), pp. 24, 238.

70. Paul Berman, *A Tale of Two Utopias: The Political Journey of the Generation of 1968* (Norton, 1996), p. 118.

71. Michael Barone notes that the Fifty-Sixth Congress, elected in 1898, was the first in which a majority of the members of the House had served a previous term.

72. Adam Clayton Powell representing New York City, Harlem; Robert Nix from Philadelphia; William Dawson from Chicago and Charles Diggs and John Conyers from Detroit.

73. Jonathan Rauch, *Demosclerosis: The Silent Killer of American Government* (Times Books, 1994), p. 84.

74. Daniel Yankelovich, *Moral Leadership in Government: A Public Agenda Foundation Report*, September 1976.

75. Quoted in Ione Malloy, *Southie Won't Go: A Teacher's Diary of the Desegregation of South Boston High School* (University of Illinois Press, 1986), p. 189.

76. University of Michigan National Election Studies, www.umich.edu/~nes/nesguide/toptables/tab6d_5.htm

PART VI
REGENERATION

1. Letter to Evangeline Bruce, quoted in R. Merry, *Taking on the World: Joseph and Stewart Alsop—Guardians of the American Century* (Viking, 1997), p. 525.

2. I thank Michael Ledeen for making me aware of this remark. Michael Ledeen, *Machiavelli on Modern Leadership* (St. Martin's, 1999).

3. Quoted in Daniel Yankelovich, *New Rules: Searching for Self-Fulfillment in a World Turned Upside Down* (Random House, 1981), p. 165.

4. Just for the record: In 1999 the United States spent approximately $45 billion on imported oil, or half what it did in 1980, before adjusting for inflation.

5. The winners:
   Chemistry, William N. Lipscomb of Harvard;
   Economics, Milton Friedman of the University of Chicago;
   Literature, Saul Bellow;
   Medicine, Baruch Blumberg of the Institute for Cancer Research and D. Carleton Gajdusek of the National Institutes of Health, and Physics, Burton Richter of Stanford and Samuel Ting of MIT.
   No peace prize was awarded in 1976.

The United States nearly did it again in 1993, winning the prizes for chemistry, economics, literature, medicine and physics. Only Nelson Mandela's peace prize spoiled the sweep.

6. Ramsay MacMullen, *Roman Government's Response to Crisis, A.D. 235–337* (Yale University Press, 1976), p. 198.

7. Richard Warren Lewis, "Whaddya Want for $135,000?" *New West*, July 5, 1976, p. 35.

8. Gurney Breckenfeld, "Is the One Family House Becoming a Fossile? Far From It," *Fortune*, April 1976, p. 84.

9. Quoted in Robert Skidelsky, *The Road from Serfdom* (Allen Lane, 1996), p. 88.

10. Quoted in Herbert Stein, *The Fiscal Revolution in America* (AEI Press, 2nd ed., 1996), p. 376. The "high interest rates" JFK excoriated included a 4.82% average prime rate for the year 1960 and a 2.93% Treasury bill.

11. Quoted in J. Bradford De Long, *Slouching Towards Utopia? The Economic History of the Twentieth Century* (www.econ161.berkeley. edu/TCEH/Slouch_title.html), Chapter 23, pp. 2–3.

12. James Tobin, *The New Economics One Decade Later* (Princeton University Press, 1974), pp. 100–01.

13. *The Fiscal Revolution in America*, p. 539.

14. Burns's counterparts in the other industrial democracies proved laxer still. In the twelve months ending in July 1975, the United States, West Germany, Austria, and Switzerland were the only industrial democracies to post inflation rates of less than 10 percent. France and Japan suffered inflation of more than 11 percent, Italy of more than 17 percent, and Britain of more than 26 percent.

15. Neil Sheehan, *A Bright Shining Lie: John Paul Vann and America in Vietnam* (Random House, 1988), pp. 733.

16. *Ibid.*, p. 784.

17. Henry Kissinger, *Years of Renewal* (Simon & Schuster, 1999), pp. 466–67.

18. *New York Times*, May 23, 1974, p. 14.

19. Quoted in *Years of Renewal*, p. 502.

20. *Years of Renewal*, pp. 518–19.

21. The *New York Times*, November 1, 1979, p. D–1. The economist is Robert Lekachman of the City University of New York.

22. The authors of the report tremulously reported, for example, a 300 percent increase in the price of lead over the previous thirty years, but omitted to mention that the purchasing power of the dollar had fallen by more than that over the same period. In constant 1987 dollars, a pound of lead cost 50 cents in 1942, 45 cents in 1972 and 20 cents in 1999.

23. Simon's proper title was Director of the Federal Energy Office. The Office was the precursor of the Department of Energy.

24. William Simon, *A Time For Truth* (Reader's Digest Press, 1979), p. 51.

25. M. A. Adelman, *The Genie out of the Bottle: World Oil Since 1970* (MIT Press, 1995), p. 56.

26. *New York Times*, March 10, 1971, p. 1.

27. Daniel Yankelovich, *The New Morality: A Profile of American Youth in the 1970s* (McGraw Hill, 1974), p. 71.

28. *The Economist*, February 1974, p. 37.

29. *New York Times*, July 15, 1975, p. 1 and p. 16.

30. See the Bureau of Transportation Statistics website, www.bts.gov/btsprod/nts/chp4/tbl4x22.html

31. C. Eugene Steurle, *The Tax Decade: How Taxes Came to Dominate the Public Agenda* (Urban Institute, 1992), Charts A–2 and A–3, pp. 214–15.

32. *Ibid.*, Chart A–3, pp. 216–17.

33. F. A. Hayek, *The Road to Serfdom* (University of Chicago, 1944), p. 182.

34. Quoted in Daniel Yergin and Joseph Stanislaw, *The Commanding Heights: The Battle Between Government and the Marketplace That Is Remaking the Modern World* (Simon & Schuster, 1998), p. 367.

35. Irving Kristol, "Socialism: An Obituary for an Idea," in *Reflections of a Neoconservative: Looking Back, Looking Ahead* (Basic Books, 1983), p. 114.

36. Stephen Breyer, *Regulation and Its Reform* (Harvard University Press, 1982), p. 205.

37. John Jacobs, *A Rage for Justice: The Passion and Politics of Phillip Burton* (University of California, 1995), pp. 257–58.

38. *Washington Post*, July 20, 1972, p. A–6.

39. Jane Austen, *Emma* (Oxford University Press, 3ᵈ Ed., 1933), p. 29.

40. Robert Reich, *The Work of Nations* (Alfred A. Knopf, 1991), p. 48.

41. Frederick Lewis Allen, *The Big Change: America Transforms Itself, 1900–1950* (Harper Brothers, 1952), p. 47.

42. *Ibid.*, p. 45.

43. Roger Starr, *The Rise and Fall of New York City* (Basic Books, 1985), p. 33.

44. All figures from U.S. Census. Summarized at www.census.gov/hhes/www/censhsg.html

45. National Research Council, *Inner-City Poverty in the United States*, ed. Laurence E. Lynn Jr. & Michael G.H. McGreary (National Academy Press, 1990), p. 34.

46. *Ibid.*, pp. 36–37.

47. Christopher Jencks, "Is the American Underclass Growing?" in *The Urban Underclass*, ed. Christopher Jencks & Paul E. Peterson (Brookings, 1991), p. 56.

48. *Ibid.*, p. 55.

49. *Ibid.*, pp. 88–93.

50 Joleen Kirschenman and Kathryn M. Neckerman, "The Meaning of Race for Employers" in *The Urban Underclass*, p. 216.

51. Mauricio Rojas, *The Rise and Fall of the Swedish Model*, trans. Roger Tanner (Social Market Foundation 1998), p. 36.

52. *The New Morality*, p. 93.

53. U.S. ambassador to Guatemala, John Gordon Mein, was gunned down in the streets of Guatemala City on August 28 1968—the first American ambassador to be slain in the line of duty. Cleo A. Noel Jr., the U.S. ambassador to the Sudan, along with another American diplomat and the Belgian charge d'affaires, were murdered by the PLO's Black September on March 1, 1973. Rodger P. Davies, U.S. Ambassador to Cyprus, was shot to death during a riot in front of the Nicosia embassy by Greek Cypriote nationalists on August 19, 1974.

Francis E. Melroy, the U.S. Ambassador to Lebanon, his driver and an aide were kidnapped and murdered by Palestinian terrorists in Beirut on June 16, 1976. Black September assassinated Jordanian Prime Minister Wasfi al Tall in Cairo on November 28, 1971. Spanish Prime Minister Carreo Blanco was killed by Basque terrorists on December 20, 1973. Jurgen Ponto, chairman of the Dresdner Bank was shot and killed at his home near Frankfurt, on July 30, 1977. Aldo Moro, a former Christian Democratic premier and the probable next president of Italy, was kidnapped and his five bodyguards killed in a bloody shootout on March 16, 1978. His body was found in the back of the trunk of a car on May 9. The Irish Republican Army planted a bomb on the boat of the Earl Mountbatten and detonated it on August 27, 1979, killing him, his grandson, and a boatboy. Mountbatten's daughter, her husband, and another grandson were seriously hurt. Anwar Sadat was machine-gunned to death by fundamentalist Islamists at a review of troops on October 6, 1981. Alexander Haig, supreme NATO commander, barely missed being blown to pieces by a bomb while being driven to work in Brussels on June 25, 1979. Pope John Paul II was shot and nearly fatally wounded on May 13, 1981, by a Turkish assassin recruited by Bulgarian intelligence. It could be said that the most notorious terrorist killing of the 1970s claimed the life of a relatively low-level diplomat: Daniel A. Mitrione, a U.S. aid official in Uruguay. His murder on July 31, 1970, inspired the Costa-Gavras movie *State of Siege*, a classic apologetic for terrorism.

54. Sean Kendall Anderson and Stephen Sloan, *Historical Dictionary of Terrorism*, (Scarecrow Press, 1995), p. 201.

55. Jillian Becker, *Hitler's Children: The Story of the Baader-Meinhoff Terrorist Gang* (J.B. Lippincott & Co., 1977), p. 262.

56. *Ibid.*, p. 18.

57. *New York Times*, May 2, 1979, p. 1.

58. *New York Times*, November 21, 1979, p. A-13.

59. Morris Janowitz, *The Last Half Century* (University of Chicago Press, 1978), p. 111.

60. Richard Scammon and Ben Wattenberg, *The Real Majority* (Coward, McCann, 1970), p. 162n.

61. Jonathan Rieder, *Canarsie: The Jews and Italians of Brooklyn Against Liberalism* (Harvard University Press, 1985), p. 3.

62. Quoted in Peter N. Carroll, *It Seemed Like Nothing Happened* (Rutgers University Press, 2nd ed., 1990), p. 194.

63. *The New Morality*, pp. 119–20.

64. Ibid.

CONCLUSION

1. Edmund Burke, *Reflections on the Revolution in France* (Everyman ed., 1971), p. 7.

2. Alexis de Tocqueville, *Democracy in America* (Alfred A. Knopf, 1945), Volume II, pp. 87–88.

3. See Albert Venn Dicey, *The Relationship Between Law and Public Opinion in England in the Nineteenth Century* (Macmillan, 2nd ed., 1926).

4. Francis Fukuyama, "Cheer Up, Conservatives!" *The Wall Street Journal*, Feb. 11, 1999, p. A–26.

5. Janelle Erlichman, "Names and Faces," *The Washington Post*, March 27, 1999, p. C–3.

6. Edward O. Laumann, John H. Gagnon, Robert T. Michael and Stuart Michaels, *The Social Organization of Sexuality: Sexual Practices in the United States* (University of Chicago, 1994), pp. 199–205.

INDEX

Printed in the United States
97053LV00001B/1/A